Higher CHEMISTRY
for CfE

John Anderson, Eric Allan

and **John Harris**

HODDER
GIBSON
AN HACHETTE UK COMPANY

The Publishers would like to thank the following for permission to reproduce copyright material:

Photo credits
p.1 (background) and Unit 1 running head image © Lawrence Lawry/Photodisc/Getty Images; p.1 (inset left) © Sondra Paulson/ iStockphoto.com, (inset centre) © Dimitri Vervitsiotis/Photographer's Choice/Getty Images, (inset right) © RIA NOVOSTI/SCIENCE PHOTO LIBRARY; p.2 (t) © Sondra Paulson/ iStockphoto.com, (b) © Redfx / Alamy; p.16 © ASTRID & HANNS-FRIEDER MICHLER/SCIENCE PHOTO LIBRARY; p.21 (t) © Positive image / Alamy, (bl) (clockwise from tl) © CSeigneurgens – Fotolia.com, © auris – Fotolia, © iStockphoto.com/ sweetym, © Ashley Whitworth – Fotolia, © Fatman73 – Fotolia, © Milos Luzanin/iStockphoto.com, (br) © Alfredo Dagli Orti/The Art Archive/Corbis; p.22 (l) © RIA NOVOSTI/SCIENCE PHOTO LIBRARY, (tr) © imagebroker / Alamy, (br) © Alex Segre / Alamy; p.23 (t) © CHARLES D. WINTERS/SCIENCE PHOTO LIBRARY, (b) © PASIEKA/SCIENCE PHOTO LIBRARY; p.24 (r) © CHARLES D. WINTERS/SCIENCE PHOTO LIBRARY; p.25 © Russell Kord / Alamy; p.28 (tl) © Kevin Wheal / Alamy, (cr) © CHARLES D. WINTERS/SCIENCE PHOTO LIBRARY; p.29 (l) © PASIEKA/SCIENCE PHOTO LIBRARY, (r) © SHEILA TERRY/SCIENCE PHOTO LIBRARY; p.30 © Dimitri Vervitsiotis/Photographer's Choice/Getty Images; p.31 (r) © Fabrizio Troiani / Alamy; p.32 © Imagestate Media; p.33 © Trinity Mirror / Mirrorpix / Alamy; p.38 © Stockbyte/Stockdisc/Getty Images; p.41 (left) © Milos Luzanin/iStockphoto.com, (right) © Peter Dazeley / Getty Images; p.42 © THOMAS HOLLYMAN/SCIENCE PHOTO LIBRARY; p.58 © Imagestate Media (John Foxx); p.63 (background) and Unit 2 running head image © Imagestate Media (John Foxx); p.63 (inset left) © SHEILA TERRY/SCIENCE PHOTO LIBRARY, (inset right) © Andy Sachs/ Stone/ Getty Images; p.69 (bl) © Andy Sachs/ Stone/ Getty Images; p.75 (t) © Ingram Publishing Limited, (bl) © J. Schwanke / Alamy, (br) © Mike Smith Photography/ borderfields.co.uk; p.80 © MARTYN F. CHILLMAID/SCIENCE PHOTO LIBRARY; p.86 © evgenyb – Fotolia.com; p.97 © KENNETH EWARD/BIOGRAFX/SCIENCE PHOTO LIBRARY; p.104 © ANDREW LAMBERT PHOTOGRAPHY/SCIENCE PHOTO LIBRARY; p.116 © SHEILA TERRY/SCIENCE PHOTO LIBRARY; p.123 (background) and Unit 3 running head image © Albaimages / Alamy; p.123 (inset left) © MAXIMILIAN STOCK LTD/SCIENCE PHOTO LIBRARY, (inset right) © Helen Sessions / Alamy; p.124 (l) © Paul Murphy, (r) © STEVE LINDRIDGE / Alamy; p.127 © Leslie Garland Picture Library / Alamy; p.128 © ROBERT BROOK/SCIENCE PHOTO LIBRARY; p.160 (l) © Phil Degginger / Alamy, (r) © MAXIMILIAN STOCK LTD/SCIENCE PHOTO LIBRARY; p.173 © Skatebiker / Wikipedia Commons; p.179 © Helen Sessions / Alamy; p.186 © MICHAEL DONNE/SCIENCE PHOTO LIBRARY; p.197 © COLIN CUTHBERT/SCIENCE PHOTO LIBRARY.

All other photos © John Anderson.

Acknowledgements
Extracts from past exam papers are reproduced with the permission of the Scottish Qualifications Authority.

Every effort has been made to trace all copyright holders, but if any have been inadvertently overlooked the Publishers will be pleased to make the necessary arrangements at the first opportunity.

Although every effort has been made to ensure that website addresses are correct at time of going to press, Hodder Gibson cannot be held responsible for the content of any website mentioned in this book. It is sometimes possible to find a relocated web page by typing in the address of the home page for a website in the URL window of your browser.

Hachette Livre UK's policy is to use papers that are natural, renewable and recyclable products and made from wood grown in sustainable forests. The logging and manufacturing processes are expected to conform to the environmental regulations of the country of origin.

Whilst every effort has been made to check the instructions of practical work in this book, it is still the duty and legal obligation of schools to carry out their own risk assessments.

Orders: please contact Bookpoint Ltd, 130 Park Drive, Abingdon, Oxon OX14 4SE. Telephone: (44) 01235 827720. Fax: (44) 01235 400454. Lines are open 9.00–5.00, Monday to Saturday, with a 24-hour message answering service. Visit our website at www.hoddereducation.co.uk. Hodder Gibson can be contacted direct on: Tel: 0141 848 1609; Fax: 0141 889 6315; email: hoddergibson@hodder.co.uk

© John Anderson, Eric Allan, John Harris 2012
First published in 2012 by
Hodder Gibson, an imprint of Hodder Education,
An Hachette UK Company
2a Christie Street
Paisley PA1 1NB

Without Answers
Impression number   5 4 3 2
Year   2016 2015 2014
ISBN: 978 1444 158601

With Answers
Impression number   4
Year   2016 2015
ISBN: 978 1444 167528

Cover photo © CROWN COPYRIGHT/HEALTH & SAFETY LABORATORY/SCIENCE PHOTO LIBRARY
Illustrations by Fakenham Prepress Solutions
Typeset in Minion Pro 11pt by Fakenham Prepress Solutions, Fakenham, Norfolk, NR21 8NN
Printed in Italy

A catalogue record for this title is available from the British Library

Contents

Preface

This book is designed to be used by students studying Higher Chemistry for Curriculum for Excellence. It closely follows the SQA arrangements for Higher Chemistry and attempts to stimulate the reader's appetite for learning new chemistry. In addition to the core text, this book also offers the following features:

Study Questions

A variety of question types are offered throughout the text and at the end of each chapter to allow the student to become familiar with answering chemical questions, and to test knowledge and understanding. Questions marked with an asterisk (*) are SQA past exam questions. There is also an *End of Course Questions* section which offers readers the chance to revise and consolidate their knowledge and understanding, and to apply their learning from the whole course to SQA past exam questions. The *With Answers* version of this book gives full answers to all questions in the book.

Researching Chemistry

Practical assignments in chemistry help to bring the subject to life and offer students an insight into working in the chemistry laboratory. To aid students' understanding of practical chemistry, *Researching Chemistry* offers students explanations of common laboratory techniques and use of apparatus, and covers the basics of data analysis that will be useful for the Higher course.

For Interest

The material in the *For Interest* sections of the book contains chemistry that is likely to be of interest to the reader, but is not examinable under the current SQA arrangements. This includes chemical phenomena, historical anecdotes, and applications of chemistry that make use of the chemistry presented in the chapter.

Checklist for Revision

A short summary of the key learning points is given at the end of each chapter. Students can use this to self-check their learning and to help them revise for assessments.

Key terms and Chemical Dictionary

Useful words and phrases are summarised at the end of the chapter to aid the student learning chemistry. A *Chemical Dictionary* is provided at the end of the book for the student to check their knowledge of the key terms.

Updates and syllabus changes: important note to teachers and students from the publisher

This book covers all course arrangements for Higher Chemistry for Curriculum for Excellence, to be examined 2015 onwards.

A significant proportion of the text is also appropriate for teaching the Revised Higher syllabus being examined 2012–2015 (please see our webpage at www.hoddereducation.co.uk/HigherScience for more details). Please note that this book does not attempt to give advice on any 'added value assessments' or 'open assignments' that may form part of a final grade in the Higher exam.

Please remember that syllabus arrangements change from time to time. We make every effort to update our textbooks as soon as possible when this happens, but – especially if you are using an old copy of this book – it is always advisable to check whether there have been any alterations to the arrangements since this book was printed. You can check the latest arrangements at the SQA website (www.sqa.org.uk), and you can also check for any specific updates to this book at www.hoddereducation.co.uk/HigherScience.

We make every effort to ensure accuracy of content, but if you discover any mistakes please let us know as soon as possible – see contact details on back cover.

Syllabus update 2014

Please note that the book you are holding is from the third (or a subsequent) printing of this title, which was revised following the publication of updated syllabus documents by SQA in 2014. A new topic on ionisation energy has been added to Chapter 3 (on page 38) and the corresponding answer section has been updated.

A note from the authors

Eric Allan and John Harris are synonymous with Higher Chemistry. Their earlier textbooks have been used by countless schools and colleges in Scotland and have helped to guide many students and teachers through the Higher Chemistry course. In writing this new book for CfE Higher, I relied on the wisdom, patience, attention to detail and insightful chemical knowledge to help bring the previous Higher Chemistry textbook up to date with the new syllabus. This book is a product of our collaboration and I am grateful for the time and energy they devoted to reviewing the text and offering ideas to help improve the book. It is our hope that this textbook will serve as an excellent guide through the Higher Chemistry course, and will hopefully inspire students to study chemistry beyond Higher too.

I am grateful to Claire, Ellie and Finlay for their patience, support and love.

John Anderson, 2012

Unit 1

Chemical Changes and Structure

Chemists make new substances by carrying out chemical reactions. An understanding of the factors that affect the rate of chemical reactions is essential for studying and practising chemistry. Once we have developed our understanding of reaction rates, we consider the properties of elements and compounds.

We examine the properties of the elements and study the underlying patterns of these properties. This leads us to consider the bonds that are formed when elements combine and how this influences the intermolecular bonding of compounds. We then examine the properties of compounds and relate this to their bonding.

The concepts introduced in this unit are referred to throughout Higher Chemistry as they are used to explain the properties of compounds we will meet in Units 2 and 3.

1 Controlling the rate of reaction

From your experience of chemistry, you are probably well aware that chemical reactions occur at different rates. For example, if you add some magnesium to hydrochloric acid it reacts vigorously with hydrogen

Figure 1.1 Fireworks exploding – a very fast reaction

Figure 1.2 The rusting of a bike chain – a very slow reaction

gas produced at a very fast rate. If you repeat the experiment with some iron, the reaction rate is much slower. In everyday life the varying rates of chemical reactions can also be witnessed from the slow rusting of an iron object to the fast burning of compounds when a firework is ignited.

Chemists need to have an understanding of the factors that affect the rate of a chemical reaction. Once they have an understanding, they can look at ways to:

1   increase the rate of the reaction – this will result in the product being made more quickly and therefore increase the profit of a manufacturing process

2   slow a reaction down – if a reaction is too fast there is a risk of thermal explosion!

In this chapter, we will investigate the methods used to monitor a chemical reaction and examine collision theory which offers us some explanations about why some reactions are faster than other reactions. We will then examine the energy changes that occur during a reaction as these will also influence the choice of route to making a new compound.

Observing factors that affect the rate of reaction by experiment

Changing the concentration or particle size of a reactant, or changing the temperature of an experiment, does affect the rate of reaction. We can observe this simply by watching experiments under different conditions and then using our senses to compare the experiments, but a more scientific approach to assessing the rate of a reaction involves taking measurements of the reaction at fixed time intervals to allow the rate to be calculated.

For example, if two runners completed a 100 m race with times of 11 s and 14 s, we would know that the 11 s runner was faster. Likewise for chemical reactions: if two experiments produced 100 cm^3 of gas with one experiment producing the gas in 11 s and the other taking 14 s, we would know that the 11 s experiment was faster (had the higher rate of reaction).

We can go further and calculate the rate of the reaction using the measurements made in the same way that the speed of a runner can be calculated by dividing the distance by the time taken. A simple experimental setup is shown in Figure 1.3 that could be used to measure the volume of hydrogen gas released from reacting magnesium with hydrochloric acid.

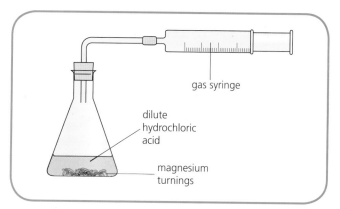

Figure 1.3 The volume of hydrogen gas can be measured at fixed time intervals to monitor the rate of the reaction.

Reacting marble chips with acid

A useful reaction to study is that between marble chips (calcium carbonate) and hydrochloric acid using the apparatus shown in Figure 1.4.

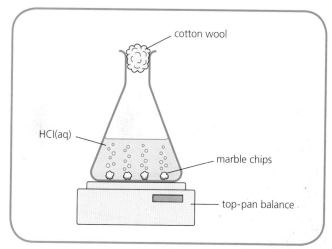

Figure 1.4 When marble chips react with acid, the mass decreases as carbon dioxide escapes from the flask.

Time/s	Mass of flask and contents/g	Decrease in mass/g	Concentration of acid/mol l⁻¹
0	149.00	–	4.00
30	147.75	1.25	2.86
60	147.08	1.92	2.25
90	146.60	2.40	1.82
120	146.24	2.76	1.49
150	145.94	3.06	1.22
180	145.68	3.32	0.98
210	145.48	3.52	0.80
240	145.32	3.68	0.65
270	145.19	3.81	0.54
300	145.08	3.92	0.44
360	144.89	4.11	0.27
420	144.77	4.23	0.15
480	144.70	4.30	0.09
540	144.65	4.35	0.04
600	144.65	4.35	0.04

Table 1.1

As the reaction proceeds, carbon dioxide gas is released and hence the mass of flask and contents decreases. A loose cotton wool 'plug' is used to prevent loss of acid spray during effervescence while allowing the gas to escape. The balanced equation for this reaction is as follows:

$$CaCO_3(s) + 2HCl(aq) \rightarrow CaCl_2(aq) + CO_2(g) + H_2O(l)$$

Specimen results from an experiment in which 15 g of marble chips were added to 50 cm³ of 4 mol l⁻¹ hydrochloric acid are given in Table 1.1. Using these quantities ensures that the marble chips are present in excess, which means that the acid will be completely neutralised.

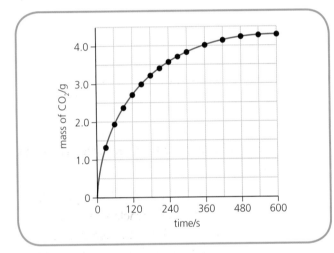

Figure 1.5 Mass of CO_2 against time

The decrease in mass is the mass of carbon dioxide released and this quantity can be plotted against time as shown in Figure 1.5. From the loss in mass it is also possible to carry out a mole calculation using the balanced equation to find the concentration of the acid at the various times. These calculated results are shown in Table 1.1 and are plotted against time in Figure 1.6.

The **rate of reaction** is the change in concentration of reactants or products in unit time. As can be seen from Figures 1.5 and 1.6, the slope of the graph is steepest at the beginning of the reaction and levels off as time passes. This shows that the rate of reaction is greatest initially and decreases with time. This is true whether we consider the rate at which gas is released or the rate at which acid is consumed. We will find out why the rate changes when we examine collision theory.

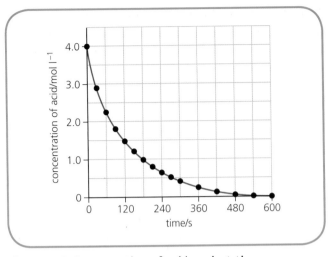

Figure 1.6 Concentration of acid against time

It is difficult to measure the actual rate at any one instant since the rate is always changing, but it is possible to calculate the average rate over a certain period of time. In this experiment the average rate would be calculated from the decrease in mass or decrease in acid concentration which occurs in a certain time interval. The method of calculation is shown in the following worked example.

Worked Example 1

Use the data given in Table 1.1 to calculate the average rate of reaction between 30 s and 60 s in terms of

a) the mass of carbon dioxide produced

b) the decrease in the concentration of hydrochloric acid.

a) Mass of CO_2 released between 30 s and 60 s
$$= 1.92 - 1.25$$
$$= 0.67 \text{ g}$$
$$\text{Average rate} = \frac{\text{mass of } CO_2}{\text{time interval}}$$
$$= \frac{0.67}{30}$$
$$= 0.022 \text{ g s}^{-1}$$

b) Decrease in concentration of HCl(aq) between 30 s and 60 s
$$= 2.86 - 2.25$$
$$= 0.61 \text{ mol l}^{-1}$$
$$\text{Average rate} = \frac{\text{decrease in acid concentration}}{\text{time interval}}$$
$$= \frac{0.61}{30}$$
$$= 0.020 \text{ mol l}^{-1}\text{s}^{-1}$$

Where it is difficult to measure a change in the chemical reaction, the time for the reaction is used to calculate the relative rate of reaction. This is done by calculating the reciprocal of time $\left(\frac{1}{t}\right)$ i.e.

$$\text{rate} = \frac{1}{\text{time}}$$

For example, a reaction that took 40 s to reach completion would have a relative rate of $\frac{1}{40} = 0.025\,\text{s}^{-1}$

We will consider how the relative rate can be used to monitor a reaction on pages 9–11.

Questions

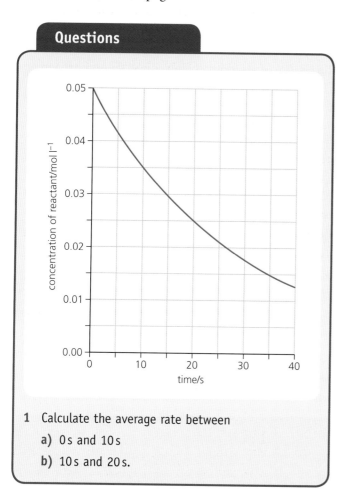

1 Calculate the average rate between

   a) 0 s and 10 s

   b) 10 s and 20 s.

Particle size

Solid logs placed onto an open fire burn very slowly. But if you break the logs up into much smaller pieces, or sawdust, they burn much faster. This is an everyday illustration of the fact that reactions in which one of the reactants is a solid can be speeded up or slowed down by altering the particle size of the solid. Breaking up a large lump into smaller pieces increases the overall surface area. Since chemical reactions happen at the surface of a solid, increasing the surface area will lead to an increase

in the speed of reaction. The fact that reactions happen on the surface of a solid is illustrated nicely when an apple is exposed to the air by cutting it in half. Browning of the apple quickly occurs, but only at the exposed surface. If the apple is cut up into lots of smaller pieces, browning occurs on all the surfaces as they are exposed to the oxygen in the air.

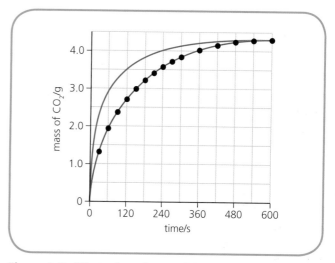

Figure 1.7 Effect of smaller particle size (green curve) on the rate of reaction

The reaction between marble chips and acid provides a good example of the effect of particle size on the speed of a chemical reaction. If the marble chips are replaced by an equal mass of smaller pieces of marble, the reaction proceeds more quickly since the surface area exposed to the acid has increased. If the mass loss against time is compared with the results shown in Figure 1.6, then a graph with a steeper slope will be obtained (see Figure 1.7).

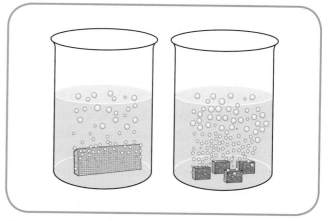

Figure 1.8 Breaking up a large lump into smaller pieces increases the surface area which speeds up the reaction.

Concentration

You will already be aware that the concentration of a reactant affects the rate of a reaction. The reaction between marble and hydrochloric acid, for example, can be speeded up by increasing the concentration of the acid. When investigating the relationship between the rate of reaction and the concentration of a reactant, a 'clock reaction' may be used. In a clock reaction, a time lapse occurs before a sudden end point is reached. This is described in more detail on pages 9 and 10.

Temperature

There are many applications of the fact that a small change in temperature has a marked effect on the rate of a reaction. For example, roasting a chicken weighing 2 kg takes about 1 hour 30 mins in a hot oven (200 °C) and twice as long in a moderate oven (150 °C). If a slow-cooking pot is used, the cooking time increases to several hours, since the temperature is not much over 100 °C. Food can be stored in a freezer for much longer than in a domestic fridge due to lower temperatures which slow down decomposition reactions (mainly involving micro-organisms such as bacteria).

When the temperature of a chemical reaction is increased, we generally state that the reaction rate will also increase. In reality, it is more complex than this. For example, if the chemical reaction is controlled by an enzyme, increasing the temperature can *decrease* the reaction rate as the increase in temperature can cause the enzyme to denature (see Unit 2 for a discussion of the effect of heat on protein structure). A denatured enzyme is one that has changed shape and is much less likely to catalyse the reaction it was designed for. Consequently, the reaction rate will significantly reduce. This can also occur when a chemical reaction is controlled by other catalysts, such as a transition metal or metal compound, as the high temperature can make the catalyst less efficient. Overall, this can lead to a decrease in reaction rate or can lead to the reaction failing to take place. The effect of temperature on reaction rate must also be carefully considered for reversible reactions. (In Unit 3, you will study the effect of temperature on reversible reactions at equilibrium). Sometimes an increase in temperature can increase the production of product; in other cases an increase in temperature will increase the break-down of product, resulting in a much lower yield. Thus, chemists must consider a variety of factors when considering how temperature is likely to affect the rate of reaction.

Temperature control is often essential in industrial processes. In the manufacture of nitric acid by the Ostwald Process, ammonia is catalytically oxidised to produce nitrogen monoxide according to the following equation:

$$4NH_3(g) + 5O_2(g) \rightarrow 4NO(g) + 6H_2O(g)$$

The reaction is operated at about 900 °C and approximately 96% conversion of ammonia occurs. The reaction is highly exothermic and, if the temperature rises too much, damage to the platinum–rhodium catalyst may occur. A higher temperature also increases the chance of ammonia being converted to nitrogen. This would decrease the yield of nitrogen monoxide and consequently affect the production of nitric acid. Refer to page 152 for a more detailed description of the effect of temperature on a chemical reaction.

Collision theory

From an early stage in studying science, you will have been aware that all substances are made up of very small particles called atoms, ions or molecules. Furthermore, these particles are continually moving, the speed and extent of the motion depending on whether the substance is a gas, a liquid, a solid or in solution. This description is often referred to as the 'kinetic model of matter'.

For a chemical reaction to occur, the reactants must be brought together in some way so that their particles will collide. This is the basis of the **collision theory**.

> Any factor which increases the number of collisions per second between the particles of the reactants is likely to increase the rate of reaction.

More collisions occur if the particle size of a solid reactant is decreased, since its overall surface area is increased. Since it is only the particles on the surface of a solid that can react initially (since they are exposed), breaking up a solid into smaller pieces exposes more surfaces and hence more particles are available to react. Similarly, if the concentration of a reactant is increased, more collisions between particles will take place since there are now more particles occupying the same volume of space. These points are illustrated in Figure 1.9.

Questions

2   The graph shows how the volume of nitrogen dioxide increases with time when 2 g of copper turnings react with excess concentrated nitric acid. Copy the graph and add similar curves for the reaction between concentrated nitric acid and **a)** 1 g of copper powder, **b)** a 2 g piece of copper foil. Label the curves **a)** and **b)** as appropriate.

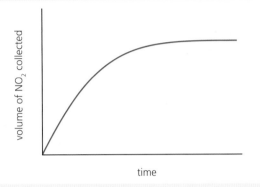

3* Excess zinc was added to 2 mol l⁻¹ sulphuric acid at room temperature and the volume of hydrogen produced was plotted against time as shown.

   a) Why does the gradient of the curve decrease as the reaction proceeds?

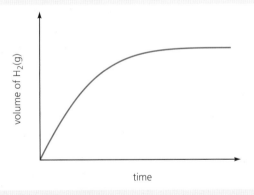

   b) Copy the graph and add corresponding curves obtained when the reaction is repeated **i)** at a higher temperature, **ii)** using an equal volume of 1 mol l⁻¹ sulphuric acid. Label the curves **i)** and **ii)** as appropriate.

Raising the temperature at which the reaction occurs does more than merely increase the number of collisions between particles. Temperature can be regarded as a measure of the average kinetic energy of the particles in a substance. Hence, at a higher temperature the particles have greater kinetic energy and will collide with greater force.

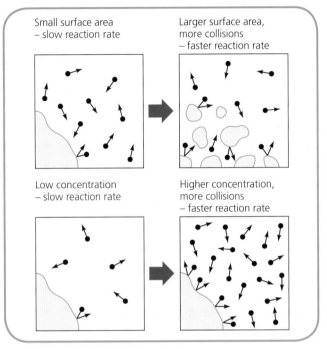

Figure 1.9 Effect of particle size and concentration on the rate of reaction

Reactions occur, then, when reactant particles collide. However, it would appear that not all collisions result in a successful reaction. If they did, all reactions would be virtually instantaneous. Reactions in which covalent substances take part are often slow, even when the substances are gases. Think about a Bunsen burner or gas hob. Unless ignited by a flame, a mixture of methane and oxygen will not react to any appreciable extent at room temperature. This is despite the fact that, as gases, their molecules are separate and will mix rapidly by diffusion and many collisions between molecules will occur per second.

Not all reactions involving covalent substances are slow. The colourless gas nitrogen monoxide combines rapidly with oxygen, even at room temperature, to form brown fumes of nitrogen dioxide.

$$2NO(g) + O_2(g) \rightarrow 2NO_2(g)$$

Reactions that involve separate ions in solution are often very fast, if not instantaneous. When an acid and alkali are mixed, large numbers of the reacting particles (H^+ and OH^- ions) collide at the moment of mixing and combine rapidly to form water molecules. Similarly, mixing solutions of barium chloride and sodium sulfate brings large numbers of barium ions and sulfate ions together and insoluble $BaSO_4$ is precipitated rapidly.

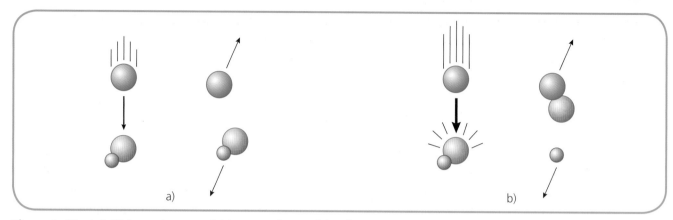

Figure 1.10 a) Collision not successful because the particles do not have enough energy. b) Collision successful as the particles do have enough energy.

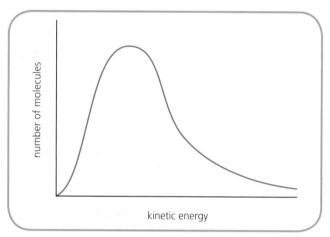

Figure 1.11

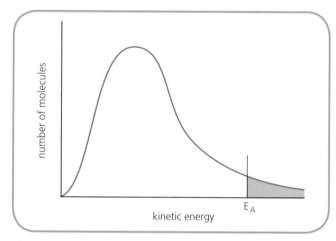

Figure 1.12 Distribution of energy including activation energy

Ionic reactions involving a solid may be slow. For example, large marble chips react slowly with dilute acid at room temperature. As you are already aware, this reaction can be accelerated by decreasing the size of the marble chips, increasing the concentration of the acid, raising the temperature or, indeed, using any combination of these factors.

In order to understand why some collisions result in successful reactions but others do not, we have to examine the work of the Swedish chemist Svante Arrhenius.

Temperature, kinetic energy and activation energy

In 1889 Arrhenius put forward the idea that for a reaction to occur, the colliding particles must have a minimum amount of kinetic energy, called the **activation energy**. The activation energy required

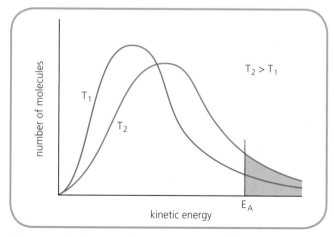

Figure 1.13 Distribution of energy at different temperatures

varies from one reaction to another. Thus, in the case of methane reacting with oxygen it must be that the activation energy for this reaction is high. In other words, methane and oxygen molecules may collide but because they do not have enough energy, the collisions do not result in a successful reaction. Conversely, the reaction between nitrogen monoxide and oxygen to form nitrogen dioxide occurs rapidly at room temperature. This suggests that this reaction has a low activation energy. The collision of nitrogen monoxide molecules with oxygen molecules results in a chemical reaction as most molecules have enough energy (equal to or greater than the activation energy) to react.

At a given temperature, individual molecules of a gas have widely different kinetic energies. Most molecules will have energy near to the average value, but some will be well below average, while others will be well above. The distribution of kinetic energy values is illustrated in Figure 1.11.

The kinetic energy of individual molecules will change continually due to collisions with other molecules. However, at constant temperature the overall distribution of energies remains the same.

Figure 1.12 shows the same distribution of kinetic energy but it also incorporates the activation energy, E_A. The shaded area represents all of the molecules that have energy greater than the activation energy, in other words the proportion of molecules that have sufficient energy to react. If the activation energy is greater, then the shaded area would be smaller thus representing a smaller proportion of the total number of molecules.

The distribution of energy changes when the temperature changes. The effect of a small rise in temperature, from T_1 to T_2, is shown in Figure 1.13.

The average energy is increased but the most significant feature is the considerable increase in the area that is shaded. In other words at a higher temperature there are many more molecules with energy equal to or greater than the activation energy.

This is the real reason why a small change in temperature can have such a marked effect on the rate of a reaction. A small rise in temperature causes a significant increase in the number of molecules that have energy greater than the activation energy.

Questions

4   A piece of phosphorus ignites when touched with a hot wire, while magnesium ribbon needs strong heating before it will catch fire.

    What does this suggest about the activation energies of these two reactions?

The following two experiments illustrate how the effect of concentration and temperature can be assessed when investigating reaction rates.

1 The effect of concentration on the rate of reaction

The reaction between hydrogen peroxide and acidified potassium iodide solution can be used to see how the rate of this reaction depends on the concentration of iodide ions. This is an example of a 'clock reaction' as referred to earlier. The equation for the reaction is as follows:

$$H_2O_2(aq) + 2H^+(aq) + 2I^-(aq) \rightarrow 2H_2O(l) + I_2(aq)$$

Starch solution and sodium thiosulfate solution, $Na_2S_2O_3(aq)$, are also included in the reaction mixture. Iodine molecules produced in the reaction are immediately changed back into iodide ions by reacting with thiosulfate ions according to the following equation:

$$I_2(aq) + 2S_2O_3{}^{2-}(aq) \rightarrow 2I^-(aq) + S_4O_6{}^{2-}(aq)$$

While this is happening the reaction mixture is colourless. When all of the thiosulfate ions have reacted, a blue–black colour suddenly appears as iodine – produced by the first reaction – is detected by starch.

As Figure 1.14 shows, potassium iodide solution, starch solution, sodium thiosulfate solution and dilute sulfuric acid are mixed. Hydrogen peroxide solution is added and the time taken for the mixture to turn blue–black is measured. The experiment is repeated using smaller volumes of the iodide solution but adding water so that the total volume of the reacting mixture is always the same. The concentrations and volumes of all other solutions are kept constant.

The number of moles of thiosulfate ions is the same in each experiment so that when the blue–black colour appears, the same extent of reaction has occurred. Since rate is inversely proportional to time, the reciprocal of time (1/t) is taken to be a measure of the rate of the reaction.

Specimen results are given in Table 1.2 and the graph of rate against volume of KI(aq) is shown in Figure 1.15.

The graph of rate against volume of potassium iodide solution shows a straight line. Since the total volume

is always the same, we can take the volume of KI(aq) to be a measure of iodide ion concentration.

The straight-line graph means that the rate of this reaction is directly proportional to the concentration of iodide ions. In other words, if the concentration of iodide ions is doubled then the rate of reaction doubles.

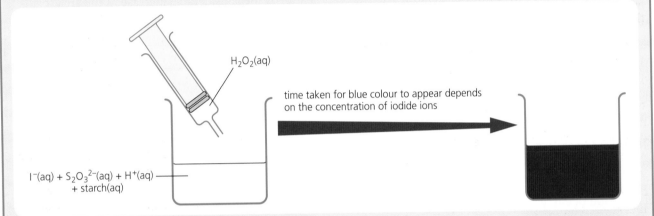

Figure 1.14

Volume of KI(aq)/cm³	Volume of H₂0/cm³	Time (t)/s	Rate (1/t)/s⁻¹
25	0	23	0.043
20	5	29	0.034
15	10	39	0.026
10	15	60	0.017
5	20	111	0.009

Table 1.2

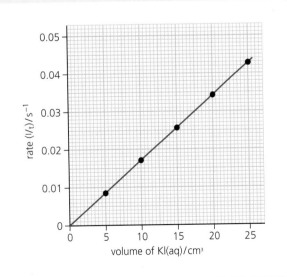

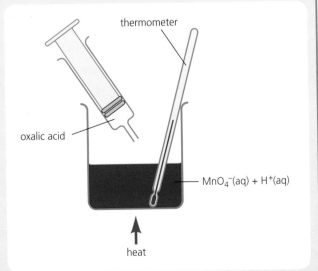

Figure 1.16

Figure 1.15

2 The effect of temperature on reaction rate

The effect of changing the temperature on the rate of a reaction can be studied using the following reaction. Acidified potassium permanganate solution, which is purple due to the presence of permanganate ions (MnO_4^-), is decolourised by an aqueous solution of oxalic acid, $(COOH)_2$. This reaction is very slow at room temperature but is almost instantaneous above 80 °C. The equation for this reaction is given below.

$$5(COOH)_2(aq) + 6H^+(aq) + 2MnO_4^-(aq) \rightarrow 2Mn^{2+}(aq) + 10CO_2(g) + 8H_2O(l)$$

This experiment is carried out at temperatures ranging from about 40 °C to about 70 °C. Volumes and concentrations of all the reactants are kept constant. As shown in Figure 1.16, the reaction starts when the oxalic acid is added to the permanganate solution previously acidified with dilute sulfuric acid. The time taken for the solution to become colourless is measured. The temperature is measured at the end point of the reaction.

Since the number of moles of permanganate ions is the same in each experiment, the same amount of reaction has occurred when the end point has been reached.

As in the previous experiment the reciprocal of the time taken to reach the end point ($\frac{1}{t}$) is taken to represent the rate of reaction.

Specimen results for the experiment are given in Table 1.3 and the graph of rate against temperature is shown in Figure 1.17.

Temperature/°C	Time (t)/s	Rate (1/t)/s^{-1}
38	87	0.011
50	35	0.029
59	18	0.056
70	8	0.125

Table 1.3

As expected, the rate of reaction increases with rising temperature. However, since the graph of rate against temperature is a curve, as can be seen from Figure 1.17, the rate is not directly proportional to the temperature. In fact it can be seen from the graph that the rate of reaction doubles if there is a temperature rise of about 10 °C. This experimental finding helps to support the activation energy theory.

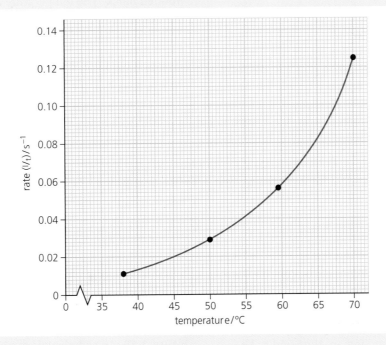

Figure 1.17

Collision geometry

Some collisions will not produce a successful reaction even if the particles collide with the correct energy. Another factor which must be considered is **collision geometry**. Consider the example of an alkene reacting with bromine. The reactive part of the alkene molecule is the carbon to carbon double bond. The neighbouring carbon and hydrogen atoms are relatively unreactive. If a bromine molecule collides with the neighbouring carbon and hydrogen atoms, and not the double bond, we would say that a reaction is unlikely to happen as the collision geometry is not correct. Direct collision with the carbon to carbon double bond is more favourable and would be more likely to result in a reaction.

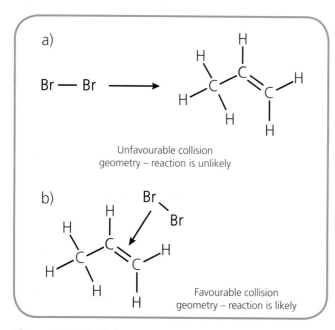

Figure 1.18 Collision geometry in a reaction

Reaction profiles
Exothermic and endothermic reactions

During your study of chemistry you will have often observed that when chemical reactions occur they are accompanied by a significant change in energy. Most of the reactions that you have come across will have involved a release of energy to the surroundings, usually in the form of heat, and are thus said to be exothermic.

Examples of such reactions include:

- combustion of elements, carbon compounds and other fuels
- neutralisation of acids by alkalis and reactive metals
- displacement of less reactive metals.

Energy may also be released in a chemical reaction in other forms, such as light (for example when magnesium burns) or sound (such as hydrogen–oxygen and hydrogen–chlorine explosions).

Reactions in which heat is absorbed from the surroundings are said to be **endothermic**. Although less frequent, such reactions do occur, and examples include:

- dissolving certain salts in water (such as ammonium nitrate or potassium nitrate)
- neutralising ethanoic acid with ammonium carbonate or sodium hydrogencarbonate.

The reaction between barium hydroxide and ammonium thiocyanate is a classic example of an endothermic reaction (see Figure 1.19).

The reactants are mixed together in a beaker on a wet wooden block. The temperature of the reacting mixture falls well below 0 °C, sufficient to freeze the water and cause the beaker to stick to the block.

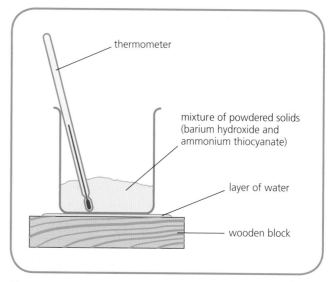

Figure 1.19 An endothermic reaction

During an exothermic reaction, energy possessed by the reactants – potential energy – is released to the surroundings. Hence the products of an exothermic reaction have less potential energy than the reactants. This can be illustrated in a potential energy diagram (Figure 1.20) which shows the energy pathway as the reaction proceeds from reactants to products.

Conversely, in an endothermic reaction, the reactants absorb energy from the surroundings so that the products possess more energy than the reactants. The potential energy diagram in Figure 1.21 shows this.

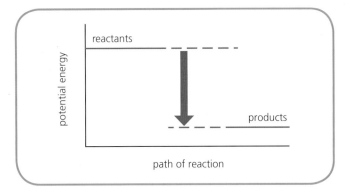

Figure 1.20 Exothermic reaction

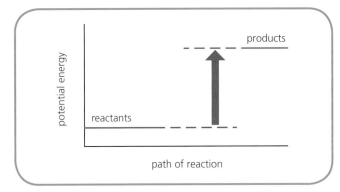

Figure 1.21 Endothermic reaction

Enthalpy change

The potential energy diagrams in the previous section (Figures 1.20 and 1.21) show the change in energy during exothermic and endothermic reactions. The difference in potential energy between reactants and products is called the **enthalpy change**, denoted by the symbol ΔH. Enthalpy changes are usually quoted in kilojoules per mole of reactant or product, abbreviated to $kJ\,mol^{-1}$.

Since the reactants lose energy in an exothermic reaction, ΔH is said to be negative, as is shown in Figure 1.22.

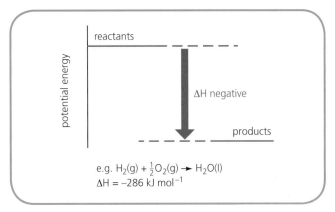

e.g. $H_2(g) + \frac{1}{2}O_2(g) \rightarrow H_2O(l)$
$\Delta H = -286\ kJ\,mol^{-1}$

Figure 1.22 Enthalpy change for an exothermic reaction

In an endothermic reaction, the reactants take in heat from the surroundings, so that the products possess more energy than the reactants. As a result, an endothermic change has a positive ΔH value, as shown in Figure 1.23.

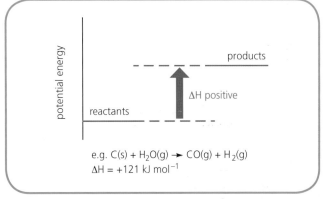

e.g. $C(s) + H_2O(g) \rightarrow CO(g) + H_2(g)$
$\Delta H = +121\ kJ\,mol^{-1}$

Figure 1.23 Enthalpy change for an endothermic reaction

It is important to note that, although it is essential to include the minus sign in front of the numerical value for the enthalpy change if the reaction is exothermic, it is not necessary to include the plus sign in the case of an endothermic reaction. The absence of a sign from the ΔH value will be taken to indicate that the reaction is endothermic.

Activation energy and activated complex

Activation energy is the minimum kinetic energy required by colliding molecules for a reaction to occur. We can also consider activation energy from the point of view of potential energy. In the potential energy diagrams shown in Figures 1.24 and 1.25, the activation

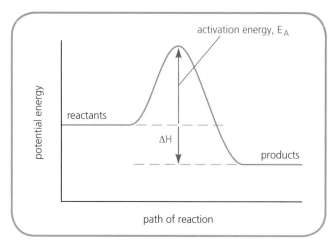

Figure 1.24 The activation energy for an exothermic reaction

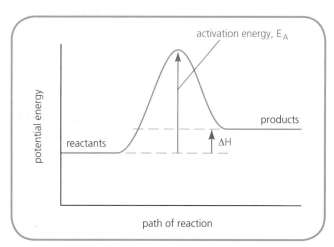

Figure 1.25 The activation energy for an endothermic reaction

energy appears as an 'energy barrier' that has to be overcome as the reaction proceeds from reactants to products. Whether a reaction is fast or slow will depend on the height of this barrier: the higher the barrier, the slower the reaction. It is worth emphasising at this point that the rate of reaction does not depend on the enthalpy change.

As the reaction proceeds from reactants to products, an intermediate stage is reached at the top of the activation energy barrier at which a highly energetic species called an **activated complex** is formed. This is illustrated in Figure 1.26, which also shows that the activation energy can be redefined as given below.

Activation energy is the energy needed by colliding particles to form the activated complex.

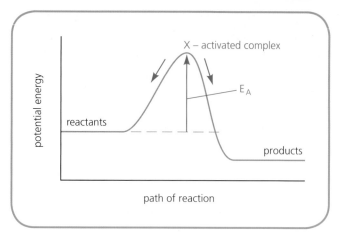

Figure 1.26 Activated complex

Activated complexes are very unstable and only exist for a very short time. From the peak of the energy barrier the complex can lose energy in one of two ways to form stable substances, in other words either to yield the products or to form the reactants again.

The addition reaction between ethene and bromine (shown in Figure 1.27) is believed to go via the

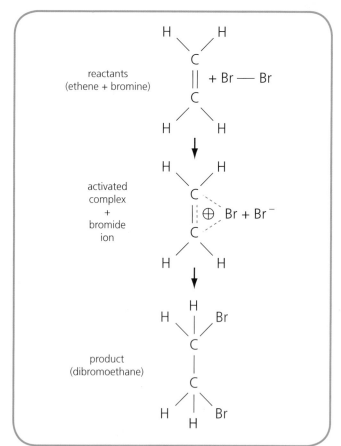

Figure 1.27 Reaction showing the formation of an activated complex

activated complex when the reaction is carried out under certain conditions. The dotted lines in the structural formula of the complex indicate partial bonding between atoms. The first step shows the formation of the activated complex and a bromide ion which combine in the second step to form dibromoethane. The first step can, however, be reversed, in other words the complex can break down to reproduce the reactants, namely ethene and bromine.

Potential energy diagrams give useful information about the energy profile of a reaction. When drawn to scale they can also be used to calculate the enthalpy change and/or the activation energy of a reaction as shown in Question 5.

Catalysts

A catalyst is a substance that alters the rate of a reaction without being used up in the reaction. Perhaps the most popular example of a catalyst is the catalytic convertor used in petrol engines as shown in Figures 1.29 and 1.30.

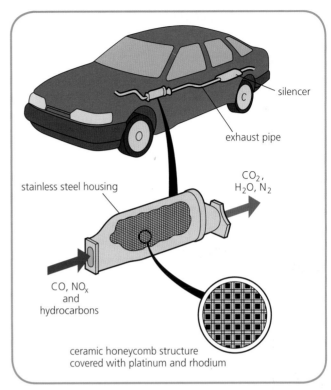

silencer

exhaust pipe

CO_2, H_2O, N_2

stainless steel housing

CO, NO_x and hydrocarbons

ceramic honeycomb structure covered with platinum and rhodium

Figure 1.29 The internal structure of a catalytic convertor

Questions

5 Potential energy diagrams of three different reactions are shown.

a) Identify the endothermic reaction(s).

b) For each reaction calculate i) its activation energy, E_A, and ii) its enthalpy change, ΔH.

c) Which reaction is likely i) to be the slowest, ii) to have the least stable activated complex?

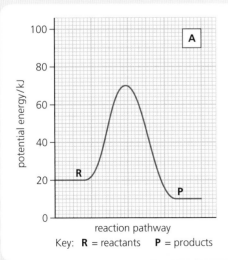

Key: **R** = reactants **P** = products

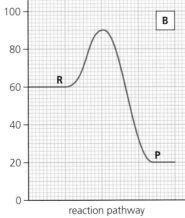

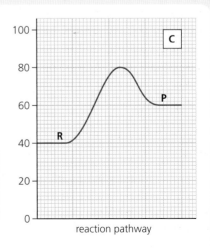

Figure 1.28

A simple example of catalysis in the lab can be shown using hydrogen peroxide. A solution of hydrogen peroxide evolves oxygen very slowly, even on heating. Oxygen is released much more rapidly when manganese(IV) oxide is added.

$$2H_2O(aq) \rightarrow 2H_2O(l) + O_2(g)$$

Catalysts play an important part in many industrial processes as illustrated in Table 1.4.

How catalysts work

Many catalysts used in laboratories and chemical plants across the world are metals or metal compounds. Catalysis occurs on the surface of the catalyst at certain points called active sites. At these sites molecules of at least one of the reactants are temporarily adsorbed (bonded to the surface). This is shown in Figure 1.31. In this example, the reactants are in a different physical state from the solid catalyst.

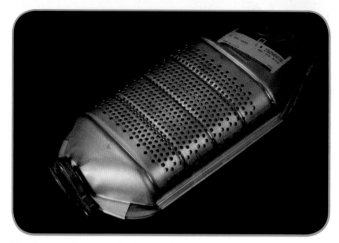

Figure 1.30 A catalytic convertor

Catalyst	Process	Reaction	Importance
Vanadium(V) oxide	Contact	$2SO_2 + O_2 \rightarrow 2SO_3$	Manufacture of sulfuric acid
Iron	Haber	$N_2 + 3H_2 \rightarrow 2NH_3$	Manufacture of ammonia
Platinum	Catalytic oxidation of ammonia	$4NH_3 + 5O_2 \rightarrow 4NO + 6H_2O$	Manufacture of nitric acid
Nickel	Hydrogenation	Unsaturated oils + $H_2 \rightarrow$ saturated fats	Manufacture of margarine
Aluminium silicate	Catalytic cracking	Breaking down long-chain hydrocarbon molecules	Manufacture of fuels and monomers for the plastics industry

Table 1.4 Common catalysts and their uses in the chemical industry

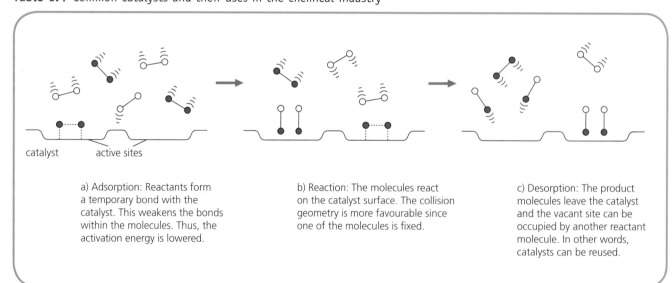

catalyst   active sites

a) Adsorption: Reactants form a temporary bond with the catalyst. This weakens the bonds within the molecules. Thus, the activation energy is lowered.

b) Reaction: The molecules react on the catalyst surface. The collision geometry is more favourable since one of the molecules is fixed.

c) Desorption: The product molecules leave the catalyst and the vacant site can be occupied by another reactant molecule. In other words, catalysts can be reused.

Figure 1.31 Catalysts provide an alternative route to the products

The diagrams shown in Figure 1.31 illustrate how a catalyst provides an alternative route for a reaction with lowered activation energy. Without the catalyst, more energy would be required to break the bonds of the reactants. When the catalyst is used, less energy is required as the catalyst helps to weaken the reactant bonds. The lowering of the activation energy is illustrated in the potential energy diagram shown in Figure 1.32.

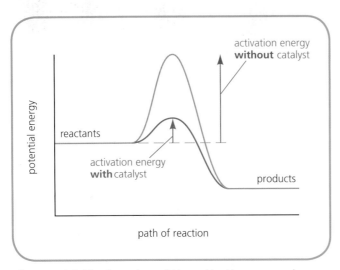

Figure 1.32 The lowering of the activation energy by a catalyst

Figure 1.31 demonstrates clearly that catalysts do take part in chemical reactions and can be reused at the end of the reaction. Practically, this is shown quite nicely by the reaction of Rochelle's salt (potassium sodium tartrate) and hydrogen peroxide. This reaction is catalysed by an aqueous solution of cobalt(II) ions as shown in Figure 1.33. This is a different type of catalysis from the previous example as here we have the reactants and catalyst in the same physical state. The immediate colour change to green is thought to be due to oxidation to form cobalt(III) ions which then catalyse the reaction. The return of the pink colour at the end of the reaction shows that cobalt(II) ions have been reformed. This sequence of colour changes shows that a catalyst may undergo a temporary chemical change during its catalytic activity.

It is worth emphasising the contrasting ways in which the use of a catalyst and the use of heat affect the rate of a reaction. Heating speeds up a reaction by increasing the number of molecules that have energy greater than the activation energy. A catalyst speeds up a reaction by lowering the activation energy. The former provides energy to overcome the energy barrier; the latter lowers the barrier. This confirms the important role played by catalysts in saving energy in many industrial processes.

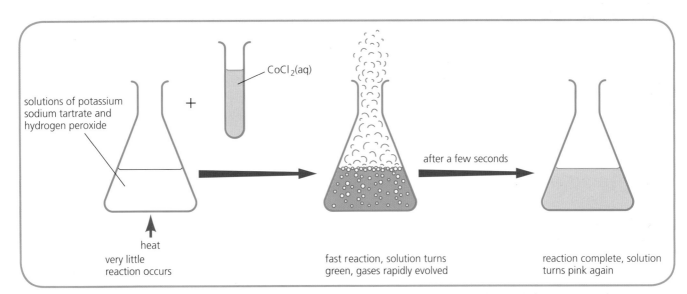

Figure 1.33 Catalysts take part in chemical reactions

Checklist for Revision

- I can calculate the rate of reaction from graphs of a changing property versus time, e.g. graphs of volume versus time.

- I can predict how the rate of a chemical reaction will be affected by changing the concentration, particle size, temperature or by using a catalyst.

- I can use collision theory to explain how these factors affect the rate of a reaction.

- I understand the concepts of collision geometry and activation energy.

- I understand why it is important for chemists to control the rate of a reaction.

- I understand energy distribution diagrams and can explain the effect of increasing the temperature, or adding a catalyst, on the rate of reaction.

- I know what is meant by the term 'activated complex'.

- I can calculate the activation energy and enthalpy change from energy profile diagrams.

- I can show the position of an activated complex on an energy profile diagram.

- I can show the effect, on an energy profile diagram, of adding a catalyst.

Key Terms

The words and phrases below were introduced in this chapter.

Their definitions are given in the chemical dictionary.

activated complex

activation energy

catalyst

collision geometry

collision theory

endothermic

enthalpy change

exothermic

rate of reaction

Find out about the Imperial Sugar Company explosion of February 2008 in the USA. What happened? Which factors led to the explosion? How can such catastrophes be avoided?

Activities

Study Questions

1*

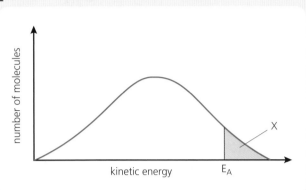

Figure 1.34

In area X

  A molecules always form an activated complex

  B no molecules have the energy to form an activated complex

  C collisions between molecules are always successful in forming products

  D all molecules have the energy to form an activated complex.

2* Hydrogen peroxide can be used to clean contact lenses. In this process, the enzyme catalase is added to break down hydrogen peroxide. The equation for the reaction is

$$2H_2O_2 \rightarrow 2H_2O + O_2$$

The rate of oxygen production was measured in three laboratory experiments using the same volume of hydrogen peroxide at the same temperature.

Experiment	Concentration of H_2O_2/mol l^{-1}	Catalyst used
A	0.2	Yes
B	0.4	Yes
C	0.2	No

Table 1.5

The curve obtained for experiment A is shown.

  a) What is the average rate of reaction between
    (i) 0 and 20 s?
    (ii) 20 and 80 s?

  b) Copy the graph and add curves to show the results of experiments B and C. Label each curve clearly.

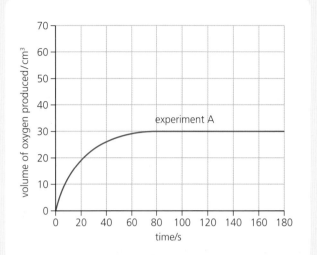

Figure 1.35

3 When a catalyst is used in a reaction

  A the enthalpy change decreases

  B the activation energy decreases

  C the enthalpy change increases

  D the activation energy increases.

4 The graph below indicates an energy diagram for the decomposition of ethanal (CH_3CHO) vapour according to the equation:

$$CH_3CHO(g) \rightarrow CH_4(g) + CO(g)$$

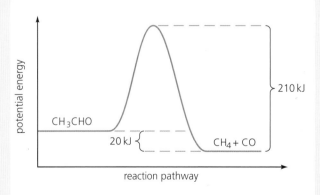

Figure 1.36

  a) What is the value for the activation energy of the reaction?

  b) What is the enthalpy change for the reaction? Is the reaction exothermic or endothermic?

c) Iodine vapour catalyses the above reaction. Copy the graph and on it indicate by means of a dotted line the reaction pathway for a catalysed reaction.

5* Methanoic acid, HCOOH, can break down to carbon monoxide and water by two different reactions, A and B.

Reaction A (catalysed)

$$HCOOH(aq) + H^+(aq) \rightarrow CO(g) + H_2O(l) + H^+(aq)$$

Reaction B (uncatalysed)

$$\overset{heat}{HCOOH(aq) \rightarrow CO(g) + H_2O(l)}$$

a) What is the evidence in the equation for Reaction A that the $H^+(aq)$ ion acts as a catalyst?

b) The energy diagram for the catalysed reaction is shown in Figure 1.37.

Copy this diagram and draw a line on it to show the reaction pathway for the uncatalysed reaction.

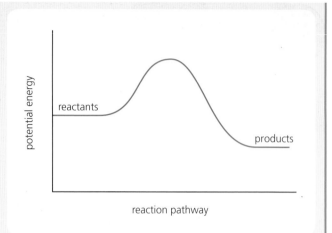

Figure 1.37

The Periodic Table: bonding and structure

Structure and bonding of the elements

The Periodic Table is used by scientists all over the world. It organises elements into **groups** and **periods** and helps us to make predictions about the properties of elements and their compounds. It is fascinating that the elements we study continue to be investigated to find out what new and exciting compounds can be made by joining the elements together. Some of these new compounds will be used to make new materials for the electronic phones and computers we use, some will help us save energy, other compounds will be used as medicines to treat and cure disease. The Periodic Table is a good starting point for any chemist who wishes to unlock the secrets of the elements which make up our Universe.

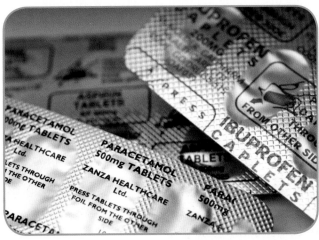

Figure 2.2 The properties of modern medicines rely on an understanding of the chemistry of elements and compounds.

The arrangement of elements in the Periodic Table

Over the years, alchemists tried in vain to change other substances into gold. While they never succeeded, they did document their experiments and thoughts

Figure 2.1 Modern electronic devices contain elements such as silicon, carbon, lithium, beryllium, lead, cadmium and many others.

Figure 2.3 The alchemists' discoveries helped shape the modern Periodic Table.

which paved the way for other chemists to discover many elements and compounds. By the nineteenth century, chemists had a bewildering mass of chemical information available to them. More elements were being discovered and their properties were being investigated. To try to simplify all the information available, they had to come up with a way of organising all of the elements that had been discovered. The Periodic Table of the elements was the solution.

The greatest step towards creating the Periodic Table was taken by the Russian scientist Dmitri Mendeleev in 1869.

Figure 2.4 Dmitri Mendeleev

Mendeleev examined all the available data on the elements and created the first Periodic Table which appeared to organise the elements in a sensible way. His main points are summarised below.

- The elements fall into a repeating pattern of similar properties if arranged in order of increasing atomic mass.

- The list was arranged into vertical and horizontal sequences. The vertical sequences were called groups and the horizontal sequences were called periods. The groups contained elements that were chemically similar.

- Unlike other scientists who tried to come up with a way of organising the elements, Mendeleev left blanks for unknown elements. He predicted the properties for the missing elements and when they were discovered later, the predictions were accurate. The missing elements included gallium

and germanium. When the noble gases were later discovered, they fitted into the Periodic Table as a separate column.

Figure 2.5 Copper and gold are both good electrical conductors and have a high lustre.

- Errors in atomic mass determinations, particularly of beryllium, were probable. Despite the great advance made, and the ready acceptance of the Periodic Law, there were still anomalies.

Figure 2.6 Chlorine and sulfur are examples of non-metal elements.

- Certain elements in the table were in reverse order of atomic mass.

- There was no easy way of placing the 'rare earths' – the elements lanthanum to lutetium.

Mendeleev was not the only scientist who organised the elements in order of atomic mass. The English chemist John Newlands noted that, when arranged in order of atomic mass, every eighth element showed similarities like musical notes in a scale. He called his idea the 'Law of Octaves'. Many scientists ridiculed Newlands' idea and so his method of organising the elements did not become established. A major flaw in Newlands' work was that he did not leave 'gaps' in his table for elements that were still to be discovered.

Unlike Mendeleev's table, the modern Periodic Table arranges elements by increasing **atomic number**. This removes the difficulties indicated in the last three bullet points and allows us to make accurate predictions about both the physical and chemical properties of the elements.

When elements are arranged in order of atomic number, each new period starts when a new layer of electrons in the atom starts to fill. Going from left to right across the Periodic Table, the number of outer electrons increases which changes completely the properties of the elements. For example, the elements towards the left-hand side of the table have metallic properties (they have a high lustre, they are malleable and they conduct electricity) whereas the elements towards the right-hand side of the table have non-metallic properties (they do not conduct electricity, they can be solid, liquid or gas etc.).

When elements are arranged in order of atomic number, each group contains elements with the same number of **electrons** in the outermost layer. This explains why elements in the same group (in other words, the same vertical column of the Periodic Table) have similar chemical properties. For example, you are probably familiar with the spectacular reactions of the group I elements with water. These elements are known as the alkali metals as they react to produce an alkali and hydrogen gas. As you go down the group, the metals become much more reactive. If we examine their electron arrangement we find that each element in group I has one outer electron. When these elements react, they readily lose this electron to achieve a much more stable electron arrangement.

23

Figure 2.7 Alkali metals, such as potassium, must be stored under oil to prevent reaction with the water and oxygen in the air.

Figure 2.8 Traditional light bulbs are filled with argon gas to prevent the tungsten filament reacting with oxygen.

The elements found in group 0, the noble gases, could not be more different from the alkali metals. They are all very unreactive and, as their name suggests, they are all gases. An examination of their electron arrangement reveals that each noble gas has a layer of outer electrons which is filled completely. This helps to explain their lack of reactivity. This lack of reactivity makes them extremely useful. For example, when reactions are carried out in air it is common for oxides to form due to elements and compounds reacting with oxygen. To prevent oxide formation, reactions are often carried out in an inert atmosphere of argon gas which allows chemists to have more control over the compounds formed.

The Periodic Table is a starting point for our journey through Higher Chemistry. When we understand the trends in the Periodic Table it makes learning chemistry so much easier. As you go through the Higher course you will use the Periodic Table regularly and develop a new understanding of the elements and their properties. As well as the alkali metals and the noble gases, you should also be able to identify the halogens, the transition metals, the metals and the non-metals.

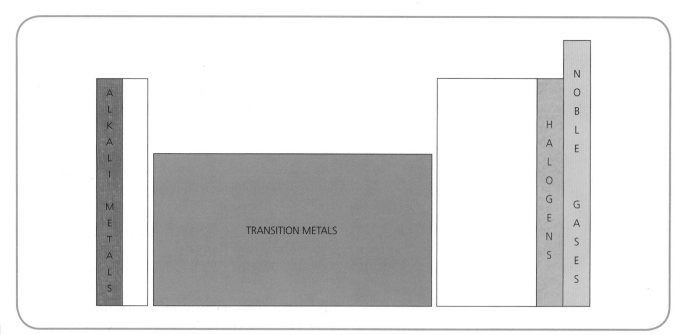

Figure 2.9

Bonding and structure in the first 20 elements

The properties and structures of elements are related to the types of bonding present. Bonding is a term that describes how atoms join together. Structure describes how the atoms in the element are arranged. The resulting characteristics of the substances, whether physical or chemical, are their properties.

Bonding in elements

In order to appreciate the properties of elements, we must understand the two main bonding types found in elements: metallic and covalent.

Metallic bonding

The fact that all metals conduct electricity and have a metallic lustre can be explained by examining the bonding present in metals. If you examine the electron arrangement of these elements, you will discover that they do not have enough electrons to allow them to achieve a full outer shell of electrons by covalent bonding (see below). Instead, we find that the outer electrons of metallic atoms are loosely held which allows them to become **delocalised**. Metallic bonding consists of the atoms losing their outer electrons to a common 'pool' of delocalised electrons. As each atom has lost one or more electrons, the atoms become positively-charged ions. The charged metal ions are now attracted to the pool of electrons. As these electrons are free to move, metals conduct electricity.

The delocalised electrons in metals are also responsible for the lustre associated with metals. When light is shone onto a metal, the delocalised electrons absorb the energy from the light and then re-emit the light which gives the metal its characteristic shiny appearance.

Figure 2.11 Metals have a high lustre.

Questions

1 Suggest why aluminium conducts electricity better than sodium.

Covalent bonding

Metallic bonding (the attraction of the negatively-charged electrons for the positive metal ions) is a form of electrostatic attraction. Covalent bonding is also electrostatic, but this time the atoms are held together by the attraction between their positive **nuclei** and negatively-charged shared pairs of electrons. This attraction is the 'glue' that holds atoms together. Figure 2.12 illustrates how two hydrogen atoms can bond by covalent bonding, in other words the sharing of electrons. If the atoms are too close together, the

nuclei and inner-shell electrons
i.e. positive ions

delocalised outer-shell electrons

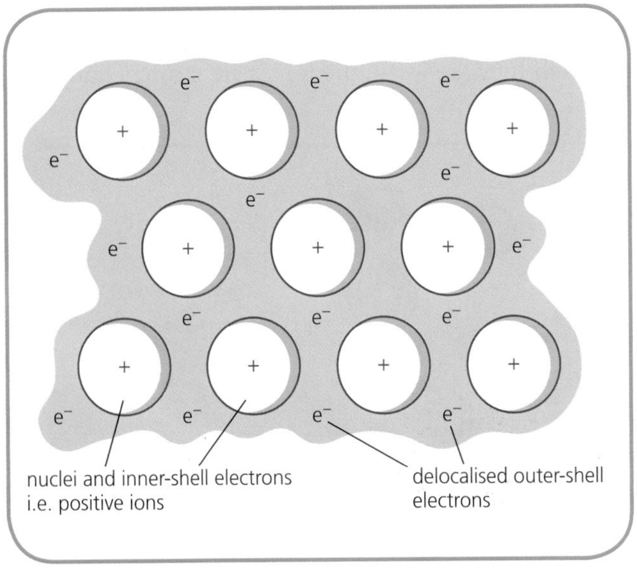

Figure 2.10 Metallic bonding

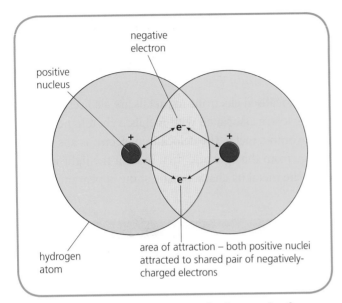

Figure 2.12 labels:
- negative electron
- positive nucleus
- e⁻
- +
- +
- e⁻
- hydrogen atom
- area of attraction – both positive nuclei attracted to shared pair of negatively-charged electrons

Figure 2.12 Two hydrogen atoms sharing a pair of electrons

nuclei will repel each other. If the atoms are too far apart, the electrons will not be attracted to both nuclei.

The covalent bond is the shared pair of electrons. Since all the atoms in an element are alike in terms of **protons** and electrons, the bonding electrons are shared equally. We say that the covalent bond is **non-polar**. In some compounds the electrons in the covalent bond are not shared equally between the two atoms. This is known as a polar covalent bond which we will meet in Chapter 3.

Intermolecular forces

Particle models for the three states of matter help us to understand the bonding in elements.

For example, sodium exists as a metallic **lattice** where sodium ions are held together by metallic bonds. It exists as a solid at room temperature because the temperature is not high enough to break the strong metallic bonds. If the temperature is increased to the melting point of sodium, some of the metallic bonds break and liquid sodium is formed. It is quite straightforward to think about the three states of matter for metals and imagine the metallic bonds holding the structure together as a solid. We can think of the melting point as a measure of how strong the metallic bonds are between the metal ions. Thus, we could predict that iron would have stronger metallic bonds than sodium since iron has a higher melting point.

When we consider the non-metals, our explanation is slightly more complex. Consider argon. We know that the noble gases are very unreactive which makes it very difficult for them to form ionic or covalent bonds. But if argon is cooled, it will form a liquid and then a solid. So what is holding the argon atoms together in the liquid and solid state? The answer is **London dispersion forces**. These are very weak forces of attraction which can operate between all atoms and **molecules**. These forces are caused by the uneven distribution of the constantly moving electrons around the nuclei of the atoms. This causes the formation of **temporary dipoles** on the atoms (see Figure 2.14). The atoms then attract each other. The dipoles are constantly changing, but there are always some in existence.

London dispersion forces are very weak compared with **ionic**, covalent and metallic bonds. However, although they are weak, the forces are strong enough to

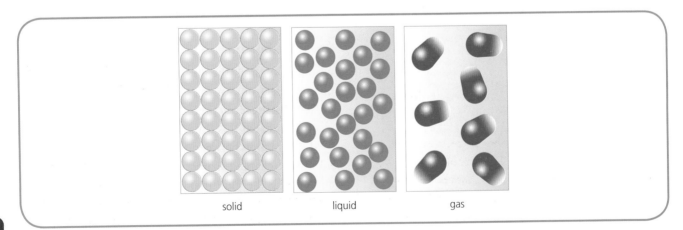

solid   liquid   gas

Figure 2.13 The three states of matter

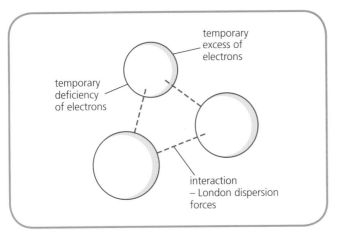

Figure 2.14 London dispersion forces

Figure 2.15 Nitrogen is very unreactive and is used in the packaging of crisps.

allow the noble gases to liquefy and solidify if they are cooled enough to remove the thermal kinetic energy of the atoms. Not surprisingly, helium, with only two electrons per atom, has the weakest London dispersion forces between its atoms and is the most difficult element to condense and freeze. It only freezes in temperatures near to absolute zero (−273°C).

Because the other noble gases have increasing numbers of electrons, the London dispersion forces, and hence melting and boiling points, increase down the group.

London dispersion forces are an example of an **intermolecular force** – in other words, a force between molecules. The other intermolecular forces (also referred to as intermolecular bonds) will be discussed in Chapter 3.

Covalent molecular elements

Hydrogen, nitrogen, oxygen, the halogens, phosphorus, sulfur and the fullerenes are known as covalent molecular structures. That is, they consist of groups of small numbers of atoms joined by covalent bonds.

Nitrogen

Nitrogen is the most common gas in the air. It is very unreactive and is used widely in the food industry as a packaging gas to prevent food from spoiling.

Nitrogen atoms, with three unpaired electrons, form diatomic molecules with a triple covalent bond. If we were asked to write the formula for nitrogen we would write N_2 regardless of whether we were talking about solid, liquid or gaseous nitrogen. To show the states we would simply place the correct state symbol after

the formula, such as $N_2(s)$, $N_2(l)$ or $N_2(g)$. Going from a solid to a liquid to a gas does not change the bonds between nitrogen atoms. The triple covalent bond in nitrogen remains. Nitrogen molecules, however, are held together by London dispersion forces. The fact that nitrogen has a very low melting and boiling point demonstrates that the forces of attraction are very weak in nitrogen; it does not take much energy to overcome the intermolecular forces of attraction to change nitrogen from a solid to liquid or liquid to gas. It is important to note that the covalent bonds (the intramolecular bonds, in other words those within the molecule) are not broken when nitrogen is melted or boiled.

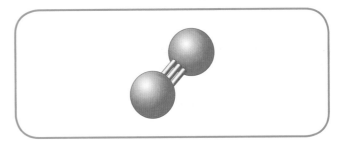

Figure 2.16 Nitrogen forms a strong triple bond between its atoms, but the forces of attraction between its molecules are very weak.

Oxygen

This vital gas sustains life and takes part in so many reactions on Earth such as combustion and rusting. Each oxygen atom uses its two unpaired electrons to form two covalent bonds with one other oxygen atom (except when the rarer form ozone, O_3, is formed). As

27

Figure 2.17 Oxygen can be cooled to produce liquid oxygen which is easier to store.

in nitrogen, oxygen molecules are attracted to other oxygen molecules by London dispersion forces. It is these weak forces that are overcome when oxygen changes state.

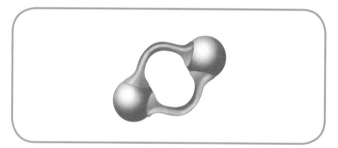

Figure 2.18 Diatomic oxygen has a very strong double covalent bond between its atoms, but the forces of attraction between oxygen molecules are very weak.

The halogens

The halogen group (group VII of the Periodic Table) contains a number of very reactive and potentially dangerous elements. The harmful nature of these elements allows them to be used as disinfectants. For example, iodine solutions are used to kill bacteria on the skin prior to surgery and both iodine and chlorine are used in water treatment.

The halogens all have a single unpaired outer electron and can form one covalent bond. As a result, they exist as diatomic molecules (F_2, Cl_2, Br_2 and I_2).

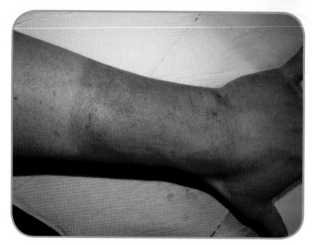

Figure 2.19 Iodine solutions are used to sterilise the skin.

Figure 2.20 Chlorine exists as a gas at room temperature.

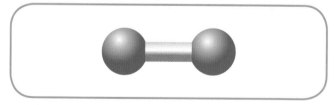

Figure 2.21 Chlorine atoms are held together by a strong covalent bond. The forces of attraction between chlorine molecules are very weak.

Sulfur

Sulfur is a very attractive yellow solid whose compounds can often be recognised by their bad smells. For example, hydrogen sulfide is responsible for the 'rotten egg' smell, while the powerful repellent released by a skunk contains sulfur compounds.

Figure 2.22 Sulfur exists as a solid at room temperature.

Figure 2.24 The discovery of phosphorus (painting by Joseph Wright, 1771)

As sulfur has the ability to form two or more bonds, sulfur atoms can bond to more than one other atom. Sulfur can even form closed, eight-membered, puckered rings. The London dispersion forces are much greater between molecules of sulfur which results in the element being a solid at room temperature. In other words, when compared with oxygen, it takes much more energy to overcome the forces of attraction to change solid sulfur into liquid sulfur.

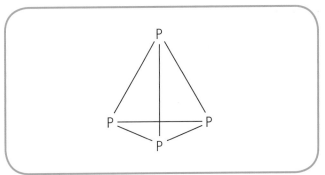

Figure 2.25 Phosphorus (P_4) molecule

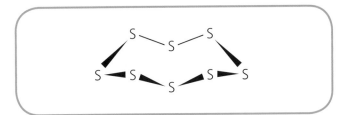

Figure 2.23 Bonding in sulfur (S_8)

molecules are strong which allows it to exist as a solid at room temperature.

Phosphorus

We owe the discovery of phosphorus to Hennig Brand, a German scientist who extracted the element from urine in the seventeenth century. The fact that phosphorus glows in the dark proved to be most entrancing to early chemists who developed many uses for this highly poisonous element.

Phosphorus makes use of single bonds to three other atoms to form tetrahedral P_4 molecules. Like sulfur, the London dispersion forces between phosphorus

Fullerenes

Discovered in 1985, the fullerenes are discrete, covalently-bonded molecules of carbon. The smallest is spherical and is named buckminsterfullerene after Buckminster Fuller, an American architect who designed large geodesic dome structures consisting of five- and six-sided panels. The spherical molecule of buckminsterfullerene (C_{60}) has five- and six-membered rings of carbon atoms producing the overall shape. Other molecules with elongated shapes can exist, such

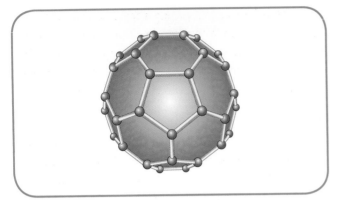

Figure 2.26 Fullerene structure

Figure 2.27 An uncut and a cut diamond

as C_{70}, and there are also much longer 'nanotubes', but all contain five- and six-membered carbon atom rings.

In the elements of groups VII, VI and V, the **intramolecular forces**, in other words the bonds within the molecule, are covalent. The intermolecular forces, those between the molecules, are the very weak London dispersion forces. Most of these elements are therefore quite volatile, even if solid at room temperature, since only the intermolecular forces have to be broken to melt and boil them.

Covalent network structures

Covalent networks are huge structures where each atom is covalently bonded to other atoms. Unlike covalent molecular substances which consist of only a few atoms bonded together, covalent network structures consist of many thousands of atoms bonded together by covalent bonds. These structures have extremely high melting points as covalent bonds must be broken for the solid to melt. For the Higher Chemistry course, we will consider carbon diamond, carbon graphite, silicon and boron.

Carbon diamond

One of the most expensive forms of an element, carbon in the form of diamond is formed when carbon-containing compounds, or other forms of carbon such as graphite, are exposed to very high pressures and specific temperatures. In nature this happens deep within the Earth's crust but the process can also be created in the laboratory to make synthetic diamonds.

Diamonds are highly valued for their beauty, which makes them an expensive stone to use in jewellery. They are also highly valued for their high thermal conductivity

(they feel cold when we touch them) and their hardness. Their hardness and strength allow diamonds to be used to cut other hard materials such as stone.

In the carbon diamond structure, each carbon atom is covalently bonded to four other carbon atoms in a tetrahedral arrangement as shown in Figures 2.28 and 2.29.

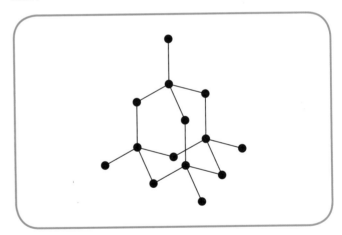

Figure 2.28 Diamond structure

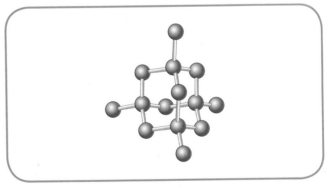

Figure 2.29 Carbon in the form of diamond exists as a covalent network compound.

The resultant structure is exceptionally hard and rigid. There are no discrete molecules, each atom being linked to all other atoms in the sample of element. There are no free electrons to allow electrical conduction but 'tunnels' between the atoms allow light to pass through, thus making diamonds transparent.

Carbon graphite

This is the form of carbon that is found in pencils.

Graphite has a structure based on three covalent bonds from each atom, forming layers of hexagonal rings. Each carbon atom contributes its fourth unpaired electron to the delocalised pool between the layers. The result is strong bonding within the layers but only weak interaction between the layers. Since the delocalised electrons are held quite weakly, they can flow across the layers. Graphite therefore conducts in a similar way to a metal. The layers separate easily so graphite is flaky, but because the layers are offset with respect to each other, light cannot pass through, so graphite is opaque.

Silicon

Silicon is the second most common element found on planet Earth. It is found in a variety of compounds, such as sand, which is silicon oxide. As an element, it is perhaps most famous for its use in the electronics industry as the 'silicon chip'.

Silicon forms a rigid covalent network with the same structure as carbon diamond.

Figure 2.32 Silicon

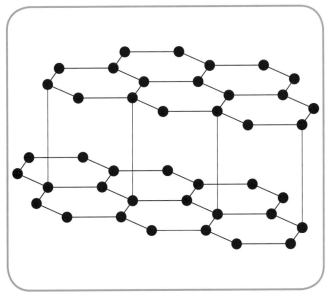

Figure 2.30 Graphite structure

Boron

Boron compounds are probably used every day by the practising chemist. Pyrex® glassware owes its strength and ability to withstand high temperatures to boron oxide which is used in the manufacture of Pyrex. Boron forms a structure made of B_{12} groups, which are bonded with other groups. The result is an element almost as hard as diamond.

Questions

2 Explain why diamond has a higher melting point than sulfur.

Monatomic elements: the noble gases

Passing electricity through a noble gas results in a colourful glow. As a result of this property, the noble gases are used in the familiar advertising signs, the so-called 'neon' lights, that light up our shops at night.

Figure 2.31 Graphite is used in pencil 'lead'.

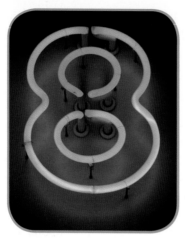

Figure 2.33 Noble gases emit light when electricity is passed through them.

The bonding in the elements is least complex at the right-hand side of the Periodic Table, in other words for the noble gases. These elements, with the exception of helium, always have an outer layer of eight electrons which is an especially stable arrangement. Because of the stability of the outer electrons, the noble gases do not form either covalent or ionic bonds between their atoms. They are **monatomic**, consisting of only one atom. When cooled, the atoms move closer together to form a liquid and then solid as they are held together by London dispersion forces.

Key properties of elements related to bonding

If we now look at some of the physical properties of these first 20 elements, we can see how these properties relate to the bond types present.

Melting and boiling points

Figure 2.35 shows that where the elements consist of discrete molecules (the monatomic and diatomic gases and P_4 and S_8), the melting and boiling points are low. This is because only the weak, intermolecular London dispersion forces have to be overcome in melting and boiling the element. The strong, covalent, intramolecular forces are unaffected.

In the covalent network solids carbon and silicon, covalent bonds must be broken when melting or

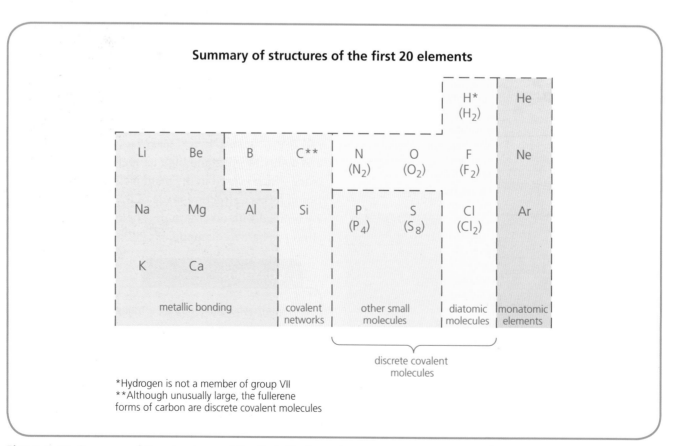

Summary of structures of the first 20 elements

						H* (H_2)	He
Li	Be	B	C**	N (N_2)	O (O_2)	F (F_2)	Ne
Na	Mg	Al	Si	P (P_4)	S (S_8)	Cl (Cl_2)	Ar
K	Ca						
	metallic bonding		covalent networks	other small molecules		diatomic molecules	monatomic elements

discrete covalent molecules

*Hydrogen is not a member of group VII
**Although unusually large, the fullerene forms of carbon are discrete covalent molecules

Figure 2.34 Summary of the structures of the first 20 elements

boiling takes place – this is much more difficult. Melting and boiling points are therefore much higher.

Similarly for group I, II and III elements, their very strong metallic bonds have to be overcome and these elements also have high melting and boiling points compared with covalent molecular elements.

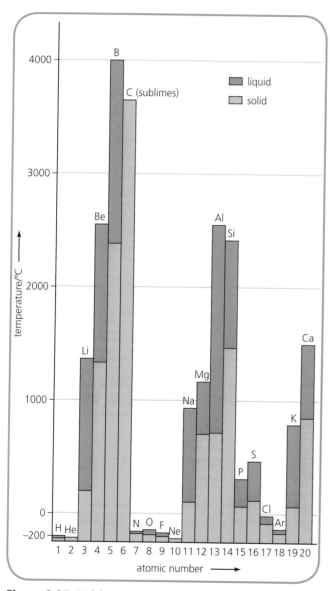

Figure 2.35 Melting and boiling points of elements 1–20

The history of the discovery of the Periodic Table and the history of the uses of its elements are fascinating. Every element has a story to tell and every story demonstrates the power of chemistry. As new discoveries are made, we learn more about the elements which fill our Universe and use this knowledge to make new substances for the benefit of mankind. Sadly, history has shown us that chemistry can also be used to destroy our precious lives. The following examples look at the use of chlorine and phosphorus as weapons of war.

On 22 April 1915, allied soldiers fighting the Germans in the First World War noticed a green haze sweeping over the battlefields as evening fell. Chaos descended on the trenches as people began to struggle for breath. The German army were using chlorine gas in an act of chemical warfare. The effects of such a poisonous element were horrific, leading to the deaths of many soldiers.

Figure 2.36 Chlorine gas was used as a chemical weapon in the First World War.

The use of chemicals in war accelerated after the First World War. Governments devoted resources to developing new chemical weapons which would have devastating consequences for populations attacked with these agents.

Another element used as a chemical weapon was phosphorus. White phosphorus was used as a chemical weapon throughout the twentieth century where its horrific effects on humans and its terrifying explosive properties were used to help defeat enemy soldiers during conflict. White phosphorus is extremely reactive and is usually stored under water to prevent it reacting with oxygen. Given its horrific properties, many organisations have been campaigning for it to be banned.

Fortunately, chemists around the world work hard to tame the properties of the elements which can cause harm. This usually involves converting these elements into compounds and examining the properties of the compounds produced.

Checklist for Revision

- I can identify groups and periods in the Periodic Table.

- I know where to find the metals, non-metals, alkali metals, halogens, noble gases and transition metals on the Periodic Table.

- I can explain the reactivity of elements by considering their electron arrangements.

- I can discuss the bonding and structure of:

  - the metallic elements (Li, Be, Na, Mg, Al, K, Ca)

  - the covalent molecular elements (H_2, N_2, O_2, F_2, Cl_2, P_4, S_8 and C_{60})

  - the covalent network elements (B, C (diamond, graphite), Si)

  - the monatomic elements (the noble gases).

- I can use my knowledge of bonding and structure to discuss the different physical properties of elements, for example, why sulfur has a higher melting point than chlorine.

Key Terms

The words and phrases below were introduced in this chapter.

Their definitions are given in the chemical dictionary on page 225.

atomic number
covalent bonding
covalent network
delocalised electrons
electrons
groups
intermolecular forces
intramolecular forces
ionic
lattice
London dispersion forces
metallic bonding
monatomic
nuclei
periods
temporary dipoles

Activities

1 Produce a presentation outlining the key dates and discoveries which led to the development of the modern Periodic Table.

2 Produce an information leaflet on the first 20 elements. Highlight the key points about their bonding and structure.

3 Find out about the different forms of phosphorus and its many uses from bombs to matches.

Study Questions

In questions 1–3 choose the correct word(s) from the following list to copy and complete the sentence.

> covalent bonds   molecular   network
> London dispersion forces

1 A fullerene is a form of carbon which has a covalent _____ structure.

2 The low melting point of sulfur is due to _____ between molecules.

3 Silicon is an example of a covalent _____ structure.

4 Which element has discrete covalent molecules?

  A Fluorine

  B Carbon diamond

  C Lithium

  D Boron

5 When liquid chlorine evaporates

  A covalent bonds are broken

  B covalent bonds are formed

  C London dispersion forces are broken

  D London dispersion forces are formed.

6 A certain element contains only London dispersion forces. This element must be

  A an alkali metal

  B a noble gas

  C a transition metal

  D a halogen.

7 Which of the following statements is not true?

  A Diamond is very hard due to its covalent network structure.

  B Aluminium conducts electricity as it has delocalised electrons.

  C Nitrogen has weak covalent bonds since it is a gas at room temperature.

  D Phosphorus has a low melting point due to London dispersion forces.

8* Diamond and graphite are well-known forms of the element carbon. New forms of pure carbon have recently been made. They exist as individual molecules of different sizes and are called fullerenes. The main fullerene has the formula C_{60}.

  a) How does the structure of a fullerene differ from that of diamond?

  b) Fullerenes were first made by passing a high current of electricity through a graphite rod in an atmosphere of helium. This caused the graphite to vaporise. Suggest why helium gas was used.

  c) Fullerenes can be made into hydrocarbons. One such hydrocarbon has the formula $C_{60}H_{36}$. Describe a chemical test which could be carried out on a solution of $C_{60}H_{36}$ to show whether the hydrocarbon is saturated or unsaturated.

9* The first 20 elements of the Periodic Table can be categorised according to their bonding and structure:

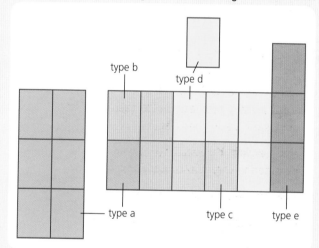

Figure 2.37

Copy and complete the following table by adding the appropriate letter for each type of element.

Type	Bonding and structure at normal room temperature and pressure
	Monatomic gases
	Covalent network solids
	Diatomic covalent gases
	Discrete covalent molecular solids
	Metallic lattice solids

Table 2.1

3 Trends in the Periodic Table

In this chapter we will consider the trends of covalent radius and electronegativity.

Covalent radius – a measure of atomic size

We often imagine atoms as little balls with a centre (the nucleus) and a definite size. One of the problems with this model is that atoms have electrons which are constantly moving. This makes it very difficult to judge where the 'edge' of the atom is located. Instead of measuring an atom from 'edge to edge', the measure of atomic size most commonly used is the **covalent atomic radius**. This is defined as half the distance between the nuclei of two covalently bonded atoms of the element.

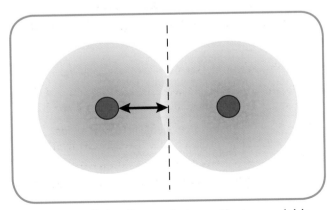

Figure 3.1 The distance between the two nuclei is the bond length of the molecule.

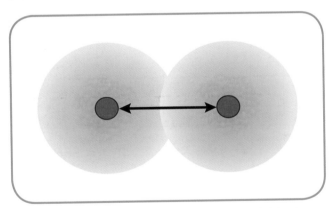

Figure 3.2 Half the distance between the two nuclei is the covalent radius.

The distance between two nuclei can be measured accurately by a technique known as X-ray diffraction. This distance is known as the bond length. Once this distance has been determined, the answer is halved to give the covalent radius. For example, the distance between the nuclei of two chlorine atoms in a molecule of chlorine is 1.98×10^{-10} m. This allows us to calculate the covalent radius of chlorine as 0.99×10^{-10} m. As these numbers are extremely small, chemists prefer to use picometres as the unit. One picometre (1 pm) is equal to 1×10^{-12} m. So, the covalent radius of chlorine would be quoted as 99 pm.

Trends in covalent radius

We are interested in the trend in the size of atoms as we go down a group or across a period in the Periodic Table. These trends are obvious when the covalent radius is graphed against atomic number as shown in Figure 3.3 on page 37.

From examining this graph, two trends are obvious:

1 Going across a period, atomic size decreases.

2 Going down a group, the atomic size increases.

There are two factors that must be considered to help us explain the trends in atomic size:

- the nuclear charge of the atom
- the number of filled electron shells.

Element	Li	Be	B	C	N	O	F
Atomic number	3	4	5	6	7	8	9
Nuclear charge	3+	4+	5+	6+	7+	8+	9+
Electron arrangement	2,1	2,2	2,3	2,4	2,5	2,6	2,7
Covalent radius/pm	134	129	90	77	75	73	71

Table 3.1 Trends in covalent radii across a period

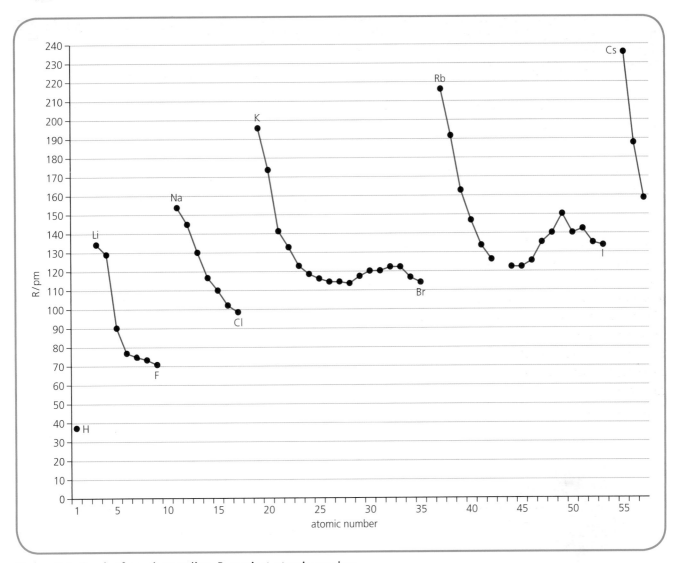

Figure 3.3 Graph of covalent radius, R, against atomic number

Going across a period, the nuclear charge increases. Consider the period from lithium to fluorine as shown in Table 3.1.

The atomic number increases by one as we move from one element to its neighbour. An increase in atomic number means that the number of protons in the nucleus is increasing. Since protons have a positive charge, increasing the atomic number results in the nuclear charge increasing. Electrons are negatively charged; an increase in atomic number results in the electrons being more strongly attracted to the nucleus which means that the size of the atom gets smaller.

Going down a group, the elements have the same number of outer electrons, but one more energy level is occupied by electrons in each succeeding element. Consider the elements in group I as shown in Table 3.2.

Although nuclear charge increases, its effect is outweighed by the much greater radius of successive electron layers. Each extra layer of electrons 'shields' the outer electrons from the positive nucleus so that the outer electrons are less strongly attracted to the nucleus. This results in the atomic size becoming larger. This **shielding** effect is also known as screening.

Element	Li	Na	K	Rb	Cs
Atomic number	3	11	19	37	55
Nuclear charge	3+	11+	19+	37+	55+
Electron arrangement	2,1	2,8,1	2,8,8,1	2,8,18,8,1	2,8,18,18,8,1
Covalent radius/pm	134	154	196	216	235

Table 3.2 Trends in covalent radii down a group

Summary

- The atomic size decreases across a period due to the increase in nuclear charge.
- The atomic size increases down a group due to the increase in number of electron shells which shield outer electrons from the nuclear charge.

Questions

1 Explain why
   a) the potassium atom is larger than the sodium atom
   b) the chlorine atom is smaller than the sodium atom.

For Interest   Atomic size and medicinal chemistry

Concepts like covalent radius can often appear to be highly theoretical with little relevance to our everyday lives. But to chemists, knowledge of the covalent radius can be used to help them solve many problems in their quest to make new products. For example, medicinal chemists design new medicines by investigating chemical structures such as enzymes. Quite often they will design a new medicine which can fit into the active site of an enzyme in the human body, which results in the enzyme working better or stops the enzyme working altogether. In order to build medicines which can fit into enzymes, medicinal chemists use their knowledge of atomic size to help them build molecules with different sizes and shapes. Sometimes a molecule can be made more effective simply by changing one atom for another. For example, changing from chlorine to fluorine – which is smaller – might help the molecule fit into an enzyme more readily, making it a more effective medicine.

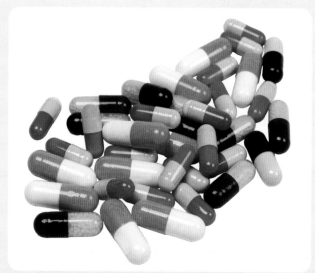

Figure 3.4 Atomic size is often considered when designing new medicines whose molecules have a specific size and shape.

First ionisation energy (or enthalpy)

The alkali metals are very reactive as they can easily lose their outer electron. A measure of how easy it is to remove an electron is the **ionisation** energy. This is defined as the energy required to remove one mole of electrons from one mole of gaseous atoms.

There are three important parts to this definition which allow fair comparisons to be made between the elements of the Periodic Table:

1 Atoms are being ionised by loss of electrons to form positive ions.

2 The atoms must be in the gaseous state.

3 One mole of atoms is compared.

The ionisation energy is an **enthalpy change** and is represented by a ΔH value. Enthalpy will be investigated further in Chapter 16.

For sodium, 502 kJ of energy is required to remove the first electron from one mole of sodium atoms in the gaseous state:

$$Na(g) \rightarrow Na^+(g) + e^- \qquad \Delta H = 502 \text{ kJ mol}^{-1}$$

This is known as the first ionisation energy of sodium since it is a measure of the energy required to remove the first, or outermost, electron from sodium. The enthalpy change has a positive value which informs us that we must use energy to remove an electron from sodium.

The second ionisation energy is the enthalpy change associated with:

$$Na^+(g) \rightarrow Na^{2+}(g) + e^- \qquad \Delta H = 4560 \text{ kJ mol}^{-1}$$

In other words, this is the energy required to remove a second electron from sodium after the first electron has been removed.

Adding together the first and second ionisation energies of sodium gives us the quantity of energy needed to remove two moles of electrons from one mole of sodium atoms in the gaseous state. The equation which represents this change is:

$$Na(g) \rightarrow Na^{2+}(g) + 2e^-$$

The enthalpy change for this reaction is:

$$502 + 4560 = 5062 \text{ kJ mol}^{-1}$$

The values for some first ionisation energies are shown in Table 3.3 (units are kJ mol^{-1}).

These values are plotted, together with second ionisation energies, for the first 20 elements in Figure 3.5.

From this information, two general trends emerge:

1 Going down a group, the first ionisation energy decreases.

2 Going across a period, first the ionisation energy increases.

As with covalent radius, there are two factors that must be considered to help us explain the trends in ionisation energy:

- the nuclear charge of the atom
- the number of filled electron shells.

Going down a group, an electron is being removed from the layer of electrons which is furthest from the nucleus. This layer is increasingly distant from the nuclear attraction and hence, although the nuclear charge is also increasing, less energy is required to remove an electron.

An additional factor is the screening effect of electrons in inner shells. These inner electrons reduce the attraction of the nucleus for outermost electrons, hence reducing the ionisation energy.

Going across a period, the pattern is less straightforward, but there is an overall increase. The electron being removed is in the same layer for any element in the same period, such as Li–Ne or Na–Ar. As already pointed out, the nuclear charge is increasing across each period. The outermost electrons are therefore more strongly held and so the energy required to remove them, the ionisation energy, increases along each period.

Finally it is worth noting that within each period, the noble gas has the highest value for first ionisation energy. This goes some way to explaining the great stability of filled electron shells and the resistance of the noble gases to forming compounds. It should be noted, however, that electrons can be removed from noble gas atoms. If some other change can compensate for the energy required then ionic compounds of the noble gases can be made.

Trends in the second ionisation energies can be explained by considering the nuclear charge and where the electron is being removed from. For example, lithium has a very low first ionisation energy but an extraordinarily high second ionisation energy. The reason for this becomes obvious when we consider the electron arrangement of lithium: 2,1. Removal of the second electron involves taking an electron from the completely filled first shell, which is much closer to the nucleus and therefore the electrons are very strongly held.

Li 526	Be 905	B 807	C 1090	N 1410	O 1320	F 1690	Ne 2090
Na 502	Mg 744	Al 584	Si 792	P 1020	S 1010	Cl 1260	Ar 1530
K 425	Ca 596	Ga 577	Ge 762	As 947	Se 941	Br 1150	Kr 1350
Rb 409	Sr 556	In 556	Sn 709	Sb 834	Te 870	I 1020	Xe 1170

decrease down group →

increase across period →

Table 3.3 First ionisation energies

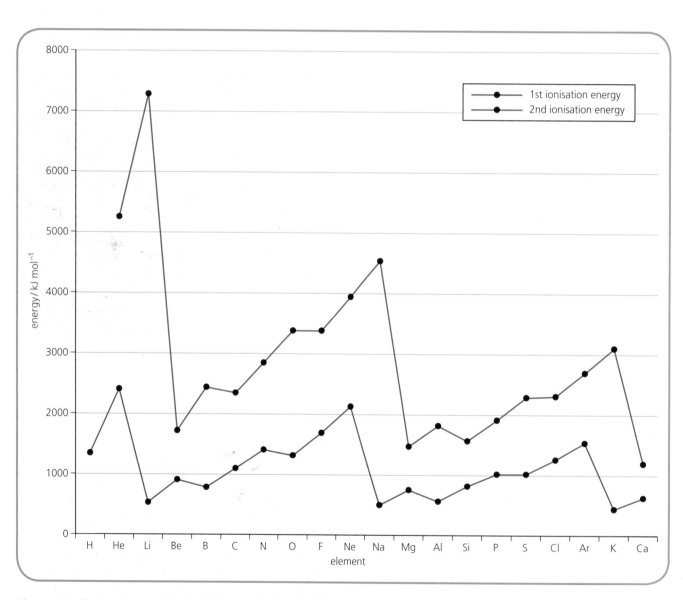

Figure 3.5 First and second ionisation energies for the first 20 elements

Scientists describe radiation as ionising or non-ionising. Ionising radiation can be harmful to human health if we are exposed to high doses of the radiation whereas non-ionising radiation is generally considered to be safe. For example, radio waves that allow a car radio to play music transmitted from a radio station and microwaves that allow mobile phones to work are referred to as non-ionising forms of radiation. In other words, radio waves and microwaves do not have enough energy to ionise an atom or molecule which would suggest that they are unlikely to be harmful to health. Health effects have been linked to non-ionising radiation, but it is likely that these effects are a result of the heating that occurs during exposure to the radiation for a certain length of time.

Examples of ionising radiation include X-rays, gamma rays and UV light. These are forms of radiation which have much higher energy – enough energy to ionise an atom or molecule, which can lead to ill effects if exposure is high. For example, it is well known that significant exposure to X-rays can be harmful to a person's health. On the other hand, scientists can make use of the ionising ability of these radiations to treat and prevent disease. For example, UV light can be used to sterilise water, while gamma rays can be used to treat certain cancers. Scientists use their knowledge of ionisation energy to help them assess how harmful radiation can be and how it can be used.

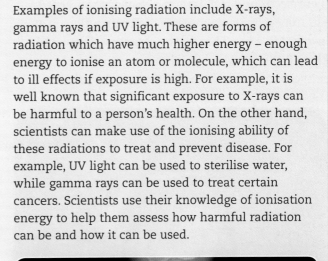

Figure 3.6 Mobile phones use non-ionising radiation.

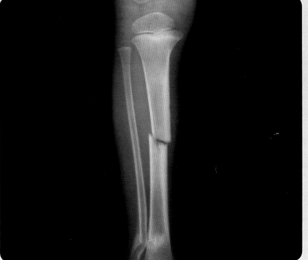

Figure 3.7 X-rays can be harmful as they have enough energy to ionise atoms.

Question

2 Use your data booklet to calculate the energy required for the following changes:

a) $Ca(g) \rightarrow Ca^{2+}(g) + 2e^-$

b) $Al(g) \rightarrow Al^{3+}(g) + 3e^-$

3 The first compounds of the noble gases were formed from xenon (Xe). Suggest why this was the case.

Electronegativity

The celebrated chemist Linus Pauling, who is the only person in history to have won a Nobel Prize for chemistry and a Nobel Prize for peace, wrote a very famous chemistry text called *The Nature of the Chemical Bond*. In this text, Pauling presented many theories which we now use to help us understand how atoms can form chemical bonds. In particular, Pauling quantified the concept that some atoms attract electrons in a bond more strongly than other atoms. This concept is known as **electronegativity**.

In a covalent bond formed by the sharing of an electron pair between two atoms, the attraction of the atoms for these electrons depends on the elements concerned. Electronegativity is a measure of the attraction an atom involved in a bond has for the electrons of the bond. Linus Pauling devised the electronegativity scale where each element is given an electronegativity value.

Figure 3.8 The famous Nobel Prize-winning chemist Linus Pauling

Elements with high electronegativity values attract electrons very strongly whereas elements with low electronegativity values attract electrons only weakly. Electronegativity values for some elements are given in Table 3.4.

Trends in electronegativity

Two general trends emerge:

1 Going down a group, the electronegativity decreases.

2 Going across a period, the electronegativity increases.

As with covalent radius, there are two factors that must be considered to help us explain the trends in electronegativity:

● the nuclear charge of the atom

● the number of filled electron shells.

In general, the electronegativity increases from left to right along a period since nuclear charge increases in the same direction. The increase in nuclear charge causes the atom to attract bonded electrons more strongly, so electronegativity values increase.

Going down a group, the atomic size increases as there are more shells of electrons. The increase in the electron shells shields the bonded electrons from the nuclear charge which means that electrons are less strongly attracted to the atom. Consequently, electronegativity decreases going down a group.

The electronegativity scale can be used to explain why some elements join to form covalent bonds while other elements join to form ionic bonds. For example, hydrogen atoms join to form diatomic H_2 molecules where the two hydrogen atoms are joined by a covalent

H 2.2						
Li 1.0	Be 1.5	B 2.0	C 2.5	N 3.0	O 3.5	F 4.0
Na 0.9	Mg 1.2	Al 1.5	Si 1.9	P 2.2	S 2.5	Cl 3.0
K 0.8	Ca 1.0	Ga 1.6	Ge 1.8	As 2.2	Se 2.4	Br 2.8
Rb 0.8	Sr 1.0	In 1.7	Sn 1.8	Sb 2.1	Te 2.1	I 2.6
Cs 0.8	Ba 0.9					

decrease down group

increase across period

Table 3.4 Electronegativity values

bond. According to Pauling's scale, the hydrogen atoms both have an electronegativity of 2.2. In this case, the electrons are attracted equally to both hydrogen nuclei so a pure covalent bond is formed. If sodium chloride is considered, sodium has a value of 0.9 and chlorine has a value of 3.0. In this case, the electrons are more strongly attracted to the chlorine. In fact, the strength of attraction is so strong that the electrons are not shared between these two atoms. Instead, an ionic bond forms between the sodium and chlorine.

Key Terms

The words and phrases below were introduced in this chapter. Their definitions are given in the chemical dictionary.

covalent atomic radius

electronegativity

screening

Checklist for Revision

- I know how to use the covalent radius to state the size of an atom.
- I can explain the meaning of electronegativity.
- I can use the data booklet to find out the covalent radius and electronegativity values for elements.
- I can explain the trend in covalent radius and electronegativity going across a period or down a group.

Study Questions

1 Which of the following increases when a chlorine atom changes to a chloride ion?

A The atomic number

B The charge of the nucleus

C The mass number

D The number of full energy levels

2 When compared with potassium, lithium has

A a greater number of electron shells

B a greater electronegativity

C a lower melting point

D a greater covalent radius.

3 Which of the following statements is true?

A Magnesium is more electronegative than sulfur.

B Sulfur is a covalent molecular solid.

C Magnesium has a smaller covalent radius than sulfur.

D Sulfur has a lower relative atomic mass than magnesium.

4* a) Atoms of different elements have different attractions for bonded electrons. What term is used as a measure of the attraction an atom involved in a bond has for the electrons of the bond?

b) Atoms of different elements are different sizes. What is the trend in atomic size across the period from sodium to argon?

5* Figure 3.9 relates the ionic radii of some elements to their atomic numbers.

a) Copy the graph and plot the ionic radii you would predict for the ions of the elements with atomic numbers 13 and 15. You may wish to refer to a Periodic Table in the data booklet to help you.

b) The value quoted for hydrogen is for the hydride ion (H^-).

   i) Why is no value quoted for the H^+ ion?

   ii) Why is the H^- ion larger than the Li^+ ion?

c) Why is there a large increase in ion size from boron to nitrogen?

6* On crossing the Periodic Table, there are trends in the sizes of atoms and ions.

a) Why is the atomic size of chlorine less than that of sodium?

b) Why is there a large increase in ionic radius on going from Si^{4+} to P^{3-}?

Ion	Ionic radius/pm
Si^{4+}	42
P^{3-}	198

Table 3.5

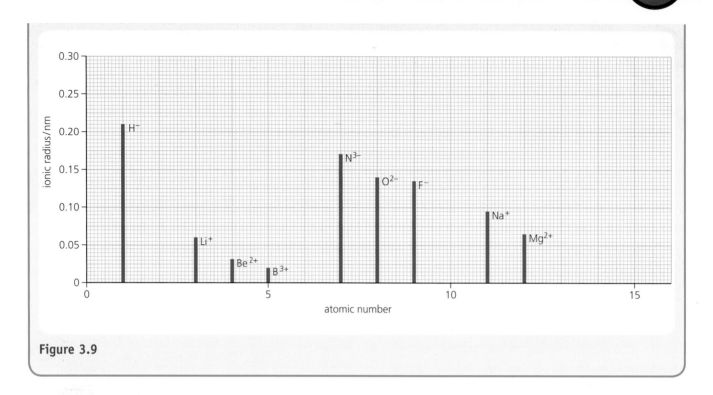

Figure 3.9

4 Bonding in compounds

Our study of the Periodic Table showed us that diatomic elements, such as hydrogen, exist as pairs of atoms joined chemically by a covalent bond. Electronegativity helps us appreciate that the electrons in the covalent bond, between the two atoms of hydrogen, are shared equally as both atoms have an equal 'pull' on the shared electrons. When we consider compounds, we find that the electrons in a bond are not always shared equally. This unequal sharing gives rise to two types of bonding: polar covalent bonding and ionic bonding.

As we study the bonding of compounds we will examine two types of intramolecular bond, pure covalent and polar covalent, and we will also study ionic bonding. In addition, we must also consider the bonds that occur between molecules, in other words the intermolecular bonds. When we surveyed the elements, we discovered that London dispersion forces were an example of an intermolecular bond. In this chapter, we will discover that there are several types of intermolecular bonds between molecules: London dispersion forces, permanent dipole–permanent dipole interactions and hydrogen bonds.

We will also consider how the different bonds found in compounds can influence the properties of the compound.

Ionic bonding

Ionic bonding is an electrostatic attraction between the positive ions of one element and the negative ions of another element.

The greater the difference in electronegativity between two elements, the less likely they are to share electrons; in other words the less likely they are to form covalent bonds. The element with the greater value of electronegativity is more likely to gain electrons to form a negative ion and the element with the smaller value is more likely to lose electrons to form a positive ion. This means electrostatic attraction results in ionic bonding, rather than covalent bonding. Elements far apart in the Periodic Table are more likely to form ionic

bonds than elements close together. In practice, this means ionic compounds result from metals combining with non-metals. Typical ionic compounds are sodium fluoride and magnesium oxide. Caesium fluoride is the compound with the greatest degree of ionic bonding. It is worth noting, however, that metals can form covalent bonds with non-metals in certain situations. It is important to examine the properties of the compound to help us decide the bonding.

Polar covalent bonding

Many covalent compounds are formed by elements with different electronegativities. In these compounds, the bonding electrons are not shared equally. The atom with the greater share of electrons will end up with a slight negative charge by comparison with the other atom. For example, in hydrogen chloride the chlorine is more electronegative than the hydrogen and in water the oxygen is more electronegative than the hydrogen. Hydrogen chloride and water can be represented as in Figure 4.1. The symbols $\delta+$ and $\delta-$ mean 'slightly positive' and 'slightly negative', respectively. Covalent bonds with unequal electron sharing are called **polar covalent bonds**.

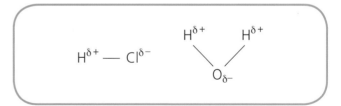

Figure 4.1 Hydrogen chloride and water have polar covalent bonds.

Pure covalent bonding

Pure covalent bonding, or non-polar covalent bonding, occurs where there is equal sharing of electrons. For example, when nitrogen is joined to chlorine the covalent bond between both atoms is a pure covalent bond. Both atoms have the same attraction for bonded electrons (both have an electronegativity value of 3.0) resulting in equal sharing of electrons. All diatomic elements contain pure covalent bonds as both atoms have the same electronegativity value.

The bonding continuum

Labelling a compound as ionic, polar covalent or pure covalent is convenient as it helps us understand how elements bond when forming compounds. In reality, however, these labels can be quite rigid as they do not reflect the wide variety of bonding found in compounds. Within these categories we find that some ionic compounds have stronger ionic properties than others and some covalent compounds have stronger covalent properties than others. This should not be too surprising when the electronegativity scale is considered: compounds with the greatest difference in electronegativity would be expected to be most ionic while compounds with the least difference in electronegativity would be expected to be the most covalent. The concept of a '**bonding continuum**' can be used to help us appreciate the differences in bonding. The bonding continuum places ionic bonding and pure covalent bonding at opposite ends, with polar covalent bonding in the middle. This is illustrated in Figure 4.2 where some of the fluorides of the period 2 elements are shown.

There is no straightforward rule that allows us to decide whether a compound is ionic, covalent or polar covalent. In general, metal compounds tend to be ionic and non-metals bonded to non-metals tend to be covalent, but this is not always the case. Tin(IV) iodide is an example of a metal compound which has polar covalent, rather than ionic, bonds.

Differences in electronegativity can be helpful when considering types of bonding since compounds with 'large' differences will be ionic. However, it can be difficult to judge whether a compound is likely to be ionic or polar covalent based on electronegativity alone. For example, sodium hydride is an ionic compound where the difference in electronegativity is 1.3 whereas hydrogen fluoride is a polar covalent compound where the difference in electronegativity is 1.8. In order to decide whether a compound is ionic, polar covalent or pure covalent, we must look at the properties of the compound.

Questions

1 Calculate the difference in electronegativity for the elements in the following compounds and indicate which compound will be the most ionic and which the least ionic:

   a) KBr   **b)** NaI   **c)** CsCl

2 The electronegativities of potassium and hydrogen are 0.8 and 2.2, respectively. Suggest what kind of bonding potassium hydride might have.

Ionic or covalent bonding?

Ionic compounds do not form molecules. Instead the positive and negative ions come together into various three-dimensional structures called lattices. Electrostatic attraction holds the oppositely-charged ions together in appropriate numbers so that the total charge is zero. For example, in sodium chloride (NaCl)

Compound	LiF	BeF_2	NF_3	OF_2	(F_2)
Difference in electronegativity	3.0	2.5	1.0	0.5	0.0

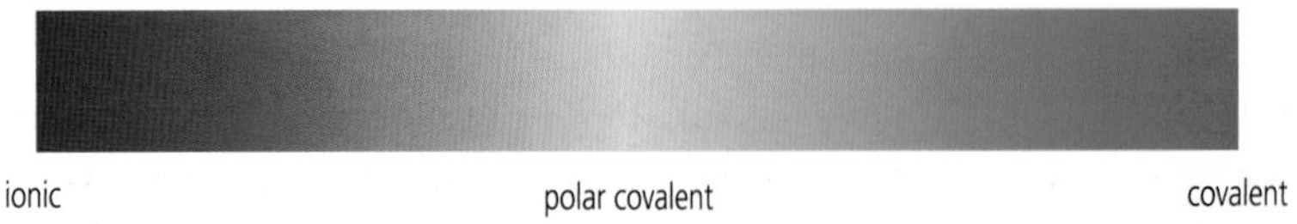

ionic   polar covalent   covalent

Figure 4.2 The bonding continuum

there are equal numbers of Na^+ and Cl^- ions, but in calcium fluoride (CaF_2) there are twice as many F^- ions as Ca^{2+}. The ionic lattice is a very stable arrangement of ions. Consequently, ionic compounds tend to have high melting points as lots of energy must be used to overcome the strong attraction between the ions in the lattice.

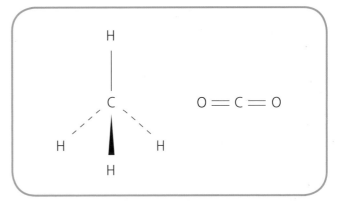

Figure 4.4 Covalent compounds can exist as small molecules.

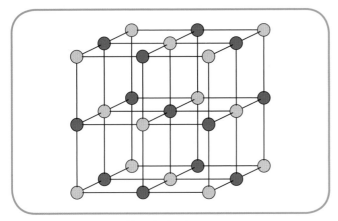

Figure 4.3 Sodium chloride lattice

Questions

3 Which of the following ionic compounds would you expect to have a sodium chloride-type lattice: Na_2O, KBr, MgF_2, MgO?

Another consequence of the ionic lattice is that solid ionic compounds do not conduct electricity. The lattice structure holds the ions in place and prevents them from moving easily when a current is applied. Ionic compounds do conduct when they are molten or in solution as the ions are now free to move when a current is passed through the compound. This property of conductivity can be used to distinguish between ionic and covalent compounds since covalent compounds do not conduct electricity.

The melting point of covalent compounds varies enormously as covalent compounds can exist in huge network structures with very high melting points (such as SiO_2, mp 1610 °C) or they can exist as small molecules with much lower melting points (for example CH_4, mp −182.5 °C). To understand the variety of melting points we encounter with covalent compounds we have to examine their intermolecular bonding.

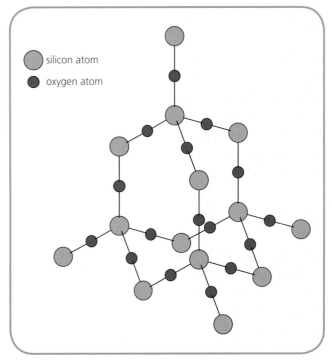

○ silicon atom

● oxygen atom

Figure 4.5 Covalent compounds can exist as huge networks such as silicon dioxide.

Intermolecular forces and properties of compounds

When we cool a covalent substance, molecules come together to form a solid. The attractive forces which hold the molecules together are known as intermolecular forces, in other words forces of attraction between molecules. The intermolecular forces acting between molecules are known as **van der Waals' forces**. When we heat a solid compound, energy is taken in by the molecule and is used to break the van der Waals' forces which hold the molecules together. There are three main types of van der Waals' forces: London dispersion forces, permanent dipole–permanent dipole interactions and hydrogen bonding. Examining the melting or boiling point of a compound gives us a good indication of the strength of the van der Waals' forces.

London dispersion forces

London dispersion forces are the weakest of all intermolecular forces and occur between all atoms and molecules. We considered this force of attraction in Chapter 2 where we examined the properties of elements such as the halogens and noble gases. In compounds, London dispersion forces are significant for non-polar molecules.

Permanent dipole–permanent dipole interactions

Permanent dipole–permanent dipole interactions occur between polar molecules. This is an example of an electrostatic force which is much stronger than London dispersion forces.

Some molecules containing polar bonds end up with an overall polarity because the bonds are not arranged symmetrically in the molecule. Hydrogen chloride and water are good illustrations of this, as is ammonia (Figure 4.6). Such molecules are said to have a **permanent dipole** where electrons are pulled to one side of the molecule. In other words, one side of the molecule has a slight positive charge while the other side has a slight negative charge.

Other molecules have a symmetrical arrangement of polar bonds and the polarity cancels out over the molecule as a whole. Consider carbon dioxide (Figure 4.7): one oxygen atom pulls electrons to the left of the molecule, but at the same time, the other oxygen atom is pulling electrons to the right of the molecule. Overall, the molecule is non-polar as there is no slight

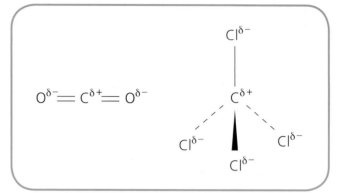

Figure 4.7 Carbon dioxide and tetrachloromethane are non-polar molecules.

positive or slight negative charge at either side of the molecule. This is also the case in other symmetrical molecules such as tetrachloromethane, also shown in Figure 4.7. These are examples of non-polar molecules which have polar bonds.

Questions

4   Draw the structures of hydrogen sulfide, phosphorus hydride, hydrogen bromide and iodine monochloride showing polarities, where appropriate.

Heptane, like all alkanes, has polar bonds (the difference in electronegativity is 0.3) but overall the molecule is non-polar as the molecule is symmetrical. For this reason, most hydrocarbons are non-polar molecules. Ethanol has one very polar O–H bond giving the molecule an overall polarity. Chloroform ($CHCl_3$), unlike tetrachloromethane (CCl_4), is polar overall because of the unsymmetrical arrangement of the C–Cl bonds. These structures are shown in Figure 4.9.

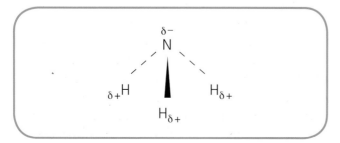

Figure 4.6 Polar bonds are present in ammonia.

The experiment shown in Figure 4.8 can be used to test whether a molecule is polar or non-polar. Rubbing a plastic rod creates an electric charge on the rod which can be used to attract charged objects. Since polar molecules have a permanent dipole, they can be attracted to the rod. Non-polar molecules are not affected by the charged rod since they do not have an overall charge.

Heptane and CCl_4 behave as in Figure 4.8(a); ethanol and chloroform as in Figure 4.8(b).

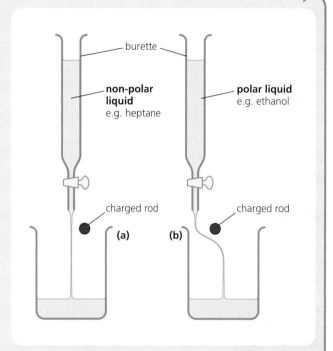

Figure 4.8 The behaviour of non-polar and polar liquids in an electric field

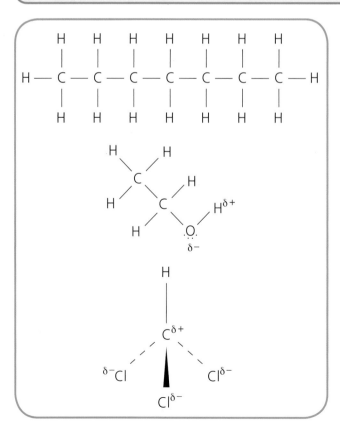

Figure 4.9 Bonding in heptane, ethanol and trichloromethane (chloroform)

Questions

5   In which way would you expect the following liquefied gases to behave in an electric field: HCl, O_2, NH_3, CH_4?

Boiling points of polar and non-polar compounds

Another consequence of molecules having an overall polarity is that their boiling points are higher than those of non-polar molecules with a similar number of electrons. Propanone and butane, shown in Figure 4.10, are good examples of this behaviour. Both molecules have a similar number of electrons but their boiling points are very different. (The strength of London dispersion forces increases as the number of electrons in a molecule increases. When making comparisons, it is important to compare molecules with a similar number of electrons so that any difference in properties must be due to an intermolecular force other than London dispersion forces.) Since propanone is polar, the molecules can attract each other as shown in Figure 4.11. In other words, the permanent dipole in one propanone molecule is attracted to the permanent dipole in another propanone molecule. This type of van der Waals' force is a permanent dipole–permanent dipole interaction. It is much stronger than London dispersion forces which are caused by temporary dipoles. Butane is non-polar; consequently, butane molecules in the liquid state are held together by London dispersion forces. It takes much less energy to overcome these weaker forces, so butane has a much lower boiling point than propanone.

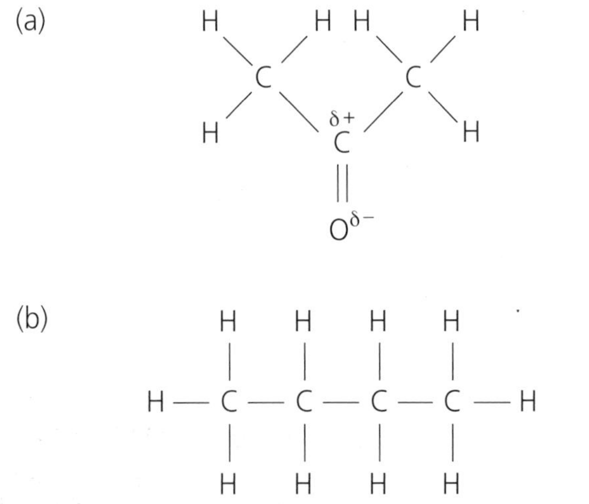

Figure 4.10 a) Propanone: boiling point 56 °C, b) butane: boiling point 0 °C

Hydrogen bonding

The accompanying graph, Figure 4.12, shows the expected increase in boiling point for the group IV hydrides. In the other three groups, however, the values of boiling points for NH_3, H_2O and HF are higher than would be expected since these molecules have the fewest electrons. These anomalous properties would appear to indicate stronger bonding between the molecules than the expected London dispersion forces and simple permanent dipole–permanent dipole attraction.

The compounds showing these properties all contain bonds which are very polar, in other words O–H, N–H and F–H, as shown by the electronegativity differences in Table 4.1. These molecules can therefore interact as shown in Figure 4.13.

H–C	H–N	H–O	H–F
0.3	0.8	1.3	1.8
	H–P	H–S	H–Cl
	0.0	0.3	0.8
		H–Se	H–Br
		0.2	0.6
		H–Te	H–I
		0.1	0.4

Table 4.1 Electronegativity differences

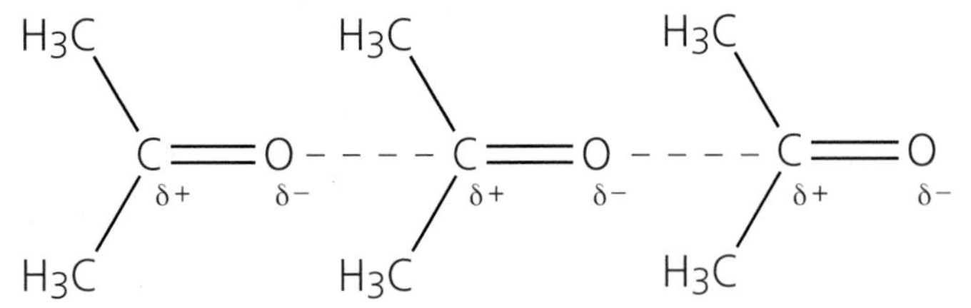

Figure 4.11 Propanone molecules bond to each other by permanent dipole-permanent dipole interactions.

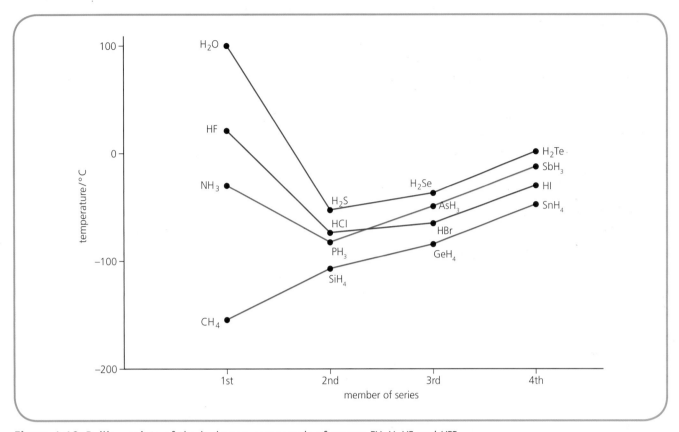

Figure 4.12 Boiling points of the hydrogen compounds of groups IV, V, VI and VII

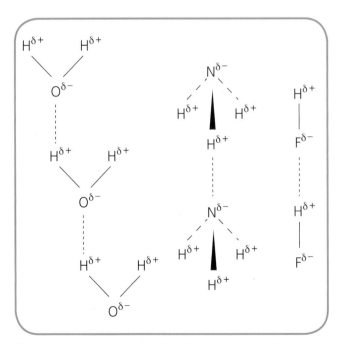

Figure 4.13 Hydrogen bonding in water, ammonia and hydrogen fluoride

This interaction is called **hydrogen bonding** since it occurs only for compounds containing a strongly electronegative element linked to hydrogen. The pull of electrons away from the hydrogen results in a positive charge located on the hydrogen atom. As hydrogen is an extremely small atom, this results in the hydrogen having a very high positive charge density. This creates a very strong permanent dipole–permanent dipole interaction as shown in Figure 4.13. Hydrogen bonding is an example of a van der Waals' force. It is stronger than London dispersion forces and stronger than ordinary permanent dipole–permanent dipole attractions but weaker than covalent bonds.

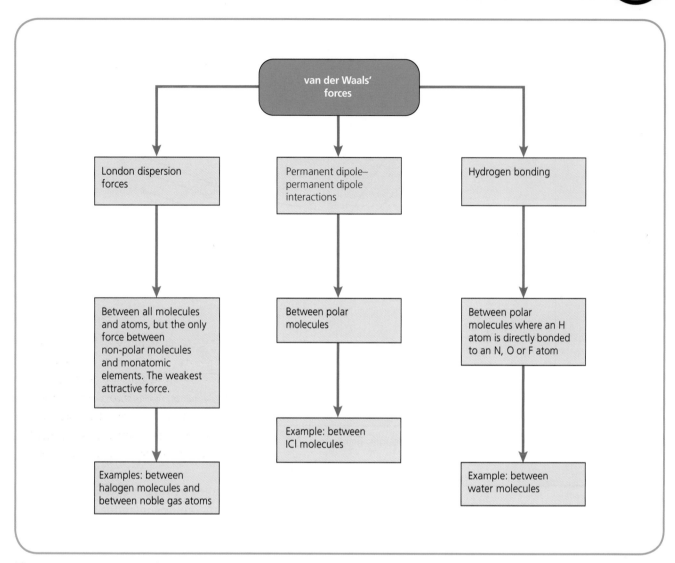

Figure 4.14 A summary of intermolecular forces

Relating properties to intermolecular forces

Melting and boiling points

As we have already discovered, melting and boiling points give an indication of the amount of energy that must be supplied to overcome the intermolecular forces between molecules. Where molecules are non-polar, we have to consider London dispersion forces. Hydrocarbons are good examples of non-polar compounds which are held together in the liquid and solid state by London dispersion forces. An examination of the boiling points of the **alkanes** (see

Figure 4.15 which shows the boiling points of the alkanes pentane to octane) shows a gradual increase in boiling point as the molecules increase in size.

This is a general trend where the strength of the London dispersion force increases as the molecular mass increases. In general, this happens because molecules with higher molecular mass tend to have more electrons, and we know that London dispersion forces increase in strength when there are more electrons. Overall, more energy must be supplied to overcome the stronger forces which hold octane molecules together than to overcome the London dispersion forces between pentane molecules.

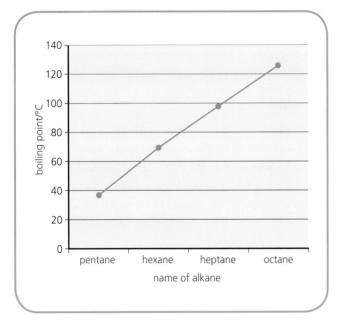

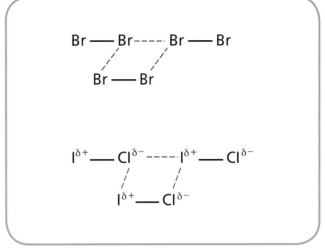

Figure 4.16 Bromine and iodine monochloride

Figure 4.15 Boiling points of selected alkanes

When the melting points of a polar and non-polar substance are compared, there is usually an obvious difference. Bromine and iodine monochloride (ICl) are good examples as they both have 70 electrons yet their melting points are very different: Br_2 has a melting

point of $-7\,°C$, ICl has a melting point of $+27\,°C$. As they have the same number of electrons we would expect them to have the same strength of London dispersion forces between molecules. If we examine the electronegativities of the atoms, we find that bromine is a non-polar molecule whereas iodine monochloride is polar. Consequently, more energy must be put in

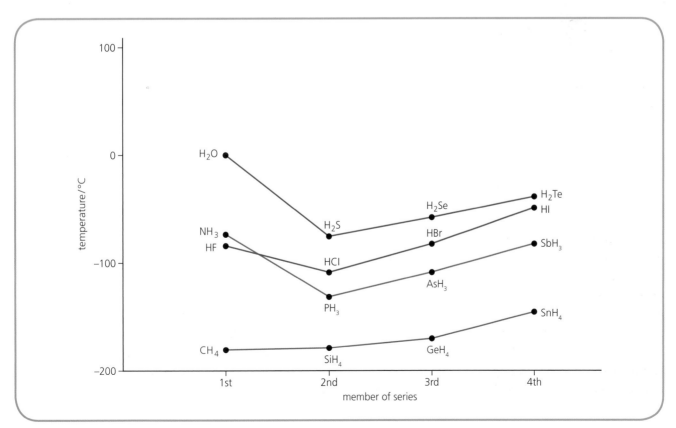

Figure 4.17 Melting points of the hydrogen compounds of groups IV, V, VI and VII

to overcome the permanent dipole–permanent dipole attractions between ICl molecules, hence the higher melting point. For bromine, it is only the weak London dispersion forces that hold the molecules together so less energy is needed to overcome these forces which hold the molecules together in the solid state (see Figure 4.16).

Where there is a significant difference in melting or boiling point between polar molecules, it is worth considering whether hydrogen bonding is present. For example, water has a much higher melting point than hydrogen sulfide, despite the latter having more electrons and therefore stronger London dispersion forces between its molecules. Both molecules are polar so their melting points suggest that hydrogen bonds between water molecules are much stronger than permanent dipole–permanent dipole interactions between hydrogen sulfide molecules.

Viscosity

Comparison of the liquid fractions obtained from the distillation of crude oil shows that viscosity normally increases as the molecules increase in size. This is a result of the bigger molecules having more electrons which results in stronger London dispersion forces. The stronger the intermolecular forces between molecules in a liquid, the more viscous the liquid will be.

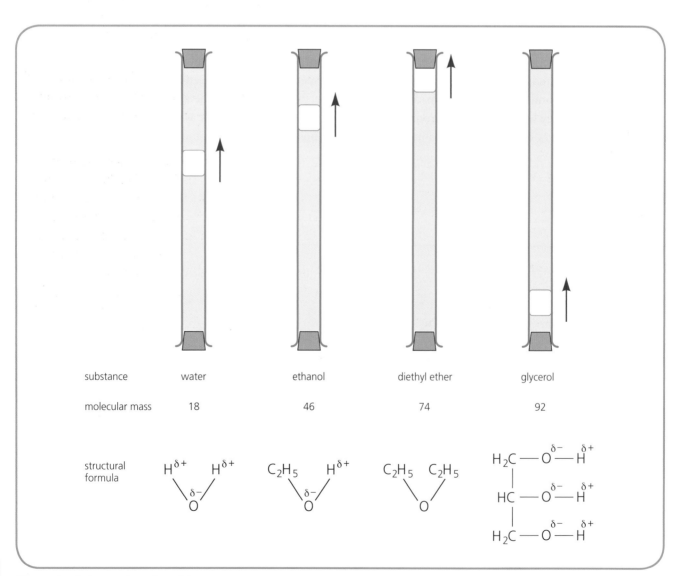

Figure 4.18 Comparing viscosities

The experiment illustrated in Figure 4.18 allows viscosities to be compared in a quick and simple way. If the tubes are inverted at the same time, the air bubble reaches the top fastest in the liquid of lowest viscosity. The results from this experiment clearly illustrate the effect of the strength of intermolecular forces on viscosity. The most viscous liquid is glycerol, followed by water, ethanol and diethyl ether. This is directly related to the intermolecular forces between the molecules: glycerol has three highly polar –OH groups which allow very strong hydrogen bonds to form between glycerol molecules. Hydrogen bonding between water molecules is more effective than that between ethanol molecules. Diethyl ether molecules are not linked by hydrogen bonds as there are no –OH bonds present. Consequently, the intermolecular forces in diethyl ether are much weaker than those in all the other liquids which results in the ether having the lowest viscosity.

Solubility

Because of its polar nature, water is capable of dissolving other polar and ionic substances. It is a general rule that polar and ionic substances are more likely to dissolve in polar solvents and non-polar substances are more likely to dissolve in non-polar solvents. For example, salt dissolves in water but not in heptane whereas wax dissolves in heptane but not in water. Water is unable to dissolve wax as wax is non-polar; it does not have positive or negative charges to attract water to bond to it. Instead, the water molecules bond to themselves leaving the wax intact. Heptane, on the other hand, is a non-polar molecule which bonds to other heptane molecules by London dispersion forces. Since wax is non-polar, it will bond to other wax molecules by London dispersion forces, but heptane will also bond to wax by London dispersion forces causing the wax to dissolve in heptane.

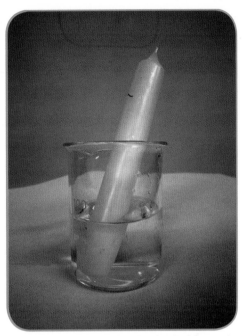

Figure 4.19 Wax does not dissolve in water.

Hydrogen chloride is an example of a polar compound which is very soluble in water. Figure 4.20 shows how the polar HCl molecules are attracted to the polar water molecules.

The dissolving of the hydrogen chloride results in the uneven breaking of the H–Cl bond giving a strongly acidic solution – hydrochloric acid. Similarly, ionisation occurs when the other hydrogen halides, HBr and HI, are dissolved in water and when pure sulfuric acid, also polar covalent, is dissolved in water. All give rise to strongly acidic solutions, in other words fully ionised solutions, despite their original structures being polar covalent. If any of the hydrogen halides are dissolved in non-polar toluene, ionisation does not occur and the solutions are not acidic.

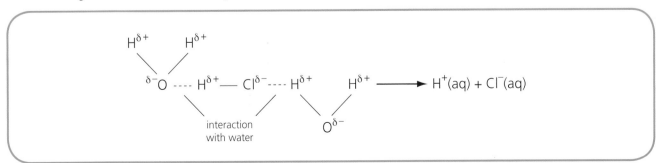

Figure 4.20 Hydrogen chloride dissolving in water

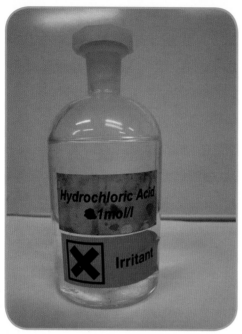

Ionic substances dissolve in a similar way, but of course the ions already exist in the initial lattice. The attraction drags ions out of the lattice and they go into solution surrounded by water molecules. The process is illustrated by Figures 4.22, 4.23 and 4.24. Ions surrounded by a layer of water molecules, held by electrostatic attraction, are said to be **hydrated**.

When thinking about solubility, it is useful to apply the rule 'like dissolves like'. In other words, polar solvents (solvents with $\delta+$ and $\delta-$) will dissolve polar and ionic solutes since these solutes also have particles which are charged. Non-polar solvents will dissolve non-polar solutes.

Figure 4.21 Hydrogen chloride gas dissolves in water to form hydrochloric acid.

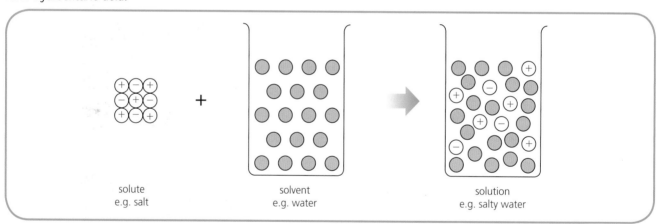

Figure 4.22 Salt dissolving in water

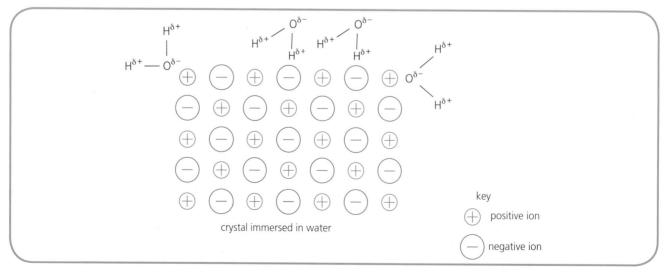

Figure 4.23 The ionic lattice is broken up by the water molecules which can bond to the + and − ions.

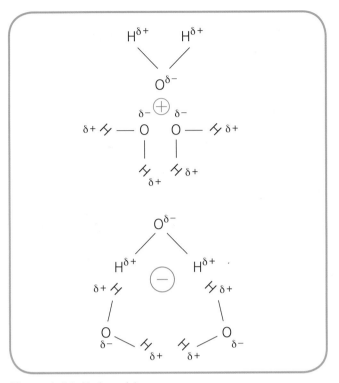

Figure 4.24 Hydrated ions

Miscibility

Miscible liquids mix thoroughly without any visible boundary between them. A glance at an alcoholic drink reveals that the ethanol (the alcohol) must mix thoroughly with the water in the drink as we cannot see two layers. Ethanol and water are examples of two liquids that are miscible. They are both polar molecules that can hydrogen bond to each other which helps them to mix. Other polar liquids are also miscible with water; for example propanone dissolves readily in water.

Figure 4.26 Propanone is miscible with water.

Oil and water are classic examples of two liquids which are immiscible. Oil is a non-polar liquid whereas water is polar. The water molecules continue to bond to themselves as they are unable to bond to the non-polar oil molecules. The immiscibility of liquids can also be

Figure 4.27 Oil and water are immiscible.

Figure 4.25 Alcohol and water are miscible.

Figure 4.28 Hexane and water are immiscible.

observed in the laboratory when hexane (non-polar) is mixed with water.

Density of water

An important consequence of hydrogen bonding is the unusual way in which water freezes. As with all liquids, water contracts on cooling, but when it reaches 4 °C it begins to expand again. At its freezing point it is less dense than the water which is about to freeze (see Figure 4.29). The reason for this is the ordering of molecules into an open lattice, shown in Figure 4.30, as the hydrogen bonds are able to overcome the decreasing thermal motion of the molecules. This open lattice structure of water molecules in ice is less dense than the arrangement of water molecules found in liquid water. As a result, ice floats on water, seas freeze from the top downwards – allowing fish to survive in the unfrozen water beneath – and, of course, pipes burst when water freezes inside them as the frozen water takes up more space than the liquid water.

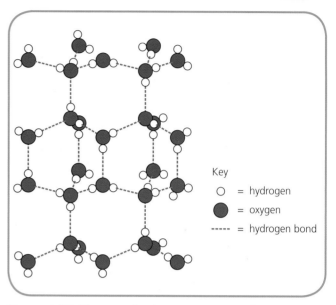

Figure 4.30 The open lattice arrangement of water molecules in ice

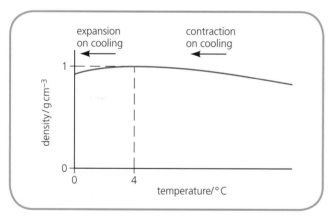

Figure 4.29 Water – change in density on cooling

Figure 4.31 Ice floats on water.

The next time you fill a test tube with water in the lab, think about the extraordinary fact that the level of water actually goes above the lip of the test tube without spilling! Water has a very high surface tension as the water molecules strongly attract each other due to hydrogen bonding. This allows small insects to 'walk' on water without the surface breaking. This can also be illustrated by placing a pin or paper clip onto the surface of water as shown in Figure 4.33.

Figure 4.33 The weight of a paper clip can be supported on the surface of water.

Figure 4.32 Water has a very high surface tension.

Many commercial products have been developed which take advantage of hydrogen bonding. For example, some disposable nappies contain polymers known as hydrogels which are able to absorb several times their own mass in water. Hydrogels are polymers with many carboxylic acid groups which are ionised so that the hydrogel has lots of negatively-charged oxygen atoms throughout the molecule. Water molecules can hydrogen bond to these oxygen ions which means that the water is absorbed onto the hydrogel. Similar hydrogels are used by gardeners as the water absorbed by the hydrogel can be released slowly into the soil over time. This reduces the need to water plants so frequently and also reduces the likelihood of over-watering the plant.

Figure 4.34 Hydrogels are found in disposable nappies.

Checklist for Revision

- I can describe how ionic and covalent bonding arise.

- I can identify a molecule as being polar or non-polar.

- I understand how London dispersion forces, permanent dipole–permanent dipole interactions and hydrogen bonding arise.

- I can relate the properties (melting points, boiling points, solubility, viscosity and miscibility) to the bonding present.

- I can explain some of the properties of water by discussing water's ability to hydrogen bond.

- I understand the concept of the bonding continuum.

Key Terms

The words and phrases below were introduced in this chapter.

Their definitions are given in the chemical dictionary.

bonding continuum

hydrated

hydrogen bonding

ionic bonding

lattice

miscibility

non-polar covalent bond

permanent dipole–permanent dipole interaction

polar covalent bond

van der Waals' forces

Study Questions

In questions 1–3 choose the correct word(s) from the following list to copy and complete the sentence.

> hydrogen bonding   large   molecular
> non-polar   polar   small
> London dispersion forces

1   A liquid can be shown to have _____ molecules if it is attracted to a charged rod when it flows out of a burette.

2   When there is a _____ difference in electronegativity between two elements they are likely to combine by ionic bonding.

3   Ice has a relatively high melting point due to _____ between molecules.

4   Substance X melts below 2000 °C and conducts electricity when solid and when liquid. Substance X could be

   A   copper

   B   graphite

   C   silicon dioxide

   D   calcium chloride.

5   Which of the following molecules would you expect to be the most polar?

   A   Hydrogen fluoride

   B   Hydrogen chloride

   C   Hydrogen bromide

   D   Hydrogen iodide

6   Which type of bond forms when water vapour condenses?

   A   Covalent

   B   Metallic

   C   Hydrogen

   D   Ionic

7   Molecules of iodine monochloride, ICl, have a permanent dipole. The attraction between molecules of ICl will be

   A   weaker than London dispersion forces but stronger than hydrogen bonds

   B   stronger than both London dispersion forces and hydrogen bonds

   C   stronger than London dispersion forces but weaker than hydrogen bonds

   D   weaker than both London dispersion forces and hydrogen bonds.

8 Hydrogen bonds are present in

A $H_2(g)$

B $CH_4(g)$

C $HI(l)$

D $NH_3(l)$.

9* Carbon dioxide is a gas at room temperature while silicon dioxide is a solid because

A London dispersion forces are much weaker than covalent bonds

B carbon dioxide contains double covalent bonds and silicon dioxide contains single covalent bonds

C carbon–oxygen bonds are less polar than silicon–oxygen bonds

D the relative formula mass of carbon dioxide is less than that of silicon dioxide.

10* a) Explain the change in atomic (covalent) radius of the elements

   i) across the Periodic Table from lithium to fluorine

   ii) down group I from lithium to caesium.

   b) Which two elements, of all those considered in a), form the compound with most ionic character?

11* State whether you would expect each of the following to conduct electricity appreciably when connected to a low voltage source:

   a) solid rubidium chloride

   b) liquid gallium (element 31)

   c) liquid nitrogen.

   Give your reasons briefly in terms of the type of bonding present.

12* a) From the information given, which of the compounds in Table 4.2 contain hydrogen bonding in the liquid state?

   b) Why does hydrogen bonding affect the boiling point of a substance?

   c) In the table we have compared substances of similar molecular mass. Why is molecular mass significant in this case?

Compound	Formula	Molecular mass	Boiling point/°C
Ethane	CH_3CH_3	30	−89
Methanol	CH_3OH	32	64
Hydrazine	NH_2NH_2	32	113
Silane	SiH_4	32	−112

Table 4.2

13* The American scientist Linus Pauling devised a scale to compare the attraction of atoms for bonded electrons. This scale is called the electronegativity scale. Some electronegativity values are shown in the data booklet.

   a) Which group of the Periodic Table contains elements with no quoted values for electronegativity?

   b) Use the electronegativity values to explain why carbon disulfide contains pure covalent bonds.

   c) Explain the trend in the electronegativity values of the group VII elements.

14* The graph shows the boiling points of the group VI hydrides.

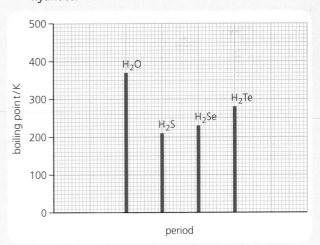

Figure 4.35

   a) Explain why the boiling points increase from H_2S to H_2Te.

   b) Why does H_2O have an unusually high boiling point compared with the other group VI hydrides?

15* Hydrogen cyanide, HCN, is highly toxic. Information about hydrogen cyanide is given in the table.

Structure	H — C ≡ N
Molecular mass	27
Boiling point	26°C

Table 4.3

Although hydrogen cyanide has a similar molecular mass to nitrogen, it has a much higher boiling point. This is due to the permanent dipole–permanent dipole attractions in liquid hydrogen cyanide.

a) What is meant by permanent dipole–permanent dipole attractions?

b) Explain how they arise in liquid hydrogen cyanide.

16* Hydrogen gas has a boiling point of –253 °C. Explain clearly why hydrogen is a gas at room temperature. (In your answer you should name the intermolecular forces involved and indicate how they arise.)

17* Compared with other gases made up of molecules of similar molecular masses, ammonia (NH_3) has a relatively high boiling point. In terms of the intermolecular bonding present, explain clearly why ammonia has a relatively high boiling point.

Activities

1 Create a flow diagram that will allow you to work out whether a compound is ionic, polar covalent or non-polar covalent.

2 Find out about Linus Pauling and his electronegativity scale.

3 Create compound cards which list the name and formula of a compound on one side and the type of intermolecular bond on the other side. Use the cards to test a partner on how quickly they can work out the type of bonds between molecules.

Unit 2

Nature's Chemistry

Organic chemistry is the study of carbon compounds. This unit offers us a glimpse of the chemistry of carbon compounds we encounter in the food and drink we consume, the soaps we use to clean, and the products we use to protect our skin. You will learn to appreciate the chemistry behind familiar products and learn how the principles of bonding can help us understand the properties and uses of the compounds we find in everyday life.

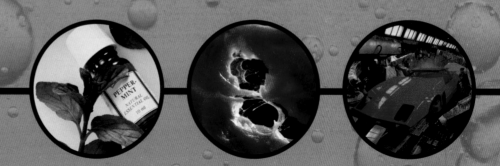

5 Alcohols, carboxylic acids and esters

From your previous chemistry studies you will appreciate that alcohols, carboxylic acids and esters are simple, yet important organic molecules found in a variety of everyday products. We start this unit by reviewing the chemistry of these compounds and by examining how they react.

What is an alcohol?

In everyday language the word 'alcohol' is used to represent an alcoholic drink. From a chemical point of view, an alcohol is a carbon compound that contains the hydroxyl **functional group**, –OH. As far as naming is concerned, an alcohol is characterised by the name ending '-ol'.

Ethanol, or ethyl alcohol as it is traditionally called, is the most important alcohol and is the alcohol present in alcoholic drinks. The structure of ethanol is shown in Figure 5.1.

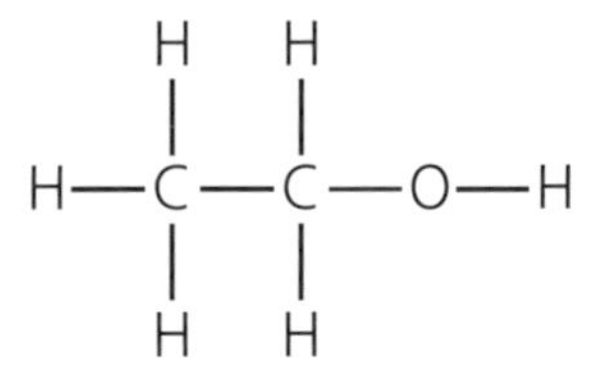

Ethanol is based on ethane where one of the hydrogens has been substituted by a **hydroxyl group**. Replacing the H of an alkane with the –OH functional group produces a family of alcohols that is commonly encountered in chemistry laboratories. The name of these common alcohols is obtained by replacing the final letter of the corresponding alkane by the name ending '-ol' (see Table 5.1).

Structural formulae and isomers

Methanol has no isomers. Ethanol does have an isomer but its isomer does not have an –OH group and is therefore not an alcohol.

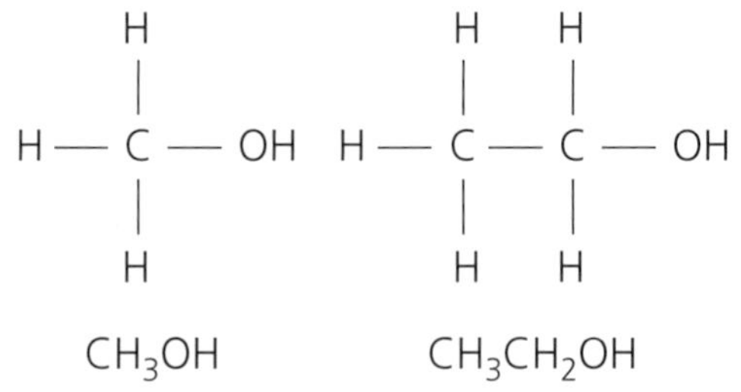

H — C — OH
(with H above and below)
CH_3OH
methanol

H — C — C — OH
(with H atoms above and below each C)
CH_3CH_2OH
ethanol

Figure 5.2 The structural formulae of methanol and ethanol

H — C — C — O — H
(ethanol structure with H atoms)

Figure 5.1 Ethanol

Alkanes		Alcohols	
Methane	CH_4	Methanol	CH_3OH
Ethane	C_2H_6	Ethanol	C_2H_5OH
Propane	C_3H_8	Propanol	C_3H_7OH
Butane	C_4H_{10}	Butanol	C_4H_9OH
Pentane	C_5H_{12}	Pentanol	$C_5H_{11}OH$
Hexane	C_6H_{14}	Hexanol	$C_6H_{13}OH$
Heptane	C_7H_{16}	Heptanol	$C_7H_{15}OH$
Octane	C_8H_{18}	Octanol	$C_8H_{17}OH$
General formula:	C_nH_{2n+2}	General formula:	$C_nH_{2n+1}OH$ or $C_nH_{2n+2}O$

Table 5.1

Carboxylic acids

It is probably impossible to go through life without using a carboxylic acid or a compound derived from a carboxylic acid. The most common carboxylic acid you are likely to encounter is ethanoic acid, which is present in vinegar. Bee venom and ant stings also contain a carboxylic acid: methanoic acid.

A carboxylic acid is characterised by its functional group, called the **carboxyl group**, and by its name ending, '-oic acid'.

The carboxyl functional group is shown in Figure 5.3.

One of the most important reactions of alcohols and carboxylic acids is their reaction to make the sweet-smelling compounds known as esters.

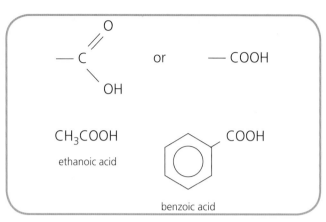

Figure 5.3 The carboxyl functional group and some examples

The table below shows the alkanoic acids. These are examples of carboxylic acids.

Name of acid	Structural formulae
Methanoic acid (formic acid)	HCOOH
Ethanoic acid (acetic acid)	CH_3COOH
Propanoic acid	CH_3CH_2COOH
Butanoic acid	$CH_3CH_2CH_2COOH$
Pentanoic acid	$CH_3CH_2CH_2CH_2COOH$
Hexanoic acid	$CH_3CH_2CH_2CH_2CH_2COOH$
Heptanoic acid	$CH_3CH_2CH_2CH_2CH_2CH_2COOH$
Octanoic acid	$CH_3CH_2CH_2CH_2CH_2CH_2CH_2COOH$
General formula	$C_nH_{2n}O_2$

Table 5.2

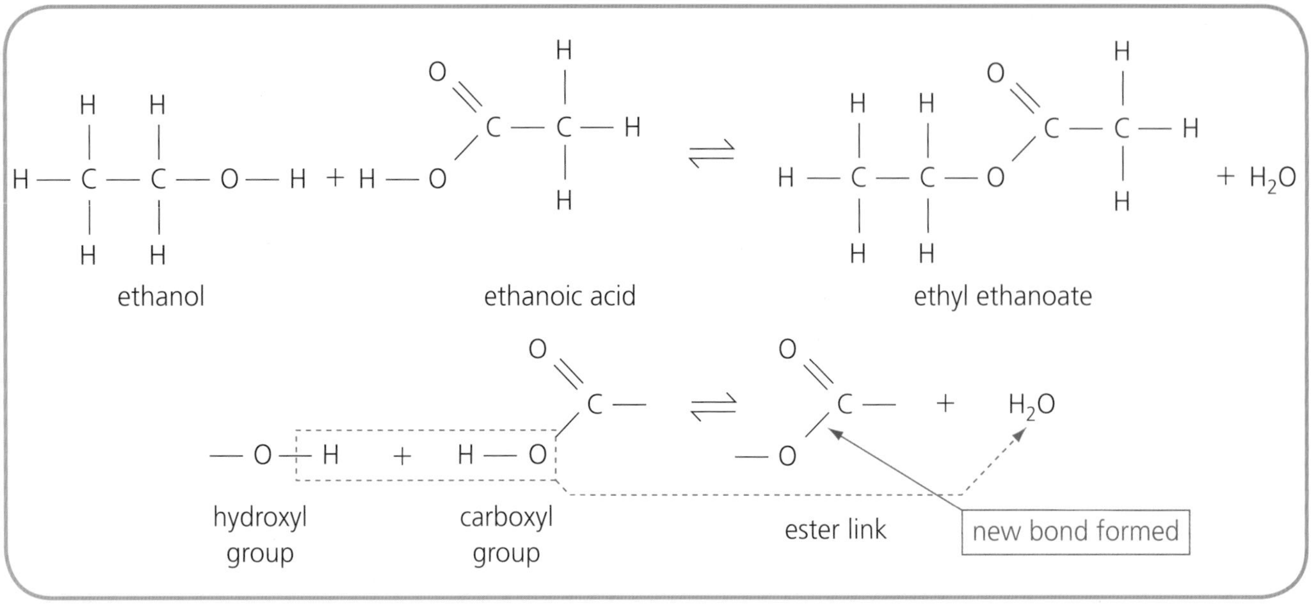

Figure 5.4 Formation of an ester, also showing how the functional groups interact

Esters

When ethanol reacts with ethanoic acid, the ester ethyl ethanoate and water are formed:

$$CH_3CH_2OH + HOOCCH_3 \rightleftharpoons CH_3CH_2OOCCH_3 + H_2O$$
ethanol   ethanoic acid   ethyl ethanoate

The hydroxyl and carboxyl groups in the reactants come together to form the ester link and a molecule of water. Hence, the process of making an ester is known as a **condensation reaction**. Figure 5.4 shows how the functional groups interact to form an ester.

Making an ester in the lab

Esters are very simple to prepare in the laboratory. An easy method of preparing an ester is described below.

A small volume of alcohol and an equal volume of a carboxylic acid are mixed together and a few drops of concentrated sulfuric acid are added. This mixture is heated, as shown in Figure 5.5, for several minutes.

The test tube is removed from the hot water bath and its contents added to sodium hydrogencarbonate solution as shown in Figure 5.6. This solution neutralises the sulfuric acid, as well as any unreacted carboxylic acid, releasing carbon dioxide in the process. The ester appears as an immiscible layer on the surface of the solution. The ester can also be detected by its characteristic smell.

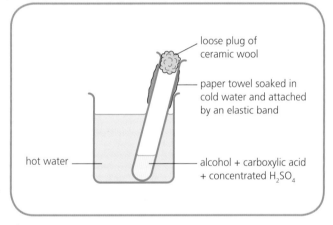

Figure 5.5

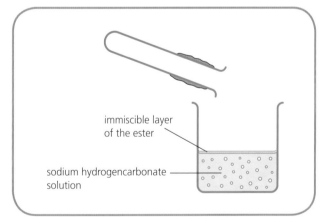

Figure 5.6

This simple lab method of preparing an ester gives us lots of information about the properties of esters and the reaction:

1 Concentrated sulfuric acid plays an important part in the reaction. It provides hydrogen ions which act as a catalyst. It also helps to increase the yield of ester by absorbing water, the other product. This should become obvious if you look at the equation for forming ethyl ethanoate in Figure 5.4. The equation shows that the reaction is reversible. The concentrated sulfuric acid is able to absorb the water and thus prevent the newly formed ester from reacting with the water and reforming the alcohol and acid. (See Chapter 14 for further details on reversible reactions.)

2 The carboxylic acid and alcohol used to make an ester contain polar O–H bonds while the ester produced does not. Hydrogen bonding between molecules in alcohols, and also in carboxylic acids, means that these types of carbon compounds have relatively high boiling points. Furthermore, short-chain alcohols and carboxylic acids are miscible with water. As esters do not have an O–H bond they cannot form hydrogen bonds. As a result esters tend to have much lower boiling points and do not dissolve in water. Consequently, the ester produced tends to form as an oily layer on top of the aqueous base used to neutralise the acids.

Naming esters

The name of an ester depends on which alcohol and which carboxylic acid have been used in preparing it. The first part of the name, which ends in '-yl', comes from the alcohol and the second part, which ends in '-oate', comes from the acid. Two examples

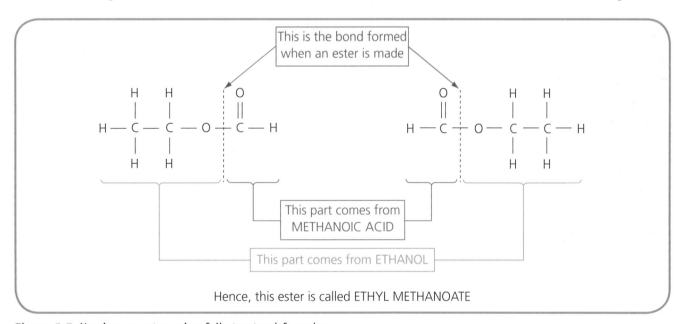

Figure 5.7 Naming an ester using full structural formulae

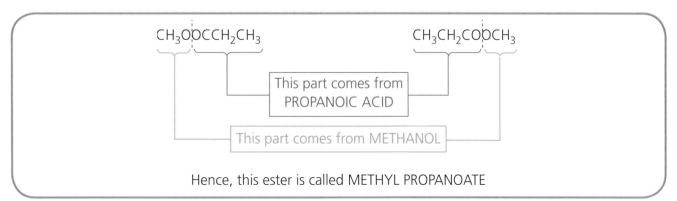

Figure 5.8 Naming an ester using shortened structural formulae

are illustrated in each of Figures 5.7 and 5.8. In these figures, note that the ester structures are shown twice, the second time in reverse. Ester formulae can be, and frequently are, written either way.

When naming an ester formed from an alcohol, the first part of the name is derived by deleting the letters '-anol' from the name of the alcohol and replacing them with the ending '-yl'. Thus, pentanol produces pentyl esters, octanol produces octyl esters, etc.

If an ester is prepared using a carboxylic acid, the second part of the ester's name ends in '-oate'. Thus, butanoic acid produces a butanoate ester, hexanoic acid produces a hexanoate ester, etc. Table 5.3 gives examples of esters produced from combining the alcohols and carboxylic acids listed.

Name of alcohol	Name of carboxylic acid	Name of ester
Ethanol	Methanoic acid	Ethyl methanoate
Propanol	Ethanoic acid	Propyl ethanoate
Methanol	Butanoic acid	Methyl butanoate

Table 5.3

Esters prepared from alcohols and carboxylic acids that have the same total number of carbon atoms will, as a result, have the same molecular formula. For example, ethyl ethanoate and methyl propanoate are isomers with the molecular formula: $C_4H_8O_2$. Butanoic acid, C_3H_7COOH, is also isomeric with these esters although it belongs to a different homologous series.

> ### Questions
>
> 1 Draw the full structural formulae of methanol, ethanoic acid and the ester produced by reacting them together. Name the ester.
>
> 2 Draw the shortened structural formulae of butanoic acid, propan-1-ol and the ester produced by reacting them together. Name the ester.

Uses of esters

Esters have a variety of uses. If you have prepared or smelled some esters, you will be well aware of the fruity aromas associated with several of them. This property makes them useful in making deodorants and as artificial flavourings in the food industry. Table 5.4 lists several esters and the flavours associated with them.

An examination of the ingredients label from a can of deodorant, aftershave or perfume reveals many exotic chemical names such as isobornyl acetate and cyclohexyl salicylate. These traditional names for the chemicals are still used in the cosmetics industry. Nevertheless, the names reveal that the compounds are esters. Isobornyl acetate has the smell of pine needles; cyclohexyl salicylate has a very sweet balsamic smell. These esters can be made to order by synthetic chemists and then added in the appropriate proportion to the scent being created.

In terms of quantity used, the principal use of esters is as solvents. As they are non-polar, esters are able to dissolve a variety of compounds which would be insoluble in water. Another advantage of using an ester as a solvent is that those with a small number of carbon atoms, such as ethyl ethanoate, have low boiling points

Name	Structural formula	Flavour
Propyl ethanoate	$CH_3CH_2CH_2OOCCH_3$	Pear
3-methyl but-1-yl-ethanoate	$CH_3CH(CH_3)CH_2CH_2OOCCH_3$	Banana
Octyl ethanoate	$CH_3(CH_2)_7OOCCH_3$	Orange
Methyl butanoate	$CH_3OOCCH_2CH_2CH_3$	Pineapple/apple
Pentyl butanoate	$CH_3(CH_2)_4OOCCH_2CH_2CH_3$	Apricot

Table 5.4

Figure 5.9 Scented products often contain both natural and synthetic esters.

and therefore evaporate easily. Ethyl ethanoate is one of the solvents used in nail varnish. It is ideal for this purpose as it acts as a good liquid for applying the varnish, but quickly evaporates to leave the varnish on the nail. It is also used as the solvent for car body paints.

Figure 5.10 Esters are used as solvents in car body paints.

Figure 5.11 Nail varnish contains ethyl ethanoate as the solvent.

Esters also have medicinal uses. Methyl salicylate or 'oil of wintergreen' is used in analgesic rubs for strains and sprains. Aspirin is another ester derived from salicylic acid, which is an aromatic carboxylic acid.

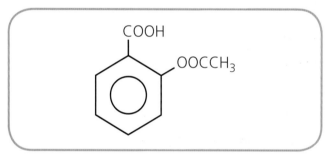

Figure 5.12 The chemical structure for aspirin

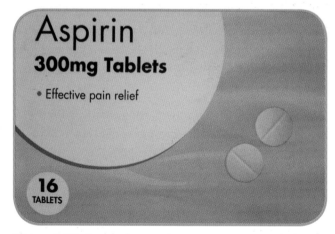

Figure 5.13 Aspirin is an ester.

Hydrolysis of esters

The equations for the formation of an ester given in Figure 5.4 show that the reaction is reversible. The reverse process, in which the ester is split by reaction with water to form an alcohol and a carboxylic acid, is an example of **hydrolysis**. Therefore, hydrolysis is the opposite of condensation, which occurs when an ester is formed. The C–O bond formed when an ester is made is the bond that is broken when the ester is hydrolysed (look back at Figure 5.4).

Although hydrolysis is the process by which water breaks down a carbon compound, in practice, water on its own is rarely successful in achieving this. Hydrolysis of an ester is usually carried out by heating it in the presence of a dilute acid, such as $HCl(aq)$ or $H_2SO_4(aq)$, to provide hydrogen ions to catalyse the hydrolysis.

The equation for the acid-catalysed hydrolysis of ethyl ethanoate is as follows:

$$CH_3CH_2OOCCH_3 + H_2O \rightleftharpoons CH_3CH_2OH + HOOCCH_3$$

   ethyl ethanoate   ethanol   + ethanoic
acid

Acid-catalysed hydrolysis is reversible and, as a consequence, will be incomplete. Complete hydrolysis can, however, be achieved by adding the ester to a strong alkali, such as $NaOH(aq)$ or $KOH(aq)$, and heating under reflux for about 30 minutes as shown in Figure 5.14. Heating under reflux involves heating the mixture with a condenser attached. This ensures that the volatile compounds (mainly the ester and alcohol) do not escape from the reaction flask. Heating under reflux allows the reaction to take place at a higher temperature without losing the reactants or products through evaporation.

The products of the hydrolysis using an alkali are the alcohol and the salt of the carboxylic acid since the carboxylic acid formed will immediately react with

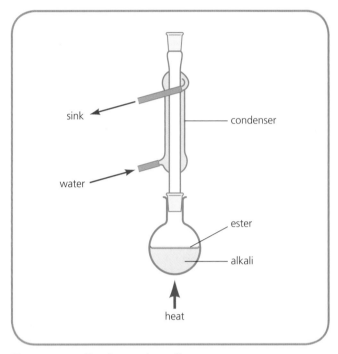

Figure 5.14 Heating under reflux

the alkali present. For example, if ethyl ethanoate is hydrolysed using a sodium hydroxide solution, the products are ethanol and sodium ethanoate. The equation for this is shown below:

$$CH_3COOCH_2CH_3(l) \rightarrow CH_3COO^-Na^+(aq) + HOCH_2CH_3(l)$$
$$+\ NaOH(aq) \qquad\quad \text{sodium ethanoate} \qquad \text{ethanol}$$

Full structural formulae for this reaction are shown in Figure 5.15.

The products from this reaction can be separated by distillation using the reassembled apparatus shown in Figure 5.16. The alcohol is distilled off and the salt of the carboxylic acid is left behind in the aqueous solution. When this solution is acidified with hydrochloric acid, the salt is converted to the carboxylic acid as shown in the equation below:

$$CH_3COO^-Na^+(aq) + HCl(aq) \rightarrow CH_3COOH(aq) + NaCl(aq)$$
$$\text{ethanoic acid}$$

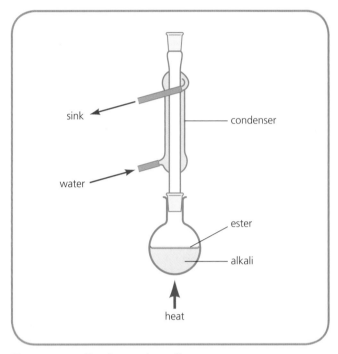

Figure 5.15 Alkaline hydrolysis of an ester

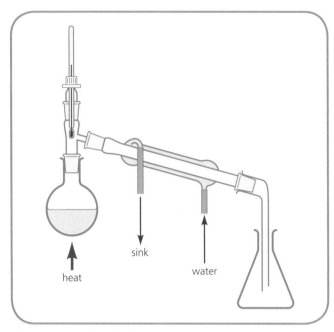

Figure 5.16 Distillation

Alkaline hydrolysis of an ester has two main advantages over acid-catalysed hydrolysis.

1   Alkaline hydrolysis is not reversible and hence there should be a higher yield of products.

2   It is usually easier to separate the products when alkaline hydrolysis has been used.

Ester hydrolysis, especially by alkali, is an important process in the manufacture of soap from fats and oils. This will be dealt with in more detail in Chapter 6.

Prevention of ester hydrolysis is also important in the food, cosmetic and pharmaceutical industries as esters are found in foods, cosmetics and medicines. If they hydrolyse easily then the properties of the product will completely change. Expiry dates are predicted, along with other factors, to take into account how quickly the product is likely to hydrolyse. A classic example of this is aspirin. If you have ever smelled some 'old' aspirin tablets you will notice the aroma of ethanoic acid as aspirin hydrolyses to produce ethanoic acid. Modern foil packaging of medicines helps to preserve them for longer as it minimises exposure to moisture in the air which causes hydrolysis. Perfumes and aftershaves suffer in the same way as the esters which give rise to the fruity smells will eventually hydrolyse to produce carboxylic acids which can have rather unpleasant smells.

Questions

3   Name the following esters and draw the full structural formulae of the alcohols and carboxylic acids produced when they are hydrolysed.

   a) $CH_3CH_2CH_2OOCH$

   b)

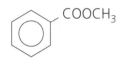

Figure 5.17

4   Write equations, giving shortened structural formulae for the carbon compounds involved, for the following reactions. Beneath each carbon compound write its name.

   a) Hydrolysis of ethyl butanoate by KOH(aq).

   b) Acid-catalysed hydrolysis of pentyl ethanoate.

Checklist for Revision

●   I can identify the carboxyl group and draw the structures of carboxylic acids if told their names.

●   I can name carboxylic acids if shown their structure.

●   I can predict the products formed when a carboxylic acid reacts with a base.

●   I can name and draw the structure of an ester if told the parent alcohol and acid.

●   I can name and draw the alcohol and acid used to form an ester if told the name or shown the structure of an ester.

●   I can state some uses for esters and relate the use to the ester structure.

●   I can name and draw the structures for the products of hydrolysis of an ester.

Key Terms

The words and phrases below were introduced in this chapter.

Their definitions are given in the chemical dictionary.

alkanoic acid

carboxyl group

condensation reaction

ester

hydrolysis

pickling

strong acid

weak acid

1 Review the labels of ingredients from scented products found in the home (air fresheners, deodorants, aftershaves etc.). How many contain esters? Can you find out the structures of these esters? Why are these esters used?

2 'We are surrounded by esters!' How true is this statement? Find out which products contain esters or have used esters in their production. Find out about the esters found in flower and fruit scents.

Study Questions

1 Which compound is an ester?

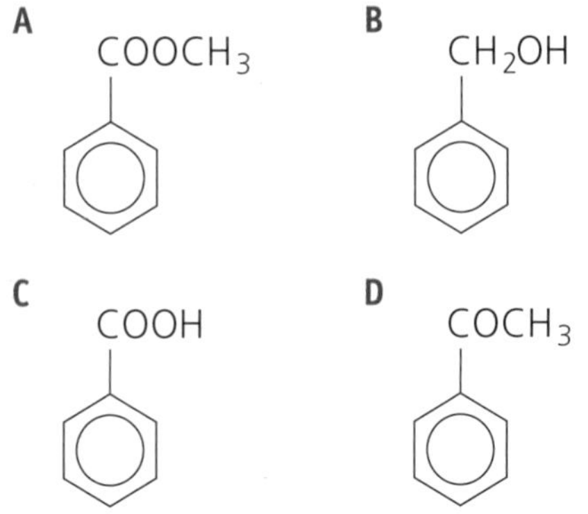

A COOCH₃

B CH₂OH

C COOH

D COCH₃

Figure 5.18

2 $HCOOCH_3 + H_2O \rightarrow HCOOH + CH_3OH$

The type of reaction shown above is

A hydration

B condensation

C addition

D hydrolysis.

3* Which ester is an isomer of butanoic acid?

A Ethyl ethanoate

B Ethyl methanoate

C Ethyl propanoate

D Propyl ethanoate

4* a) Esters are formed when carboxylic acids react with alcohols, for example

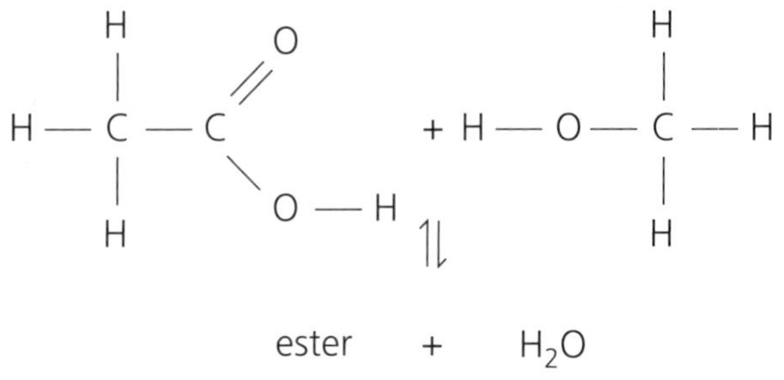

ester + H₂O

Figure 5.19

i) Name the ester formed in this reaction.

ii) Name the type of reaction which takes place.

iii) To find out which atoms of the alcohol and carboxylic acid go to form the water molecule, the reaction was carried out using an alcohol in which the ¹⁶O atom was substituted by the ¹⁸O isotope. All of the ¹⁸O was found in the ester and none in the water.

Copy the equation and circle the atoms in the acid and the alcohol which combine to form the water molecule.

b) Esters can be prepared in the laboratory by heating an alcohol and a carboxylic acid with a few drops of concentrated sulfuric acid in a water bath. After 10 minutes or so, the reaction mixture is poured into sodium hydrogencarbonate solution.

i) What evidence would show that the ester has been formed?

ii) Give two reasons for using the concentrated sulfuric acid.

5 Draw the structural formula of the ester formed when pentan-2-ol reacts with methanoic acid.

6 The structural formula for a plum-flavoured ester is shown below.

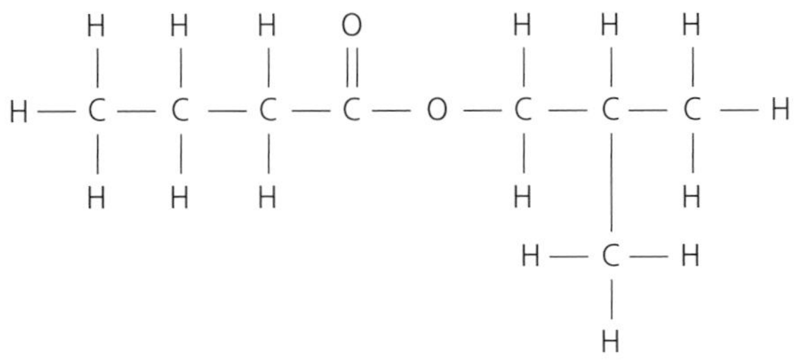

Figure 5.20

Name the alcohol and acid formed when this ester is hydrolysed.

7* One of the chemicals released in a bee sting is an ester that has the structure shown.

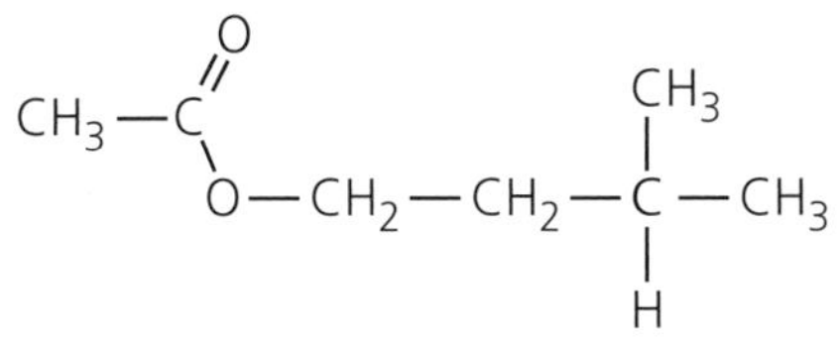

Figure 5.21

This ester can be produced by the reaction of an alcohol with an alkanoic acid.

a) Name this acid.

b) The ester can be prepared in the lab by heating a mixture of the reactants with a catalyst.

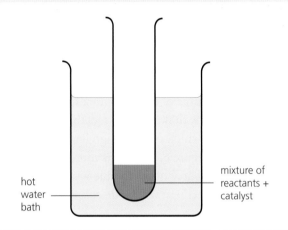

Figure 5.22

Suggest why a hot water bath is used to heat the reactants rather than a Bunsen burner.

8* The full structural formula for an ester found in pineapples is shown.

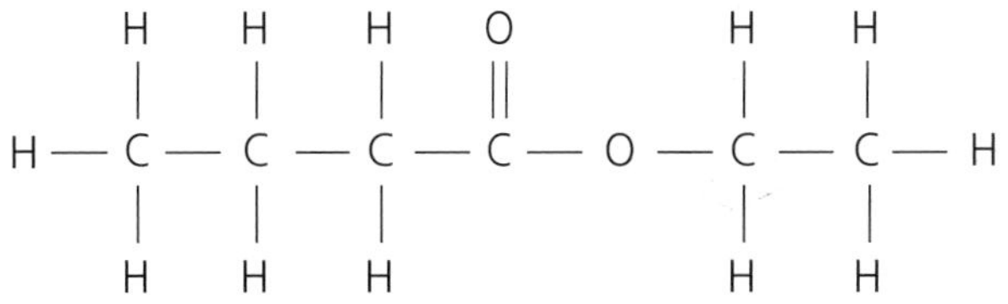

Figure 5.23

a) Name the ester.

b) What would be observed if this ester was added to water?

6   Fats, oils and soaps

Fats and oils

Fats and **oils** are an essential part of the human diet. They are a good source of energy with a high satiety level, in other words, they help you feel fuller for longer. Examples of foods which contain high levels of fats and oils are shown in Figure 6.1. Perhaps more importantly, fats and oils are a source of fat-soluble vitamins and essential fatty acids (these will be discussed later).

Unfortunately fats and oils have received a poor reputation which has led many people to severely restrict their intake. This can be an unhealthy approach as missing out on fats and oils can also mean missing out on these essential vitamins and fatty acids. For example, vitamin D is made by our skin when we are exposed to strong sunlight containing UVB radiation. Sun exposure to cause this in Scotland usually occurs between April and September. Recent health advice has tried to promote short periods of sun exposure, without sunscreen, to ensure our bodies are making vitamin D. For the rest of the year, however, our bodies rely on receiving enough vitamin D from our diet. If we do not consume enough food that is rich in the fats

and oils which store vitamin D – such as fish, eggs, milk and meat – our bodies start to suffer from vitamin D shortage which has been linked to many illnesses. Thus, fats and oils are an important group of natural products for chemists to study. In this chapter, we will explore the structure of fats and oils and examine how their properties are related to their structure.

Fats and oils can be of animal, vegetable or marine origin as shown in Table 6.1.

Vegetable	Animal	Marine
Olive oil	Lard (pork fat)	Cod liver oil
Rapeseed oil	Mutton fat	Whale oil
Palm oil	Beef fat	
Linseed oil		
Castor oil		
Soya bean oil		

Table 6.1

Vegetable oils are usually pressed out of the seed of the appropriate plant. Rapeseed has been grown traditionally on British farms as a way of keeping fields free of weeds and to promote fertility of the soil. Now, rapeseed oil has grown in popularity for its use as cooking oil and for producing biodiesel.

Cod liver oil continues to be used as a dietary supplement as it contains high levels of vitamins A, D and the omega 3 fatty acids. In the past, children would endure the unpleasant taste of this oil as they were given their daily dose first thing in the morning. Nowadays, cod liver oil capsules are available which offer the benefits of consuming the oil without having to endure the foul taste!

Figure 6.1 Examples of foods rich in fats and oils

Figure 6.2 A field of oil-seed rape. A typical scene in Scotland in May.

Figure 6.3 Harvested rapeseed

Figure 6.4 Extra virgin rapeseed oil

The structure of fats and oils

Fats and oils have very similar chemical structures. Physically, oils have lower melting points than room temperature so they are liquids whereas fats have much higher melting points so they are solids at room temperature. Under cold conditions some vegetable oils may become cloudy or even solidify.

Fat and oil molecules belong to the ester family. They are formed by the **condensation reaction** of a molecule of **glycerol** (propane-1,2,3-triol) with carboxylic acid molecules. This produces a structure known as a **triglyceride** such as that shown in Figure 6.7. A triglyceride may be formed from three different carboxylic acids, as shown in Figure 6.7, or with two different carboxylic acids or, indeed, with all three the same.

Figure 6.5 Cod liver oil is an example of an oil of marine origin.

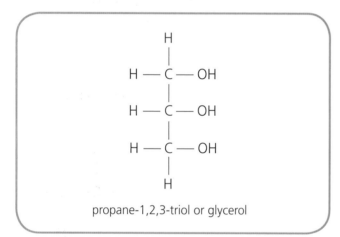

propane-1,2,3-triol or glycerol

Figure 6.6 Glycerol is an example of an alcohol.

The carboxylic acids which attach to the glycerol are referred to as **fatty acids**. Many are straight-chain carboxylic acids that may be **saturated** or **unsaturated** and which contain even numbers of carbon atoms ranging most often from C_{14} to C_{24} but primarily C_{16} and C_{18}. Some contain –OH substituent groups.

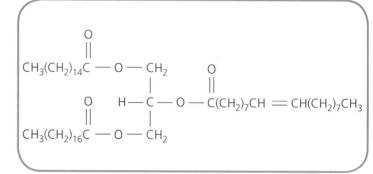

Figure 6.7 An example of a triglyceride

Table 6.2 gives examples of saturated and unsaturated fatty acids.

The names used in the table are the common or 'trivial' names. Stearic acid, for example, is systematically named octadecanoic acid.

Fats and oils contain glycerol combined with fatty acids in the ratio of one mole of glycerol to three moles of fatty acid.

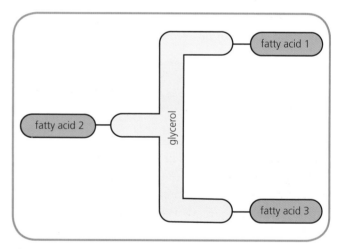

Figure 6.8 The structure of a fat or oil

Name of fatty acid	Chemical formula
Palmitic acid	$CH_3(CH_2)_{14}COOH$
Stearic acid	$CH_3(CH_2)_{16}COOH$
Oleic acid	$CH_3(CH_2)_7CH=CH(CH_2)_7COOH$
Linoleic acid	$CH_3(CH_2)_3(CH_2CH=CH)_2(CH_2)_7COOH$
Ricinoleic acid	$CH_3(CH_2)_5CH(OH)CH_2CH=CH(CH_2)_7COOH$

Table 6.2

Questions

1 Write the structural formula of the triglyceride made from propane-1,2,3-triol and ethanoic acid. Circle the ester linkages.

The higher melting points of fats compared with oils is caused by fats containing more saturated fatty acids than oils. In other words, fats contain more carbon–carbon single bonds compared with oils. A simple test with bromine water can confirm this: shaking of oils with bromine water results in the bromine water being readily decolourised. The bromine's decolourisation is the standard test for unsaturation. If a solution of fat is treated this way, decolourisation is not so rapid. The test can be modified to estimate quantitatively the degree of unsaturation of various oils and fats.

Fats and oils are roughly 'tuning-fork' shaped, with the three limbs consisting of hydrocarbon chains (Figures 6.9 and 6.10). If the chains are saturated, the molecules can pack neatly together, even at quite high temperatures. This efficient packing of molecules allows the van der Waals' attraction to be strong enough to hold the structure together at room temperature. When the fat is heated, the van der Waals' attractions are easily broken and the fat melts.

If the chains contain one or more double bonds, the zig-zag chains become more distorted and close packing of molecules is more difficult. This results in weaker van der Waals' attractions. Unless the substance is cooled to remove more thermal energy, it will not solidify (therefore oils have lower melting points).

The only chemical difference between fats and oils is that the oils contain many more double bonds. Hence, 'hardening' of oils can be carried out by **addition** of hydrogen across the double bonds. Ethene can be

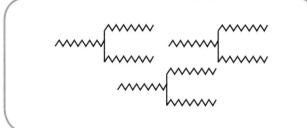

Figure 6.9 Fat molecules are able to pack closely together.

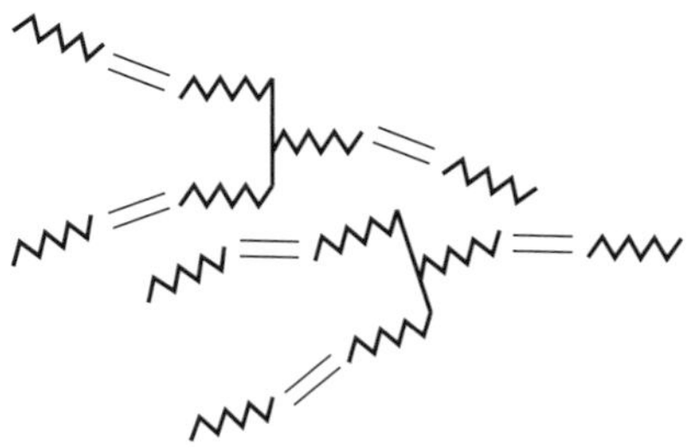

Figure 6.10 An exaggerated picture of oil molecules

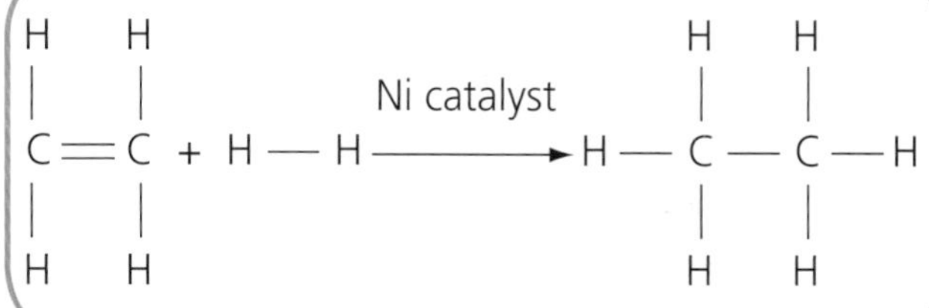

$$H_2C=CH_2 + H-H \xrightarrow{\text{Ni catalyst}} H_3C-CH_3$$

Figure 6.11 Hydrogenation of ethene

converted to ethane by addition of hydrogen, as shown in Figure 6.11.

Similarly oils can be converted to fats by the use of hydrogen with nickel catalysts (see Figure 6.12).

The degree of unsaturation is now less than that of the original oil.

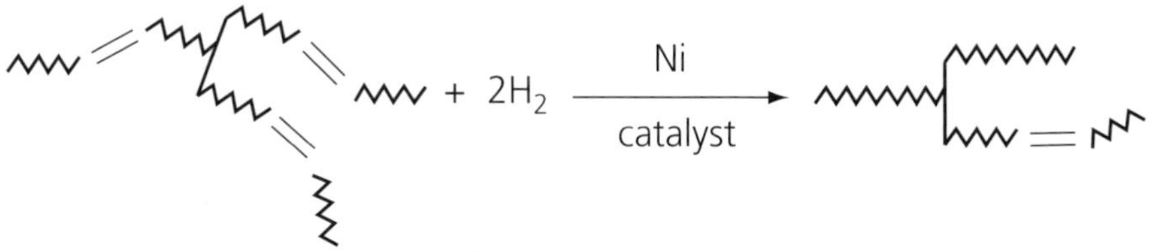

Figure 6.12 Partial hydrogenation of an oil molecule

For Interest   Trans fats

If you have ever looked at the ingredients list of some cakes or biscuits, you will have probably noted the term 'hydrogenated fats'. The process of converting liquid oils into a more solid form has been used by the food industry for over 100 years. Margarine was one of the most successful food products created by hydrogenation of vegetable oils. It was marketed as a healthier alternative to butter so long as it contained added fat-soluble vitamins – a requirement in the UK. It was also favoured by many people for baking as it was much easier to use. Ironically, it is for health reasons that many countries have passed legislation which effectively bans hydrogenated fats from foods. 'Trans' fats are one of the products of hydrogenating oils. These are not naturally found in the human diet in such large quantities. Research since the 1950s has linked trans fats with heart disease, cancer and several other illnesses. In 2003, Denmark became the first country to act on this scientific research by passing legislation which regulates the sale of trans fats in food. In the UK, many supermarkets have acted to ensure that their own-brand produce is free from trans fats.

Figure 6.13 Hydrogenated fats have been removed from many processed foods.

Relating structure to function

Fats and oils are insoluble in water. They are said to be **hydrophobic** which means 'water hating'. Indeed, scientists often refer to parts of a molecule as the 'fatty part' to describe molecules that do not dissolve in water. Fats and oils do not dissolve in water because they are non-polar. The long hydrocarbon chains cannot bond to water and there are no polar –OH groups or ions that can bond to water. When we examine the structure of fats and oils, we can also begin to appreciate why certain vitamins are classed as fat- or water-soluble. For example, the structures of vitamin C and vitamin A are shown in Figures 6.14 and 6.15. Vitamin A is classed as a fat-soluble vitamin whereas vitamin C is classed as a water-soluble vitamin. Vitamin C has several polar –OH groups that can bond to water by hydrogen bonding. As it is such a polar molecule, it will not bond to fats and oils that are non-polar. Vitamin A is a less polar molecule as it is mainly composed of hydrocarbon groups. This means that the bulk of the molecule cannot bond to water, but it will be able to bond to fats and oils by London dispersion forces since fats and oils are largely non-polar too.

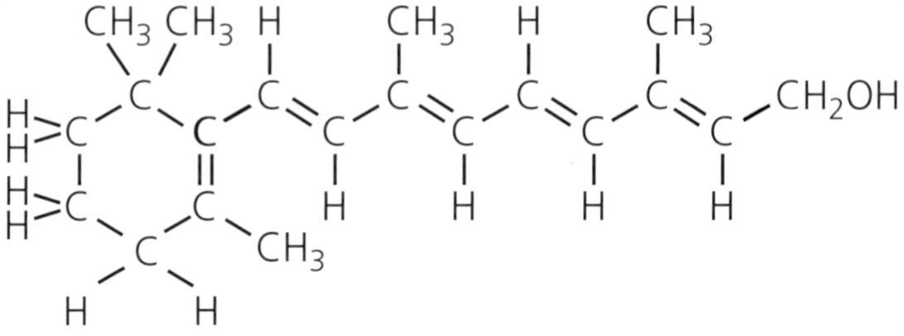

Figure 6.14 Vitamin A

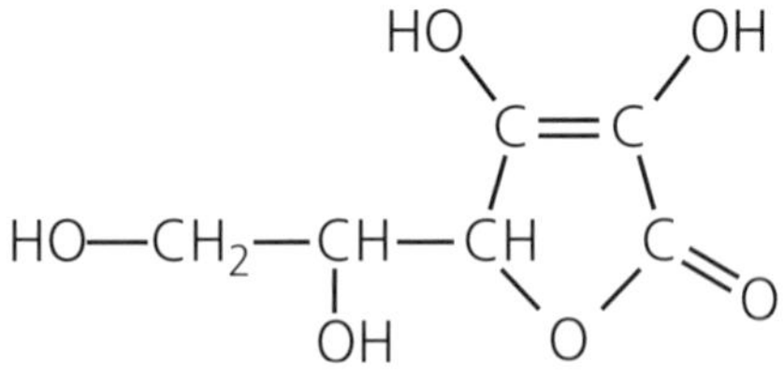

Figure 6.15 Vitamin C

Using fats and oils to make soap

Soaps

Soaps are derived from fats and oils by treating the fat or oil with an alkali such as sodium hydroxide or potassium hydroxide. This results in alkaline **hydrolysis** of the three ester links in the fat or oil, and produces glycerol and the sodium salt or potassium salt of the fatty acids. These salts are 'soap'.

Since they are soluble, soaps must be extracted from the hydrolysis mixture by adding a large excess of sodium chloride, after which the soap can be filtered off. Some famous brand names of soap, such as Palmolive®, take their name from the oils that are hydrolysed to produce the soap; in this case palm oil and olive oil. Another example is SR toothpaste. The SR refers to the name of the soap sodium ricinoleate, made from castor oil, which was described as an ingredient in early TV advertising. The by-product from making soap, glycerol, is usually chemically cleaned (to ensure that there is no excess alkali) and sold on.

The cleaning action of soap

When we cover our hands in oil from a cycle chain or fat from handling butter, rinsing our hands under water does not remove the greasy residue. This should not be surprising now that we know that fats and oils are non-polar molecules and so they are not attracted to polar water molecules. If soap is used, however, we can make the greasy residue dissolve in the water. The structure of the soap gives us some clues as to how this is made possible.

Figure 6.16 Soaps have been made and used since ancient times by hydrolysis of fats and oils.

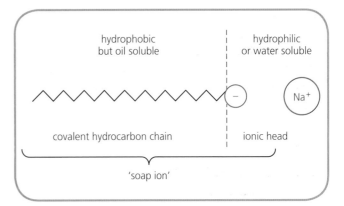

Figure 6.18 The structure of soap

$$CH_3(CH_2)_{14}COO^-$$
Hydrophobic tail   Hydrophilic head

Figure 6.19 A soap ion

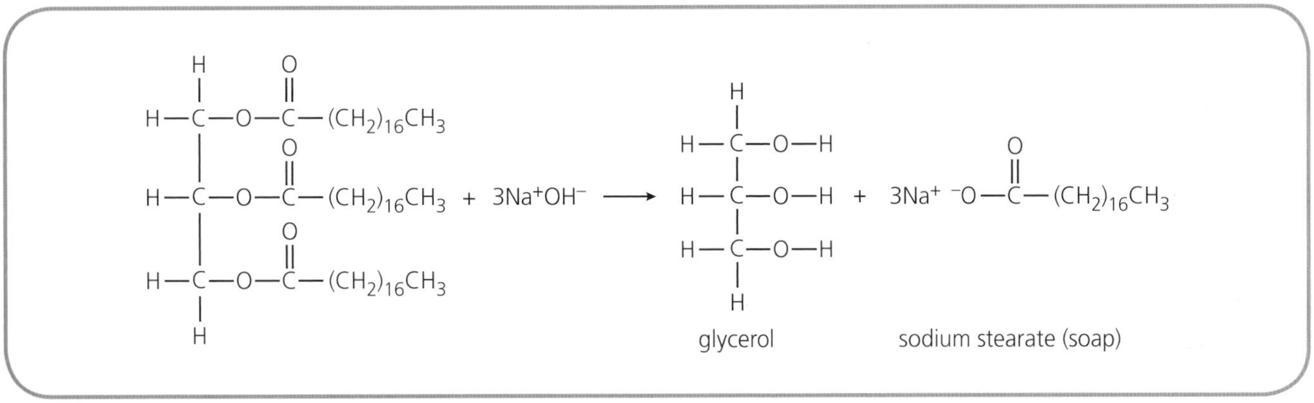

Figure 6.17 Hydrolysis of this fat produces soap and glycerol.

This representation of a soap molecule illustrates that soaps have two parts to them:

1 an ionic head (the carboxylate ion) which is water soluble

2 a covalent hydrocarbon tail which is soluble in oil/ grease.

As the covalent 'tail' is a hydrocarbon chain, it is non-polar and can bond easily to the greasy material on fabric or skin. This part of the soap does not bond to water and is therefore said to be hydrophobic (water hating). The ionic head is attracted to the polar covalent water molecules; this part of the soap molecule is said to be **hydrophilic** (water loving). This results in globules of grease dispersed in water as shown in Figure 6.20.

Detergents

In many regions of the UK, particularly the south east of England, the water is said to be 'hard'. Hard water contains dissolved calcium and magnesium ions. When hard water is mixed with soap, instead of forming a soapy lather, a precipitate is formed, for example

$$CH_3(CH_2)_{14}COO^-(aq) + Ca^{+2}(aq) \rightarrow (CH_3(CH_2)_{14}COO)_2Ca(s)$$

The precipitates reduce the cleansing action of soap and build up to leave a 'scum' around baths, sinks and shower heads.

Figure 6.21

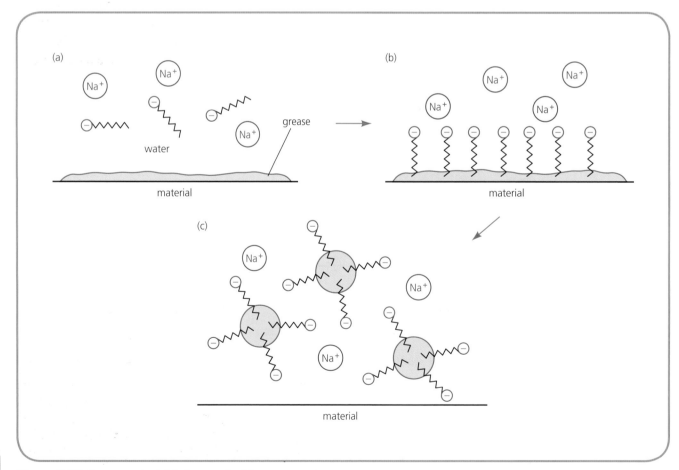

Figure 6.20 Greasy material being washed by soapy water

In hard water areas it is best to use a soapless detergent. These compounds have a soap-like structure, but do not form precipitates when mixed with hard water. An example of a soapless detergent is dodecylbenzenesulfonate:

$$CH_3(CH_2)_{11}C_6H_4SO_3^-$$

Like soaps, the detergent dodecylbenzenesulfonate contains a hydrocarbon tail, which is oil soluble, and an ionic head, which is water soluble. Unlike soaps, this ion will not react with calcium or magnesium ions to form a precipitate.

Emulsions

Grease particles mixed in soapy water is an example of an **emulsion**: small droplets of one liquid dispersed in another liquid. The grease and water would normally separate out to form two separate layers, but the soap acts as an emulsifier as it helps to bring the two substances together. Emulsions in food are very common. For example, as we learned at the start of this chapter, milk is an important source of fat-soluble vitamins. Milk is mostly water but it also contains lots of fats and fat-soluble compounds, yet when we look at a glass of milk we cannot see two separate layers. Milk contains naturally occurring emulsifiers such as sodium caseinate as well as compounds called phospholipids. These compounds help the fatty parts of milk to be dispersed throughout the water in milk. Thus, milk is an example of an emulsion. Mayonnaise is another classic example of an emulsion. It is formed by mixing oil, such as olive oil, vinegar and egg yolk. Lecithin in the egg yolk acts as the emulsifier helping the vinegar (mostly water) to stay mixed with the oil. The structure of lecithin is shown in Figure 6.22. If we examine the structure we can see that the molecule consists of a hydrophilic part and a hydrophobic part. The charged phosphate and nitrogen are attracted to water while the long hydrocarbon chains are attracted to oil.

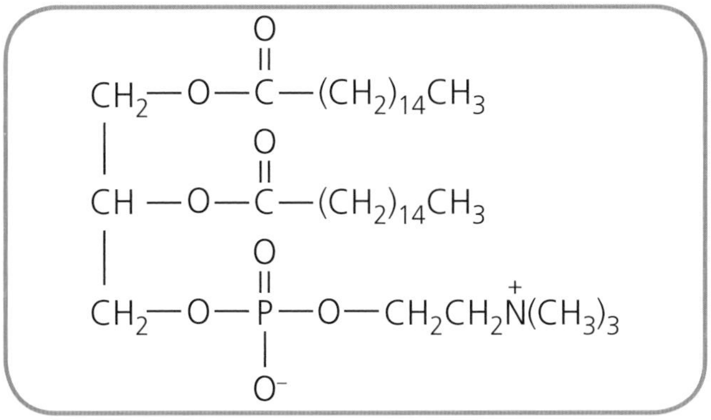

If we examine the ingredients labels of some common foodstuffs, such as those shown in Figure 6.24, mono- and diglycerides of fatty acids are referred to frequently. These are emulsifiers that are often referenced by their E number E471. An example of a monoglyceride is shown in Figure 6.25. The mono refers to the glycerol

Figure 6.22 Lecithin is found in egg yolk and acts as an emulsifier.

Figure 6.23 Milk and mayonnaise are examples of emulsions.

INGREDIENTS: Reconstituted skimmed milk, sugar, glucose-fructose syrup, glucose syrup, emulsifier (mono and diglycerides of fatty acids), stabili... carrageenan), natural vanilla flavouring from Madagascar, vanilla bean colour (mixed carotenes).

Figure 6.24 Emulsifiers are present in many foods.

structure having just one OH reacted with a fatty acid to form an ester; two of the OH groups remain free. This can act as an emulsifier as the OH groups are

polar, allowing the molecule to dissolve in water, while the fatty acid is non-polar (oil soluble).

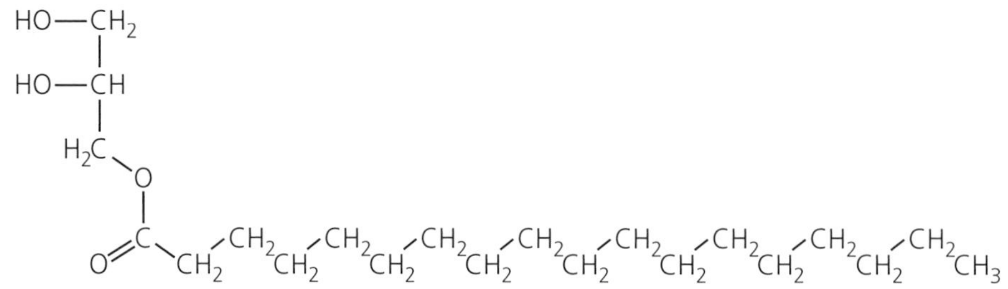

Figure 6.25 An example of a monoglyceride of a fatty acid

Checklist for Revision

- I can explain the function of fats and oils in the human diet.
- I can identify glycerol and draw its structure.
- I know that fats and oils are tri-esters formed by reacting glycerol with three fatty acid molecules.
- I can look at the structure of a fat, oil or fatty acid and state whether it is saturated or unsaturated.
- I can explain why oils have lower melting points than fats.
- I can draw the products of hydrolysis of a fat or oil.
- I know how soaps are produced from fats and oils.
- I can describe how soaps and detergents work.
- I can identify an emulsion and I know why they are used.

Key Terms

The words and phrases below were introduced in this chapter.

Their definitions are given in the chemical dictionary.

  condensation reaction
  emulsion
  fatty acid
  glycerol
  hardening
  hydrolysis
  hydrophilic
  hydrophobic
  soap
  triglyceride

Study Questions

1* Fats have higher melting points than oils because when comparing fats and oils

   A fats have more hydrogen bonds

   B fats have more cross-links between molecules

   C fat molecules are more loosely packed

   D fat molecules are more saturated.

2* Which one of the following substances would act as a soap?

   A Glycerol

   B Stearic acid

   C Potassium stearate

   D Ethyl stearate

3* Which of the following is the structural formula for glycerol?

A CH_2OH
   |
   CH_2
   |
   CH_2OH

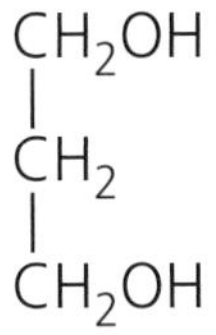

B CH_2OH
   |
   CH_2OH

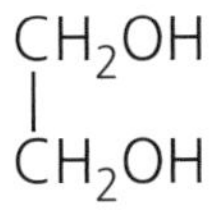

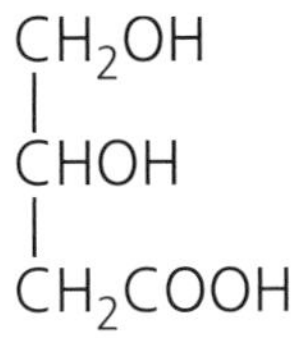

C CH_2OH
   |
   $CHOH$
   |
   CH_2COOH

D CH_2OH
   |
   $CHOH$
   |
   CH_2OH

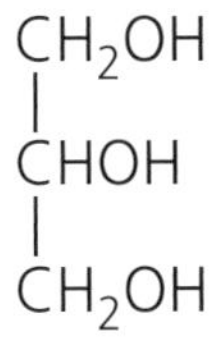

Figure 6.26

4* Both fats and oils are mixtures of triglycerides. Each triglyceride molecule contains three ester linkages and the majority of the molecules contain carbon–carbon double bonds.

a) Why does the triglyceride molecule contain three ester linkages?

b) Oils can be converted into fats by a process called hardening. What happens to the triglyceride molecules when oils are hardened?

c) On exposure to air, oils turn rancid more rapidly than fats. In this process, the triglyceride molecules are broken up into smaller, 'foul-smelling' molecules.

At what functional group within the triglyceride molecule is the breaking likely to occur?

5 Hydrolysis of the triglyceride shown in Figure 6.27 yields an alcohol and carboxylic acids.

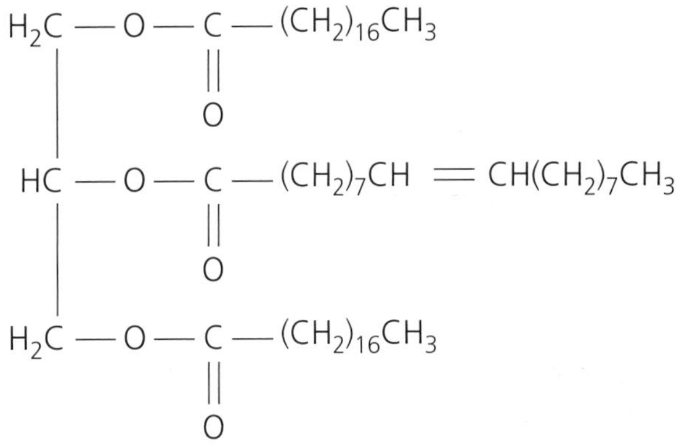

$$H_2C - O - C - (CH_2)_{16}CH_3$$
$$\quad\quad\quad \| $$
$$\quad\quad\quad O$$

$$HC - O - C - (CH_2)_7CH = CH(CH_2)_7CH_3$$
$$\quad\quad\quad \| $$
$$\quad\quad\quad O$$

$$H_2C - O - C - (CH_2)_{16}CH_3$$
$$\quad\quad\quad \| $$
$$\quad\quad\quad O$$

Figure 6.27

a) How many different acids will be produced?

b) Give the molecular formula of the saturated acid produced on hydrolysis.

c) Name the alcohol produced and give its structural formula.

6* Biodiesel is a mixture of esters which can be made by heating rapeseed oil with methanol in the presence of a catalyst.

a) Name compound X in Figure 6.28.

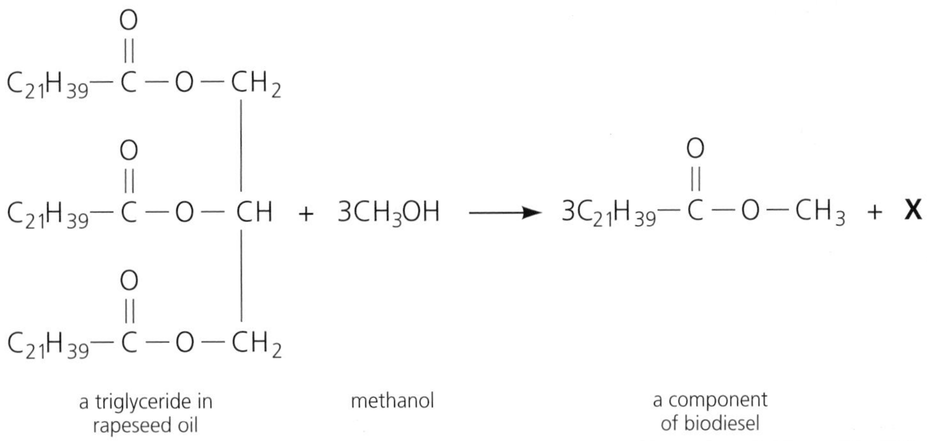

$$
\begin{array}{c}
O \\
\| \\
C_{21}H_{39} - C - O - CH_2 \\
\\
O \\
\| \\
C_{21}H_{39} - C - O - CH \quad + \quad 3CH_3OH \quad \longrightarrow \quad 3C_{21}H_{39} - C - O - CH_3 \quad + \quad \mathbf{X} \\
\\
O \\
\| \\
C_{21}H_{39} - C - O - CH_2
\end{array}
$$

a triglyceride in rapeseed oil   methanol   a component of biodiesel

Figure 6.28

b) A typical diesel molecule obtained from crude oil has the molecular formula $C_{16}H_{34}$ (hexadecane). Other than the ester group, name a functional group present in biodiesel molecules which is not present in hexadecane.

c) Vegetable oils like rapeseed oil are converted into fats for use in the food industry. Suggest how this is done.

7* Small children can find it difficult to swallow tablets or pills so ibuprofen is supplied as an 'infant formula' emulsion.

The emulsifier used is polysorbate 80. Its structure is shown below.

a) Explain why this molecule acts as an emulsifier.

b) The emulsion contains 2 g of ibuprofen in every 100 cm³ of emulsion.

The recommended dose for treating a 6-month-old baby is 0.050 g.

Calculate the volume, in cm³, of infant formula needed to treat a 6-month-old baby.

8 Explain fully why fats have higher melting points than oils.

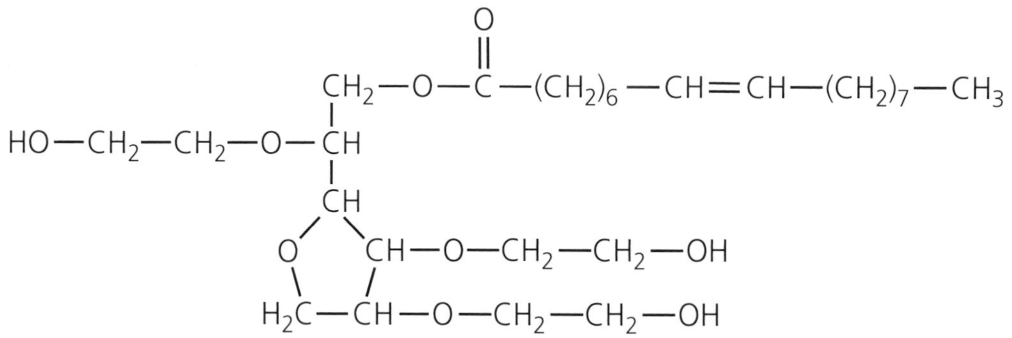

$$CH_2—O—\overset{\overset{\textstyle O}{\|}}{C}—(CH_2)_6—CH=CH—(CH_2)_7—CH_3$$

$$HO—CH_2—CH_2—O—CH$$
$$CH$$
$$O \quad CH—O—CH_2—CH_2—OH$$
$$H_2C—CH—O—CH_2—CH_2—OH$$

Figure 6.29

1 Research the structures of vitamins which are fat soluble and those which are water soluble. Can you relate the structure of the vitamin to its solubility?

2 Investigate the debate over saturated and unsaturated fats in our diets.

3 Find out about the soap-making process. Where does the fat/oil come from? What happens to the glycerol? How is the pH of the soap brought down to an acceptable level?

7 Proteins

Proteins make up a huge variety of animal and plant material of which the following are examples:

- peas and beans
- meat
- fish
- cheese
- eggs
- hides and skin
- wool and silk

Without proteins, the human body could not survive. Proteins are the major structural materials of animal tissue and they are also involved in the maintenance and regulation of life. Examples of proteins and their functions are shown in Table 7.1.

All proteins yield acrid-smelling alkaline gases on heating with soda lime (Figure 7.3), a concentrated alkaline mixture of sodium and calcium hydroxides. Such gases are all amines or ammonia, in other words, nitrogen-containing substances. Hence we can deduce that all proteins contain nitrogen and we can begin to understand why plants require soluble nitrogen

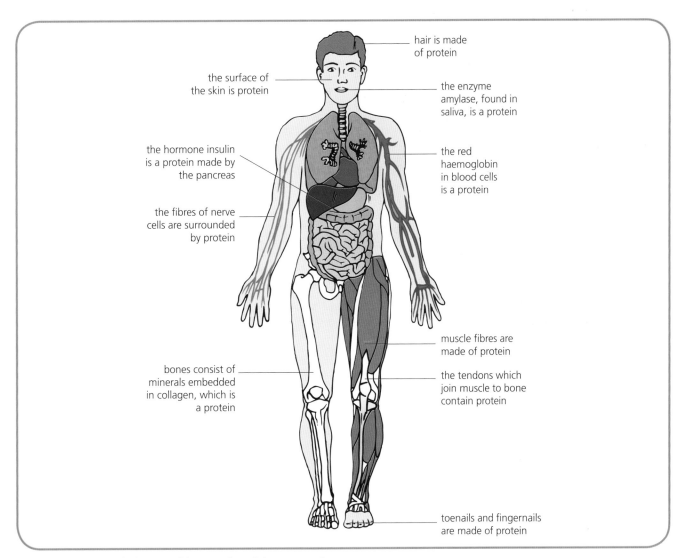

hair is made of protein

the surface of the skin is protein

the enzyme amylase, found in saliva, is a protein

the hormone insulin is a protein made by the pancreas

the red haemoglobin in blood cells is a protein

the fibres of nerve cells are surrounded by protein

muscle fibres are made of protein

bones consist of minerals embedded in collagen, which is a protein

the tendons which join muscle to bone contain protein

toenails and fingernails are made of protein

Figure 7.1 Human beings could not exist without proteins.

Name of protein	Where found	Function
Collagen	Tendons, muscle and bone	Structural support
Keratin	Hair, skin and nails	Structural support
Myosin	Muscles	Helps muscles to contract
Insulin	Pancreas	Hormone which helps to control blood glucose levels
Haemoglobin	Red blood cells	Transports oxygen around the body
Immunoglobins	Blood, tears, saliva, skin	Fight infection
Amylase	Saliva and pancreas	An enzyme which breaks down starch

Table 7.1

compounds as an essential nutrient. Without them plants cannot synthesise protein.

Animals cannot synthesise protein from simple nitrogen compounds but they can reconstruct vegetable protein or other animal protein from food which they have eaten. All protein derives, therefore, from the fixation of atmospheric nitrogen as nitrates in soil.

If protein is hydrolysed using 50% hydrochloric acid, refluxing the mixture for several hours, the protein breaks down into its constituents called **amino acids**. Figure 7.4 illustrates suitable apparatus for a small-scale experiment.

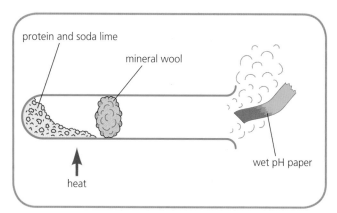

Figure 7.2 Blood sugar levels are controlled by the hormone insulin. Diabetics measure their blood glucose levels.

Figure 7.3 Protein mixed with soda lime and then heated

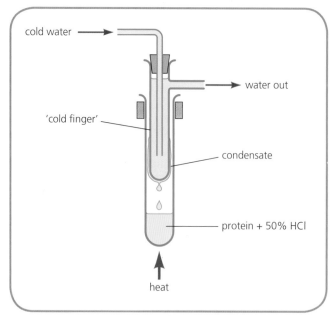

Figure 7.4 Protein being hydrolysed with hydrochloric acid

These amino acids have a typical structure, as shown in Figure 7.5.

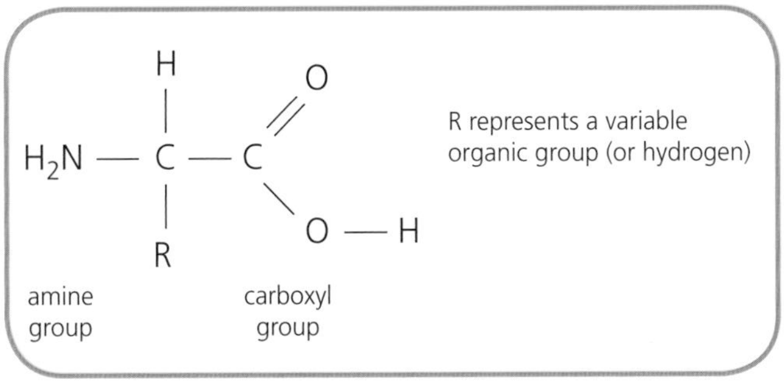

Figure 7.5 Amino acid structure

Figure 7.6 shows the structures of some common amino acids. The simplest amino acids are glycine and alanine.

Twenty amino acids occur frequently in proteins, another six occur occasionally. The amino acids produced by hydrolysis of proteins can be identified by chromatography as discussed in Chapter 17.

Making proteins

Protein chains can contain several thousand amino acids and hence protein molecules have huge molecular masses. The variety of proteins is caused by arranging the amino acids in a specific order. It is a bit like using the letters of the alphabet to form words; a small number of letters can form a small word and a large number of letters can form a large word. Likewise, arranging letters in different orders will produce different words. In effect, an alphabet of amino acids is assembled into a dictionary full of proteins. It is fascinating that the human body is able to organise these amino acids into the correct sequence to make the proteins our bodies need to keep us alive and healthy.

Proteins comprise a large part of an animal's diet. During digestion the animal and vegetable proteins in foodstuffs are broken down (hydrolysed) into amino acids which are small enough to pass into the bloodstream. Proteins required for the body's specific needs are built up from amino acids in the body cells according to information supplied by DNA in the cell nuclei.

When amino acids react together, the amino group joins with the hydroxyl group to form an **amide link** and a water molecule. This type of reaction is known as a condensation reaction and is shown in Figure 7.7. The groups in brackets are the amide links. In proteins, these amide links are also called **peptide links**. Since proteins are very large molecules made from many thousands of amino acids, the reaction to form a protein is usually referred to as a condensation **polymerisation**.

The breakdown of proteins, which occurs during digestion, is the opposite of condensation: a hydrolysis reaction takes place where the peptide bond is broken by water molecules to produce amino acids. This process is illustrated in the structures shown in Figure 7.8.

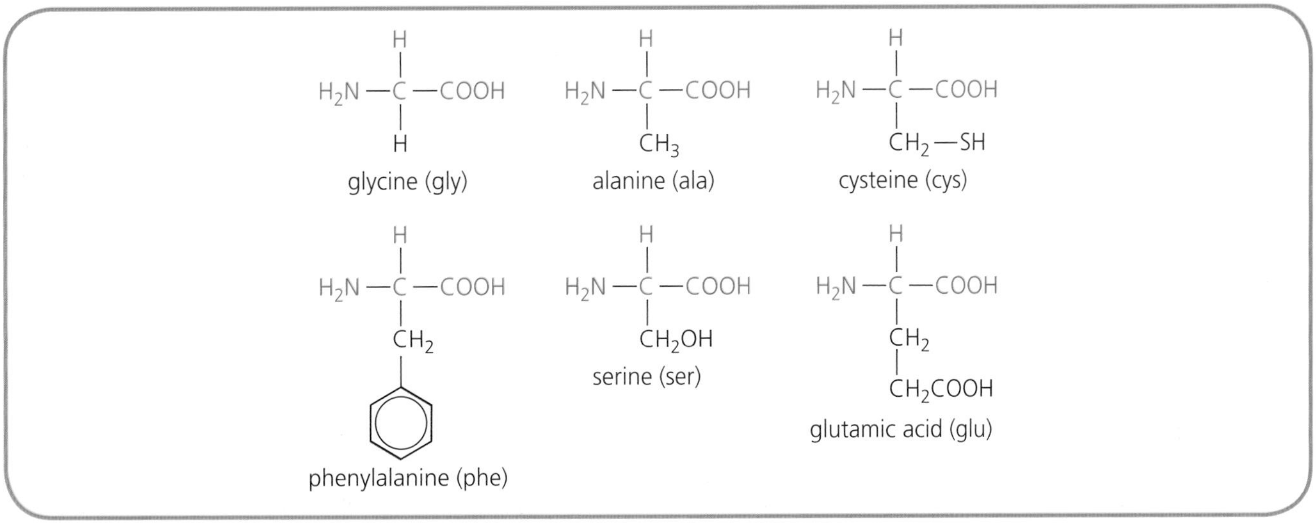

Figure 7.6 Structures of six common amino acids

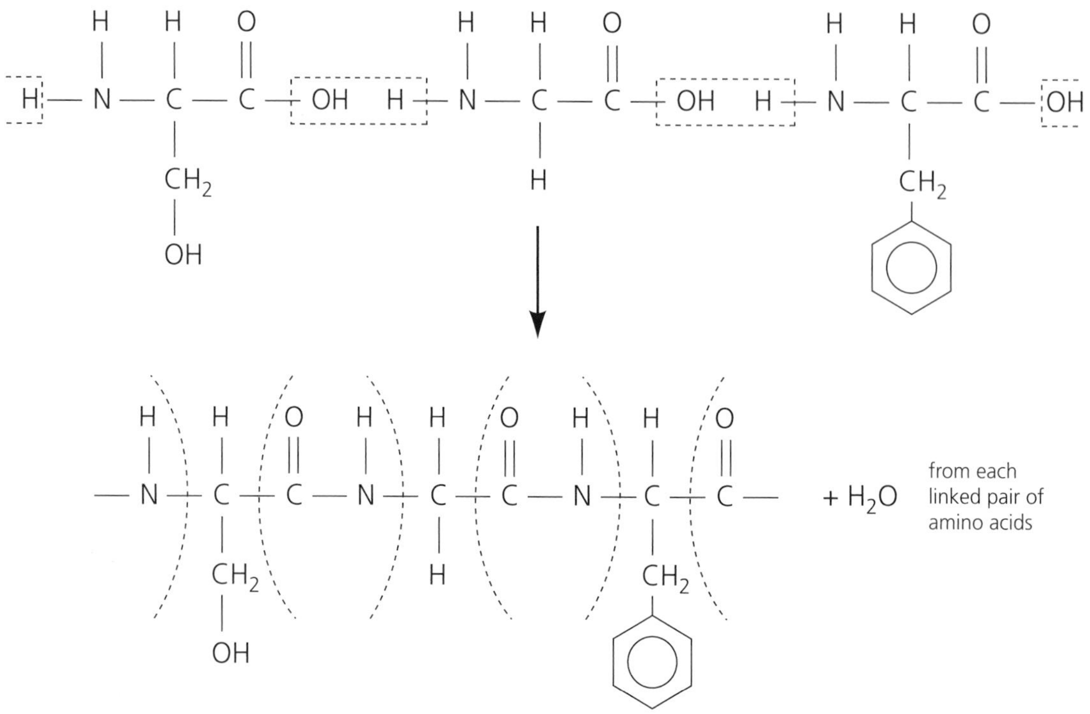

Figure 7.7 Condensation of amino acids to form amide links (shown in brackets) in a protein

This is the process also occurring in the experiment in Figure 7.4.

One of the amazing functions of the human body is its ability to carry out complex chemical reactions. Making amino acids is one of the functions that our bodies carry out on a daily basis. However, not all of the amino acids that we require can be synthesised by the body. Amino acids which cannot be made by the body are called **essential amino acids**. These must be present in our diet which is one important reason for consuming a wide variety of foods. A diet deficient in one of the essential amino acids can lead to serious health problems. Cases of malnutrition highlight the effects of, among other things, restricting the supply to the body. This is demonstrated quite horrifically when pictures of starving children are beamed across our TV screens to illustrate famine in the developing world. Kwashiorkor is the medical name for the severe malnutrition that is displayed by the children we see in the newsreels, with their swollen abdomen being the most obvious sign of

the disease. Children who have just stopped feeding on their mother's milk (which is usually a rich source of protein) suffer from the lack of protein in their diet and develop kwashiorkor after many months of eating a diet of very-low-protein meals. It is very rare to encounter kwashiorkor in the UK, although the elderly are probably most vulnerable as they are most likely to suffer from malnutrition.

Key Terms

The words and phrases below were introduced in this chapter.

Their definitions are given in the chemical dictionary.

> **amide link**
>
> **amino acid**
>
> **essential amino acid**
>
> **peptide link**

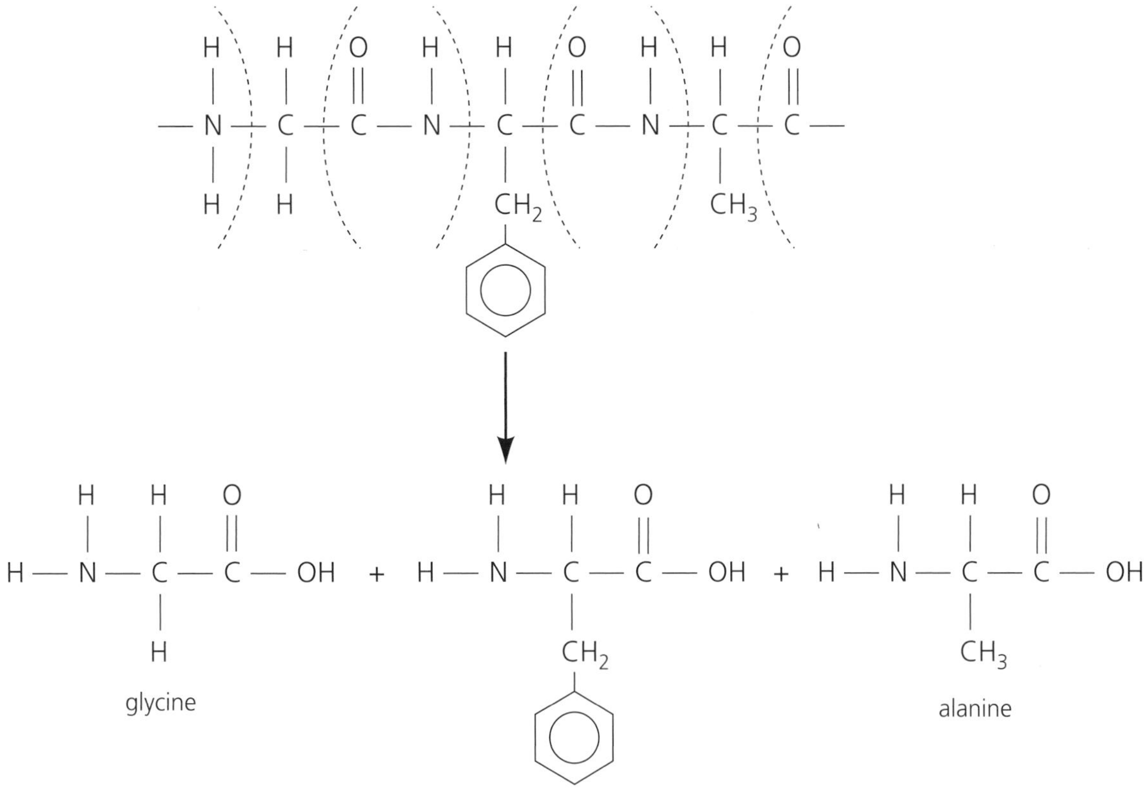

Figure 7.8 Hydrolysing a protein

Checklist for Revision

- I can identify an amino acid and recognise the amino and carboxyl functional groups.
- I can combine amino acids by forming amide links and know that this is a condensation reaction.
- I understand that joining amino acids makes proteins and that the sequence of amino acids determines the properties of the protein formed.
- I know that proteins are the major structural materials of animal tissue and that proteins are involved in the maintenance and regulation of life.
- I know that enzymes are examples of proteins.
- I can draw the amino acids formed from the hydrolysis of a protein.
- I know what is meant by the term 'essential amino acid'.

Study Questions

1* Essential amino acids come from the food we eat. Some of these are also called α-amino acids because the amino group is on the carbon atom adjacent to the acid group.

Which of the following is an α-amino acid?

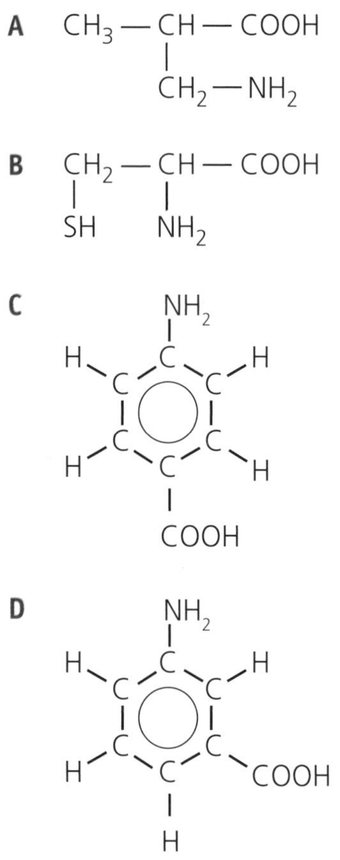

A $CH_3 - CH - COOH$
        $\quad\quad\quad |$
        $\quad\quad CH_2 - NH_2$

B $CH_2 - CH - COOH$
        $\quad | \quad\quad |$
        $\quad SH \quad\quad NH_2$

C

D

Figure 7.9

2 Proteins can be classified as

   A polyesters   **B** amino acids

   C polyamides   **D** carboxylic acids.

3* The dipeptide in Figure 7.10 forms the two amino acids aspartic acid and phenylalanine when it is hydrolysed.

  a) On a copy of the structure of this dipeptide, identify the amide link by placing brackets around it.

  b) Draw the structure of the amino acid phenylalanine.

  c) The artificial sweetener aspartame is a methyl ester of the dipeptide shown in Figure 7.10. Its

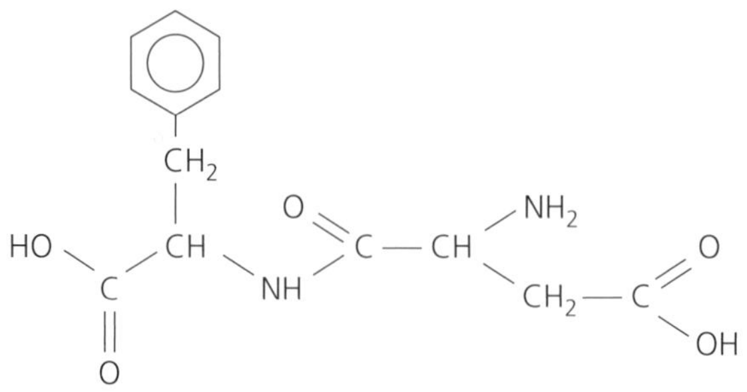

Figure 7.10

   sweetness depends on the shape and structure of the molecule.

   Suggest a reason why aspartame is not used in food that will be cooked, but is used in cold drinks, for example.

4* The structure shown is part of a protein molecule.

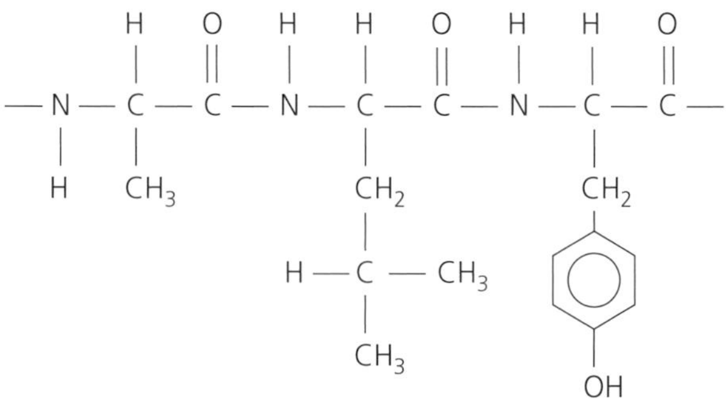

Figure 7.11

  a) Circle a peptide (amide) link in the structure.

  b) Draw the structural formula for one of the molecules which would be formed if the protein was hydrolysed.

5* Keratin, a natural polymer, is a protein found in hair. The hydrolysis of keratin produces different compounds of the type shown in Figure 7.12.

  a) What name is given to compounds like glycine, alanine and cysteine?

  b) What is meant by a hydrolysis reaction?

  c) Dacron, a synthetic polymer, is used in heart surgery. A section of the polymer is shown in Figure 7.13.

   What name is given to the link made by the shaded group of atoms in this section of the polymer?

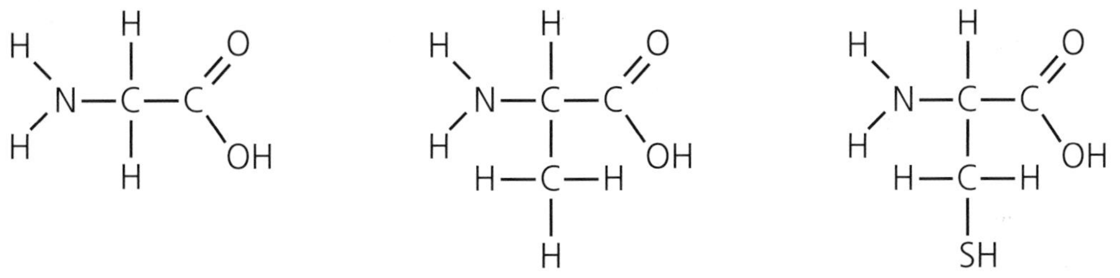

glycine   alanine   cysteine

Figure 7.12

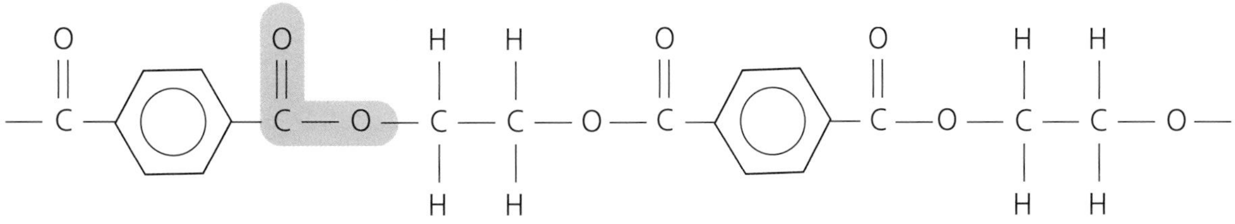

Figure 7.13

8 The chemistry of cooking and oxidation of food

Flavour in food

One of the greatest pleasures of eating a meal is savouring the variety of flavours from the foods eaten. Good cooking involves many chemical and physical reactions. The chef has to balance these reactions to create a dish that is wholesome and full of flavour. This involves:

- ensuring the cooking process (grilling, steaming, boiling etc.) does not destroy any of the flavours present in the raw food

- choosing the best cooking process to release the flavour molecules that are locked in the food

- choosing the best cooking process to create new compounds that add to the flavour of the food.

In order to understand how cooking can affect the chemistry of the food, it is important to look at

Figure 8.2 Chopping a food can release flavour molecules from the cells of the food.

the molecules responsible for the flavour in foods. 'Tasting' a food involves smelling the flavour molecules too. Molecules that evaporate easily are said to be volatile and will contribute to the flavour. Examples of molecules which give rise to familiar smells and flavours are shown in Table 8.1.

Figure 8.1 Cooking alters the chemical composition of the food.

Name	Where found?
Limonene	Lemons and oranges
Furaneol	Strawberries
Vanillin	Vanilla pods
Eugenol	Bay leaves/clove oil
Capsaicin	Chilli peppers

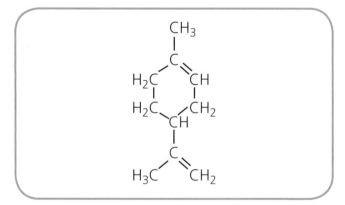

Figure 8.3 Structure of limonene

Table 8.1

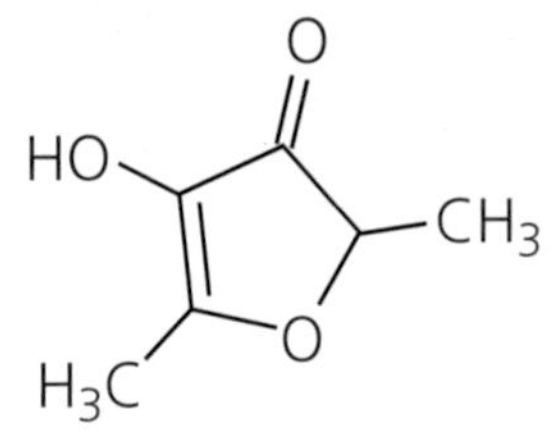

Figure 8.4 Structure of furaneol

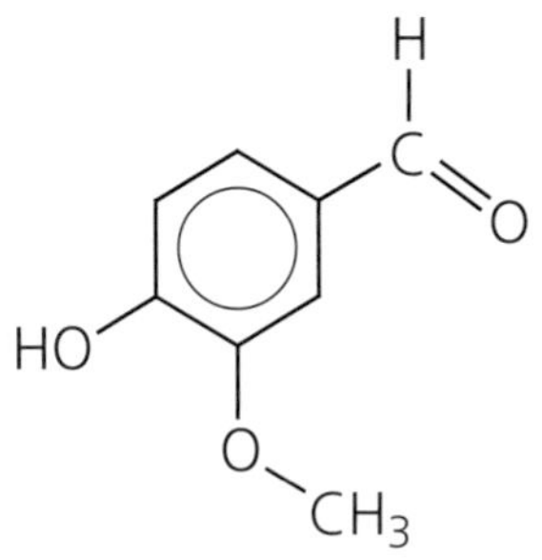

Figure 8.5 Structure of vanillin

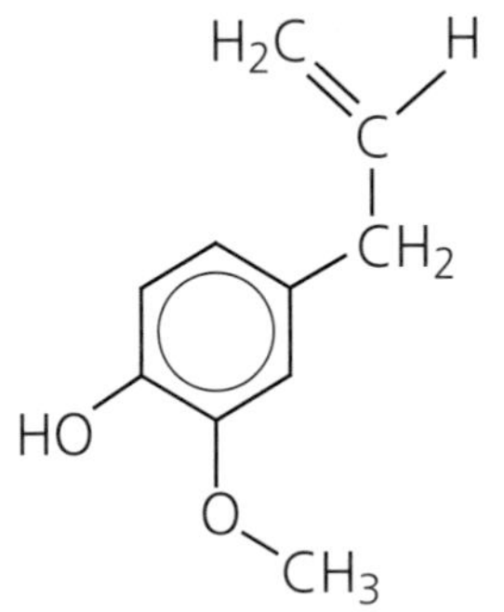

Figure 8.6 Structure of eugenol

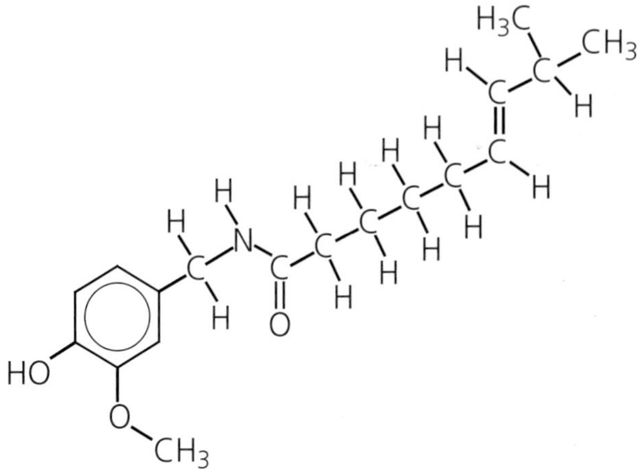

Figure 8.7 Structure of capsaicin

Changing the groups attached to a molecule can have a significant effect on the flavour. This is illustrated quite nicely when we examine the structure of vanillin (responsible for vanilla flavour), eugenol and capsaicin. All three molecules share a similar chemical structure but changing one part of the molecule alters the properties and hence the flavour. Vanillin is soluble in water. Changing the vanillin **aldehyde** group (see later in this chapter) for a hydrocarbon chain gives us eugenol which is much less soluble in water, but much more soluble in oil. Thus, when cooking with bay leaves which contain eugenol, cooking in oil should yield different flavours from cooking in water.

Figure 8.8 The vanillin molecule is found in vanilla pods.

An examination of the structures shown allows us to make some predictions about their solubility in water. For example, we would expect limonene to be completely insoluble in water as it is a non-polar molecule, whereas furaneol should be much more soluble in water as the polar –OH group (and the carbonyl oxygen and the oxygen in the centre of the ring) allows bonds to be made to water molecules.

Capsaicin is one of the molecules responsible for the hot chilli taste found in peppers such as jalapeño and habanero. Like eugenol, capsaicin is based on the vanillin molecule where the aldehyde group is replaced. This time, the aldehyde group is replaced with an amide group attached to a long hydrocarbon chain. It is therefore not that surprising that capsaicin is insoluble

Figure 8.9 Bay leaves contain eugenol.

Figure 8.10 Capsaicin is present in chilli peppers.

in cold water. Anyone who has suffered from eating a very spicy meal, where capsaicin has been one of the molecules present in the chillies consumed, will testify that drinking plenty of water does not help to reduce the burning sensation. As the capsaicin is insoluble in water, drinking water does not help to remove the molecule from the mouth. Instead, drinking some milk is recommended. As we now know, milk contains proteins, such as casein, which can act as emulsifiers. Thus, just like adding a soap to allow oil and water to mix, swishing your mouth with milk will help the capsaicin mix with water and remove it from your mouth where it is causing the nerves to tingle!

An examination of the size and structure of a molecule allows us to predict how volatile it is likely to be. In general, molecules with a molecular mass of under 300 are likely to be volatile whereas much larger molecules are not likely to be volatile. The type of bonding present will also have a significant influence

on how volatile the molecule is likely to be. This is exploited when creating perfumes that contain mixtures of molecules of differing volatility. For example, citronellol and undecanal are commonly used in perfumery. Citronellol has a floral/rose fragrance and is much less volatile than undecanal which has a lavender fragrance. An examination of the structures of these molecules alerts us to the fact that citronellol has an –OH group allowing it to form strong hydrogen bonds to neighbouring citronellol molecules. Undecanal cannot form hydrogen bonds and so the intermolecular bonds are much weaker. It is therefore more volatile.

The famous chef Heston Blumenthal started a new trend when he began to investigate the chemistry of cooking. His comments on the cooking of asparagus revolutionised the way people in the UK cook the vegetable. He was one of the pioneers who highlighted the fact that the flavour molecules in asparagus are

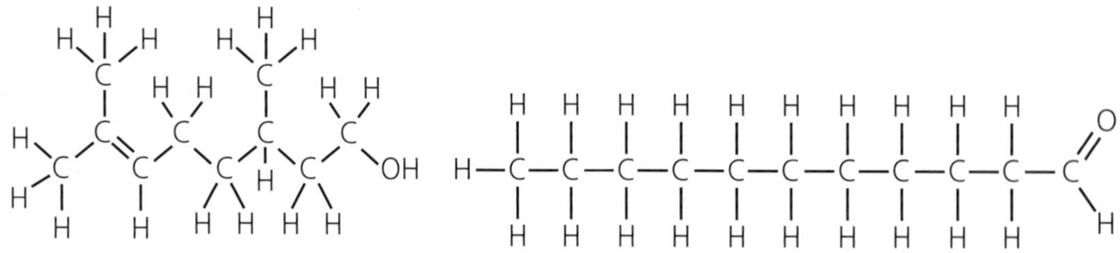

citronellol

undecanal

Figure 8.11 The structures of citronellol and undecanal

water soluble. Thus, steaming and boiling are not recommended for cooking asparagus as the flavour molecules dissolve in the cooking water and are therefore lost. Instead, Heston promoted cooking asparagus in olive oil and/or butter. Cooking in oil or fat prevents the flavour molecules 'escaping' as they are not very soluble in the oil or fat. Applying similar chemical principles, he also advises cooking broccoli in water as the opposite is true for broccoli: it contains flavour molecules that are more soluble in oil than they are in water.

An understanding of the chemical composition of food also gives us an insight into how best to preserve the nutritional value of food. For example, as mentioned in the previous chapter, vitamins can be classed as water soluble or fat soluble. Vitamin C (see Figure 8.14) is

an example of a water-soluble vitamin that is found in many fruits and vegetables such as apples, kiwis and peppers. Cooking vegetables in boiling water can extract the water-soluble vitamins, such as vitamin C, into the cooking water thus robbing the food of these important vitamins.

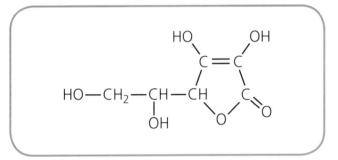

Figure 8.14 Vitamin C is a polar molecule. It dissolves in water.

Figure 8.12 The flavour molecules in asparagus are soluble in water.

Figure 8.15 Peppers are a good source of vitamin C.

Changing the structure of food by heating

Frying an egg is the classic example of an everyday chemical reaction. The most visible sign of a reaction is the hardening and change in colour of the egg 'white'. In order to understand the chemistry of the changes that occur, we need to examine the structure of the molecules that are found in the egg white.

Figure 8.13 The flavour molecules in broccoli are soluble in oil.

Figure 8.16 Chemical changes occur when an egg is fried.

Egg whites are a great source of protein. We learned in the previous chapter that proteins are made from amino acids joining together in a condensation polymerisation. The proteins which form are able to form hydrogen bonds to themselves and other protein molecules through the polar CO and NH groups of the amide links.

$$\underset{\delta+}{}C \underset{\delta-}{=} O \quad \text{and} \quad \underset{\delta-}{}N \underset{\delta+}{-} H$$

Figure 8.17 These polar groups allow protein molecules to form hydrogen bonds with each other.

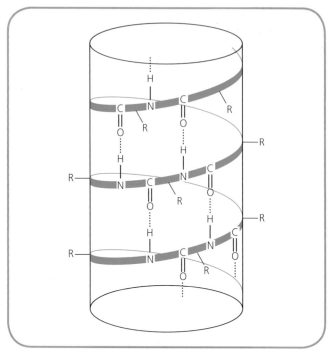

Figure 8.18 The alpha helix

Hydrogen bonding between the protein molecules occurs readily and causes the protein molecule to produce many complex structures such as the alpha helix (Figure 8.18) and the beta-pleated sheet (Figure 8.19). When two or more protein molecules bond to each other, very complex shapes emerge such as the structure shown in Figure 8.20. This shows the protein haemoglobin which has a specific shape that allows it to carry out its function of transporting oxygen around the body.

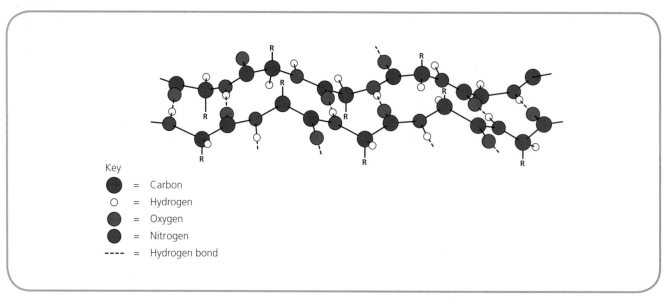

Key

● = Carbon
○ = Hydrogen
● = Oxygen
● = Nitrogen
---- = Hydrogen bond

Figure 8.19 The beta-pleated sheet

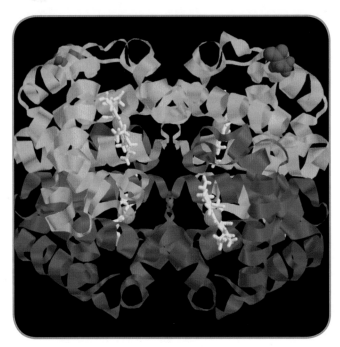

Figure 8.20 A computer graphic of the complex shape of haemoglobin

Enzymes work on the principle of having a specific shape which allows them to catalyse a limited number of reactions. Their shape comes from the twisting and folding of the protein molecules (see Figure 8.21).

In the egg white, the protein is an example of a globular protein where the protein chains are wrapped around each other and form a ball of molecules (a bit like a ball of string). The structure is held together by hydrogen bonds. When an egg is heated, the heat energy breaks the hydrogen bonds between the protein chains, causing the long chains to unfold. This changes the shape and allows the uncurled protein molecules to form hydrogen bonds with other molecules which have also uncurled during the heating process. Overall, the

structure of the protein has changed into a new shape completely. This process is known as **denaturing**. It also occurs when we expose enzymes to high temperatures. Denaturing the enzyme can stop it catalysing reactions as it no longer possesses the specific shape that allows it to interact with the reactant molecules.

Cooking meat involves many chemical reactions including the denaturing of protein structures. An examination of a cut of meat, such as the one shown in Figure 8.22, shows a thin film which holds layers of muscle together. This is the protein collagen, which is found in animals and helps to keep muscles attached together and to the bone. Weight-bearing muscles and muscles that are used a lot during the animal's life (such as the legs, chest and rump) have high levels of collagen. Older animals have high levels of collagen too. An examination of the structure of collagen reveals that it is composed of protein molecules which wrap round each other in spirals, just like the twine in a

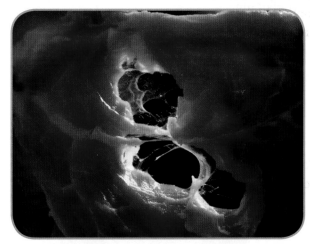

Figure 8.22 Collagen is the tough protein which holds meat together.

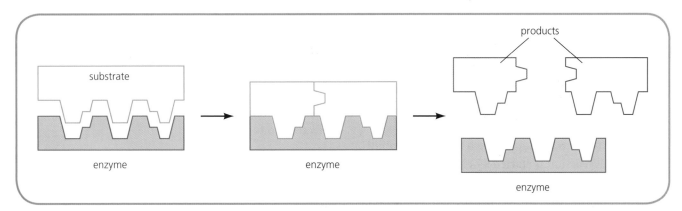

Figure 8.21 The 'lock and key' principle. The specific shape of an enzyme comes from the folding of proteins.

rope. This gives collagen a very tough structure that makes it undesirable for eating. Collagen in meat starts to break down as the meat is heated. The heating causes the protein molecules to unwind, which changes the shape of the molecule and makes the protein less tough. Experiments have shown that the meat must be heated to at least 60 °C to cause such changes.

Oxidation of food

Packing food in the correct environment can help prolong its freshness. You will no doubt have noticed that many foods are now foil packed to preserve the freshness of the product. A closer examination of the packaging usually reveals that the food is also packaged in an inert gas. Usually, this means that the food is packaged under nitrogen gas rather than air. Air contains moisture and oxygen that can spoil the food. Nitrogen is an inert gas that will not react with the food. Thus, the food is preserved for a much longer period of time.

Figure 8.23 Many foods are packaged in an inert gas to prolong their shelf life.

One of the great battles of food preservation is to prevent oxidation of the food. Exposing foods to oxygen causes them to spoil through the process of oxidation. If you cut an apple or expose a banana to the air for any length of time, you will witness the familiar browning that causes the fruit to spoil rapidly. This natural reaction is started by exposing the fruit to oxygen which helps to start further reactions in the fruit. Sealing the fruit, by keeping the skin on, prevents the surface being exposed to the oxygen. To prevent

Figure 8.24 Apples deteriorate rapidly when exposed to oxygen.

food spoiling by oxidation, several methods have been developed which are employed by the food industry. In order to understand the chemistry of these processes we need to examine the process of chemical oxidation.

Traditionally, oxidation was the name used to describe the reaction of a substance with oxygen. For example, when a strip of magnesium is held in a Bunsen flame, the magnesium reacts with oxygen to produce magnesium oxide:

$$Mg(s) + O_2(g) \rightarrow 2Mg^{2+}O^{2-}(s)$$

A more general view of oxidation is a reaction where one of the atoms or ions loses electrons. In the magnesium example, the magnesium atom loses two electrons to form a magnesium ion (Mg^{2+}). We say that the magnesium has been oxidised. The 'lost' electrons are gained by another reactant. In this case the oxygen gains the two electrons from the magnesium. This reaction is known as a reduction reaction. Reactions which do not involve oxygen can therefore still be classed as oxidation reactions. For example, the reaction of sodium with chlorine to make sodium chloride:

$$2Na(s) + Cl_2(g) \rightarrow 2Na^+Cl^-(s)$$

The sodium atom has been oxidised (it has lost one electron to form Na^+).

The chlorine molecule has been reduced (each Cl atom has gained one electron to form Cl^-).

Oxidation of alcohols

From your previous chemistry knowledge, you will be aware that alcohols are useful fuels. For example, ethanol can be burned completely to produce carbon dioxide and water:

$$C_2H_5OH(l) + 3O_2(g) \rightarrow 2CO_2(g) + 3H_2O(l)$$

This is an example of the complete oxidation of an alcohol. This occurs when there is a plentiful supply of oxygen and some energy is supplied to start the reaction. However, alcohols also undergo much milder oxidation reactions which do not involve such a drastic change to the structure of the alcohol. As we shall see, only a few specific bonds will be affected. Furthermore, whether the alcohol is a primary, secondary or tertiary alcohol has an important bearing on what happens.

Types of alcohol

Alcohols can be subdivided into three different types depending on the position of the hydroxyl group. These are summarised in Table 8.2.

Primary, secondary and tertiary alcohols can be represented as shown in Figure 8.25, where the symbols R, R^1 and R^2 stand for **alkyl groups**, such as methyl CH_3-, ethyl C_2H_5-, etc.

Methanol and ethanol are examples of primary alcohols.

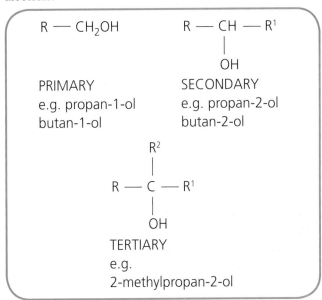

Figure 8.25

Type	Primary	Secondary	Tertiary
Position of –OH group	Joined to the *end* of the carbon chain	Joined to an *intermediate* carbon atom	Joined to an *intermediate* carbon atom which also has a branch attached

Characteristic group of atoms	$-CH_2OH$	— CH —
		    OH
			— C —
			    OH

Table 8.2

Questions

1 Write down the systematic name and type of each of the following alcohols:

a)
$$CH_3CH_2\overset{\overset{\displaystyle CH_3}{|}}{\underset{\underset{\displaystyle OH}{|}}{C}}CH_3$$

b)
$$HOCH_2\overset{\overset{\displaystyle CH_3}{|}}{\underset{\underset{\displaystyle CH_3}{|}}{C}}CH_2CH_3$$

c)
$$CH_3\overset{\overset{\displaystyle CH_3}{|}}{C}HCH_2\underset{\underset{\displaystyle OH}{|}}{C}HCH_3$$

Figure 8.26

Primary and secondary alcohols can be oxidised by various oxidising agents but tertiary alcohols do not undergo oxidation readily. Acidified potassium dichromate solution is a suitable oxidising agent. When mixed with a primary or secondary alcohol and heated in a water bath, the alcohol is oxidised. You can see this as the dichromate changes colour from orange to blue-green. A different smell may also be detected, showing that the alcohol has changed.

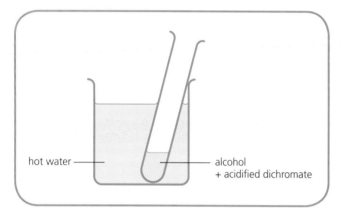

Figure 8.27 Oxidation of an alcohol using a mild oxidising agent.

The electrons lost by the alcohol are gained by the dichromate ion:

$$Cr_2O_7^{2-} + 14H^+ + 6e^- \rightarrow 2Cr^{3+} + 7H_2O$$

The orange colour due to dichromate ions changes to a blue-green colour showing that chromium(III) ions have been formed. The ion–electron equation shows

that this reaction will only occur in the presence of H^+ ions. This explains why **acidified** dichromate must be used.

Oxidation can also be achieved by passing the alcohol vapour over heated copper(II) oxide as shown in Figure 8.28. During the reaction the copper oxide is reduced to copper. If ethanol is used, it is oxidised to form a compound called ethanal. The equation for the reaction is:

$$CH_3CH_2OH + CuO \rightarrow CH_3CHO + Cu + H_2O$$

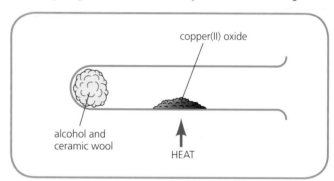

Figure 8.28 Alcohols can be oxidised using hot copper(II) oxide.

The following tables show what happens to alcohols when they react with either of these oxidising agents (acidified dichromate or hot copper(II) oxide).

When primary alcohols are oxidised they produce **aldehydes**.

When secondary alcohols are oxidised they produce **ketones**.

Alcohol	Aldehyde
Ethanol	Ethanal
CH_3CH_2OH	CH_3CHO
The structure of ethanol	The structure of ethanal

Table 8.3 Oxidation of ethanol produces ethanal.

Alcohol	Aldehyde
Propan-1-ol	Propanal
$CH_3CH_2CH_2OH$	CH_3CH_2CHO
The structure of propan-1-ol	The structure of propanal

Table 8.4 Oxidation of propan-1-ol produces propanal.

Alcohol	Ketone
Propan-2-ol	Propanone
$CH_3CH(OH)CH_3$	CH_3COCH_3
The structure of propan-2-ol	The structure of propanone

Table 8.5 Oxidation of propan-2-ol produces propanone.

Alcohol	Ketone
Butan-2-ol	Butanone
$CH_3CH_2CH(OH)CH_3$	$CH_3CH_2COCH_3$
The structure of butan-2-ol	The structure of butanone

Table 8.6 Oxidation of butan-2-ol produces butanone.

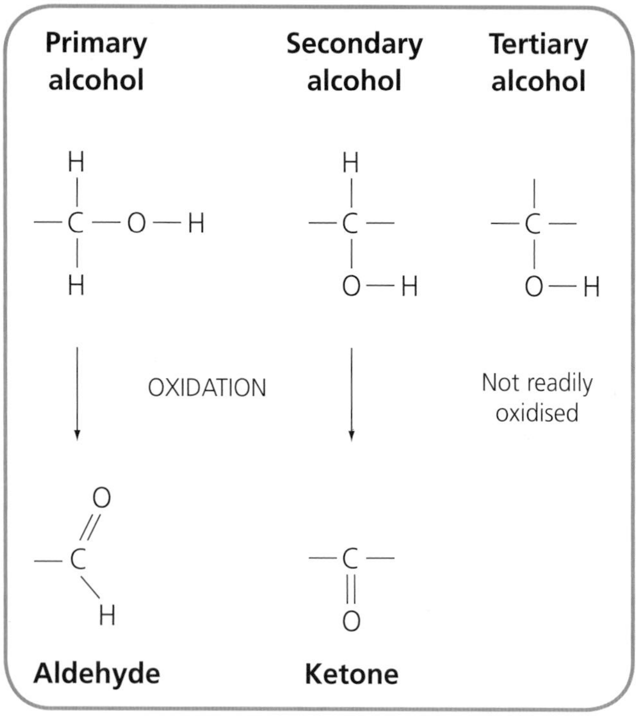

Figure 8.29 Oxidation of alcohols

3-methylbutanal   3-methylpentan-2-one

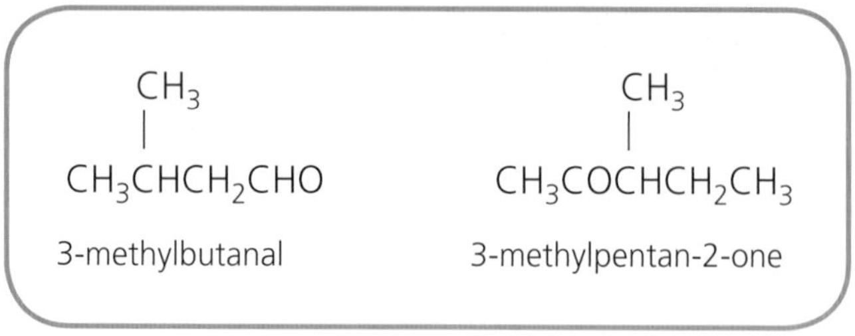

Figure 8.30

A tertiary alcohol cannot be oxidised since it does not have a hydrogen atom attached to the carbon atom which is adjacent to the hydroxyl group. Figure 8.29 illustrates these points.

Table 8.7 shows the functional group, general formula and the first few members of the aldehydes and ketones. Traditional names of some of these compounds are given in brackets.

Note that in the shortened structural formula of an aldehyde, the functional group is written as –CHO and not –COH, which would imply that the hydrogen atom is joined to the oxygen atom. Writing –CHO implies that the H atom is joined to the C atom by a single bond and the O atom is joined to the C atom by a double bond.

Aldehydes and ketones can be identified by the presence of a carbon–oxygen double bond, C=O, which is known as the **carbonyl group**. In an aldehyde, the carbonyl group is at the end of the carbon chain and has a hydrogen atom attached to it. In a ketone, the carbonyl group is joined to two other carbon atoms.

When primary alcohols are oxidised to aldehydes and secondary alcohols are oxidised to ketones, two hydrogen atoms are removed:

- the hydrogen atom of the –OH group
- a hydrogen on the adjacent carbon atom.

Branched aldehydes and ketones do exist. When naming these, the position of the functional group again takes precedence over the position of the branch, as shown in the examples in Figure 8.30. Note that there is no need to indicate a number for the functional group when naming an aldehyde as it must always be at the end of the chain. However, when naming a ketone it is usually necessary to specify the number of the carbonyl group.

Aldehydes	Ketones
Methanal (formaldehyde) $HCHO$ Ethanal (acetaldehyde) CH_3CHO Propanal CH_3CH_2CHO Butanal $CH_3CH_2CH_2CHO$	Propanone (acetone) CH_3COCH_3 Butanone $CH_3CH_2COCH_3$
General formula: $C_nH_{2n}O$ ($n \geq 1$) Functional group: 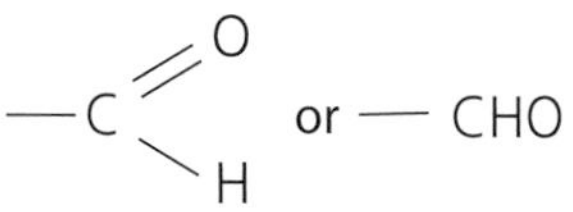 	General formula: $C_nH_{2n}O$ ($n \geq 3$) Functional group: 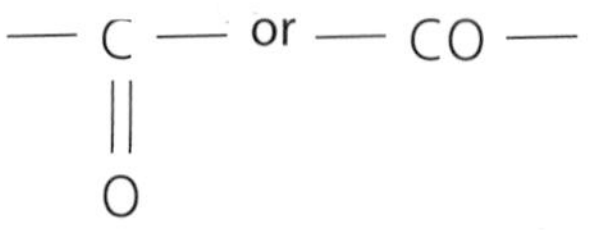

Table 8.7

Questions

2 For each of the following compounds **i)** draw its structural formula and **ii)** name the alcohol which produces it on oxidation.

a) 4-methylpentanal

b) 3-methylbutan-2-one

3 Name the following compounds.

a)

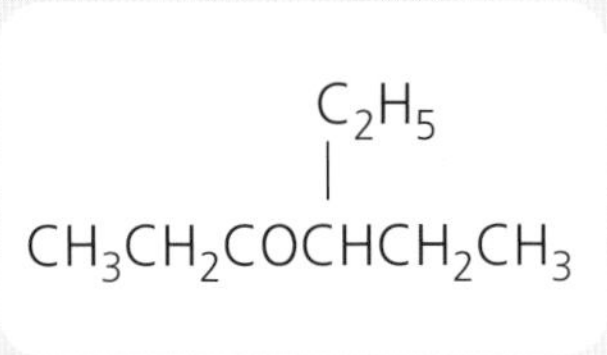

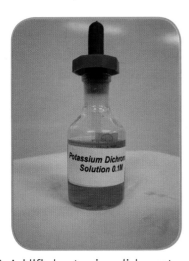

$$CH_3CH_2COCHCH_2CH_3$$

with C_2H_5 attached above the CH.

Figure 8.31

b)

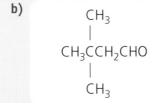

$$CH_3CCH_2CHO$$

with CH_3 above and CH_3 below the second carbon.

Figure 8.32

Oxidation of aldehydes

So far we have tended to emphasise the similarity between aldehydes and ketones in that both types of compound contain the carbonyl group and are obtained by oxidation of alcohols. They do have several chemical properties that are similar, as you will discover if you study chemistry beyond Higher level.

However, there is one important reaction which shows a difference between aldehydes and ketones, namely that aldehydes are readily oxidised whilst ketones are not. Several oxidising agents can be used to distinguish aldehydes from ketones. The three most common are shown in Figures 8.33, 8.34 and 8.35.

Figure 8.33 Acidified potassium dichromate solution, $Cr_2O_7^{2-}(aq)/H^+(aq)$

Figure 8.34 Fehling's solution, $Cu^{2+}(aq)$ in alkaline solution

Figure 8.35 Tollens' reagent (ammoniacal silver(I) nitrate solution), $Ag^+(aq)/NH_3(aq)$

Teachers may wish to consult SSERC's *Science and Technology Bulletin*, Number 196 (Spring 1999) for a discussion on the use of Benedict's, Fehling's and other solutions. The article suggests that Fehling's solution gives a distinction between propanal and propanone, but that Benedict's solution does not do so.

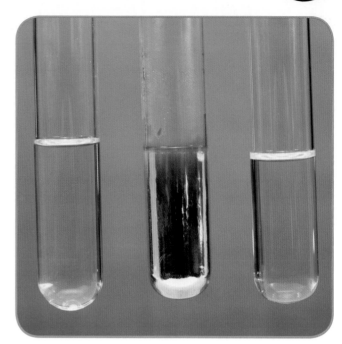

Figure 8.36 A silver mirror is produced when an aldehyde is warmed with Tollens' reagent.

Oxidising agent	Observations	Explanation
Acidified potassium dichromate solution	Orange → blue-green	$Cr_2O_7^{2-}(aq)$ reduced to $Cr^{3+}(aq)$
Fehling's solution	Blue → orange/red	$Cu^{2+}(aq)$ reduced to $Cu_2O(s)$ i.e. $Cu^{2+} + e^- \rightarrow Cu^+$
Tollens' reagent	Colourless → silver	$Ag^+(aq)$ reduced to $Ag(s)$ i.e. $Ag^+ + e^- \rightarrow Ag$

Table 8.8

These oxidising agents oxidise an aldehyde to form a **carboxylic acid**. This is shown in Tables 8.9 and 8.10.

Aldehyde	Carboxylic acid
Ethanal	Ethanoic acid
CH_3CHO	CH_3COOH
The structure of ethanal	The structure of ethanoic acid

Table 8.9 Oxidation of ethanal produces ethanoic acid.

Aldehyde	Carboxylic acid
Butanal	Butanoic acid
$CH_3CH_2CH_2CHO$	$CH_3CH_2CH_2COOH$
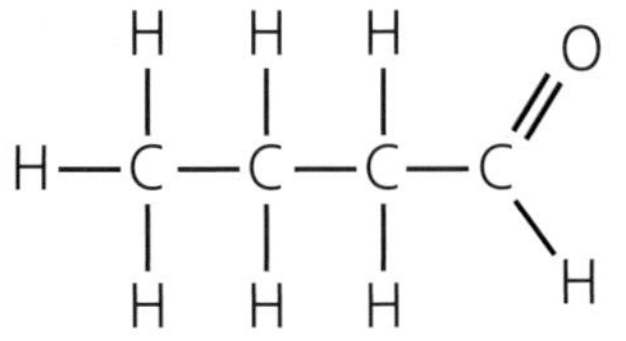 The structure of butanal	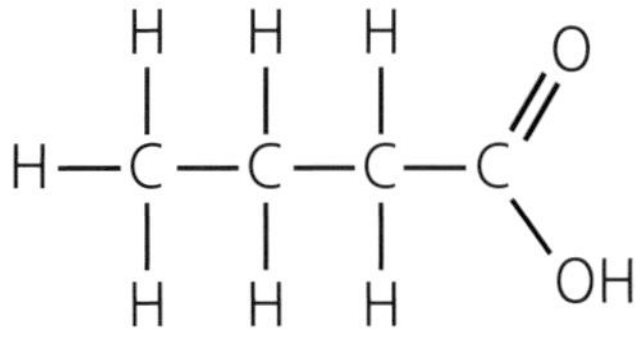 The structure of butanoic acid

Table 8.10 Oxidation of butanal produces butanoic acid.

Overall, the change that occurs to the functional group when an aldehyde is oxidised is shown in Figure 8.37.

This shows that during the oxidation of an aldehyde, the C–H bond next to the carbonyl group is broken and the hydrogen atom is replaced by a hydroxyl group. This cannot happen with a ketone since it does not have a hydrogen atom attached to its carbonyl group.

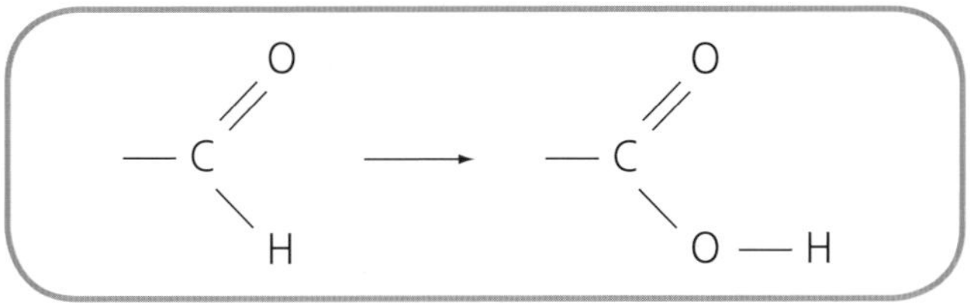

Figure 8.37 Oxidation of an aldehyde produces a carboxylic acid.

Summary

The oxidation of alcohols can be summarised as follows:

1 Primary alcohol → Aldehyde → Carboxylic acid
2 Secondary alcohol → Ketone (not readily oxidised)
3 Tertiary alcohol (not readily oxidised)

Reactions of carboxylic acids

Acids such as hydrochloric and sulfuric acid are acidic because they break up completely when added to water, to produce hydrogen ions (H^+). Acids that ionise completely when added to water are known as **strong acids**.

$$HCl(ag) \rightarrow H^+(aq) + Cl^-(aq)$$

Carboxylic acids also produce H^+ ions when added to water, but not to the same extent as the strong acids. Carboxylic acids are known as **weak acids** as they partially ionise when they are added to water. This is shown in the equation below:

$$CH_3COOH(l) \rightleftharpoons CH_3COO^-(aq) + H^+(aq)$$

Ethanoic acid, like all water-soluble carboxylic acids, exists as a mixture of molecules and ions when in aqueous solution.

Carboxylic acids can undergo the same type of chemical reactions as the other common lab acids such as hydrochloric. For example, when sodium hydroxide is added to hydrochloric acid, sodium chloride and water are produced:

$$HCl(aq) + NaOH(aq) \rightarrow NaCl(aq) + H_2O(l)$$

When acids react in this way, the H^+ of the acid is replaced by a positive ion, in this case the Na^+.

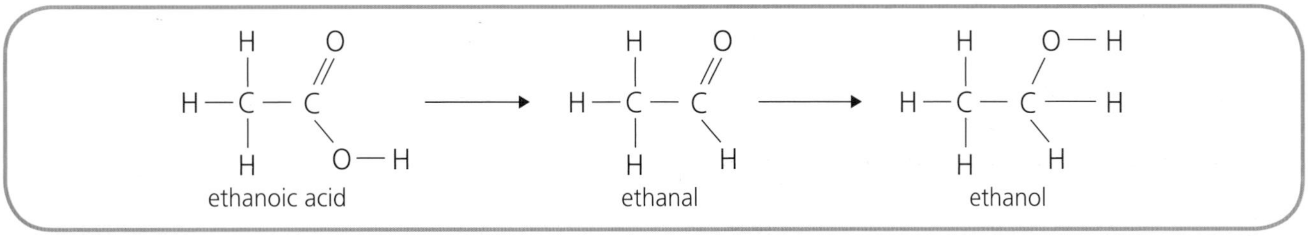

Figure 8.38 Reduction of a carboxylic acid

Carboxylic acids react with bases to produce salts which contain the carboxylate ion ($-COO^-$). Thus, when ethanoic acid reacts with sodium hydroxide, the products are sodium ethanoate and water:

$$CH_3COOH(aq) + NaOH(aq) \rightarrow CH_3COONa(aq) + H_2O(l)$$

When propanoic acid is reacted with calcium hydroxide, calcium propanoate and water are produced:

$$2C_2H_5COOH(aq) + Ca(OH)_2\,(aq) \rightarrow (C_2H_5COO)_2Ca(aq) + 2H_2O(l)$$

Salts of carboxylic acids are widely used as preservatives in the food industry. For example, calcium propanoate is used widely as a preservative (E282) as it is able to stop the growth of moulds which can spoil food.

The reaction of carboxylic acids with bases is demonstrated in spectacular fashion when vinegar is reacted with bicarbonate of soda. This is often carried out in an old film canister so that it produces a mini chemical rocket!

$$CH_3COOH(aq) + NaHCO_3(s) \rightarrow CH_3COONa(aq) + H_2O(l) + CO_2(g)$$

The rapidly produced CO_2 ensures that the canister lid is propelled into the air!

Sodium benzoate, E211, has similar properties and is used in bottled sauces and fruit juices.

Carboxylic acids are produced by the oxidation of alcohols and aldehydes. The reverse process can also occur, i.e. carboxylic acids can be reduced to form aldehydes and alcohols. For example, ethanoic acid can be reduced to form ethanal and ethanol, as shown in Figure 8.38 on page 103.

When we examine the oxidation of carbon compounds, we notice that there is a change in the oxygen to hydrogen ratio. Let us apply this specifically to alkanols. The ratio of oxygen atoms to hydrogen atoms is quoted for each compound.

In each of the examples in Tables 8.11 and 8.12 we can see that oxidation of an alcohol or an **aldehyde** has resulted in an increase in the oxygen:hydrogen ratio. The reverse of these reactions would be reductions and would involve a decrease in the oxygen:hydrogen ratio.

Primary alcohol	Aldehyde	Carboxylic acid
Ethanol	Ethanal	Ethanoic acid
CH_3CH_2OH	CH_3CHO	CH_3COOH
O:H ratio 1:6	O:H ratio 1:4	O:H ratio 1:2

Table 8.11

Secondary alcohol	Ketone
Propan-2-ol	Propanone
$CH_3CH(OH)CH_3$	CH_3COCH_3
O:H ratio 1:8	O:H ratio 1:6

Table 8.12

Although it is possible to write ion–electron equations to show that the above changes are oxidations, it is often considered more appropriate when dealing with carbon compounds to define oxidation and reduction in terms of the O:H ratio as follows:

- Oxidation occurs when there is an increase in the oxygen to hydrogen ratio.

- Reduction occurs when there is a decrease in the oxygen to hydrogen ratio.

Antioxidants and food preservation

Many flavour and aroma molecules are aldehydes and ketones. Table 8.13 lists examples of aldehydes and ketones that are responsible for some of the aromas and flavours of familiar foods.

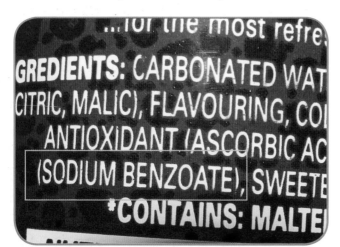

Figure 8.39 Salts of benzoic acid are commonly added to soft drinks as a preservative.

Compound name	Where found
Cinnamaldehyde	Cinnamon
Furfural	Coffee
2,3-butanedione	Butter
1-(2-pyridinyl)ethanone	Popcorn
Heptan-2-one	Blue cheese

Table 8.13

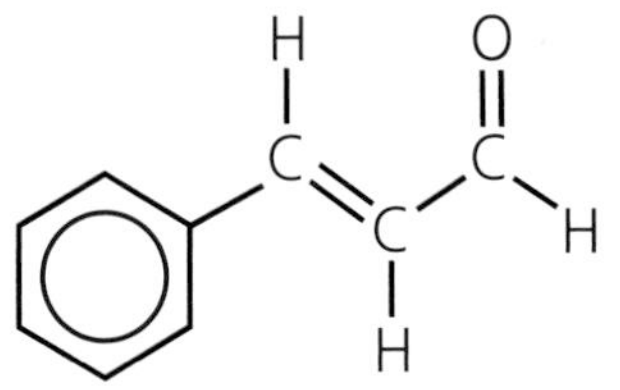

Figure 8.40 The structure of cinnamaldehyde

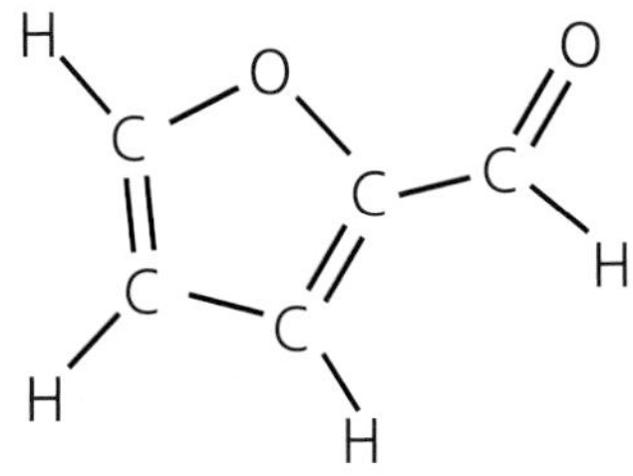

Figure 8.41 The structure of furfural

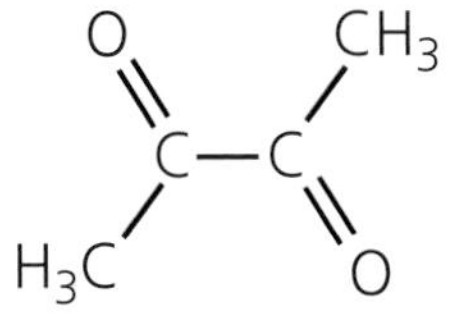

Figure 8.42 The structure of 2,3-butanedione

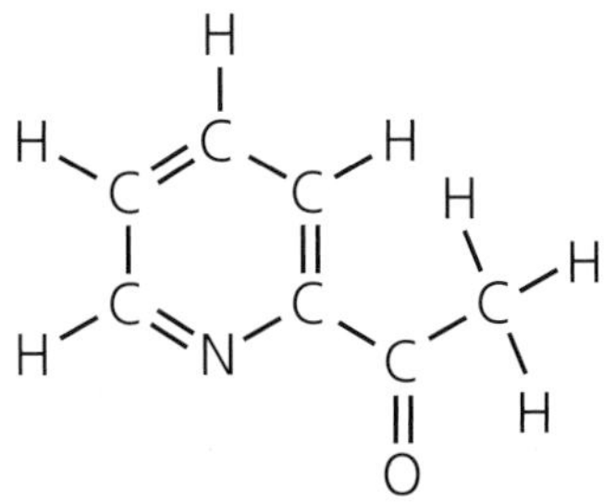

Figure 8.43 The structure of 1-(2-pyridinyl)ethanone

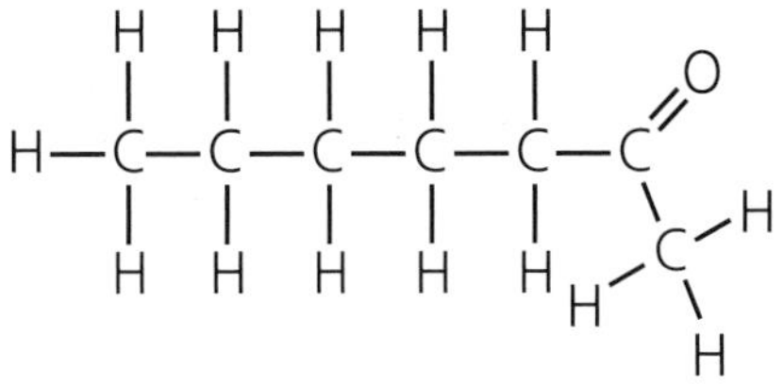

Figure 8.44 The structure of heptan-2-one

It is important to appreciate that the aroma and flavour of a food or drink is rarely due to one molecule. Usually, many hundreds of molecules are responsible. If, however, the flavour and aroma molecules undergo changes, our senses of smell and taste are powerful enough to detect this. Thus, when a food 'spoils' we can often taste and smell the products of oxidation. For example, oxidation of aldehydes will lead to carboxylic acids being produced. This completely alters the taste (making it more acidic) and will usually cause us to reject the food. Consequently, food manufacturers use several methods to stop oxidation happening. As previously mentioned, many foods are packaged in an inert atmosphere of nitrogen gas to prevent oxidation. This works well but the food can often spoil quite quickly when exposed to the air. A common method of preventing oxidation involves adding an **antioxidant** to the food. One of the most common antioxidants used is ascorbic acid, which is also known as vitamin C. Ascorbic acid acts as an antioxidant as it will readily undergo oxidation and thus save the food from becoming oxidised:

$$C_6H_8O_6 \rightarrow C_6H_6O_6 + 2H^+ + 2e^-$$

The most noticeable example of food oxidation is the reaction of oxygen with edible oils. This produces particularly rancid flavours as the oils are oxidised. Food manufacturers use fat/oil-soluble antioxidants to prevent the oxidation of the oil. A good example of this is found in the manufacture of dog food which contains

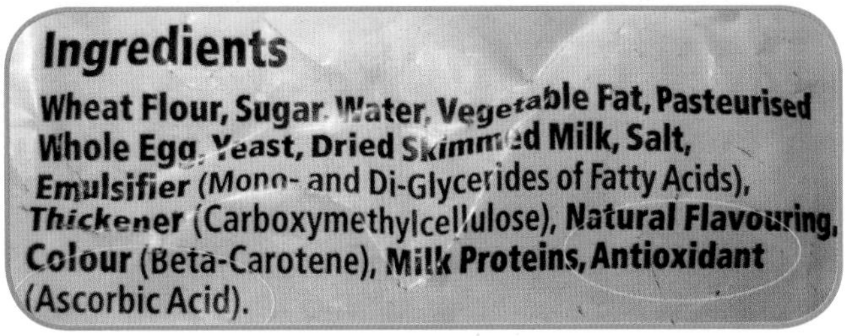

Ingredients

Wheat Flour, Sugar, Water, Vegetable Fat, Pasteurised Whole Egg, Yeast, Dried Skimmed Milk, Salt, Emulsifier (Mono- and Di-Glycerides of Fatty Acids), Thickener (Carboxymethylcellulose), Natural Flavouring, Colour (Beta-Carotene), Milk Proteins, Antioxidant (Ascorbic Acid).

Figure 8.45 Many foods contain antioxidants to prevent them from spoiling.

107

a significant quantity of fat. Dried dog food contains preservatives such as butylated hydroxytoluene (BHT), butylated hydroxyanisole (BHA) and tocopherols (vitamin E). These compounds are added to prevent oxidation of the fats/oils.

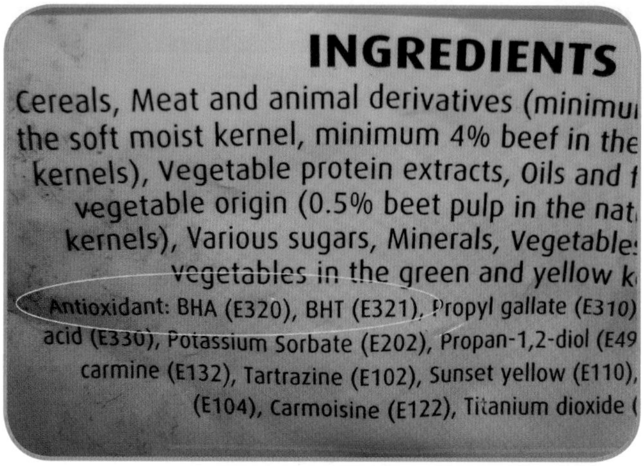

INGREDIENTS

Cereals, Meat and animal derivatives (minimu the soft moist kernel, minimum 4% beef in the kernels), Vegetable protein extracts, Oils and f vegetable origin (0.5% beet pulp in the nat kernels), Various sugars, Minerals, Vegetable: vegetables in the green and yellow k Antioxidant: BHA (E320), BHT (E321), Propyl gallate (E310) acid (E330), Potassium Sorbate (E202), Propan-1,2-diol (E49 carmine (E132), Tartrazine (E102), Sunset yellow (E110), (E104), Carmoisine (E122), Titanium dioxide (

Figure 8.46 An ingredients label from a brand of dried dog food.

Questions

4 a) 'Oxidation occurs when methanol is converted to methanal and then to methanoic acid.' Justify this statement by working out the oxygen to hydrogen ratio in each compound shown in the following sequence:

$$CH_3OH \rightarrow HCHO \rightarrow HCOOH$$

b) Write similar oxidation sequences for

i) butan-1-ol

ii) pentan-2-ol.

Show that the reactions involve oxidation by reference to O:H ratios.

For Interest   Alcohol

The ethanol consumed by a person when drinking alcoholic beverages could cause serious harm if allowed to remain in the body as toxic ethanol. Fortunately, the human body has developed enzymes to break down the ethanol so that it can be eliminated from the body. Alcohol dehydrogenase is one of these enzymes which catalyses the oxidation of ethanol to ethanal, while aldehyde dehydrogenase is responsible for oxidising the ethanal to ethanoic acid, which is not toxic. The levels and speed of activity of these enzymes vary. For example, men tend to have greater levels of these enzymes compared with women, and different ethnic populations may also have different versions. Some scientists have commented on the fact that alcoholism is often lower in populations that have 'fast' alcohol dehydrogenases (which rapidly convert

the ethanol into ethanal) and 'slow' aldehyde dehydrogenases. As ethanal is toxic and causes nasty side effects (such as nausea, face flushing and rapid heartbeat) people with this combination of enzymes will have a build up of ethanal in their body and, some studies show, will, therefore, prefer not to consume as much alcohol as it is such an unpleasant experience.

The oxidation performed by these enzymes can be blocked deliberately to allow a build up of toxic ethanol. This is the basis of the medicine Antabuse which contains a compound that blocks the aldehyde dehydrogenase enzyme. The medicine can be prescribed as part of a treatment programme for alcoholics to help them abstain from drinking alcohol.

Checklist for Revision

● I can predict whether a molecule is likely to be fat/oil soluble or water soluble by examining the functional groups present.

● I can predict how volatile a molecule is likely to be by examining the size and structure of the molecule.

● I can describe how heating a protein can change the structure of the protein.

● I can state whether an alcohol is primary, secondary or tertiary and whether it is likely to be oxidised.

● I can name common agents capable of oxidising alcohols and aldehydes.

● I can name and draw the products formed when an alcohol or aldehyde is oxidised.

● I can describe the oxidation of a carbon compound in terms of the oxygen:hydrogen ratio.

● I can state the function of an antioxidant.

Key Terms

The words and phrases below were introduced in this chapter.

Their definitions are given in the chemical dictionary.

aldehyde

antioxidant

carbonyl group

denaturing

ketone

Study Questions

In questions 1–4 choose the correct word from the following list to complete the sentence.

| blue-green | carbonyl | decreased | hydroxyl |
| increased | secondary | orange-red | tertiary |

1 Pentan-3-ol is an example of a _____ alcohol.

2 When an alcohol is oxidised the ratio of oxygen atoms to hydrogen atoms is _____.

3 The functional group in a ketone is known as the _____ group.

4 When acidified potassium dichromate solution reacts with an aldehyde, the colour of the solution changes to _____.

5 Which of the structures in Figure 8.47 is a ketone?

6 Which of the following is a pair of isomers?

   A Ethanol and ethanal

   B Butanoic acid and butanal

   C Propan-2-ol and propanal

   D Pentan-2-one and pentanal

7 Which of the following can form a silver mirror with Tollens' reagent?

A

$$H-\underset{\underset{H}{|}}{\overset{\overset{H}{|}}{C}}-\underset{\underset{OH}{|}}{\overset{\overset{H}{|}}{C}}-\underset{\underset{H}{|}}{\overset{\overset{H}{|}}{C}}-H$$

B

$$H-\underset{\underset{H}{|}}{\overset{\overset{H}{|}}{C}}-C\overset{\displaystyle O}{\underset{\displaystyle OH}{}}$$

C

$$H-\underset{\underset{H}{|}}{\overset{\overset{H}{|}}{C}}-\underset{\underset{O}{||}}{C}-\underset{\underset{H}{|}}{\overset{\overset{H}{|}}{C}}-H$$

D

$$H-\underset{\underset{H}{|}}{\overset{\overset{H}{|}}{C}}-C\overset{\displaystyle O}{\underset{\displaystyle H}{}}$$

Figure 8.47

A $CH_3CH_2CH(OH)CH_3$

B $CH_3CH_2CH_2CHO$

C $CH_3COCH_2CH_3$

D $CH_3CH_2CH_2CH_2OH$

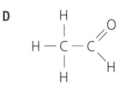

8

$$\overset{1}{\text{HCHO}} \rightarrow \overset{2}{\text{HCOOH}} \rightarrow \text{CH}_3\text{OH}$$

In the reaction sequence shown above

A both steps involve oxidation

B step 1 is reduction and step 2 is oxidation

C both steps involve reduction

D step 1 is oxidation and step 2 is reduction.

9* Copy the carbon skeleton in Figure 8.48 three times.

Add a hydroxyl group to each skeleton to make

a) a primary alcohol

b) a secondary alcohol

c) a tertiary alcohol.

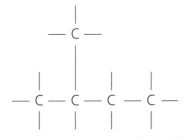

Figure 8.48

10* Compound X is a secondary alcohol.

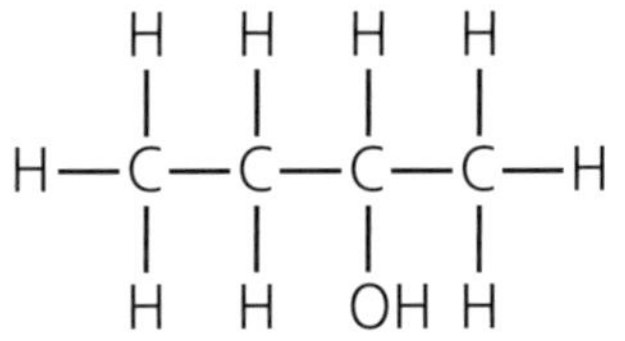

$$\begin{array}{c} \text{H} \quad \text{H} \quad \text{H} \quad \text{H} \\ | \quad | \quad | \quad | \\ \text{H}-\text{C}-\text{C}-\text{C}-\text{C}-\text{H} \\ | \quad | \quad | \quad | \\ \text{H} \quad \text{H} \quad \text{OH} \quad \text{H} \end{array}$$

Figure 8.49

a) Name compound X.

b) Draw a structural formula for the tertiary alcohol that is an isomer of compound X.

11* There are four isomeric alcohols of molecular formula C_4H_9OH. Their structural formulae are as follows:

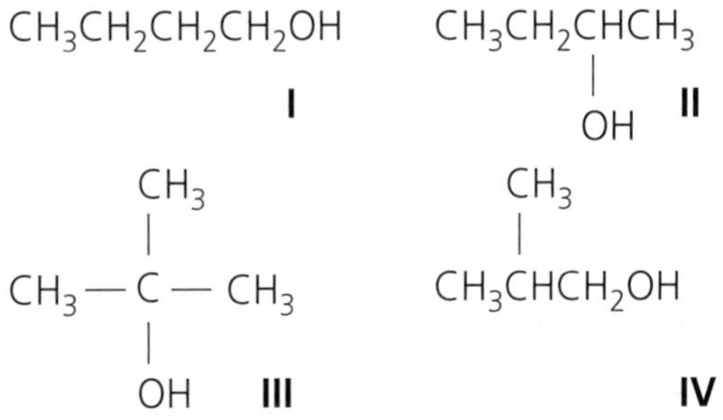

$$\text{CH}_3\text{CH}_2\text{CH}_2\text{CH}_2\text{OH} \qquad \text{CH}_3\text{CH}_2\text{CHCH}_3$$
$$\qquad\qquad \textbf{I} \qquad\qquad\qquad\qquad\qquad | $$
$$\qquad\qquad\qquad\qquad\qquad\qquad\qquad \text{OH} \quad \textbf{II}$$

$$\begin{array}{c} \text{CH}_3 \\ | \\ \text{CH}_3-\text{C}-\text{CH}_3 \\ | \\ \text{OH} \quad \textbf{III} \end{array} \qquad \begin{array}{c} \text{CH}_3 \\ | \\ \text{CH}_3\text{CHCH}_2\text{OH} \\ \\ \textbf{IV} \end{array}$$

Figure 8.50

a) Give systematic names for I, II, III and IV.

b) State which of the compounds I–IV are primary, which are secondary and which are tertiary alcohols.

c) The four alcohols are contained, separately, in four bottles marked A, B, C and D. From the following information decide which bottle contains which alcohol. State your reasoning briefly at each stage.

   i) The contents of A, B and C can readily be oxidised by acidified potassium dichromate solution, while those of D cannot.

   ii) A and B, on complete oxidation by the dichromate, give acids of formulae C_3H_7COOH. C does not give this acid.

   iii) All four substances can be dehydrated to give alkenes. A and D can both form the same alkene. B and C can both form the same alkene, which is an isomer of that formed by A and D.

12* Perfumes normally contain three groups of components called the top note, the middle note and the end note.

a) The top note components of a perfume form vapours most easily. Two compounds found in top note components are geranyl acetate and p-cresyl acetate (see Figure 8.51).

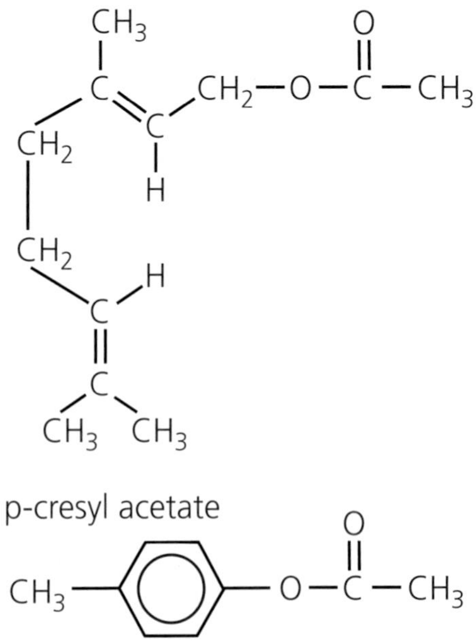

geranyl acetate

p-cresyl acetate

Figure 8.51

i) With reference to the structure of these compounds, why are they likely to have pleasant smells?

ii) Describe a chemical test which would distinguish between these two compounds and give the result of the test.

b) The middle note compounds form vapours less readily than the top note compounds. A typical compound of the middle note is 2-phenyl ethanol:

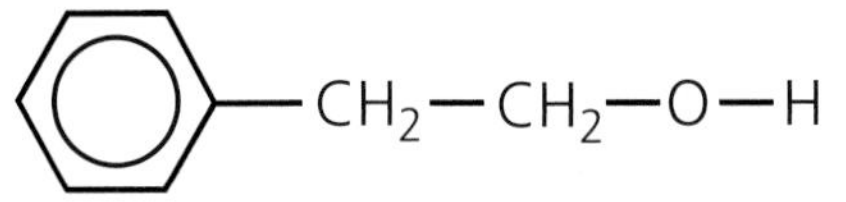

Figure 8.52

Due to hydrogen bonding 2-phenylethanol forms a vapour less readily than p-cresyl acetate.

Draw two molecules of 2-phenylethanol and use a dotted line to show where a hydrogen bond exists between the two molecules.

c) The end note of a perfume has a long-lasting odour which stays with the user.

An example of an end note compound is civetone (see Figure 8.53).

Draw the structure of the alcohol which would be formed by the reduction of civetone.

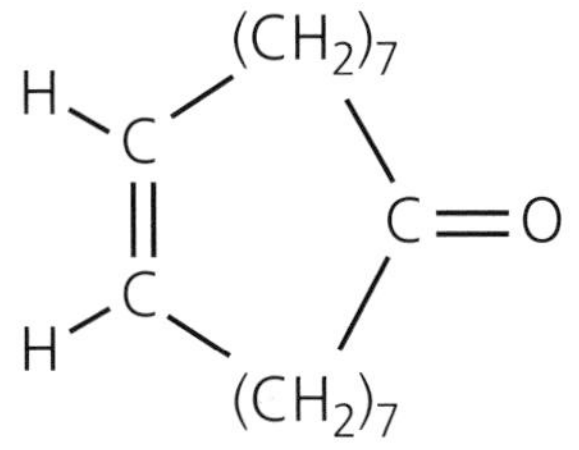

Figure 8.53

13 Although aldehydes and ketones have different structures, they both contain the carbonyl functional group.

a) In what way is the structure of an aldehyde different from that of a ketone?

b) As a result of the difference in structure, aldehydes react with Fehling's (or Benedict's) solution and Tollens' reagent but ketones do not.

i) What colour change would be observed when propanal is heated with Fehling's (or Benedict's) solution?

ii) In the reaction of propanal with Tollens' reagent, silver ions are reduced to form silver metal.

Complete the following ion–electron equation for the oxidation.

$$C_3H_6O \rightarrow C_2H_5COOH$$

1 Vitamin C and vitamin E are both antioxidants. Find out why it is common to find both vitamins being used together to prevent oxidation.

2 Investigate the structure of the compounds present in a perfume. Predict which compound will be **a)** most and **b)** least volatile. Check your prediction by researching the boiling and melting points of your chosen compounds.

3 Find out about the toxicity of methanol and ethylene glycol. Why are they toxic? What is used to treat someone who has consumed methanol or ethylene glycol?

9 Fragrances

Essential oils

Perfumes are found in most consumer products to make them more appealing. If a product smells pleasant, we are more likely to use it. A close examination of the ingredients list of deodorants, cosmetics and cleaning products reveals exotic names such as camphene, limonene, lavendulol and geraniol. Some of the names hint at the origin of the compound, such as limonene from lemons, lavendulol from lavender, geraniol from geranium. These are examples of **essential oils**. Essential oils are concentrated extracts of the aroma compounds from plants. They are usually volatile, insoluble in water and composed of mixtures of organic compounds. They can be derived from almost any part of the plant. For example, lavendulol is derived from the flowers of the lavender plant whereas cinnamon is derived from the bark of the cinnamon tree. It is worth noting that the word 'essential' means 'derived or extracted from essences' and is not the same as 'essential' amino acids, as discussed in Chapter 7.

Figure 9.2 Cinnamon

The most common compounds found in essential oils are the family of compounds known as the **terpenes**. Examples of terpenes found in essential oils are shown in Table 9.1.

Terpenes are compounds based on isoprene (2-methylbuta-1,3-diene) which has the molecular formula C_5H_8.

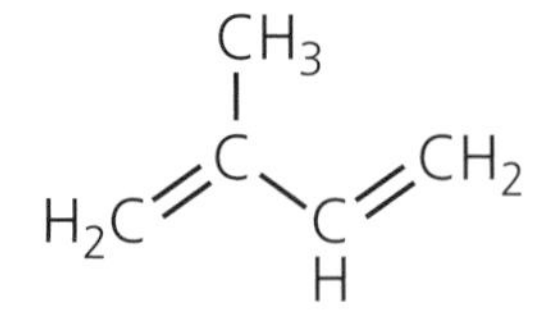

$$\text{H}_2\text{C} = \overset{\overset{\textstyle CH_3}{|}}{\underset{}{\text{C}}} - \overset{}{\underset{\underset{\textstyle H}{|}}{\text{C}}} = \text{CH}_2$$

Figure 9.3 The structure of isoprene

Figure 9.1 Lavender plant

Limonene	Carvone	Myrcene
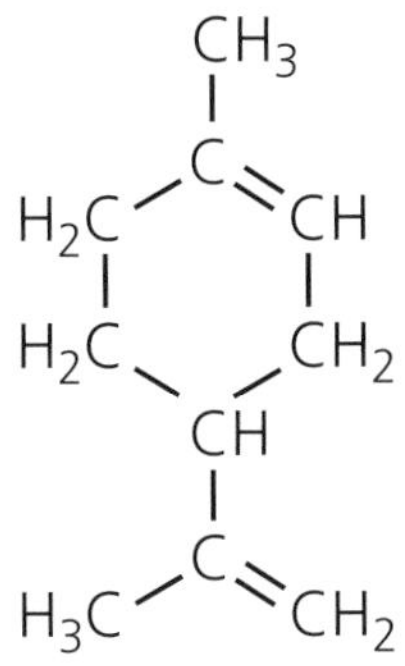	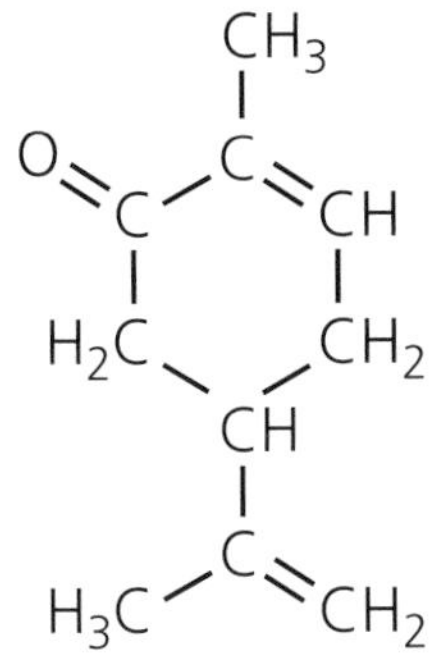	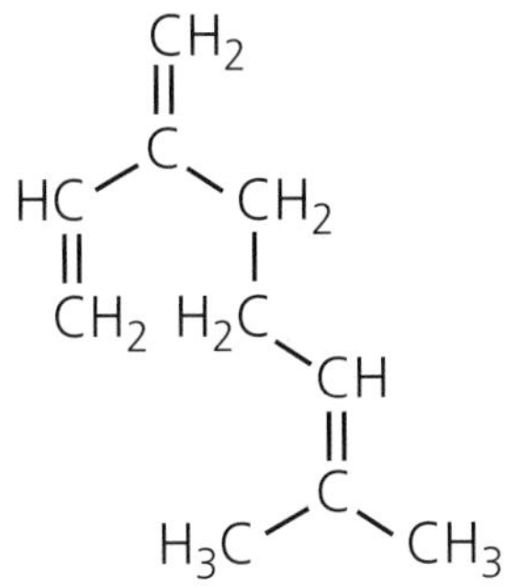
Citrus	Spearmint	Woody smell

Table 9.1 Examples of terpenes found in essential oils

All terpenes contain isoprene units joined together. In general, terpenes are based on $(C_5H_8)_n$ where n is the number of terpene units joined together. For example, limonene, carvone and myrcene all contain two isoprene units. Figure 9.4 shows how two isoprene units join to form myrcene.

Many terpenes found in nature have larger molecules containing more than two isoprene units joined. For example, Figures 9.5 and 9.6 represent farnesol, a terpene found in the essential oils of rose and cyclamen, and squalene, a terpene found in shark oil. The isoprene units are highlighted in each case: farnesol, with 15 carbons, is based on three isoprene units; squalene, with 30 carbons, is based on six isoprene units.

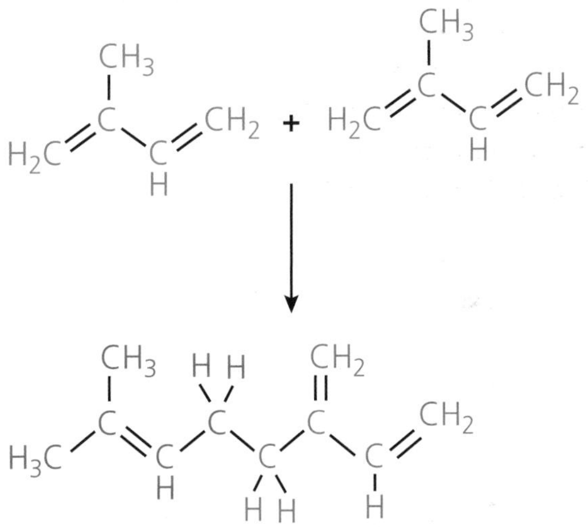

Figure 9.4 Myrcene is formed from two isoprene units.

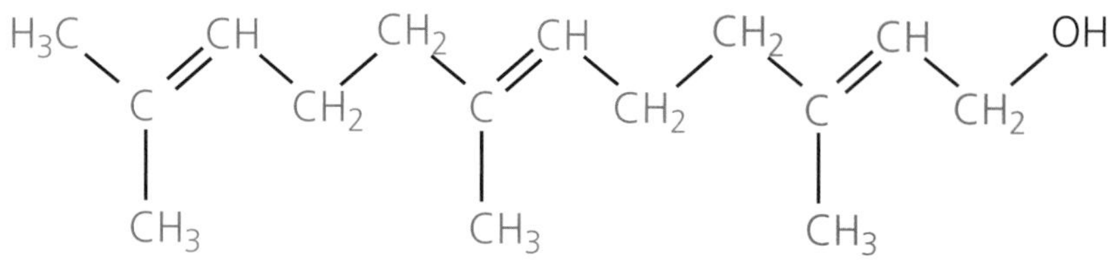

Figure 9.5 Farnesol

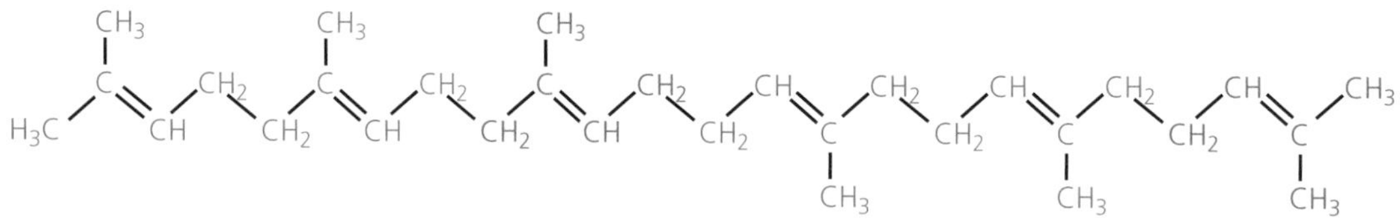

Figure 9.6 Squalene

Oxidation of terpenes

Since many of the essential oils are used in perfumes and household cleaning products, chemists have studied the reactions of the terpenes found in the essential oils to ensure that they remain stable for the lifetime of the product. Again, chemists have found that terpenes can be oxidised to form new compounds which have different properties from the original terpene. These can alter the fragrance and other properties of a product. For example, tea tree oil is sold in many health food stores and is used as an antiseptic. One of the terpenes found in tea tree oil is known as alpha terpinene. When tea tree oil is left exposed to the air, oxidation occurs which changes the smell and properties of the oil. For example, oxidation of the alpha terpinene forms p-cymene and ascaridole. It is believed that many people suffer allergic reactions to tea tree oil when their skin is in contact with these oxidation products. Consequently, manufacturers will often seal the tea tree oil in brown bottles (to prevent photo-oxidation), will advise users to re-seal the bottle after use and will label the

Figure 9.7 Tea tree oil is used as an antiseptic.

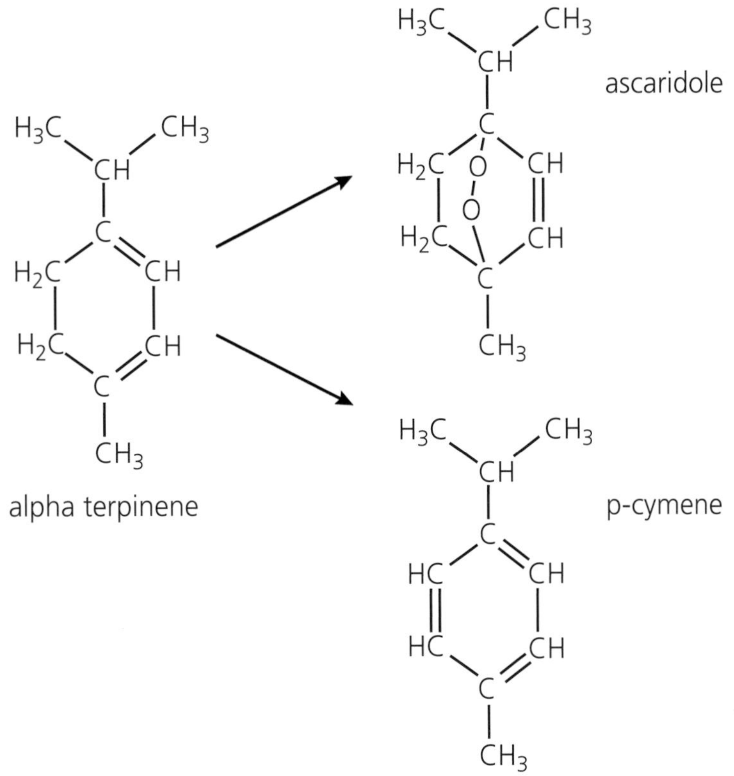

Figure 9.8 Oxidation of alpha terpinene

bottle with a use-by date. Despite these measures, it is likely that a significant amount of the terpenes will still oxidise and form these unwanted and potentially harmful products.

Another example of terpene oxidation occurs when orange juice is left exposed to air. After a few days, the limonene oxidises to produce carvone (structures are shown in Table 9.1) which alters the taste of the juice.

In nature, oxidation of terpenes produces many of the compounds responsible for the aroma of spices derived from plants. For example, peppermint oil contains the terpene menthol and the oxidation product of menthol, menthone. Both compounds contribute to the peppermint flavour of the oil. Another example is nerol which is found in lemongrass along with citral. It can be seen that citral is the oxidation product of nerol. The structures of these compounds are shown in Table 9.2.

Terpene	Oxidised terpene	Where found?
Menthol 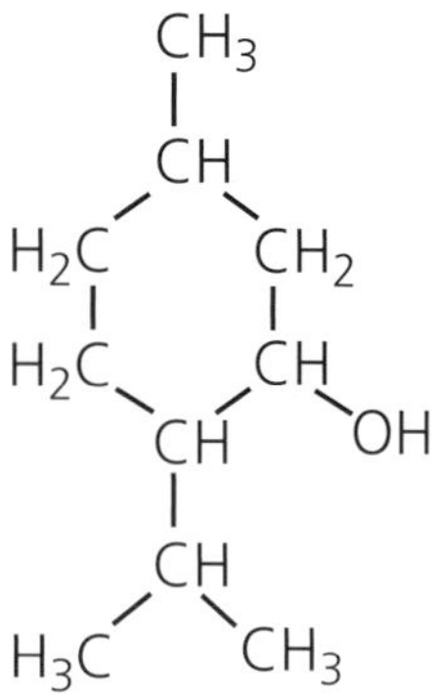	Menthone 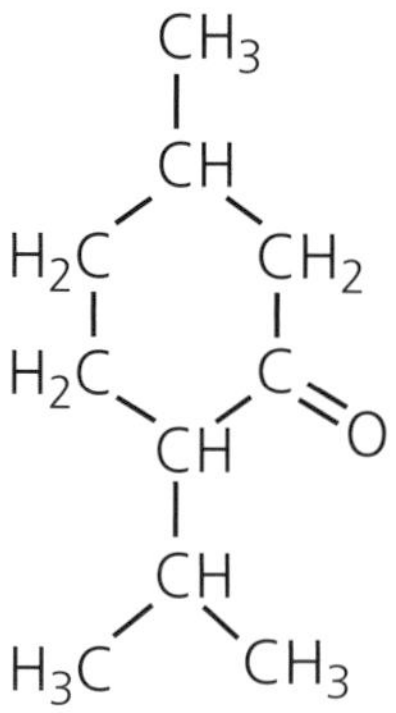	Peppermint oil 
Nerol 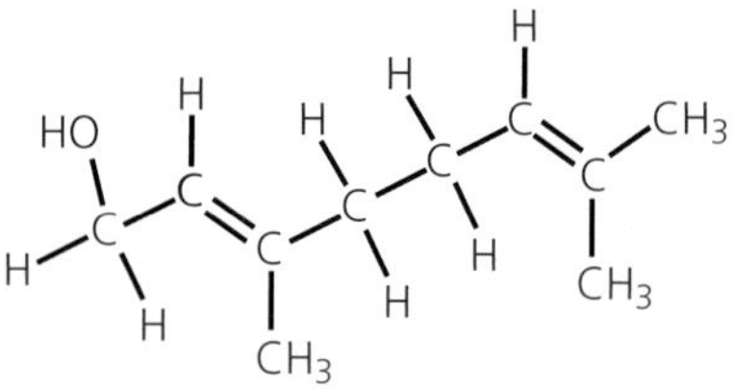	Citral 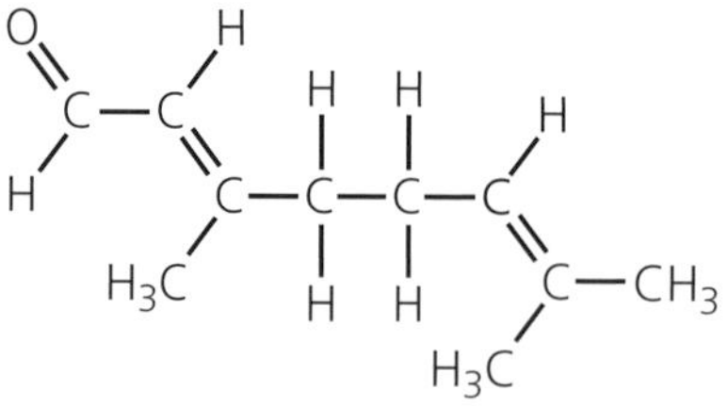	Lemongrass 

Table 9.2 Terpenes and their oxidation products

Checklist for Revision

- I can define the term essential oil.
- I can identify and draw the terpene unit, isoprene.
- I can state whether or not a compound is a terpene.
- I can predict the products formed when a terpene is oxidised.

Key Terms

The words and phrases below were introduced in this chapter.

Their definitions are given in the chemical dictionary.

essential oils

terpenes

Study Questions

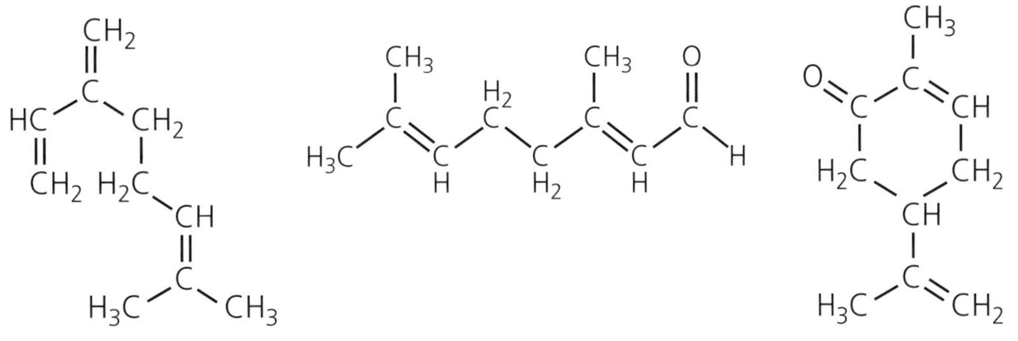

Figure 9.9 Compounds A, B and C

1 Compounds A, B and C above belong to a large group of compounds known as terpenes.

   a) The molecular unit from which terpenes are synthesised is 2-methylbuta-1,3-diene.

   Draw the structural formula of 2-methylbuta-1,3-diene.

   b) A 0.019 mol sample of one of the above terpenes required 47.5 cm³ of 1.20 mol l⁻¹ bromine solution for complete reaction.

   Identify, by calculation, the terpene used in the reaction. Show your working.

   c) Compound A cannot be reduced easily, but B and C can be reduced easily.

   Draw the structural formula of the organic product formed on reducing B.

2* To create a fragrance for men, the compound civetone (see Figure 9.10) is added.

   a) Draw a structural formula for the alcohol that can be oxidised to form civetone.

   b) To make a shower gel produce a cold, tingling sensation when applied to the skin, menthol is added.

   Like terpenes, menthol is formed from isoprene (2-methylbuta-1,3-diene).

   Copy the menthol structure and circle an isoprene unit on your diagram.

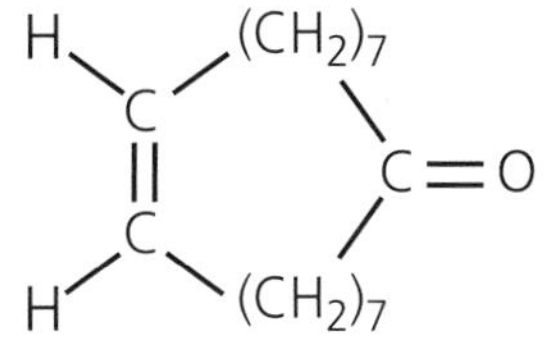

Figure 9.10 Civetone

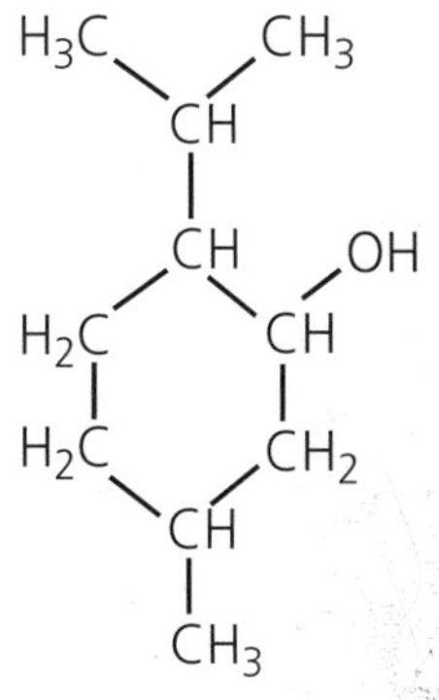

Figure 9.11 Menthol

10 Skin care

Life on Earth could not exist as it does today without the influence of sunlight. Its role is perhaps most obvious in the chemical reactions which take place in a plant during photosynthesis. Without light, plants would not produce the oxygen that animals rely on to live. Given that our survival is dependent on photosynthesis, scientists have spent many years researching the role of light in chemical reactions. This branch of chemistry is known as photochemistry and is used in almost every field of human endeavour including medicine, engineering, art preservation and dentistry, to name but a few examples. In this chapter we will explore some chemical reactions that are started by light and use this knowledge to understand how cosmetic chemists create new creams and lotions to protect our skin from damage that can occur from excessive exposure to the sun.

UV and sun block

When we consider sunlight, we have to appreciate that it is composed of many types of light. From earlier science you are probably familiar with the fact that white light is composed of a rainbow of colours from red through to violet, with all the shades in between. This is known as the visible spectrum of light. Sunlight also bathes us with light that we cannot see. As chemists, we are interested in light in the ultraviolet region (UV light) since this has enough energy to break chemical bonds. It is the UV light that causes chemical reactions to occur in our skin to make vitamin D, to give us a 'tan', to give us sunburn and to age our skin. As sunburn has been linked to skin cancer, many products have now been developed to protect our skin from the damaging effects of too much sun exposure. To prevent sunburn, chemists have developed the products we know as sun blocks and sun screens. Sun screens contain compounds that filter the UV light so that less UV reaches the skin. Sun block contains compounds such as titanium dioxide that reflect the UV so that it does not reach the skin at all.

Free radical reactions

A covalent bond contains two electrons shared between two atoms. Both electrons are attracted to the positive nuclei of the two atoms. To 'break' the covalent bond, high energy is required to overcome this attraction. UV light has enough energy to break covalent bonds into two atoms with unpaired electrons. For example,

Figure 10.1 Sun screens filter UV light.

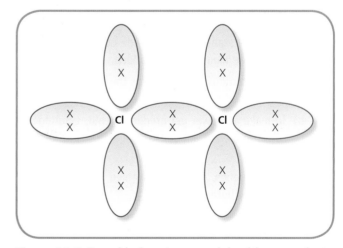

Figure 10.2 Two chlorine atoms are joined by a covalent bond.

a chlorine molecule contains two chlorine atoms as shown in Figure 10.2.

When UV light is shone onto chlorine (Cl_2), the covalent bond breaks to form two chlorine atoms. These atoms are highly reactive as they each have an unpaired electron and are known as **free radicals**. Note that the chlorine atoms produced are electrically neutral (they do not have a charge). They are reactive because they have seven outer electrons rather than the stable noble gas arrangement they achieved through sharing electrons as a molecule.

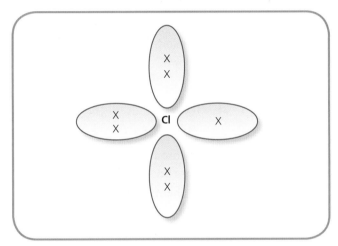

Figure 10.3 A chlorine free radical

Free radicals will react quickly with neighbouring atoms to form new bonds. For example, when chlorine (Cl_2) and hydrogen (H_2) gases are mixed together in a dimly lit room, no reaction occurs. However, when UV light is shone on the mixture they react explosively! A chemical mechanism for this reaction is shown below. This shows all the bonds that are broken and formed when the hydrogen and chlorine react. There are three steps to this: **initiation**, **propagation** and **termination**.

Step 1: Initiation
The UV light breaks some Cl–Cl bonds to form two chlorine free radicals.

$$Cl{-}Cl \rightarrow Cl^{\cdot} + Cl^{\cdot}$$

Step 2: Propagation
The highly reactive chlorine free radicals react with hydrogen molecules. This produces hydrogen free radicals that can react with chlorine molecules.

$$Cl^{\cdot} + H{-}H \rightarrow H{-}Cl + H^{\cdot}$$

$$H^{\cdot} + Cl{-}Cl \rightarrow H{-}Cl + Cl^{\cdot}$$

Step 3: Termination
The free radicals can react with other free radicals.

$$Cl^{\cdot} + Cl^{\cdot} \rightarrow Cl_2$$

$$H^{\cdot} + H^{\cdot} \rightarrow H_2$$

$$H^{\cdot} + Cl^{\cdot} \rightarrow H{-}Cl$$

Important points to note

1   The initiation step starts the reaction. The Cl–Cl bond breaks rather than the H–H bond as the Cl–Cl bond is much weaker. You can check this for yourself by looking up the bond enthalpy in the data booklet. This is a measure of how much energy is required to break the bond. For chlorine it is $243\,\text{kJ}\,\text{mol}^{-1}$ and for hydrogen it is $432\,\text{kJ}\,\text{mol}^{-1}$.

2   The propagation step keeps the reaction going. In this case, the highly reactive chlorine radical collides with a hydrogen molecule. A new bond is formed between a chlorine and hydrogen to create H–Cl. This leaves a hydrogen radical. This hydrogen radical collides with a chlorine molecule to form another molecule of H–Cl and a chlorine radical. Forming a chlorine radical in the propagation step is crucial to this chemical reaction as the chlorine radical was responsible for the reaction in the first place. Now that it has been created again, the whole process continues again and again and again until there are no more reactants left or termination occurs. Hopefully you can see why this is called a chain reaction.

   If we add together the two equations for the propagation steps, we obtain the equation for the overall reaction:

$$H_2 + Cl_2 \rightarrow 2HCl$$

3   At any point in the reaction two radicals can collide and form a stable molecule. Since radicals are required to keep this reaction going, once they have all combined to form a stable molecule the reaction will stop. This is known as termination.

Reaction of alkanes with halogens

Alkenes rapidly decolourise when added to bromine water as the double bond breaks to form an addition product with the bromine. If the same reaction is carried out with an **alkane** in the presence of UV light, the bromine will also decolourise. This time, the reaction is a free radical reaction. The steps for the reaction of bromine with methane, in the presence of UV, are outlined below:

Initiation

$$Br–Br \rightarrow Br^• + Br^•$$

Propagation

$$Br^• + CH_4 \rightarrow {}^•CH_3 + HBr$$

$${}^•CH_3 + Br_2 \rightarrow CH_3Br + {}^•Br$$

Termination

$$Br^• + Br^• \rightarrow Br_2$$

$${}^•CH_3 + Br^• \rightarrow CH_3Br$$

$${}^•CH_3 + {}^•CH_3 \rightarrow C_2H_6$$

Important points to note

1   When UV light is shone on bromine and methane, either the Br–Br bond can break or the C–H bond. The Br–Br bond breaks more readily as it is much weaker.

2   Propagation always follows the same routine: the radical produced in the initiation step ($Br^•$) reacts with the other reactant (CH_4). The second step of the propagation must recreate the $Br^•$ radical so that the process can continue.

3   Termination is straightforward as it requires combining any two radicals to produce a stable molecule.

Questions

1   Write out the initiation, propagation and termination steps for the reaction between chlorine gas and ethane under the action of UV light.

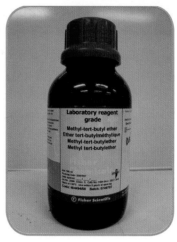

Figure 10.4 Many chemicals are stored in brown bottles to stop light initiating reactions that could cause the stored chemical to break down.

Storage of chemicals

If you look around the chemistry lab you will notice that some chemicals are stored in brown glass bottles rather than colourless glass bottles. Brown glass filters light and is used to store chemicals that can degrade when exposed to light. For example, chemicals known as ethers can form oxide radicals when exposed to light which combine to form highly explosive peroxides!

Free radical scavengers

Given that UV light can cause free radicals to form on our skin, which leads to ageing of the skin, cosmetic chemists have developed compounds that combine with these free radicals to form stable molecules.

Figure 10.5 Many cosmetic creams contain free radical scavengers such as vitamin E.

These compounds are known as **free radical scavengers**. As they form stable molecules, they help to stop the free radical chain reactions that cause the skin to form wrinkles.

The most common free radical scavengers used in anti-ageing creams are vitamin C and vitamin E. However, as these compounds are unstable it is usually an ester of these vitamins that is used, such as tocopheryl ethanoate (an ester of vitamin E) and ascorbyl-2-phosphate (an ester of vitamin C). Once these esters penetrate the skin, they hydrolyse to produce vitamin C and vitamin E which can then combine with free radicals to form stable molecules.

Of course, free radical scavengers are not only added to cosmetic creams; food and drinks are often altered by adding antioxidants that slow down the rate of oxidation. Plastics too have free radical scavengers added as without them they can break down under the action of UV light and oxygen. Common free radical scavengers added to plastics include butylated hydroxyanisole (BHA) and butylated hydroxytoluene (BHT). When these compounds are used in plastics for storing food, they have the advantage that they also preserve the food by reacting with the radicals that would spoil the food.

For Interest   The effect of light on art

The action of light on chemical compounds must also be carefully controlled and measured in museums and art galleries. The next time you tour an art gallery, look out for the paintings housed in dimly lit rooms and the 'no flash photography' signs. While it is usually true that the museum restricts photography to protect the copyright of a painting, many museums take the precaution as they wish to limit the light exposure their paintings receive. High-intensity light can initiate chemical reactions that could damage the painting. Many galleries around the world employ scientists to ensure that light damage of fragile paintings is prevented. This usually involves subduing the lighting in the gallery and carefully controlling the moisture and temperature in the display room. Fragile exhibits can even be housed in special glass that filters UV, thus preventing initiation of free radical reactions.

Checklist for Revision

- I understand the cause of sunburn and the role of sun block in preventing sunburn.

- I know what a free radical is and can write equations for free radical reactions which include the initiation, propagation and termination steps.

- I know what a free radical scavenger is and can give examples of their use.

Key Terms

The words and phrases below were introduced in this chapter.

Their definitions are given in the chemical dictionary.

free radical
free radical scavenger

Study Questions

1 Which of the following represents an initiation step in a chain reaction?

   A $Cl_2 \rightarrow 2Cl^{\bullet}$

   B $CH_3^{\bullet} + CH_3^{\bullet} \rightarrow C_2H_6$

   C $CH_4 + Cl^{\bullet} \rightarrow CH_3Cl + H^{\bullet}$

   D $CH_3^{\bullet} + Cl_2 \rightarrow CH_3Cl + Cl^{\bullet}$

2 The mechanism for the bromination of methane is outlined below.

   a) State what is required at *(a)* to initiate the reaction.

   b) What names are given to stages *(g)* and *(h)*?

   c) Complete the mechanism by writing formulae for *(b)–(f)*.

   $Br_2 \overset{(a)}{\rightarrow} (b)$ initiation

   $(c) + CH_4 \rightarrow HBr + (d)$ }
   $(e) + Br_2 \rightarrow CH_3Br + (f)$ } *(g)*

   $CH_3^{\bullet} + Br^{\bullet} \rightarrow CH_3Br$ }
   $CH_3^{\bullet} + CH_3^{\bullet} \rightarrow C_2H_6$ } *(h)*

3 Write the initiation, propagation and termination steps for the following reactions:

   a) fluorine reacting with propane

   b) bromine reacting with hydrogen.

4 In the previous examples, initiation always involves creating halogen radicals. Explain why halogen radicals are produced rather than hydrocarbon radicals.

Activities

1 Find out about CF_3SF_5. Why is it known as a 'supergreenhouse gas'? How is it formed?

2 Examine the labels from commercial sun blocks. Identify the compounds that can act as sun blocks.

3 Debate the pros and cons of wearing sun block. How can it be used sensibly?

4 Examine the ingredients labels from cosmetic creams for the skin. Identify the free radical scavengers and explain how they work.

Unit 3

Chemistry in Society

Chemists make new products which benefit society. The goal of the global chemical industry is to design chemical reactions to make these products so that waste is minimal and maximum profit is generated.

This unit allows you to develop skills in calculations that can be applied to chemical reactions. This will allow you to find out how chemists calculate some of the factors they must take into account when designing a new reaction, and how they can alter a reaction to make the most of the resources available.

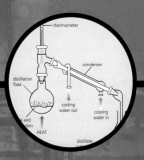

11 Getting the most from reactants: designing an industrial process

Introduction

If you walk into a supermarket, it is almost impossible to find one product that has not been touched by chemistry. From the fertilisers used to help fruit and vegetables grow, to the antioxidants added to bakery products to prolong their shelf life, chemists have been involved at some stage in the process of getting all supermarket produce into the shop. The chemicals used in the manufacture and analysis of everyday products are manufactured by the chemical industry. This chapter considers how the chemical industry manufactures chemicals on a large scale.

Figure 11.1 Chemists are involved in the making and analysing of everyday goods.

Plastics	Cosmetics & toiletries
Paints	Disinfectants
Detergents	Domestic polishes & cleaners
Explosives	Veterinary health products
Adhesives	Inks, dyestuffs & pigments
Pharmaceuticals	Chemicals used in treating
Aerosols	water, metals, paper & fabrics
Fertilisers	Intermediates for making
Herbicides	synthetic fibres
	Pesticides

Table 11.1 Some examples of products manufactured by the chemical industry.

The UK chemical industry makes a major contribution to the quality of life in this country. Some idea of the influence of chemicals in everyday life can be gained by a close look at Table 11.1 which lists the main applications of products from the chemical industry.

In Scotland the chemical industry is indebted to the pioneering work of James 'Paraffin' Young in obtaining many useful materials from shale oil during the latter half of the nineteenth century. These included motor spirit, fuel oil, lamp oil and paraffin wax. Many of the techniques he developed are still used in the oil industry to this day.

The UK chemical industry also plays a vital role in our national economy. Within the country it is one of the largest manufacturing industries. The UK has an excellent reputation across the world for its chemical industry and chemists. UK chemists can be found working in the chemical industry all over the world.

Figure 11.2 Many chemical companies are located in Grangemouth in Scotland.

Making a new product

Many companies, and individuals, make huge sums of money from creating new products using chemistry. They create new detergents, medicines, insect repellents and explosives, for example, or simply change existing products to make them 'better'. The ultimate goal for the chemical industry is to make products which will create maximum profit. Of course, it is also vital that in making the new product, an assessment is made of how this product will affect the environment.

Once the need for a new product has been recognised and its market potential assessed, there are several stages that a chemical company will employ before production can begin. Some of these stages are shown in the form of a flow diagram in Figure 11.3, which includes a brief description of what each stage involves.

Factor	Profit making	Profit losing
Availability, sustainability and cost of feedstock(s)	If the process relies on a feedstock which is available locally, this will help to keep costs down and maximise profit.	If the feedstock has to be transported from further afield, this will have significant cost, safety and environmental considerations. Is the feedstock likely to last for a long time or is it likely to become scarce? This could significantly affect the cost of buying the feedstock since rare materials cost more. If the feedstock is too expensive, alternatives might have to be investigated. Energy derived from oil and gas fluctuates in price, but always becomes more expensive in times of tension in the producing areas.
Opportunities for recycling	If unreacted starting materials can easily be fed back into the chemical reactor to form new products, this will improve the efficiency and profitability of the process. If water used in the process can be recycled, this reduces waste.	If it is very difficult to separate unreacted starting materials at the end of the reaction, this makes the reaction inefficient and wasteful.
Energy requirements	Exothermic reactions can be used to sustain the heat in a reaction or heat the building. This saves money on energy costs. Many chemical reactions use catalysts to speed up the rate of the reaction rather than using higher temperatures. This can allow more control of the reaction products and saves energy.	Reactions which require heating can be very costly as energy (gas, electricity) must be purchased. Reactions which require cooling can also be expensive as energy must be removed from the reaction by surrounding with a coolant.
Use of by-products	Many reactions produce more than one product. If the other product(s) can be used elsewhere in the process, this will save money. If the by-products can be sold to other companies, this will also increase profit.	If the by-products are toxic, very corrosive or environmentally damaging, it will be expensive to deal with these. For example, acidic gases like sulfur dioxide (SO_2) and the greenhouse gas carbon dioxide (CO_2) can be costly for companies to deal with.
Yield of product	A high yield of product is very profitable.	Low yields cost money as time and energy must be put in to run the reaction several times to produce enough of the desired product.

Table 11.2 Factors affecting the design of a chemical process

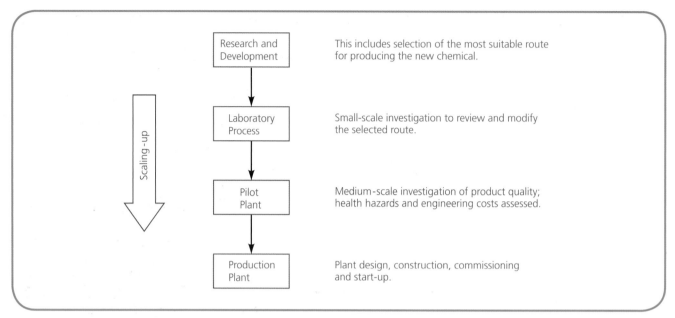

Figure 11.3 Stages in the manufacture of a new product

Several factors must be taken into consideration when considering how best to make a new product. Table 11.2 lists the main factors that influence the design of a process to make a new product.

Route 1: The direct oxidation of naphtha

> naphtha + air → ethanoic acid + several
> by-products
>
> By-products include propanone, methanoic acid and propanoic acid.
>
> Process conditions: 180 °C; 50 atmospheres pressure

Advantages	Disadvantages
Single-step process	Low yield of ethanoic acid (<50%)
By-products can be sold for profit	Lots of by-products. This means that time and energy must be spent separating the ethanoic acid from the by-products.

Table 11.3 The advantages and disadvantages of route 1

As an example, consider the production of ethanoic acid. There are several possible routes for its production. Two of these routes are summarised below.

Route 2: From methanol

> methanol + carbon monoxide → ethanoic acid
>
> Process conditions: 180 °C; 30 atmospheres pressure; rhodium/iodine catalyst

Advantages	Disadvantage
High yield of ethanoic acid (>99%)	Special materials are needed for plant construction which makes it very expensive to start up and maintain the plant.
Fewer by-products	
Flexible source of feedstock. Methanol can be made from coal, natural gas or crude oil.	

Table 11.4 The advantages and disadvantages of route 2

What is a feedstock?

A **feedstock** is a reactant from which other chemicals can be extracted or synthesised. Feedstocks are themselves derived from **raw materials** either by physical separation or by chemical reaction. Examples of raw materials include crude oil, air and water. For example, air is a raw material for the production of nitrogen and oxygen gases. Nitrogen and oxygen are examples of feedstocks: nitrogen is used to make ammonia; oxygen is used to make sulfuric acid. In the production of ethanoic acid by route 2, the feedstock for the process is methanol. This can be obtained from the raw materials coal, natural gas or crude oil.

Environmental considerations

The chemical industry is aware of how important it is to protect our environment. Strict codes of conduct must be followed to ensure that the chemicals and processes used have minimum impact on the environment. The three main environmental considerations are:

1   How can waste be minimised?

2   How can we avoid making toxic substances?

3   Can we design products that will biodegrade?

The modern chemical industry considers these factors when creating a new product. Quite often a review of these considerations will cause the company to change the process they are using so that they can minimise environmental damage.

Historically, chemical plants were sited near the coast so that waste material could be put directly into the sea. This method of disposal is no longer acceptable and most chemical companies take pride in their concern for the environment. Large chemical plants such as that at Billingham in Northern England pride themselves on reporting how they have changed processes to make them more environmentally acceptable.

Figure 11.4 The chemical plant at Billingham is located next to the sea.

Examples of changes made at Billingham include the following:

- Discharges of phosphates (which can cause algal growth and oxygen depletion in water), cyanides and heavy metals (which build up in the food chain and are toxic) declined at Billingham by about 90%.

- Waste sulfuric acid is recovered and reused rather than being pumped into the river, so reducing pollution and saving money.

- Reed beds are used to harbour microbes which break down waste organic chemicals in liquids which would otherwise deplete river water of oxygen. The water reaching the river is, therefore, clean. As a bonus, the reed beds provide an excellent wildlife habitat.

Figure 11.5 Reed beds can be used to break down chemical waste.

Many chemical companies, in developed countries at least, are involved in similar schemes. Figure 11.6 shows the consequences that failing to develop a good environmental policy might have.

In addition to dramatic accidents (see the For Interest box), the chemical industry has a history of causing long-term damage to the health of its workers. In the nineteenth century this was sometimes a consequence of a lack of concern for the safety of workers in society as a whole. Later it may have been because of ignorance of the harmful effects of particular chemicals. Nowadays, the rules governing exposure to harmful chemicals are very strict and rigorously enforced. The change in attitudes is illustrated in

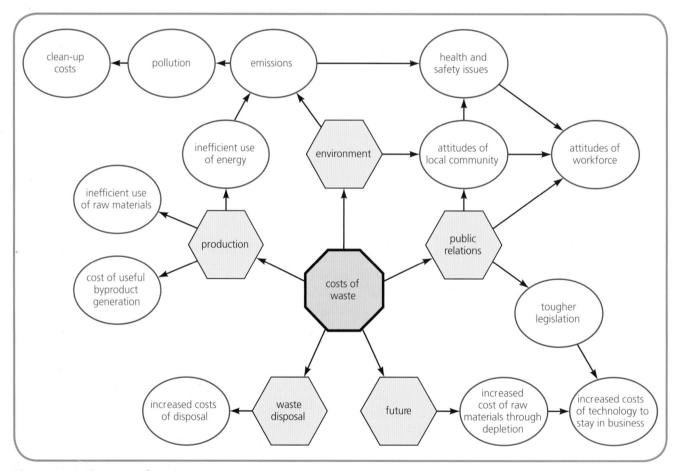

Figure 11.6 The costs of waste

Accidents in the chemical industry

In recent years, the chemical industry has developed great expertise in handling hazardous chemicals. Tragically, much of this expertise has been gained from an examination of past disasters which resulted in the loss of many lives.

The worst British chemical accident was at Flixborough, Lincolnshire, in 1974. A plant making cyclohexane to be used in polyamide manufacture suffered an explosion and fire. Twenty-eight people were killed and 104 were injured, some in neighbouring housing. The control room was destroyed along with its workers and the plant could not be shut down quickly. Lessons learnt included the building of new plants away from housing and the development of control rooms that were fire- and blast-proof. When the Fife Ethylene Plant was built at Mossmorran, Fife, a few years later, these principles were put into effect.

Year	Observations	MEL/ppm
1930s	Narcotic effects noticed Workers became drowsy	No limit in force
1962	To prevent narcotic effect, limit introduced	500
1960s	Animal experimentation showed vinyl chloride affected liver, bones and kidneys	
1971	New limit	200
1971	Three workers in US company died of liver cancer	
1975	Health and Safety Executive (UK) suggest a new limit of 25 In the same year, limit was reduced to 10	25 10
1978	Limit reduced to 7 ... ... with a maximum averaged annual limit of 3	7 3

Table 11.5 Reviewing the use of vinyl chloride and exposure limits

Table 11.5 which shows the data for vinyl chloride monomer. A long-term Maximum Exposure Level (MEL) for employees is derived from measurements made over an 8-hour working day and averaged. It must not be exceeded, and should be reduced if possible. The units are parts of substance per million parts of air.

In recent years, claims of many more deaths and of many workers being treated for cancer have increased pressure for further reductions in the MEL. The present limit in the UK is still 3 ppm (parts per million).

In the 1980s the chemical industry recognised that it needed to make a significant improvement in its safety, health and environmental performance. Through national chemical associations in the UK, the USA and Canada, a programme called Responsible Care was created in 1986. All members committed themselves to these improvements and to increasing openness about their activities. The programme has been expanded to produce the Responsible Care Global Charter (2006) and has been adopted very successfully in many countries across the world leading to significant improvements in the health, safety and environmental performance of the chemical industry.

Study Questions

1 Which of the following is a feedstock in the chemical industry?

A Natural gas

B Ethene

C Sea water

D Air

2* Acetone, widely used as a solvent, is manufactured from cumene. Cumene is oxidised by air and the cumene hydroperoxide product is then cleaved.

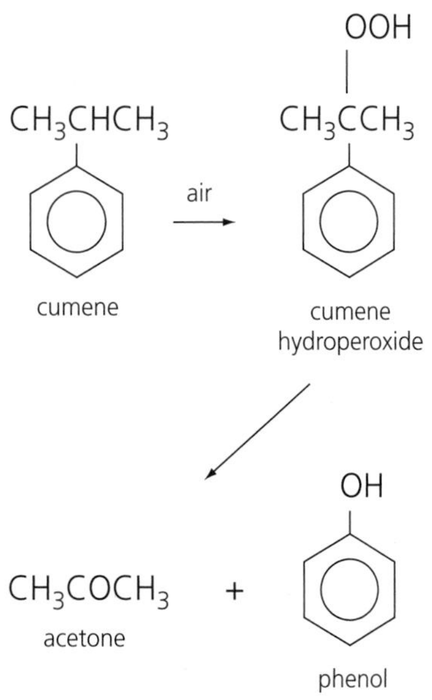

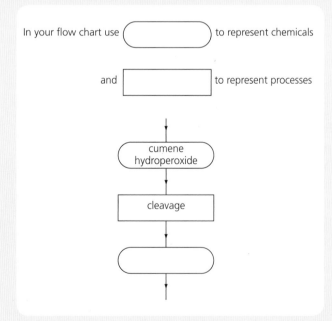

Figure 11.7

The mixture of acetone and phenol is separated by distillation.

a) Copy and complete the flow chart in Figure 11.8 to summarise the manufacture of acetone from cumene.

b) Acetone can also be manufactured by oxidising propan-2-ol. In industry, several factors influence the decision as to which route might be used. Suggest two of these factors.

Figure 11.8

3 Natural gas, steam and air are the raw materials used to make ammonia in the UK. Preparation of the nitrogen–hydrogen mixture required to synthesise ammonia is a multi-stage process.

a) Using a suitable resource, find out about the two main stages involved: **i)** the manufacture of synthesis gas and **ii)** the 'shift reaction'. For each stage write an equation and describe the conditions used, such as temperature, pressure, catalyst, etc.

b) Oxygen is removed from the air to leave nitrogen. How is this achieved?

c) Before the first main stage, any sulfur, which may be present in trace amounts in compounds in natural gas, must be removed. Suggest why the sulfur is removed.

d) The carbon dioxide produced during the 'shift reaction' must be removed prior to synthesising ammonia from nitrogen and hydrogen. One way of achieving this is to react CO_2 with potassium carbonate solution. Water is also a reactant and the only product is potassium hydrogencarbonate solution. Write the balanced equation for this reaction.

4* The flow diagram (Figure 11.9) shows how vinyl chloride ($CH_2{=}CHCl$), an important feedstock, is made in industry.

a) Write the formulae for the three substances which are recycled.

b) Write the equation for the reaction taking place in the cracker.

c) Name the process taking place in the separator units.

d) Name the type of reaction taking place in the scrubber unit.

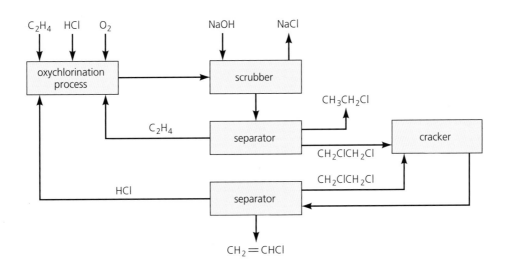

Figure 11.9

5* The flow diagram given in Figure 11.10 outlines the manufacture of sodium carbonate by the Solvay Process.

a) Name the reactants in the reaction taking place in the Solvay Tower.

b) As well as ammonia, a salt and water are produced in reaction vessel B. Write a balanced equation for the production of ammonia in this reaction vessel.

c) The sea water used in the Solvay Process can contain contaminant magnesium ions. These can be removed by the addition of sodium carbonate solution. Why is sodium carbonate solution suitable for removing contaminant magnesium ions?

d) Using the information in the flow diagram, give two different features of the Solvay Process that make it economical.

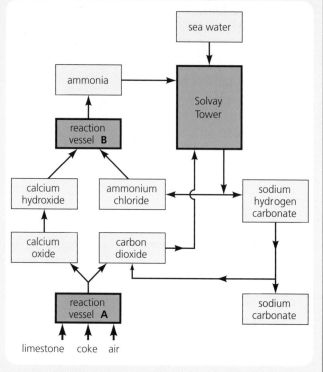

Figure 11.10

1 Propanone and ethyl ethanoate are two solvents commonly used in the chemical industry. Research the properties of these solvents. For example, how they are manufactured, what they are used for, what dangers they pose to health and the environment, and how they can be disposed of.

2 In 1984 toxic methyl isocyanate gas leaked from a chemical factory in Bhopal, India, killing several thousand people. Research this disaster and report on the lessons learned.

3 Grangemouth in Scotland is a world-leading supplier of many specialised chemicals. Find out about one of the chemical industries located at Grangemouth. What do they make? How profitable are they? What feedstocks are used? Where do these feedstocks come from? What impact do they have on the environment? How many people do they employ?

12 Calculations from equations

Making a new product requires chemists to work routinely with chemical equations so that they are able to calculate how much product they are likely to form or how much reactant they will require to make a certain quantity of product. This requires an understanding of balanced chemical equations and how to calculate the number of **moles** of material of given concentrations, volumes or masses.

The following examples illustrate this in practice.

Calculations involving mass

Questions

1 Calculate the mass of carbon dioxide produced when 64 g of methane is burned according to the following equation.

$$CH_4 + 2O_2 \rightarrow CO_2 + 2H_2O$$

2 Calculate the mass of carbon dioxide produced when 48 g of carbon is burned according to the following equation.

$$C + O_2 \rightarrow CO_2$$

Worked Example 1

Calculate the mass of water produced when 320 g of methane is burned according to the following equation:

$$CH_4 \qquad + 2O_2 \qquad \rightarrow \qquad CO_2 + 2H_2O$$

Step 1: Write a balanced chemical equation (unless already given).

1 mole $\qquad \rightarrow \qquad$ 2 moles

Step 2: Identify the two chemicals referred to in the question and write the mole ratio.

$$Mole = \frac{mass}{gfm}$$

$$= \frac{320}{16}$$

Step 3: Calculate the moles of the substance you have been given a mass for (methane). Note that gfm stands for gram formula mass.

$$= 20 \text{ moles} \qquad \rightarrow \qquad 40 \text{ moles}$$

$$Mass = moles \times gfm$$

Step 4: Use the mole ratio to calculate the number of moles of the other substance (water).

$$= 40 \times 18$$

$$= 720 \text{ g}$$

Step 5: Calculate the mass.

Calculations involving solutions

The concentration of a solution is usually expressed in moles per litre ($mol\,l^{-1}$).

A $1\,mol\,l^{-1}$ solution will contain 1 mole of a solute dissolved to make 1 litre of solution.

If you dissolved 10 moles of a substance to make 2 litres of solution, the concentration would be $5\,mol\,l^{-1}$. This tells us that to find out the concentration we divide the moles by the volume, in litres.

$$\text{concentration} = \frac{\text{number of moles}}{\text{volume}}$$

Volumes and concentrations can be used to find out about reactants and products in a balanced chemical equation in the same way that masses can be used.

Questions

3   Calculate the mass of KOH required to make up 0.5 litres of a solution with a concentration of $2\,mol\,l^{-1}$.

4   Calculate the mass of Na_2CO_3 required to make a $500\,cm^3$ solution of concentration $3\,mol\,l^{-1}$.

5   Calculate the concentration of a solution where 12.8 g of SO_2 is dissolved in 2 litres of solution.

6   Calculate the concentration of a solution where 11.2 g of KOH is dissolved in $100\,cm^3$ of solution.

Calculations involving volumes and concentrations

Worked Example 2

Calculate the concentration of hydrochloric acid used if $20\,cm^3$ of the acid was neutralised by $10\,cm^3$ of $1\,mol\,l^{-1}$ sodium hydroxide solution.

HCl	+ NaOH	$\rightarrow H_2O + NaCl$
1 mole	1 mole	

$V = 20\,cm^3$ $V = 10\,cm^3$

$C = ?$ $C = 1\,mol\,l^{-1}$

Moles of NaOH $= CV = 1 \times 0.01 = 0.01$

Since 1 mole of alkali reacts with 1 mole of acid,
Moles HCl $= 0.01$

Concentration of HCl $= \dfrac{\text{moles}}{\text{volume}}$

$= \dfrac{0.01}{0.02}$

$= 0.5\,mol\,l^{-1}$

Step 1: Write a balanced chemical equation (unless already given).

Step 2: Identify the two chemicals referred to in the question and write the mole ratio.

Step 3: Write down the volumes, in litres, and concentrations under the reactants.

Step 4: Calculate the number of moles of the chemical with most information.

Step 5: Use the mole ratio to work out the moles of the other reactant (in this case, 1 mole of acid reacts with 1 mole of alkali).

Step 6: Calculate the volume, concentration or mass of the chemical you are asked to find out.

Questions

7 What volume of sodium hydroxide, concentration 0.1 mol l^{-1}, is required to neutralise 50 cm^3 of 0.2 mol l^{-1} hydrochloric acid?

$$NaOH + HCl \rightarrow NaCl + H_2O$$

8 What volume of potassium hydroxide, concentration 0.2 mol l^{-1}, is required to neutralise 45 cm^3 of 0.1 mol l^{-1} hydrochloric acid?

Calculations involving masses, volumes and concentrations

Worked Example 3

Calculate the mass of calcium carbonate required to react completely with 300 cm^3 of 0.1 mol l^{-1} hydrochloric acid.

$$CaCO_3 + 2HCl \rightarrow CaCl_2 + CO_2 + H_2O$$

1 mole   2 moles

Moles of acid $= CV = 0.1 \times 0.3 = 0.03$

So number of moles of $CaCO_3$ = 0.015 moles

Mass of $CaCO_3$ = moles $\times$ gfm
$$= 0.015 \times 100$$
$$= 1.5\,g$$

Questions

9 Calculate the volume of 0.5 mol l^{-1} sulfuric acid required to react completely with 4 g of magnesium.

$$Mg + H_2SO_4 \rightarrow MgSO_4 + H_2$$

Calculations involving excess reactant

So far, our reactions have only considered the effect of one reactant on the quantity of product obtained. We must now consider how we decide which reactant will dictate how much product we obtain. This is done by calculating which reactant is 'in excess'. The reactant which is in excess will not control how much product is produced since some of this reactant will remain unreacted. In other words, we focus our attention on the reactant which is not in excess since this will control how much product is formed. The following example illustrates this.

Worked Example 4

4.86 g of magnesium was reacted with 100 cm^3 of 2 mol l^{-1} hydrochloric acid. Calculate the mass of magnesium chloride produced.

$$Mg + 2HCl \rightarrow MgCl_2 + H_2$$

The number of moles of magnesium $= \dfrac{4.86}{24.3} = 0.2$ moles

The number of moles of hydrochloric acid $= 2 \times 0.1$
$$= 0.2\,Moles$$

Now that we know the number of moles of each reactant, we can work out which reactant is in excess.

According to the balanced equation, 1 mole of magnesium reacts with 2 moles of hydrochloric acid.

Thus, 0.2 moles magnesium will react with 0.4 moles of hydrochloric acid.

We only have 0.2 moles of hydrochloric acid, so the magnesium must be in excess. We can calculate how much magnesium there is in excess by looking at the acid:

2 moles of acid react with 1 mole of magnesium.

0.2 moles of acid react with 0.1 moles of magnesium i.e. the magnesium is in excess by

$(0.2 - 0.1) = 0.1$ moles.

To calculate how much product is formed, we ignore the excess reagent (the magnesium in this case) and proceed as normal.

$$Mg + 2HCl \rightarrow MgCl_2 + H_2$$

2 moles HCl $\rightarrow$ 1 mole of magnesium chloride

0.2 moles HCl $\rightarrow$ 0.1 moles of magnesium chloride

Mass magnesium chloride = moles $\times$ gfm
$$= 0.1 \times 95.3$$
$$= 9.53\,g$$

Worked Example 5

15 g of calcium carbonate were reacted with 50 cm³ of 4 mol l⁻¹ hydrochloric acid.

a) Show by calculation which reactant was present in excess.

b) Calculate the mass of carbon dioxide produced.

a) $\qquad CaCO_3 + 2HCl \rightarrow CaCl_2 + CO_2 + H_2O$

$\qquad$ 1 mol $\quad$ 2 mol $\qquad\qquad$ 1 mol

$\qquad$ 100 g $\qquad\qquad\qquad\quad$ 44 g

Number of moles of $CaCO_3 = \dfrac{mass}{gfm} = \dfrac{15}{100} = 0.15\,mol$

Number of moles of $HCl = C \times V = 4 \times \dfrac{50}{1000}$

$\qquad\qquad\qquad\qquad = 0.2\,mol$

According to the equation, 1 mol of $CaCO_3$ neutralises 2 mol of HCl.

Hence, 0.1 mol of $CaCO_3$ neutralises 0.2 mol of HCl.

Since there is more than 0.1 mol of $CaCO_3$ present, this reactant is in excess.

b) To calculate the mass of carbon dioxide produced we use the quantity of the reactant which is completely reacted, in other words the acid, and not the one which is present in excess.

According to the equation, 2 mol of HCl produce 1 mol of CO_2.

Hence, 0.2 mol of HCl produce 0.1 mol of CO_2.

Mass of CO_2 = moles × gfm = 0.1 × 44

$\qquad\qquad\qquad = 4.4\,g$

4.4 g of carbon dioxide is produced.

Questions

10 A piece of magnesium ribbon weighing 0.6 g was added to 40 cm³ of 2 mol l⁻¹ hydrochloric acid.

$$Mg + 2HCl \rightarrow MgCl_2 + H_2$$

a) Show by calculation that excess acid has been used.

b) Calculate the number of moles of excess acid.

c) Describe briefly how the result in b) could be checked by experiment.

11 2.6 g of zinc dust were added to 30 cm³ of 1.0 mol l⁻¹ copper(II) sulfate solution.

$$Zn + CuSO_4 \rightarrow ZnSO_4 + Cu$$

a) Show by calculation that the zinc was in excess.

b) Calculate the mass of copper produced.

c) Describe briefly how the excess zinc could be removed and the copper obtained to check this result.

Calculations involving gases

Molar volume

When dealing with reactants or products that are gases, it is usually more appropriate to measure volume rather than mass. In order to tackle calculations involving gases, we must consider the volume of 1 mole of gas. This is known as the **molar volume** and can be determined experimentally as shown in Figure 12.1.

A round-bottomed flask can be evacuated and then weighed. It is then reweighed after being filled with a gas. The volume of the flask can be found by filling it with water and emptying it into a measuring cylinder. This can be repeated using other gases. The molar volume can then be calculated from the data obtained as illustrated in Worked Example 6.

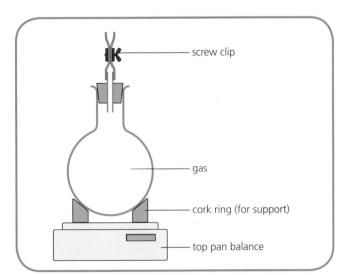

Figure 12.1 An experiment for determining the molar volume of a gas (safety screen not shown)

Another way to measure the molar volume of a gas is to use a gas syringe in place of the flask.

Calculating the molar volume

Worked Example 6

Calculate the molar volume of carbon dioxide from the following data obtained at 20 °C and 1 atmosphere pressure.

Mass of empty flask = 107.49 g

Mass of flask + carbon dioxide = 108.37 g

Volume of flask = 480 cm³

Calculation:

Mass of carbon dioxide = 108.37 − 107.49 = 0.88 g
Gram formula mass of CO_2 = 44 g

0.88 g of carbon dioxide occupies a volume of 480 cm³.

0.88 g → 480 cm³

1 g   → $\frac{480}{0.88}$ = 545.45 cm³

44 g   → 44 × 545.45 = 24 000 cm³

Hence, the molar volume of CO_2 is 24.0 litres at 20 °C and 1 atmosphere pressure.

Since the volume of a gas changes if the temperature and/or the pressure changes, it is important to specify the temperature and pressure at which a volume is being measured. If this experimental technique is repeated for other gases, we find that **the volume of 1 mole of any gas is approximately the same**. In other words, at room temperature and pressure, 20 °C and 1 atmosphere pressure, the molar volume of any gas is approximately 24 litres mol⁻¹.

It may seem surprising at first that the molar volume is the same for all gases, even at the same temperature and pressure. This is certainly not true for either solids or liquids. However, in a gas the molecules have much greater kinetic energy and are relatively far apart so that the volume of the gas does not depend on the size of the actual molecules. It is possible to calculate that in a gas at room temperature and pressure the molecules themselves only occupy about 0.1% of the volume of the gas. The rest is empty space!

Questions

12 A 100 cm³ gas syringe was weighed empty and again when filled with ethane, C_2H_6, at 20 °C and 1 atmosphere pressure. Calculate the molar volume of ethane from the following data.

Mass of syringe = 151.51 g

Mass of syringe + ethane = 151.63 g

Provided the molar volume of a gas is known, the volume of the gas can be calculated from the number of moles of gas. Alternatively, the number of moles of a gas can be calculated from its volume. The relationship between volume of a gas, number of moles and molar volume can be expressed as shown in Figure 12.2.

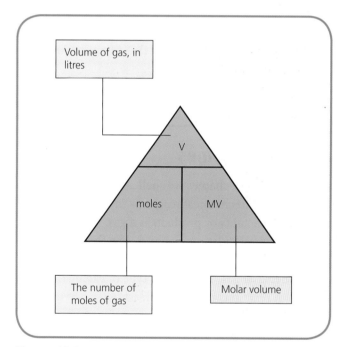

Figure 12.2

Using molar volume

Worked Example 7

The molar volume at 0 °C and 1 atmosphere pressure is 22.4 litres mol^{-1}.

Calculate a) the volume of 0.025 mol of oxygen and b) the number of moles of nitrogen in 4.48 litres under these conditions.

a) The volume of gas $= \text{moles} \times MV = 0.025 \times 22.4$
$$= 0.56 \text{ litres}$$

b) The number of moles of nitrogen $= \dfrac{V}{MV} = \dfrac{4.48}{22.4}$
$$= 0.2$$

Questions

13 At room temperature and pressure the molar volume is 24 litres mol^{-1}.

a) Calculate the volume of **i)** 0.04 mol of CO_2, **ii)** 5 mol of CH_4.

b) Calculate the number of moles in **i)** 72 litres of H_2, **ii)** 360 cm^3 of Ar.

Reacting volumes

In this part of the chapter we shall apply the idea of molar volume to chemical reactions in which at least one of the reactants or products is a gas. There are two main types of calculation involved. The first type is often used in a reaction where only one of the reactants or products is a gas. The second type of calculation deals with reactions in which at least two gases take part and the volumes of the gases are then compared with each other. The difference between the two types of calculation should become apparent in the next two sections.

Calculations involving mass and volume

Worked Example 8

Calculate the volume of carbon dioxide released when 0.4 g of calcium carbonate is dissolved in excess hydrochloric acid. The gas is collected at room temperature and pressure. The molar volume is 24 litres mol^{-1}. The equation for the reaction is

$$CaCO_3(s) + 2HCl(aq) \rightarrow CaCl_2(aq) + CO_2(g) + H_2O(l)$$

This calculation is treated in exactly the same way as previous calculations from equations except that we must consider the volume of gas rather than the mass.

1 mole of calcium $\rightarrow$ 1 mole of carbon
carbonate   dioxide gas

Number of moles of $CaCO_3 = \dfrac{0.4}{100} = 0.004 \rightarrow$
$$0.004 \text{ moles of } CO_2$$

1 mole of $CO_2 \rightarrow 24$ litres

0.004 moles $\rightarrow 0.004 \times 24 = 0.096$ litres

Questions

14 $Zn(s) + 2HCl(aq) \rightarrow ZnCl_2(aq) + H_2(g)$

Use the equation given above to calculate the volume of hydrogen produced when the following reactions go to completion. Take the molar volume to be 24 litres mol^{-1}.

a) 13.1 g of zinc are added to excess dilute hydrochloric acid.

b) Excess zinc is added to 100 cm^3 of 2 mol l^{-1} hydrochloric acid.

15 $2NH_3(g) + H_2SO_4(aq) \rightarrow (NH_4)_2SO_4(aq)$

Calculate the volume of ammonia, measured at room temperature and pressure, needed to neutralise 2.5 litres of 5 mol l^{-1} sulfuric acid. Take the molar volume to be 24 litres mol^{-1}.

Comparing volumes of gases

Let us consider the reaction in which carbon monoxide burns to form carbon dioxide.

$$2CO(g) + O_2(g) \rightarrow 2CO_2(g)$$

According to the equation, 2 moles of carbon monoxide combine with 1 mole of oxygen to form 2 moles of carbon dioxide.

Provided the volumes are measured at the same temperature and pressure, any volume of carbon monoxide will produce the same volume of carbon dioxide by reacting with half that volume of oxygen, for example:

- 2 litres CO + 1 litre O_2 produces 2 litres CO_2
- 100 cm^3 CO + 50 cm^3 O_2 produces 100 cm^3 CO_2

In many reactions which involve gases, one or more of the reactants or products may be a liquid or a solid. The volume of liquid or solid is so small compared with that of the gas or gases that it can be regarded as negligible. Thus, if a reaction produces water when all the volumes are measured at room temperature and pressure, the water is ignored as it is a liquid.

Thus 100 cm^3 of methane requires 200 cm^3 of oxygen for complete combustion and produces 100 cm^3 of carbon dioxide when the volumes are measured at room temperature and pressure. Incidentally, the volume of water formed would be about 0.1 cm^3.

Worked Example 9

Calculate

a) the volume of oxygen required for the complete combustion of 100 cm^3 of methane

b) the volume of each product.

All volumes are measured at 150 °C and 1 atmosphere pressure.

	$CH_4(g) + 2O_2(g) \rightarrow CO_2(g) + 2H_2O(g)$			
Mole ratio	1	2	1	2
Volume ratio	1	2	1	2
Volumes given in question	100 cm^3			
Volume of oxygen required		200 cm^3		
Volume of products			100 cm^3	200 cm^3

Hence 100 cm^3 of methane:

a) requires 200 cm^3 of oxygen for complete combustion

b) produces 100 cm^3 of $CO_2(g)$ and 200 cm^3 of $H_2O(g)$.

Questions

16 Nitrogen monoxide gas, NO, combines with oxygen to form brown fumes of nitrogen dioxide according to the following equation.

$$2NO(g) + O_2(g) \rightarrow 2NO_2(g)$$

Calculate the volume of oxygen needed to react completely with 60 cm³ of nitrogen monoxide and calculate the volume of nitrogen dioxide formed.

Note

Balanced equations are required in the next two questions.

17 Calculate the volume of oxygen required for the complete combustion of 20 cm³ of propane, C_3H_8, and calculate the volume of each product. All volumes are measured at 130 °C and 1 atmosphere pressure.

18 For each of the following gases, calculate
i) the volume of oxygen required for the complete combustion and **ii)** the volume of carbon dioxide produced. All gases are measured under the same conditions of room temperature and pressure.

a) 200 cm³ of methane, CH_4

b) 5 litres of butane, C_4H_{10}

Gas volume calculations involving excess reactant

At this point it is appropriate to apply the idea of excess to calculations involving gas volumes. Worked Examples 10 and 11 illustrate the application of excess reactant to the types of calculation covered in the previous two sections. In each example it is necessary to find out which reactant is in excess before calculating the volume of gaseous product.

Worked Example 10

Calculate the volume of carbon dioxide produced at room temperature and pressure when 0.4 g of calcium carbonate is added to 12 cm³ of 0.5 mol l⁻¹ hydrochloric acid. The molar volume is 24 litres mol⁻¹.

$$CaCO_3(s) + 2HCl(aq) \rightarrow CaCl_2(aq) + CO_2(g) + H_2O(l)$$

| 1 mol | 2 mol | | 1 mol | |
| 100 g | | | 24 litres | |

Number of moles of calcium carbonate $= \dfrac{0.4}{100} = 0.004$

Number of moles of hydrochloric acid $= 0.5 \times \dfrac{12}{1000}$

$$= 0.006$$

According to the equation, 1 mol of $CaCO_3$ requires 2 mol of HCl.

Therefore, 0.004 mol $CaCO_3$ require 0.008 mol HCl.

The number of moles of acid present is less than this, so the $CaCO_3$ is in excess and as a result the volume of CO_2 produced will depend on the number of moles of acid.

2 mol of HCl $\rightarrow$ 1 mol of CO_2

0.006 mol HCl $\rightarrow$ 0.003 mol CO_2

Hence, the volume of CO_2 produced $= 0.003 \times 24\,l$

$$= 0.072 \text{ litres}$$
$$(\text{or } 72 \text{ cm}^3)$$

Worked Example 11

A mixture of 20 cm³ of propane and 130 cm³ of oxygen was ignited and allowed to cool. Calculate the volume and composition of the resulting gaseous mixture. All volumes are measured under the same conditions of room temperature and pressure.

	$C_3H_8(g) + 5O_2(g) \rightarrow 3CO_2(g) + 4H_2O(l)$			
Mole ratio	1	5	3	4
Volume ratio	1	5	3	
Volumes given in question	20 cm³	130 cm³		
Volume of oxygen required from reacting 20 cm³	20 cm³	100 cm³		
Volume remaining	0 cm³	30 cm³	60 cm³	

According to the equation,

20 cm³ of propane requires 5 × 20 cm³ of oxygen, i.e. 100 cm³.

Hence, oxygen is present in excess since its initial volume is 130 cm³.

Volume of excess oxygen = (130 – 100) = 30 cm³

Volume of carbon dioxide formed = (3 × 20) = 60 cm³

Therefore the resulting gas mixture consists of 30 cm³ of O_2 and 60 cm³ of CO_2.

Questions

19 A piece of aluminium foil weighing 2.7 g was added to 100 cm³ of 2 mol l⁻¹ hydrochloric acid. The balanced equation for this reaction is

$$2Al + 6HCl \rightarrow 2AlCl_3 + 3H_2$$

a) Show by calculation which reactant is present in excess.

b) Calculate the volume of hydrogen produced. (Molar volume = 24 litres mol⁻¹)

20 In each of the following examples

i) write the balanced equation for complete combustion and show by calculation which of the reactants is present in excess

ii) calculate the volume and composition of the resulting gas mixture, assuming that all volumes are measured at the same room temperature and pressure.

a) A mixture of 10 cm³ methane, CH_4, and 25 cm³ oxygen was burned.

b) A mixture of 10 cm³ propane, C_3H_8, and 25 cm³ oxygen was burned.

Checklist for Revision

- I can calculate confidently the mass, concentration, volume and number of moles of a substance if given appropriate data.
- I can use balanced chemical equations to calculate the mass of reactants or products.
- I can use balanced chemical equations to work out which reactant is in excess.
- I can calculate the molar volume of a gas from experimental data.
- I can calculate the volume of a gas using balanced chemical equations and appropriate data.

Key Terms

The term below was introduced in this chapter.

Its definition is given in the chemical dictionary.

molar volume

Study Questions

Calculations from equations involving mass

1 Calculate the mass of water produced when 320 g of methane is burned according to the following equation:

$$CH_4 + 2O_2 \rightarrow CO_2 + 2H_2O$$

2 a) Write an equation to show the complete reaction of carbon with chlorine gas to form carbon tetrachloride.

   b) What mass of chlorine is needed to react completely with 0.6 g of carbon?

3 When sulfur reacts with oxygen gas, sulfur dioxide is produced.

   a) Write a balanced chemical equation for this reaction.

   b) Calculate the mass of sulfur dioxide produced when 12.8 g of sulfur is completely combusted.

4 When carbon is reacted with insufficient oxygen, carbon monoxide is produced.

   a) Write a balanced chemical equation for this reaction.

   b) Calculate the mass of carbon monoxide produced from 0.6 g of carbon.

5 Calculate the mass of magnesium oxide produced when 6 g of magnesium burns in oxygen.

6 Calculate the mass of water produced when 100 g of ethane is completely combusted.

7 4.46 g of lead(II) oxide is reacted with excess dilute nitric acid. Calculate the mass of lead(II) nitrate produced.

$$PbO + 2HNO_3 \rightarrow Pb(NO_3)_2 + H_2O$$

8 Calculate the mass of iron(III) oxide which, on complete reduction by carbon monoxide, will produce 558 tonnes of iron.

$$Fe_2O_3 + 3CO \rightarrow 2Fe + 3CO_2$$

Calculations from equations involving mass, concentrations and volume

You will need to write balanced chemical equations for questions 9–11.

9 40 cm³ of H_2SO_4(aq) is neutralised by 60 cm³ of 0.2 mol l⁻¹ NaOH(aq). Calculate the concentration of the H_2SO_4(aq).

10 50 cm³ of nitric acid is neutralised by 25 cm³ of 6 mol l⁻¹ sodium hydroxide. Calculate the concentration of the nitric acid.

11 Calculate the mass of calcium sulfate formed from reacting excess calcium oxide with 100 cm³ of 3 mol l⁻¹ sulfuric acid.

Calculations from equations involving excess reagent

12 $20 \, cm^3$ of $0.2 \, mol \, l^{-1}$ lead(II) nitrate solution and $10 \, cm^3$ of $0.6 \, mol \, l^{-1}$ potassium iodide solution were mixed together.

$$Pb(NO_3)_2(aq) + 2KI(aq) \rightarrow PbI_2(s) + 2KNO_3(aq)$$

a) Show by calculation which reactant was in excess.

b) Calculate the mass of precipitate formed.

13 $$Mg + H_2SO_4 \rightarrow MgSO_4 + H_2$$

A student added $8 \, g$ of magnesium to $200 \, cm^3$ of $1.0 \, mol \, l^{-1}$ sulfuric acid.

Which statement is true for this experiment?

A Excess acid has been used.

B $0.4 \, mol$ of magnesium sulfate is produced.

C All of the magnesium reacts.

D $0.4 \, g$ of hydrogen gas is released.

14 For each of the following examples of neutralisation

i) show by calculation which reactant is present in excess

ii) calculate the mass of salt produced.

a) $3.0 \, g$ lead(II) carbonate was added to $40 \, cm^3$ of $0.5 \, mol \, l^{-1}$ nitric acid.

$$PbCO_3 + 2HNO_3 \rightarrow Pb(NO_3)_2 + CO_2 + H_2O$$

b) $8.1 \, g$ of aluminium was added to $250 \, cm^3$ of $.4 \, mol \, l^{-1}$ hydrochloric acid.

$$2Al + 6HCl \rightarrow 2AlCl_3 + 3H_2$$

Calculations involving gas volumes

15 If the molar volume is 24.0 litres at room temperature and pressure, which of the following gases has a volume of 6.0 litres under these conditions?

A $4 \, g$ of oxygen

B $4 \, g$ of methane

C $4 \, g$ of helium

D $4 \, g$ of ammonia

16 $$C_2H_4(g) + 3O_2(g) \rightarrow 2CO_2(g) + 2H_2O(l)$$

When a mixture of $10 \, cm^3$ of ethene and $50 \, cm^3$ of oxygen was sparked, what was the final volume of gases? All volumes were measured at room temperature and pressure.

A $20 \, cm^3$ B $40 \, cm^3$ C $60 \, cm^3$ D $80 \, cm^3$

17 Mercury(II) nitrate decomposes when heated according to the following equation.

$$Hg(NO_3)_2(s) \rightarrow Hg(l) + 2NO_2(g) + O_2(g)$$

If the molar volume is 24.0 litres at room temperature and pressure, the total number of litres of gas produced when $0.1 \, mol$ of mercury(II) nitrate is completely decomposed by heat is

A 3.6   B 4.8   C 6.0   D 7.2

18 Silver(I) oxide decomposes when heated as shown in the equation below:

$$2Ag_2O \rightarrow 4Ag + O_2$$

Calculate the mass of silver(I) oxide that would release $120 \, cm^3$ of oxygen, measured at room temperature and pressure.

Molar volume $= 24$ litres mol^{-1}.

19 Hydrogen sulfide, H_2S, is a gas which can be made by adding an acid to a metal sulfide. The equation for the reaction between iron(II) sulfide and hydrochloric acid is shown below:

$$FeS + 2HCl \rightarrow FeCl_2 + H_2S$$

$100 \, cm^3$ of $5.0 \, mol \, l^{-1}$ hydrochloric acid was added to $30 \, g$ of iron(II) sulfide.

a) Show by calculation that excess metal sulfide was used.

b) Calculate the volume of gas produced given that molar volume $= 24$ litres mol^{-1}.

20* The following apparatus can be used to determine the relative formula masses of liquids which are easily evaporated.

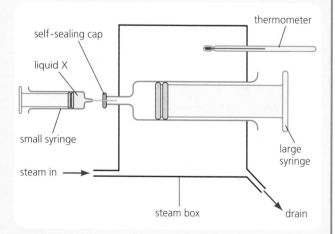

Figure 12.3

Some of liquid X is injected into the large syringe and it evaporates. The following results were obtained:

Mass of small syringe before injection $= 5.774\,g$

Mass of small syringe after injection $= 5.648\,g$

Large syringe reading before injection $= 5\,cm^3$

Large syringe reading after injection $= 89\,cm^3$

a) Calculate the relative formula mass of liquid X. (Take the molar volume of a gas to be $30.6\,litre\,mol^{-1}$.)

b) Suggest why this apparatus could not be used to determine the relative formula masses of liquids with boiling points above $100\,°C$.

21* A mixture of $80\,cm^3$ CO and $150\,cm^3$ O_2 was exploded.

a) Write a balanced equation for the reaction.

After cooling, the residual gas was shaken with sodium hydroxide solution.

b) Which gas would be absorbed by the sodium hydroxide?

c) What would be the reduction in volume of residual gas on shaking with the sodium hydroxide?

d) What volume of gas would remain? (Assume all volumes are measured at the same temperature and pressure.)

22* a) Write a balanced equation for the complete combustion of ethyne (C_2H_2).

b) If $50\,cm^3$ of ethyne is burned completely in $220\,cm^3$ of oxygen, what will be the volume and composition of the resulting gas mixture? (All volumes are measured under the same conditions of temperature and pressure.)

13   Percentage yield and atom economy

Percentage yield

Chemists carry out chemical reactions to make new products. The ideal reaction for a chemist is one where all the reactants are converted into the desired product. In reality, this does not always occur. One method of assessing a reaction is to calculate the percentage yield. The following examples will explain how this works.

Consider a simple reaction such as methane reacting with oxygen:

$$CH_4 + 2O_2 \rightarrow CO_2 + 2H_2O$$

If 16 g of methane was reacted with oxygen, we would expect 44 g of carbon dioxide to form.

(1 mole of methane, gfm = 16 g → 1 mole of carbon dioxide, gfm = 44 g)

This quantity of product, 44 g, is called the **theoretical yield**.

The **actual yield** is the quantity obtained when the experiment is carried out. Once the actual yield is known, the percentage yield can be calculated.

$$\text{percentage yield} = \frac{\text{actual yield}}{\text{theoretical yield}} \times 100$$

For example, if 16 g of methane produced 22 g of carbon dioxide, the percentage yield would be:

$$\frac{22}{44} \times 100 = 50\%$$

In other words, only 50% of the expected quantity of carbon dioxide has been produced.

Why is the yield not 100%?

There are several reasons:

1   The reaction may not go to completion. In other words, some of the reactants remain unreacted and are not converted into products. This is true of making an ester where the reaction is reversible. The technique for making an ester in the lab requires the ester to be separated from unreacted alcohol and carboxylic acid as it is known that the reaction is unlikely to have gone to completion.

2   Competing reactions (also known as side reactions) may be occurring. In the case of methane reacting with oxygen, a competing reaction would be incomplete combustion to produce carbon monoxide instead of carbon dioxide. The more incomplete the combustion, the more carbon monoxide and hence the lower the yield of carbon dioxide.

3   The final product may have to be purified from other products or reactants. Purification steps can be difficult and can lead to loss of product.

4   Human error – a clumsy chemist might lose some of the product!

In industrial processes a high percentage yield as well as high purity of product is often desirable. Where this is not possible or economically feasible, unconverted reactants are frequently recycled for further reaction, for example in the making of ammonia by the Haber Process and the making of ethanol by hydration of ethene. If the percentage yield is low because the reactants form other products, steps must be taken to minimise this. This may involve altering the reaction conditions (temperature, pressure, use of a catalyst etc.) or trying a different chemical reaction.

Driving a reaction forward by increasing the quantity of reactants is commonly carried out. When taking this approach, it is usually the least expensive reactant that will be selected to be in excess.

Worked Example 1

A sample of methyl ethanoate weighing 6.9 g was obtained from a reaction mixture containing 9.0 g of ethanoic acid, excess methanol and a small volume of concentrated sulfuric acid. Calculate the percentage yield of ester using the following equation.

$$CH_3OH + HOOCCH_3 \rightleftharpoons CH_3OOCCH_3 + H_2O$$

$$\text{1 mol} \qquad\qquad \text{1 mol}$$
$$\text{60 g} \qquad\qquad \text{74 g}$$

In theory, 60 g of ethanoic acid should yield 74 g of methyl ethanoate.

Hence, 9.0 g of ethanoic acid should yield

$9.0 \times \dfrac{74}{60} = 11.1$ g of methyl ethanoate.

In other words, the theoretical yield is 11.1 g, while the actual yield is 6.9 g.

$\% \text{ yield} = \dfrac{6.9}{11.1} \times 100$

$\qquad\quad = 62.2\%$

Questions

1   Excess ethyne was reacted with 0.1 mol of hydrogen chloride and 4.1 g of the product, 1,1-dichloroethane, were obtained. Calculate the percentage yield using the equation:

$$C_2H_2 + 2HCl \rightarrow C_2H_4Cl_2$$

2   A student hydrolyses 7.5 g of ethyl benzoate and obtains a 71% yield of benzoic acid. Calculate the actual yield of benzoic acid given that, theoretically, one mole of the ester ($C_6H_5COOC_2H_5$) produces one mole of the acid (C_6H_5COOH).

Using the percentage yield

The percentage yield allows chemists to examine the efficiency of a chemical reaction and to calculate how much money will have to be spent on reactants to produce a certain mass of product. For example, the ester propyl ethanoate is widely used as an industrial solvent (for example, for dissolving ink for use in printing). The Dow Chemical Company manufactures this ester by the acid-catalysed reaction of propan-1-ol with ethanoic acid:

$$C_3H_7OH + CH_3COOH \rightleftharpoons C_3H_7OOCCH_3 + H_2O$$

The cost of reactants will vary with market conditions but at the time of writing, the typical cost for 2.5 kg of propan-1-ol was £73 and the cost for 2.5 kg of ethanoic acid was £34.

Worked Example 2 demonstrates how the percentage yield and cost of reactants can be used to find out how much it will cost to produce a certain quantity of product.

Worked Example 2

a) Calculate the mass of reactants required to make 1 kg of the ester propyl ethanoate assuming a yield of 65%.

Moles of ester required $= \dfrac{\text{mass}}{\text{gfm}} = \dfrac{1000}{102} = 9.8$ mol

Since 1 mol of ester is formed from 1 mol of each reactant, 9.8 mol of each reactant would be required. However, this assumes a 100% yield. If the yield is only 65% then the number of moles of each reactant required will be greater than 9.8 mol.

Moles required $= \dfrac{9.8}{0.65} = 15.083$ mol

Mass of propan-1-ol = moles × gfm = 15.08 × 60
$\qquad\qquad\qquad\qquad\qquad\qquad = 904.98$ g

Mass of ethanoic acid = moles × gfm = 15.08 × 60
$\qquad\qquad\qquad\qquad\qquad\qquad\quad = 904.98$ g

b) Calculate the cost of propan-1-ol and ethanoic acid required.

2500 g propan-1-ol → £73

1 g → £0.0292

904.98 g → £26.41

2500 g ethanoic acid → £34

1 g → £0.0136

904.98 g → £12.30

Thus, £38.71 would have to be spent on the two reactants in order to make 1 kg of the product ester. Using this information, along with the energy costs for the reaction, the costs of catalysts, employee time, costs for reactants used during the purification of the product, packaging costs, plants costs, marketing costs etc., a price for the product can be set. A knowledge of the costs involved will also influence how the reaction is carried out. In this case, it would make sense to use an excess of ethanoic acid to drive this reaction forward as it is much cheaper to use ethanoic acid than propan-1-ol.

Atom economy

The percentage yield gives us information about how successful the reaction is at converting reactants into products, but it does not give us information on how many by-products are formed. A reaction which produces lots of products can be problematic and wasteful, depending on the value of the other products. By-products can also be costly if they have properties which make them difficult to handle, for example if they are toxic, corrosive, flammable etc. A reaction where most of the reactant atoms end up in the product is highly desirable. Applying the concept of **atom economy** allows chemists to examine the proportion of reactants converted into the desired product. It is calculated using the equation:

$$\text{atom economy} = \frac{\text{mass of desired product(s)}}{\text{total mass of reactants}} \times 100$$

Worked Example 3

Hydrogen gas can be obtained by reacting methane gas with steam.

$$CH_4 + H_2O \rightarrow CO + 3H_2$$

Calculate the atom economy for this reaction where hydrogen is the desired product.

Mass of desired product (from the equation)
$= 3 \times \text{gfm } H_2$
$= 3 \times 2$
$= 6 \text{ g}$

Total mass of reactants $= \text{gfm } CH_4 + \text{gfm } H_2O$
$= 16 + 18$
$= 34 \text{ g}$

Atom economy $= \frac{6}{34} \times 100$
$= 17.65\%$

Worked Example 4

Calculate the atom economy for the production of propyl ethanoate, assuming that all reactants are converted into products, according to the following equation.

$$C_3H_7OH + CH_3COOH \rightarrow C_3H_7OOCCH_3 + H_2O$$

Mass of desired product (from the equation) $= 102 \text{ g}$

Total mass of reactants $= 120 \text{ g}$

Atom economy $= \frac{102}{120} \times 100$
$= 85\%$

This is a high atom economy which suggests that making the ester by this method does not create much waste. An examination of the equation shows that the other product is water which is easy to deal with as it is not toxic, flammable or highly corrosive.

Worked Example 5

Ethylene oxide is widely used in the production of medicines, explosives, cosmetics and numerous other chemicals. It has the structure shown and can be made by a multi-step chemical reaction known as the chlorohydrin process.

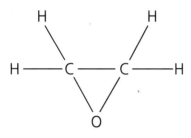

Figure 13.1 The structure of ethylene oxide (C_2H_4O)

The overall equation for the chlorohydrin process is:

$$C_2H_4 + Cl_2 + Ca(OH)_2 \rightarrow C_2H_4O + CaCl_2 + H_2O$$

This reaction has a very low atom economy and is therefore very wasteful.

A more convenient and less wasteful method is the direct oxidation of ethene using a silver catalyst:

$$C_2H_4 + \tfrac{1}{2}O_2 \rightarrow C_2H_4O$$

Show that the atom economy for the production of ethylene oxide, C_2H_4O, is 25% for the chlorohydrin process and 100% for the direct oxidation as presented in these equations.

Direct oxidation

Mass of desired product (from the equation) = 44

Total mass of reactants = $28 + \frac{1}{2} \times 32 = 44$

Atom economy $= \dfrac{44}{44} \times 100$

$\qquad\qquad = 100\%$

Chlorohydrin process

Mass of reactants = $C_2H_4 + Cl_2 + Ca(OH)_2 = 173$

Mass of ethylene oxide = 44

Atom economy $= \dfrac{44}{173} \times 100$

$\qquad\qquad = 25\%$

Note

The chlorohydrin process has a low atom economy as several by-products are produced such as $CaCl_2$.

Questions

3 Calculate the atom economy for the production of iron in the following reaction.

$$Fe_2O_3 + 3CO \rightarrow 2Fe + 3CO_2$$

4 What is the atom economy of the product of a reaction when there are no by-products?

Key Terms

The words and phrases below were introduced in this chapter.

Their definitions are given in the chemical dictionary.

   atom economy

   percentage yield

Checklist for Revision

- I can calculate the percentage yield for a reaction.

- I can use the percentage yield to comment on the quantity of reactants required to produce a certain mass of products.

- I can calculate the atom economy for a reaction.

- I can use the percentage yield and atom economy to comment on the choice of route for making a chemical.

Study Questions

1   Dichloroethane can be formed by the reaction of ethene gas with chlorine gas:

$$C_2H_4 + Cl_2 \rightarrow C_2H_4Cl_2$$

In a reaction, 700 g of ethene reacted with 2 kg of chlorine to produce 2.2 kg of dichloroethane.

a) Calculate the percentage yield of dichloroethane.

b) Calculate the atom economy for this reaction.

2   Phenylethanol has a smooth rose-like odour and is used in floral perfumes together with its propanoate ester.

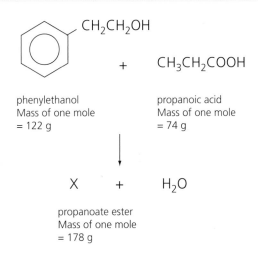

phenylethanol
Mass of one mole
= 122 g

propanoic acid
Mass of one mole
= 74 g

X   + H_2O

propanoate ester
Mass of one mole
= 178 g

Figure 13.2

a) Draw a structural formula for ester X.

b) Calculate the atom economy for the formation of ester X.

c) 3.05 tonnes of phenylethanol was refluxed with 1.48 tonnes of propanoic acid. Show, by calculation, that the phenylethanol is in excess. (1 tonne = 1000 kg)

d) The formation of the propanoate ester gives a 70% yield after refluxing. Calculate the mass of ester obtained. (Show your working clearly.)

3   In theory, one mole of benzene, C_6H_6, can be converted to one mole of methylbenzene, $C_6H_5CH_3$, which in turn can yield one mole of benzoic acid, C_6H_5COOH. In an experiment, 0.1 mole of benzene produced 4.6 g of methylbenzene which was then converted to benzoic acid, the percentage yield for this reaction being 70%. Calculate:

a) the percentage yield for the first reaction

b) the mass of benzoic acid finally obtained

c) the overall percentage yield of benzoic acid based on the original quantity of benzene.

4   Calcium oxide can be formed by

a) heating calcium with oxygen: $Ca + \frac{1}{2}O_2 \rightarrow CaO$

b) heating calcium carbonate: $CaCO_3 \rightarrow CaO + CO_2$

Calculate the atom economy for the production of calcium oxide in each reaction.

5   In the Haber Process nitrogen is reacted with hydrogen to produce ammonia gas.

$$N_2 + 3H_2 \rightarrow 2NH_3$$

Calculate the mass of ammonia obtained by reacting 2 kg of nitrogen with excess hydrogen, assuming a 30% yield of ammonia.

6   Ethanol can be formed by

a) fermentation of glucose:

$$C_6H_{12}O_6 \rightarrow 2C_2H_5OH + 2CO_2$$

b) hydration of ethene: $C_2H_4 + H_2O \rightarrow C_2H_5OH$

Calculate the atom economy for the production of ethanol in each reaction.

7* Since the 1990s, ibuprofen has been synthesised by a three-step process. The equation below shows the final step of the synthesis.

What is the atom economy of this step?

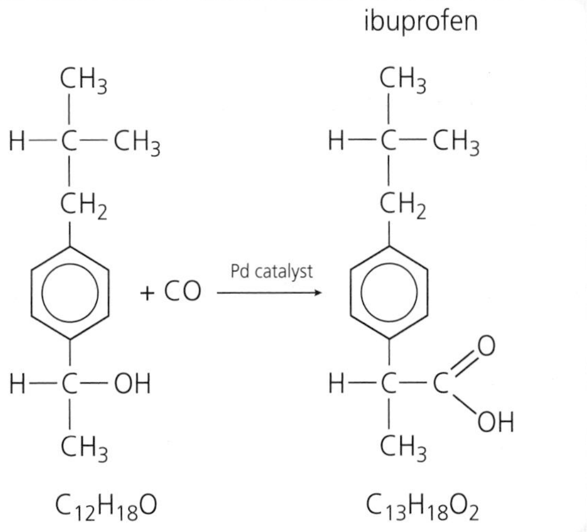

ibuprofen

H—C—CH₃ structure with Pd catalyst + CO

$C_{12}H_{18}O$ $C_{13}H_{18}O_2$

Figure 13.3

14 Equilibria

Many chemical reactions are reversible: products form but they also break back down into reactants. This can be a real challenge for chemists if the goal is to make as much product as possible. An understanding of reversible reactions is crucial to help chemists alter the reaction conditions so that the reaction always favours going forward to make products. Failure to consider this could mean that costly reactants do not get fully converted into products.

Reversible reactions and dynamic equilibrium

In order to understand reversible reactions, it is worth considering an analogy. Picture a bucket with a hole in the bottom that is half filled with water. The bucket is constantly being filled with water and emptying through the hole at the same time. If the level of water in the bucket remains the same, this must mean that the rate of water going into the bucket is the same as the rate of water leaving the bucket. If we focus on the water level in the bucket, it would be tempting to conclude that nothing much was happening as the level remains the same. This is very similar to reversible chemical reactions, which often appear to have 'stopped' as the concentrations of reactants and products remain constant. This is not true! If, in a reversible reaction, the concentration of reactants and products remain constant, then it must mean that the rate of the forward reaction (making products) is equal to the rate of the reverse reaction (making reactants). We say that reversible reactions attain a state of **equilibrium when the rate of the forward reaction is equal to the rate of the reverse reaction.**

Consider a saturated solution containing excess of the undissolved solute, in this case sodium chloride.

$$NaCl(s) \rightleftharpoons Na^+(aq) + Cl^-(aq)$$

In this situation the undissolved sodium chloride is in equilibrium with the dissociated ions. There is constant interchange of ions between the solid and the solution, but the amount of undissolved sodium chloride remains the same. The rate at which ions are dissolving is equal to the rate at which other ions are precipitated.

In bromine water, familiar from tests for unsaturation, there is the following equilibrium:

$$Br_2(l) + H_2O(l) \rightleftharpoons Br^-(aq) + BrO^-(aq) + 2H^+(aq)$$

In each of the above, when the solution is being made up, initially only the forward reactions occur.

$$NaCl(s) \rightarrow Na^+(aq) + Cl^-(aq)$$

$$Br_2(l) + H_2O(l) \rightarrow Br^-(aq) + BrO^-(aq) + 2H^+(aq)$$

The rates of these forward reactions will be related to the high initial concentrations of the solutes. As the reactions proceed, products will be formed. These products form the reactants for the reverse reactions. The reverse reactions can now start. These reactions are initially slow to proceed as their reactants are still only in low concentration:

$$Na^+(aq) + Cl^-(aq) \rightarrow NaCl(s)$$

$$Br^-(aq) + BrO^-(aq) + 2H^+(aq) \rightarrow Br_2(l) + H_2O(l)$$

The rates of the forward reactions will decrease as their reactants are consumed, and the rates of the reverse reactions will increase as their reactants increase in concentration.

Eventually the rates of the forward and reverse reactions will be the same and equilibrium is attained.

It is important to realise, however, that the reaction does not stop when equilibrium is attained. When a saturated solution of a salt such as NaCl is formed, an equilibrium is set up in which as many ions are passing into solution as are being redeposited on the solid crystals. In other words, the rate of solution equals the rate of precipitation. At equilibrium these processes do not cease. For this reason, chemical equilibrium is described as being dynamic.

It is also important to note that when equilibrium is reached, this does not imply that the equilibrium mixture consists of 50% reactants and 50% products. This will only very rarely be the case. The actual position of equilibrium can be influenced by a number of factors as we shall see later in this chapter.

Under similar conditions, the same equilibrium can be arrived at from two different starting points. This can be shown using the fact that iodine is soluble in trichloroethane, $C_2H_3Cl_3$, and also in aqueous potassium iodide solution (see Figure 14.1). Tubes X and Z represent the two starting positions. In X, iodine is dissolved in $C_2H_3Cl_3$ only and in Z it is dissolved in KI solution only. Tube Y represents the equilibrium mixture which is obtained. Equilibrium can be attained quickly by shaking the tubes or slowly by allowing them to stand.

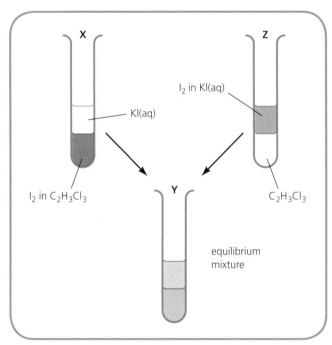

Figure 14.1 Equilibrium can be reached from either direction.

Many reactions appear to be irreversible, such as the neutralisation of a strong acid and strong base or precipitation such as:

$$Ag^+(aq) + Cl^-(aq) \rightarrow AgCl(s)$$

However, all reactions are, in fact, reversible to at least some extent. We can say that in such reactions, the equilibrium lies so far in one direction that for practical purposes they can be considered as having gone to completion.

A final point worth noting is that a state of dynamic equilibrium will only be reached in a **closed system**.

This means that the reaction must not be interfered with by any outside influence or reaction. For example, if bromine solution is left in an open test tube, a state of dynamic equilibrium will never be reached as some of the bromine will vapourise and escape from the tube. Instead, the bromine water should be placed in a sealed container so that equilibrium can be established.

Changing the position of equilibrium

We shall now consider the factors that can alter the position of equilibrium in a reversible reaction. Equilibrium is reached when the opposing reactions occur at an equal rate. Hence, we should expect that any condition which changes the rate of one reaction more than the other should change the position of equilibrium and thus the relative proportions of reactants and products in the mixture.

This section deals with the influence of changing the concentration, the pressure and the temperature on the equilibrium position. The effect of these changes can be summarised by **Le Chatelier's Principle**, which states that:

> 'If a system at equilibrium is subjected to any change, the system readjusts itself to counteract the applied change.'

Note that this statement only refers to reversible reactions that have reached equilibrium.

Changing the concentration

Let us consider the following reaction at equilibrium:

$$A + B \rightleftharpoons C + D$$

An increase in the concentration of A (or B) will speed up the forward reaction, thus increasing the concentration of C and D until a new equilibrium is obtained. A similar effect can be achieved by reducing the concentration of C (or D). These results agree with Le Chatelier's Principle, since the equilibrium has moved to the right to counteract the applied change. The following reactions can be used to illustrate these points.

Bromine water

Bromine dissolves in water, forming a red-brown solution that contains a mixture of molecules and ions:

$$Br_2(l) + H_2O(l) \rightleftharpoons Br^-(aq) + BrO^-(aq) + 2H^+(aq)$$

The equilibrium can be adjusted as shown in Figure 14.2. The addition of OH^- ions removes H^+ ions to form water, and the equilibrium shifts to the right. Adding H^+ ions moves the equilibrium back to the left.

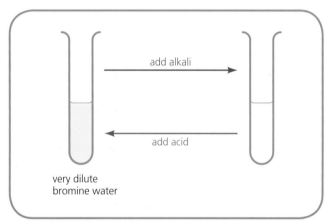

Figure 14.2 Changing the position of an equilibrium using bromine water

Iron(III) ions + thiocyanate ions (CNS⁻)

When separate solutions containing iron(III) ions and thiocyanate ions are mixed, a deep blood-red solution is formed due to the presence of complex ions such as $[Fe(CNS)]^{2+}$. This reaction is reversible:

$$Fe^{3+}(aq) + CNS^-(aq) \rightleftharpoons [Fe(CNS)]^{2+}(aq)$$

pale yellow   colourless   red

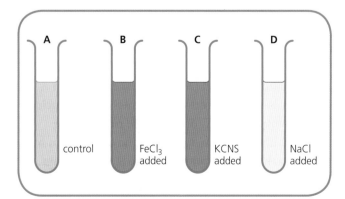

Figure 14.3 Changing the position of an equilibrium using iron(III) and thiocyanate ions

The intensity of the colour may be taken as an indication of the position of equilibrium. Some of the blood-red solution is diluted until an orange colour is obtained, and this solution is poured into four test tubes until each is half full. Tube A is kept for reference; crystals of iron(III) chloride, potassium thiocyanate and sodium chloride are added to tubes B, C and D, respectively. The results are shown in Figure 14.3.

An increase in the concentration of Fe^{3+} ions or CNS^- ions shifts the equilibrium to the right and results in the formation of more of the complex ions. The addition of NaCl removes Fe^{3+} ions due to complex formation with Cl^- ions and the equilibrium shifts to the left to compensate.

Questions

1 When chlorine is dissolved in water the following equilibrium is set up:

$$Cl_2 + H_2O \rightleftharpoons 2H^+ + ClO^- + Cl^-$$

The hypochlorite ion, ClO^-, is responsible for the bleaching action of the solution. What effect would each of the following have on the bleaching action?

a) Adding dilute nitric acid.

b) Adding sodium chloride crystals.

c) Adding potassium hydroxide solution.

(Tip: Consider the effect of the ions in each solution.)

Changing the temperature

In a reversible reaction, if the forward reaction is exothermic, then the reverse reaction must, of course, be endothermic. If a system at equilibrium is subjected to a change in temperature, the equilibrium position will adjust itself to counteract the applied change, according to Le Chatelier's Principle. Thus, a rise in temperature will favour the reaction which absorbs heat, in other words, the endothermic process, and a fall in temperature will favour the exothermic reaction. This can be seen in the following example.

Nitrogen dioxide

Brown fumes of nitrogen dioxide (NO_2) are formed when most metal nitrates are decomposed thermally or when copper is added to concentrated nitric acid. The gas produced is, in fact, an equilibrium mixture of nitrogen dioxide (a dark brown gas) and dinitrogen tetroxide, N_2O_4 (a colourless gas). This is represented in the following equation. The forward reaction is endothermic.

$$N_2O_4(g) \rightleftharpoons 2NO_2(g)$$

colourless   dark brown

Figure 14.4 illustrates the results obtained on subjecting samples of this gas mixture to different temperature conditions. An increase in temperature favours the endothermic reaction and so the proportion of NO_2 increases and the gas mixture becomes darker in colour. A drop in temperature favours the exothermic reaction and, hence, the gas mixture lightens in colour.

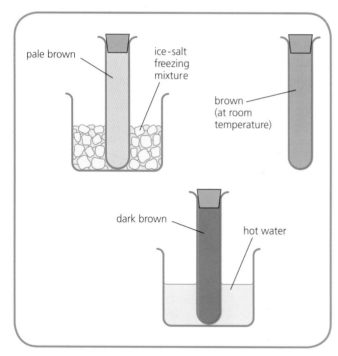

Figure 14.4 Equilibrium and temperature

Questions

2   The Contact Process to make sulfuric acid involves the following reaction:

$$2SO_2(g) + O_2(g) \rightleftharpoons 2SO_3(g) \qquad \Delta H = -197\,kJ$$

What would be the effect of raising the reaction temperature on

a) rate of reaction

b) yield of SO_3?

Changing the pressure

The pressure exerted by a gas is caused by the freely moving molecules bombarding the walls of the containing vessel. An increase in the number of molecules will be accompanied by an increase in pressure, the size of the container being kept constant. The effect of changes in pressure on a system involving gases is equivalent to the effect of changes in concentration on a system in solution.

The N_2O_4–NO_2 system is a suitable example to study in this connection.

$$N_2O_4(g) \rightleftharpoons 2NO_2(g)$$

1 mole   2 moles

An increase in pressure will cause the system to readjust to counteract this effect, in other words it will reduce the pressure within the system. Thus, the equilibrium will adjust to the left, forming more N_2O_4 molecules and reducing the number of molecules per unit volume. A suitable apparatus for the study of this effect is shown in Figure 14.5. The results are shown in Table 14.1.

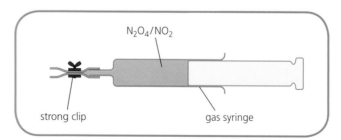

Figure 14.5 Equilibrium and pressure

Applied pressure change	Initial colour change	Final colour change
Increase (plunger in)	Darkens due to compression	Lightens as equilibrium shifts to the left
Decrease (plunger out)	Lightens due to expansion	Darkens as equilibrium shifts to the right

Table 14.1
(Authors' note: Teachers may wish to consult *School Science Review* (1978), 211, **60**:309 for an alternative explanation of the changes observed in the NO_2–N_2O_4 system.)

Generally in a reversible reaction involving a gas or gases at equilibrium, an increase in pressure will cause the equilibrium to shift in the direction which results in a decrease in the number of gaseous molecules. In a system in which there is no overall change in the total number of gaseous molecules, changes in pressure will have no effect on the equilibrium position, for example

$$CO(g) + H_2O(g) \rightleftharpoons CO_2(g) + H_2(g)$$

1 mole   1 mole   1 mole   1 mole

> **Questions**
>
> 3 Reaction 1: $H_2(g) + I_2(g) \rightleftharpoons 2HI(g)$
>
> Reaction 2: $2CO(g) + O_2(g) \rightleftharpoons 2CO_2(g)$
>
> Reaction 3: $CH_3OH(g) \rightleftharpoons CO(g) + 2H_2(g)$
>
> In which of the above reactions will an increase of pressure
> a) shift the position of equilibrium to the right?
> b) have no effect on the equilibrium position?

Catalysts and equilibrium

A catalyst speeds up a reaction by lowering the activation energy (see Chapter 1). However, in a reversible reaction it reduces the activation energy for both the forward and reverse reactions by the same amount, as shown in Figure 14.6.

Thus, a catalyst speeds up both the reactions to the same extent and does not alter the position of equilibrium. The use of a catalyst does not result in an increased yield of product. The advantage of using a catalyst in a reversible reaction is that it enables equilibrium to be reached more rapidly.

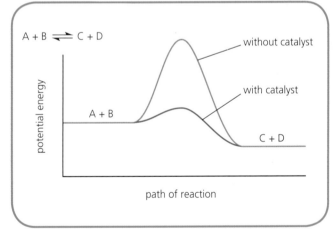

Figure 14.6 Potential energy for a catalysed and uncatalysed reaction

Summary

Change applied	Effect on equilibrium position
Concentration Addition of reactant or removal of product Addition of product or removal of reactant	Equilibrium shifts to the right Equilibrium shifts to the left
Temperature Increase Decrease	Shifts in direction of endothermic reaction Shifts in direction of exothermic reaction
Pressure Increase Decrease	Shifts in direction which reduces the number of molecules in gas phase Shifts in direction which increases the number of molecules in gas phase
Catalyst	No effect on equilibrium position; equilibrium more rapidly attained

Table 14.2

Questions

4   Propyl ethanoate is made by the reaction of ethanoic acid with propanol.

$$CH_3COOH + C_3H_7OH \rightleftharpoons CH_3COOC_3H_7 + H_2O$$

The reaction is catalysed by H^+ ions. If more H^+ ions were added to the reaction mixture, what effect would this have on

a) the speed of reaching equilibrium

b) the yield of ester?

5   Suggest why the laboratory preparation of esters makes use of concentrated sulfuric acid.

An industrial example: equilibrium and the Haber Process

In the Haber Process to synthesise ammonia, if a closed reaction vessel is used, an equilibrium is set up:

$$N_2(g) + 3H_2(g) \rightleftharpoons 2NH_3(g)$$

When the rates of the forward and reverse reactions are equal, equilibrium is reached. The same equilibrium is eventually reached whether starting from the nitrogen and hydrogen ('reactant') side or from the ammonia ('product') side. This is a general rule with any reversible reaction.

At equilibrium, the concentrations of reactants and products remain constant, but not necessarily equal.

The relative concentrations of reactants and products can be affected by altering the conditions under which the reaction is taking place. This is illustrated in Table 14.3 using the reaction:

$$N_2(g) + 3H_2(g) \rightleftharpoons 2NH_3(g) \ \Delta H = -92\,kJ$$

In the industrial manufacture of ammonia, the ammonia formed is continuously removed and the reactants are continuously fed into the reaction. This means that a true equilibrium, which requires a closed system, is not achieved.

New conditions	Equilibrium change	Explanation
Increase pressure	To right, [NH$_3$] increases	Forward direction involves a decrease in number of moles of gas (4 moles → 2 moles) and hence a decrease in volume. Decrease in volume is assisted by increase in pressure.
Decrease pressure	To left, [NH$_3$] decreases	Reverse direction involves an increase in number of moles of gas and hence in volume, assisted by reduced pressure.
Increase temperature	To left, [NH$_3$] decreases	Increasing temperature involves increasing energy of system. The reverse reaction is endothermic and will be assisted by providing energy.
Decrease temperature	To right, [NH$_3$] increases	Decreasing temperature removes energy from system, making reverse endothermic reaction less favourable, less NH$_3$ split up.
Catalyst	No change	Both forward and reverse reactions are accelerated. The equilibrium is reached more rapidly.

Table 14.3

([ ] is a recognised abbreviation for 'concentration of'. For example, [NH$_3$] means concentration of ammonia.)

In practice the operating conditions for most industrial processes involve compromises among yield, construction and maintenance costs, catalyst life and catalyst activity. The following illustrates some of these considerations for the Haber Process:

$$N_2(g) + 3H_2(g) \rightleftharpoons 2NH_3(g) \quad \Delta H = -92\,kJ$$

$$4\,vol \qquad\qquad 2\,vol$$

The conditions for maximum yield are low temperature and high pressure. Figure 14.7 shows the percentage of NH$_3$ in equilibrium when reacting nitrogen and hydrogen in a 1:3 mixture by volume at different temperature and pressures.

The lower the temperature is, the higher the percentage of NH$_3$, but the slower the reaction. The higher the pressure is, the higher the percentage of ammonia, but the greater the cost of equipment both in outlay and maintenance.

Commonly used operating conditions are: 380–450 °C; high pressure, up to 200 atmospheres; iron catalyst with potassium hydroxide promoter. About 15% ammonia is produced in each pass over the catalyst. The ammonia is condensed on cooling and unreacted nitrogen and hydrogen are topped up and recycled, resulting in an overall maximum yield of 98%.

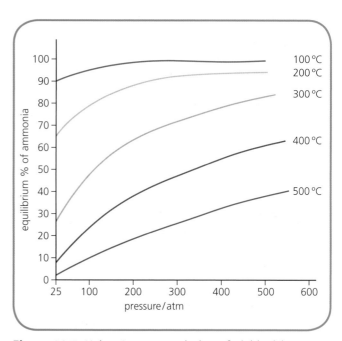

Figure 14.7 Haber Process: variation of yield with pressure and temperature

For Interest | Catalysts and industrial processes

Catalysts have revolutionised chemical reactions. In our attempt to conserve precious energy resources, catalysts are a tremendous help as they allow reactions to take place at much lower temperatures which means that less energy is used in the reaction. The Haber Process has been studied since its invention in an attempt to make the process even more economically and environmentally efficient. In early 2011, a team of German researchers discovered that they could achieve high yields of ammonia at atmospheric pressure and 50 °C. They used a catalyst based on ruthenium which proved to be very effective at breaking the H–H bond of the reactant hydrogen molecules. Their work demonstrates one of the ways scientists collaborate to devise intelligent solutions to real-world problems. Ammonia is one of the essential compounds of the chemical industry as it is used in the manufacture of so many products. Creating a catalyst that allows ammonia to be manufactured under these conditions will lead to a tremendous saving in energy and money.

Checklist for Revision

● I know what is meant by the term 'dynamic equilibrium'.

● I know what is meant by a 'closed system'.

● I understand why chemists want to alter the position of equilibrium.

● I understand and can predict the effect of changing the temperature, concentration, pressure and adding a catalyst on a system at equilibrium.

Key Terms

The words and phrases below were introduced in this chapter.

Their definitions are given in the chemical dictionary.

  closed system
  equilibrium

Study Questions

In questions 1–4 choose the correct word from the following list to complete the sentence.

> constant   decreases   endothermic   equal
> exothermic   left   increases   right

1 When a reversible reaction has reached equilibrium, the concentrations of reactants and products are

  _____.

2 Increasing the concentration of a product causes the equilibrium to move to the _____.

3 In the Haber Process, high pressure favours the production of ammonia since the number of moles of gas _____ going from reactants to product.

4 Raising the temperature shifts the equilibrium position in the direction of the _____ reaction.

5 $Cl_2(g) + H_2O(l) \rightleftharpoons Cl^-(aq) + ClO^-(aq) + 2H^+(aq)$

  Which of the following substances is least likely to alter the position of equilibrium when added to an aqueous solution of chlorine?

  A NaOH(aq)   **B** NaBr(s)   **C** HCl(aq)   **D** KCl(s)

6     $HCOOH + CH_3OH \rightleftharpoons HCOOCH_3 + H_2O$

  The use of a catalyst in the reaction shown above will

  A increase the equilibrium concentration of the ester

  B decrease the time taken to reach equilibrium

  C increase the activation energy

  D decrease the equilibrium concentration of methanol.

7 The following equation shows one of the reactions involved in obtaining the reactants for the Haber Process from natural gas and air.

$$CO(g) + H_2O(g) \rightleftharpoons CO_2(g) + H_2(g)$$

The forward reaction is exothermic. The equilibrium can be moved to the right by

A increasing the pressure

B decreasing the pressure

C increasing the temperature

D decreasing the temperature.

8 $SO_2(g) + \frac{1}{2}O_2(g) \rightleftharpoons SO_3(g)$ $\Delta H_{forward} = -94\,kJ\,mol^{-1}$

The ideal conditions for producing a high yield of sulfur trioxide are

A high pressure and low temperature

B low pressure and high temperature

C high pressure and high temperature

D low pressure and low temperature.

9* Ammonia is manufactured in industry by the reaction of nitrogen with hydrogen.

$$N_2(g) + 3H_2(g) \rightleftharpoons 2NH_3(g) \quad \Delta H_{forward} = -92\,kJ\,mol^{-1}$$

Typical conditions for an ammonia plant are:

Pressure	250 atmospheres
Temperature	380–450 °C
Catalyst	Iron containing promoters to stop catalyst poisoning
Conversion	15% by volume of ammonia

Table 14.4

a) Explain what would be expected to happen to the percentage conversion if the temperature of the ammonia plant was decreased.

b) High pressure favours conversion to ammonia. Suggest why pressures higher than 250 atmospheres are not used.

10* Synthesis gas, a mixture of hydrogen and carbon monoxide, is prepared as shown below. Nickel is known to catalyse the reaction.

$$CH_4(g) + H_2O(g) \rightleftharpoons 3H_2(g) + CO(g)$$

a) An increase in temperature increases the yield of synthesis gas. What information does this give about the enthalpy change in the forward reaction?

b) Explain how a change in pressure will affect the composition of the equilibrium mixture.

c) State how the rate of formation of synthesis gas will be affected by the use of the catalyst.

d) State how the composition of the equilibrium mixture will be affected by the use of the catalyst.

11 When bismuth(III) chloride is dissolved in water, an equilibrium is set up as shown in the following equation:

$$BiCl_3(aq) + H_2O(l) \rightleftharpoons BiOCl(s) + 2HCl(aq)$$

a) What effect, if any, will there be on the position of equilibrium on adding

i) potassium hydroxide

ii) nitric acid

iii) potassium nitrate?

b) Which of the reagents named in **a)**, if added in sufficient quantity, would dissolve the precipitate?

12* Ammonia is now one of the world's most important chemicals, about two million tonnes being produced each year in the UK alone. It is manufactured by the direct combination of nitrogen and hydrogen by the Haber Process.

$$N_2(g) + 3H_2(g) \rightleftharpoons 2NH_3(g)$$

The graph shows how the percentage of ammonia in the gas mixture at equilibrium varies with pressure at different temperatures.

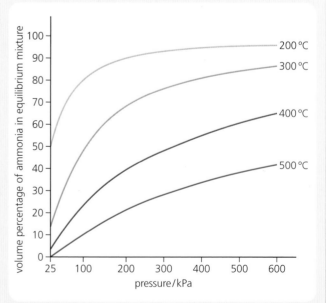

Figure 14.8

a) What does the term 'at equilibrium' mean?

b) Use the graph and the chemical equation to explain the conclusion that the reaction is exothermic.

c) i) Typical conditions for the Haber Process are approximately 400 °C and 200 kPa pressure.

Use the graph to estimate the percentage of ammonia which could be obtained if the mixture was left until equilibrium was reached at this temperature and pressure.

ii) In practice, the percentage of ammonia in the gas mixture never rises above 15%. Although the yield is low, the process is still profitable. Give one reason for this fact.

15 Chemical energy

The energy released or taken in by a chemical reaction is known as the enthalpy change. We have already met the concept of exothermic and endothermic reactions when we considered the profile of a chemical reaction. Both of these types of reaction can be put to practical use. For example, cold packs, such as the one shown in Figure 15.1, contain chemicals that react together endothermically.

Figure 15.1 An endothermic reaction

On a much larger scale, endo- and exothermic reactions can have significant cost implications. Endothermic reactions can be costly to industry as heat energy must be supplied to sustain the reaction. In an ideal situation, this energy would come from another step in the chemical process that was exothermic, thus saving money on energy. However, exothermic reactions can often be costly too. It is important for chemists to control exothermic reactions as they can lead to thermal explosions if they are left to produce a substantial amount of energy. Reactions which get too hot can also produce undesirable products as 'side reactions' take place. Thus money may have to be spent cooling an exothermic reaction to ensure that the process is safe and produces the desirable products. It is therefore important that chemists can predict whether a reaction is likely to be exothermic or endothermic. This can be done on a small scale in the lab by simply carrying out a reaction and noting whether the temperature increases or decreases. But chemical

reactions which make a product for profit will be done on a huge scale and it is therefore important that exact predictions can be made about the likely temperature increase or decrease. To do this, enthalpy calculations are carried out using our knowledge of the reactants and likely products. In this chapter we will examine how to calculate the enthalpy change for a chemical reaction from both data tables and from carrying out simple lab experiments.

Figure 15.2 Chemists monitor the temperature changes in lab chemical reactions so that they can predict the enthalpy change when the process is scaled up to a much bigger size.

Experimental measurement of enthalpy changes
Enthalpy of combustion

The enthalpy of combustion of a substance is the enthalpy change when one mole of the substance is burned completely in oxygen. Equations for the complete combustion of propane and methanol, for example, are given on the next page along with their enthalpies of combustion.

$$C_3H_8(g) + 5O_2(g) \rightarrow 3CO_2(g) + 4H_2O(l)$$
$$\Delta H = -2220\,kJ\,mol^{-1}$$

$$CH_3OH(l) + 1\tfrac{1}{2}O_2(g) \rightarrow CO_2(g) + 2H_2O(l)$$
$$\Delta H = -727\,kJ\,mol^{-1}$$

Note that

- there is a negative sign in the ΔH values since combustion is an exothermic reaction

- it is usual to write the equation showing one mole of the substance that is burning.

The equation for the combustion of methanol shows that 1.5 moles of oxygen are needed per mole of methanol. If the equation is doubled to remove half moles of oxygen, then the ΔH value is doubled. The units are then kJ, not $kJ\,mol^{-1}$, since the energy released relates to the complete combustion of 2 moles of methanol.

In order to calculate the enthalpy of combustion of a fuel:

1 the mass of the fuel burned must be known

2 the energy released for this mass of fuel must be known.

Both of these can be calculated experimentally as outlined below.

Method 1: Using a spirit burner

The enthalpy of combustion of a fuel can be determined by experiment using apparatus like that shown in Figure 15.3.

The burner containing the fuel is weighed before and after burning. This allows the mass of the fuel burned to be calculated (point 1). The fuel is allowed to burn until the temperature of the water in the copper can has been raised by, say, 10 °C before extinguishing the flame. The temperature rise of the water can be used to calculate the energy released by the fuel (point 2) using what is known as the specific heat capacity of water, which is given the symbol c and has a value of $4.18\,kJ\,kg^{-1}\,°C^{-1}$.

> In other words, to raise the temperature of 1 kg of water by 1 °C requires 4.18 kJ.

It should make sense that to raise the temperature of an even larger mass of water would require much more energy (think about using a Bunsen to boil a small volume of water versus a large volume of water). For example, to raise the temperature of 10 kg of water by 1 °C would require ten times as much energy, in other words 41.8 kJ.

Similarly, to raise the temperature of 1 kg of water by a much greater amount would require more energy. For example, to raise the temperature of 1 kg of water by 2 °C would require $2 \times 4.18 = 8.36\,kJ$.

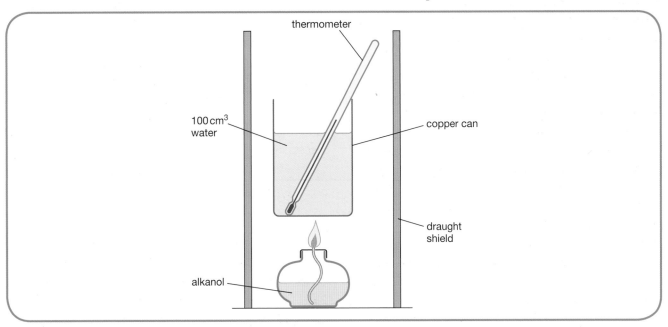

Figure 15.3 Simple lab apparatus used to measure the enthalpy of combustion of a fuel

To find out the energy released by the fuel, therefore, an equation that links the specific heat capacity of water with the mass of water heated and the temperature change can be used:

$$E_h = cm\Delta T$$

where

c is the specific heat capacity of water, $4.18\,kJ\,kg^{-1}\,°C^{-1}$
m is the mass of water heated, in kg
ΔT is the change in temperature of the water.

This is a measure of the heat released by the burning fuel and from this the enthalpy of combustion of the fuel can be calculated. The method of calculation is shown in Worked Example 1 using specimen data for the burning of methanol, which gives a result close to the accepted figure given in your data booklet.

The values for the enthalpy of combustion by experimental methods such as the one described are always much lower than the data booklet values. There are several reasons for this, but the main ones are listed:

1   Some of the heat produced by burning the fuel is 'lost' as it is absorbed by the beaker, thermometer and the air so it does not heat the water.

2   The definition of the enthalpy of combustion assumes that the substance has burned completely. The lab method will not combust the fuel completely. There will be some incomplete combustion which can usually be seen by a smoky flame and black soot (carbon) forming on the bottom of the copper beaker.

A much improved method for measuring the enthalpy of combustion is to use a calorimeter such as the one shown in Figure 15.4.

Worked Example 1

To calculate the enthalpy of combustion of methanol, CH_3OH

Data from the experiment are given in Table 15.1.

Mass of burner + methanol before burning	53.65 g
Mass of burner + methanol after burning	53.46 g
Mass of water heated, m	100 g = 0.1 kg
Temperature of water before heating	20 °C
Highest temperature of the water, after heating	30 °C

Table 15.1

Calculation:

Heat energy released, $E_h = cm\Delta T$
$\qquad\qquad\qquad\quad = 4.18 \times 0.1 \times 10$
$\qquad\qquad\qquad\quad = 4.18\,kJ$

Gram formula mass of methanol, $CH_3OH = 32\,g$

Mass of methanol burned = 0.19 g

$0.19\,g \rightarrow 4.18\,kJ$

$1\,g \rightarrow \dfrac{4.18}{0.19} = 22\,kJ$

$32\,g \rightarrow 32 \times 22 = 704\,kJ$

Enthalpy of combustion of methanol by experiment, $\Delta H = -704\,kJ\,mol^{-1}$

Note that since the reaction is exothermic, it is necessary to insert a negative sign in the final result.

Method 2: Using a calorimeter

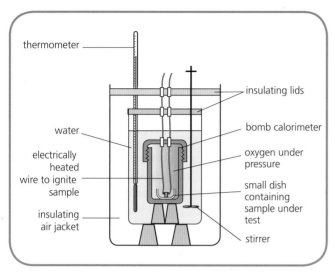

Figure 15.4 Calorimeter

The calorimeter can be used to obtain much more accurate enthalpy of combustion data as it is designed to overcome the two experimental problems that were discussed for the spirit burner.

1 Heat loss to the surroundings: as the water completely surrounds the container where the combustion occurs, most of the heat generated will be transferred to the water.

2 Incomplete combustion: the calorimeter is usually attached to an oxygen cylinder so that the sample is ignited in an oxygen-rich atmosphere. This ensures that the sample is completely burned.

Enthalpy of solution

Enthalpy changes occur when substances are dissolved in water. The enthalpy change when this happens is known as the **enthalpy of solution**. By definition, the enthalpy of solution is the enthalpy change when one mole of the substance dissolves in water.

The enthalpy of solution of a soluble substance can be determined experimentally as illustrated in Figure 15.5. The temperature of the water before adding a weighed amount of solute is measured along with the highest or lowest temperature of the final solution. A thermometer reading to the nearest 0.1–0.2 °C will enable more accurate results to be obtained. The method of calculating the enthalpy change is shown in Worked Example 2. (**Please note** that enthalpy of solution and neutralisation is not examinable in the CfE Higher course. They are included as examples of the application of CMΔT and are useful for illustrating the concept of Hess' Law.)

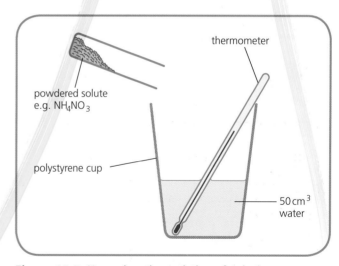

Figure 15.5 Measuring the enthalpy of solution

Questions

1 When burned, 0.01 moles of methane raised the temperature of 200 cm³ of water by 10.5 °C. Calculate the enthalpy of combustion of methane.

2 Mass of burner + propanol before burning = 84.25 g

Mass of burner + propanol after burning = 83.95 g

Mass of water heated = 120 g

Temperature of water before heating = 19.0 °C

Highest temperature of water after heating = 31.5 °C

The data given was obtained by some pupils using apparatus similar to that shown in Figure 15.3. The alkanol used was propanol, C_3H_7OH.

a) Use the data to calculate the enthalpy of combustion of propanol obtained in this experiment.

b) Compare this result with the data booklet value and describe what you consider to be the main sources of experimental error.

Worked Example 2

To calculate the enthalpy of solution of NH_4NO_3

Data from the experiment are given in Table 15.2.

Measurement	Result
Mass of solute (ammonium nitrate)	1.00 g
Mass of water used, m	0.05 kg
Temperature of water initially	20.4 °C
Highest or lowest temperature of solution	18.8 °C

Table 15.2

Calculation:

Temperature fall, $\Delta T = 1.6$ °C

Heat energy absorbed, $E_h = cm\Delta T$
$$= 4.18 \times 0.05 \times 1.6$$
$$= 0.3344 \text{ kJ}$$

Gram formula mass of ammonium nitrate = 80 g

$1.00 \text{ g} \rightarrow 0.3344 \text{ kJ}$

$80 \text{ g} \rightarrow 80 \times 0.3344 = 26.8 \text{ kJ}$

Enthalpy of solution of ammonium nitrate,
$\Delta H = 26.8 \text{ kJ mol}^{-1}$

Note that this reaction is endothermic. As mentioned earlier it is not essential to include a plus sign before the numerical value. Note also that in this calculation (as well as in Worked Example 3) two approximations are being made, namely that

1. the density of a dilute aqueous solution is the same as that of water (1 g cm^{-3}) at room temperature

2. the specific heat capacity of a dilute aqueous solution is the same as that of water ($4.18 \text{ kJ kg}^{-1} \text{°C}^{-1}$).

Questions

3. 3.03 g of potassium nitrate, KNO_3, was dissolved in 100 cm^3 of water. The temperature of the water fell by 2.5 °C.

   Calculate the enthalpy of solution of this salt.

4. Calculate the enthalpy of solution of sodium hydroxide from the following data.

Mass of solute, NaOH	= 0.80 g
Volume of water used	= 40 cm³
Temperature of water initially	= 20.2 °C
Highest temperature of solution	= 25.0 °C

Enthalpy of neutralisation

The enthalpy of **neutralisation** of an acid is the enthalpy change when the acid is neutralised to form one mole of water.

As you already know, when any acid such as hydrochloric acid is neutralised by any alkali such as sodium hydroxide, a salt – in this case sodium chloride – and water are formed.

$$HCl(aq) + NaOH(aq) \rightarrow NaCl(aq) + H_2O(l)$$

When an acid is neutralised by an alkali the reaction can be expressed by the following equation (with spectator ions omitted).

$$H^+(aq) + OH^-(aq) \rightarrow H_2O(l)$$

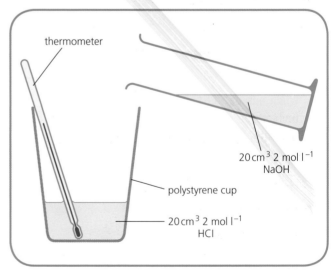

Figure 15.6 Enthalpy of neutralisation

The enthalpy of neutralisation of an acid by an alkali can be found by experiment as shown in Figure 15.6.

The temperature of each reactant is measured before mixing so that the average initial temperature can be calculated. The solutions are then mixed and the highest temperature of the neutral solution is noted. The method of calculating the enthalpy change is shown in Worked Example 3.

Worked Example 3

To calculate the enthalpy of neutralisation of HCl(aq) by NaOH(aq)

Data from the experiment are given in Table 15.3.

Measurement	Result
Solutions used	$20\,cm^3$ $2\,mol\,l^{-1}$ HCl and $20\,cm^3$ $2\,mol\,l^{-1}$ NaOH
Temperature of acid before mixing	$19.5\,°C$
Temperature of alkali before mixing	$18.5\,°C$
Highest temperature of solution after mixing	$32.5\,°C$

Table 15.3

Calculation:

Average initial temperature $= \dfrac{19.5 + 18.5}{2} = 19.0\,°C$

Temperature rise, ΔT $= 32.5 - 19.0 = 13.5\,°C$

Total volume of solution $= 40\,cm^3$

Mass of solution heated $= 40\,g = 0.04\,kg$

Heat energy released E_h $= cm\Delta T$
$= 4.18 \times 0.04 \times 13.5$
$= 2.26\,kJ$

Number of moles of acid $= CV = 2 \times 0.02 = 0.04$

Number of moles of water formed $= 0.04$ (since 1 mole of HCl $\rightarrow$ 1 mole of water)

0.04 moles of water $\rightarrow$ 2.26 kJ

1 mole of water $\rightarrow \dfrac{2.26}{0.04} = 56.4\,kJ$

Enthalpy of neutralisation, $\Delta H = -56.4\,kJ\,mol^{-1}$

In the calculation in Worked Example 3, 0.04 moles of HCl are neutralised by 0.04 moles of NaOH producing 0.04 moles of water. Hence, in the calculation, $cm\Delta T$ is divided by 0.04 so that the ΔH value obtained refers to one mole of acid being neutralised to form one mole of water.

In question 6 below, sulfuric acid, a dibasic acid, is used but the enthalpy of neutralisation is about the same as in question 5 since one mole of sulfuric acid produces two moles of water when completely neutralised by sodium hydroxide. This reaction is shown by the following equation:

$$H_2SO_4(aq) + 2NaOH(aq) \rightarrow Na_2SO_4(aq) + 2H_2O(l)$$

Monobasic or monoprotic acids are those which can yield one mole of hydrogen ions per mole of acid. Examples include hydrochloric acid (HCl), nitric acid (HNO_3) and ethanoic acid (CH_3COOH). Sulfuric acid (H_2SO_4) is an example of a dibasic or diprotic acid since it can yield two moles of hydrogen ions per mole of acid, while phosphoric acid (H_3PO_4) is a tribasic or triprotic acid.

Questions

5 Calculate the enthalpy of neutralisation of nitric acid by potassium hydroxide given that a temperature rise of 6.5 °C was observed on mixing $10\,cm^3$ of $1\,mol\,l^{-1}$ HNO_3 and $10\,cm^3$ of $1\,mol\,l^{-1}$ KOH.

6 Calculate the enthalpy of neutralisation of sulfuric acid by sodium hydroxide from the following data. Solutions used: $20\,cm^3$ of $1\,mol\,l^{-1}$ H_2SO_4 and $20\,cm^3$ of $2\,mol\,l^{-1}$ NaOH.

Temperature of acid before mixing $= 20.0\,°C$

Temperature of alkali before mixing $= 20.8\,°C$

Temperature of solution after mixing $= 34.0\,°C$

Remember that this enthalpy change relates to the formation of one mole of water.

Hess's Law

In this section we will be using enthalpy changes when applying a very important rule in chemistry called Hess's Law. This law can be stated as follows:

> 'The enthalpy change of a chemical reaction depends only on the chemical nature and physical states of the reactants and products and is independent of any intermediate steps.'

In other words, Hess's Law states that the enthalpy change of a chemical reaction does not depend on the route taken during the reaction.

Verification of Hess's Law by experiment

Hess's Law can be tested by experiment as the following example shows. This involves converting solid potassium hydroxide into potassium chloride solution by two different routes, as illustrated in Figure 15.7.

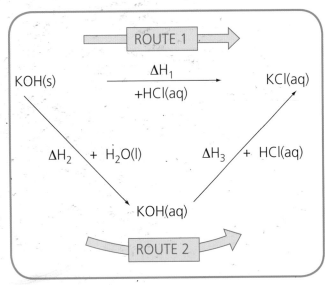

Figure 15.7 Making KCl(aq) via two routes to confirm Hess's Law

The first route is a one-step process. Solid potassium hydroxide is added to dilute hydrochloric acid to produce potassium chloride solution. Let us call the enthalpy change for this reaction ΔH_1.

Route 1: $KOH(s) + HCl(aq) \rightarrow KCl(aq) + H_2O(l)$ ΔH_1

The second route involves two steps. Firstly the solid potassium hydroxide is added to water to form potassium hydroxide solution. This solution

is neutralised in the second step by addition to hydrochloric acid.

Route 2:

Step 1: $KOH(s) + (aq) \rightarrow KOH(aq)$ ΔH_2

Step 2: $KOH(aq) + HCl(aq) \rightarrow KCl(aq) + H_2O(l)$ ΔH_3

ΔH_2 is the enthalpy of solution of KOH(s).

ΔH_3 is the enthalpy of neutralisation of hydrochloric acid by KOH(aq).

> According to Hess's Law: $\Delta H_1 = \Delta H_2 + \Delta H_3$

An experimental method for carrying out this experiment can be summarised as follows.

Route 1: $25\,cm^3$ of $1.0\,mol\,l^{-1}$ hydrochloric acid is measured out and its temperature noted. The acid is added to a known mass of solid potassium hydroxide (about 1.2 g) in a polystyrene cup and the mixture stirred. The highest temperature of the reacting mixture is noted.

Route 2 (Step 1): $25\,cm^3$ of water is measured out and its temperature noted. It is added to a known mass of solid potassium hydroxide (about 1.2 g) in a polystyrene cup. The mixture is stirred and its highest temperature is noted. This solution is allowed to cool before use in step 2.

Route 2 (Step 2): $25\,cm^3$ of $1.0\,mol\,l^{-1}$ hydrochloric acid is measured out and its temperature noted. The temperature of the potassium hydroxide solution prepared in step 1 is noted. These values are averaged to give the initial temperature. The solutions are mixed and the highest temperature recorded.

For each of these experiments, the energy released can be calculated using the relationship, $E_h = cm\Delta T$. The enthalpy change for each reaction is then obtained by dividing the energy released, E_h, by the number of moles of potassium hydroxide.

Essentially, Hess's Law is the application of the Law of Conservation of Energy to chemical reactions. This can be shown in a theoretical manner as follows. If, in the example given above, the first route was readily reversible and it was found that the sum of ΔH_2 and ΔH_3 was greater than ΔH_1, then it would be possible to create energy by carrying out steps 2 and 3 and then reversing the first route. This would violate the Law of Conservation of Energy, which states that energy cannot be created or destroyed but can only be converted from one form into another.

Calculations using Hess's Law

Hess's Law is important because it often enables us to calculate enthalpy changes which are either very difficult or even impossible to obtain by experiment. The formation of carbon compounds from their constituent elements is just one example of such a reaction.

The following worked examples illustrate the application of Hess's Law in calculating enthalpy changes which cannot be found by experiment. In the

first example, the enthalpy of formation of methane gas from carbon and hydrogen is calculated. The equation for this reaction is:

$$C(s) + 2H_2(g) \rightarrow CH_4(g)$$

Direct combination between carbon and hydrogen does not readily occur and, in any event, methane is not the only product. However, the enthalpy change for this reaction can be calculated using Hess's Law. Each of the substances shown in the equation can be burned and their enthalpies of combustion can be found by experiment. Hence an alternative route can be devised as Figure 15.8 shows. Worked Example 5 shows a similar calculation for ethanol.

Worked Example 4

$$C(s) + 2H_2(g) \rightarrow CH_4(g)$$

Calculate the enthalpy change of the above reaction using the enthalpies of combustion of carbon, hydrogen and methane.

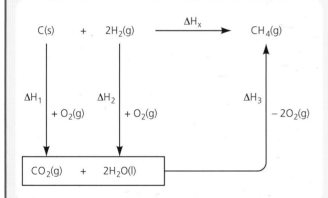

Figure 15.8

Step 1: Write equations for the enthalpy of combustion of C, H_2 and CH_4.

1 $C(s) + O_2(g) \rightarrow CO_2(g)$ $\Delta H = -394$ kJ mol^{-1}

2 $H_2(g) + \frac{1}{2}O_2(g) \rightarrow H_2O(g)$ $\Delta H = -286$ kJ mol^{-1}

3 $CH_4(g) + 2O_2(g) \rightarrow CO_2(g) + 2H_2O(g)$
   $\Delta H = -891$ kJ mol^{-1}

The target equation is $C(s) + 2H_2(g) \rightarrow CH_4(g)$.

You have to use the ΔH combustion equations and rearrange them to resemble the target equation.

Step 2:

- Multiply equation 2) $\times$ 2 to give 2 moles of H_2.

- Reverse equation 3) so that CH_4 is a product. (If you reverse the equation, you must reverse the ΔH.)

- Rewrite all three equations and add to give the target.

1 $C(s) + O_2(g) \rightarrow CO_2(g)$ $\Delta H = -394$ kJ mol^{-1}

2 $2H_2(g) + O_2(g) \rightarrow 2H_2O(g)$
   $\Delta H = 2 \times -286$ kJ mol^{-1}

3 $CO_2(g) + 2H_2O(g) \rightarrow CH_4(g) + 2O_2(g)$
   $\Delta H = +891$ kJ mol^{-1}

$C(s) + 2H_2(g) \rightarrow CH_4(g)$ $\Delta H = -394 + -572 + 891$

$= -75$ kJ mol^{-1}

Worked Example 5

The following equation shows the formation of ethanol from carbon, hydrogen and oxygen.

$$2C(s) + 3H_2(g) + \tfrac{1}{2}O_2(g) \rightarrow C_2H_5OH(l)$$

Use the enthalpies of combustion of carbon, hydrogen and ethanol to calculate the enthalpy change of this reaction.

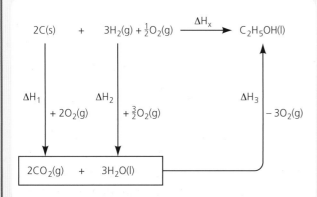

Figure 15.9

Step 1: Write equations for the enthalpy of combustion of C, H$_2$ and C$_2$H$_5$OH.

1 $C(s) + O_2(g) \rightarrow CO_2(g)$ $\Delta H = -394$ kJ mol^{-1}

2 $H_2(g) + \tfrac{1}{2}O_2(g) \rightarrow H_2O(g)$ $\Delta H = -286$ kJ mol^{-1}

3 $C_2H_5OH(l) + 3O_2(g) \rightarrow 2CO_2(g) + 3H_2O(l)$
   $\Delta H = -1367$ kJ mol^{-1}

The target equation is $2C(s) + 3H_2(g) \rightarrow \tfrac{1}{2}O_2(g) \rightarrow C_2H_5OH(l)$.

You have to rearrange the ΔH combustion equations to resemble this target equation.

Step 2:

- Multiply equation 1) × 2 to give 2 moles of C.
- Multiply equation 2) × 3 to give 3 moles of H$_2$.
- Reverse equation 3) so that C$_2$H$_5$OH is a product.
- Rewrite all three equations and add to give the target.

1 $2C(s) + 2O_2(g) \rightarrow 2CO_2(g)$ $\Delta H = 2 \times -394$ kJ mol^{-1}

2 $3H_2(g) + 1\tfrac{1}{2}O_2(g) \rightarrow 3H_2O(g)$ $\Delta H = 3 \times -286$ kJ mol^{-1}

3 $2CO_2(g) + 3H_2O(l) \rightarrow C_2H_5OH(l) + 3O_2(g)$
   $\Delta H = +1367$ kJ mol^{-1}

$2C(s) + 3H_2(g) + \tfrac{1}{2}O_2(g) \rightarrow C_2H_5OH(l)$ $\Delta H = -279$ kJ mol^{-1}

Note

Oxygen is one of the elements present in ethanol but it is not involved in deriving the required enthalpy change. The calculation is based on enthalpies of combustion. Oxygen gas supports combustion; it does not have an enthalpy of combustion.

Questions

7 Use relevant data on enthalpies of combustion and the following equation to calculate the enthalpy of formation of ethyne, C$_2$H$_2$(g).

$$2C(s) + H_2(g) \rightarrow C_2H_2(g)$$

8 Benzene reacts with hydrogen under certain conditions to yield cyclohexane according to the following equation:

$$C_6H_6(l) + 3H_2(g) \rightarrow C_6H_{12}(l)$$

Use relevant data on enthalpies of combustion to calculate the enthalpy change for this reaction.

(Enthalpy of combustion of cyclohexane, $\Delta H = -3924$ kJ mol^{-1})

The answer to question 7 is interesting as it shows that the formation of ethyne from its elements is highly endothermic. This is in contrast to the equivalent reaction for methane, which is exothermic, as shown in Worked Example 4. Figure 15.10 compares these two enthalpy changes in a potential energy diagram.

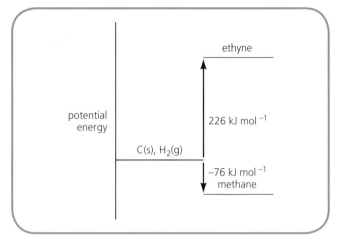

Figure 15.10

This suggests that ethyne is a much less stable compound than methane. Ethyne is a gas at room temperature and has a boiling point of −84 °C. It is liable to explode if liquefied, but it can be stored safely in cylinders if it is dissolved in propanone under pressure.

Calculation of the enthalpy change using bond enthalpies

All chemical reactions involve making new substances. In order to make something new, reactant bonds must be broken and product bonds must be formed. We can easily estimate the enthalpy change of **gas-phase** reactions if we know the bond enthalpy. The **molar bond enthalpy** is the enthalpy change when a bond in a gaseous molecule is broken. The bond enthalpy data are listed in the data booklet.

For example, the bond enthalpy of chlorine refers to the reaction:

$$Cl_2(g) \rightarrow 2Cl(g) \quad \Delta H = 243 \, kJ \, mol^{-1}$$

In other words, it takes 243 kJ of energy to break all the chlorine molecules into chlorine atoms in one mole of chlorine gas. This informs us that bond breaking is endothermic. This should make sense as energy is needed to overcome the attraction of the bonding electrons for the nuclei in both atoms. This also informs us that bond making must be exothermic. Making one mole of chlorine from its atoms would release 243 kJ of energy:

$$2Cl(g) \rightarrow Cl_2(g) \quad \Delta H = -243 \, kJ \, mol^{-1}$$

We can use this information to calculate the enthalpy change for a chemical reaction. For example, the enthalpy change for the reaction of hydrogen and chlorine to make hydrogen chloride can be calculated as shown in Worked Example 6.

A close examination of data tables for bond enthalpy reveals that some of the bond enthalpies are known

Worked Example 6

Calculate the enthalpy change, using bond enthalpies, for the following reaction:

$$H_2(g) + Cl_2(g) \rightarrow 2HCl(g)$$

The necessary data are given in Tables 15.4 and 15.5.

Bonds broken	$\Delta H/kJ \, mol^{-1}$
H–H	432
Cl–Cl	243
Total	**675**

Table 15.4

Bonds made	$\Delta H/kJ \, mol^{-1}$
H–Cl	−428
H–Cl	−428
Total	**−856**

Table 15.5

enthalpy change = total bonds + total bonds
broken made

$$\Delta H = 675 + (-856) = -181 \, kJ \, mol^{-1}$$

as mean bond enthalpies. This distinction is made as these bonds can occur in a variety of compounds. For example, the mean bond enthalpy of C–C is 346 kJ mol^{-1}. A C–C bond can occur in an alkane, a carbohydrate, an alcohol etc. The C–C bond will have a slightly different enthalpy depending on which compound is examined. The value quoted is, therefore, an average. Compare this with the bond enthalpies used in Worked Example 6. These are not mean bond enthalpies since these bonds can only occur in one molecule, for example an H–H bond can only occur in a hydrogen molecule. Likewise, an H–Cl bond can only occur in a molecule of HCl.

Questions

9 Calculate the enthalpy change, using bond enthalpies, for the following reactions:

a) $C_2H_4(g) + H_2(g) \rightarrow C_2H_6(g)$

b) $CH_4(g) + 2O_2(g) \rightarrow CO_2(g) + 2H_2O(g)$

Checklist for Revision

- I know the importance of enthalpy changes in chemical reactions.
- I can calculate the enthalpy change for a reaction using $E_h = cm\Delta T$ and appropriate data.
- I know the definition of the enthalpy of combustion.
- I can describe how enthalpy of combustion data can be obtained by experiment.
- I know the definition of Hess's Law.
- I can use Hess's Law to calculate the enthalpy change for a chemical reaction.
- I can use bond enthalpies to calculate the enthalpy change for a reaction.

Key Terms

The words and phrases below were introduced in this chapter.

Their definitions are given in the chemical dictionary.

enthalpy of combustion
enthalpy of neutralisation
enthalpy of solution
Hess's Law
molar bond enthalpy

Study Questions

1 The enthalpy of combustion of ethene relates to which of the following equations?

A $C_2H_4(g) + 2O_2(g) \rightarrow 2CO_2(g) + 2H_2(g)$

B $C_2H_4(g) + 3O_2(g) \rightarrow 2CO_2(g) + 2H_2O(l)$

C $C_2H_4(g) + 2O_2(g) \rightarrow 2CO(g) + 2H_2O(l)$

D $C_2H_4(g) + O_2(g) \rightarrow 2CO(g) + 2H_2(g)$

2 Benzene can be produced from ethyne. The equation for this reaction is

$$3C_2H_2(g) \rightarrow C_6H_6(l)$$

The enthalpy change for this reaction in $kJ\,mol^{-1}$, using enthalpies of combustion from the data booklet, is

A 632   B –632   C 1968   D –1968

3 Refer to the reaction paths shown below.

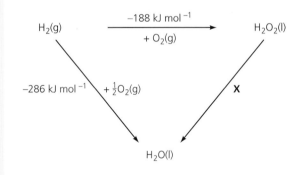

Figure 15.11

According to Hess's Law, the enthalpy change, in $kJ\,mol^{-1}$, for reaction **X** is

A –98   B 98   C –474   D 474

4

Reactant	Hydrochloric acid	Ammonia solution
Concentration/mol l^{-1}	1.0	2.0
Volume/cm³	40.0	20.0
Temperature/°C	20.5	20.5

Table 15.6

The highest recorded temperature after mixing these solutions was 28.5 °C.

Use the data given to calculate the enthalpy of neutralisation of hydrochloric acid by ammonia solution. Ammonia solution, $NH_3(aq)$, reacts as $NH_4OH(aq)$ when it neutralises an acid. The equation for the reaction with hydrochloric acid is

$$NH_4OH(aq) + HCl(aq) \rightarrow NH_4Cl(aq) + H_2O(l)$$

5 A polystyrene cup contained 50 cm³ of water at 21.2 °C. 2.53 g of powdered ammonium chloride was added and dissolved with stirring. Calculate the lowest temperature which the solution should reach given that the enthalpy of solution of NH_4Cl is 15.0 $kJ\,mol^{-1}$.

6 Two litres of water, initially at 25 °C, were heated using a butane burner as shown below.

aluminium pot containing water

BUTANE

Figure 15.12

a) Using appropriate data from your data booklet, calculate the number of moles of butane needed to boil this quantity of water.

b) In practice, some heat is lost to the surroundings. Calculate the mass of butane burned if 80% of the heat produced by the burner is transferred to the water.

7* The following results are taken from the notebook of a pupil who was trying to confirm Hess's Law.

Experiment 1 – Addition of 1.6 g of sodium hydroxide solid to 50 cm³ of 1 mol l⁻¹ hydrochloric acid

$$NaOH(s) + HCl(aq) \rightarrow NaCl(aq) + H_2O(l)$$

Mass	= 50 g
Initial temperature of HCl(aq)	= 21.7 °C
Highest temperature during experiment	= 29.9 °C
ΔT	= 8.2 °C

Experiment 2 – Addition of 25 cm³ of 2 mol l⁻¹ sodium hydroxide solution to 25 cm³ of 2 mol l⁻¹ hydrochloric acid

$$NaOH(aq) + HCl(aq) \rightarrow NaCl(aq) + H_2O(l)$$

Mass	= 50 g
Initial temperature of HCl(aq) – T_1	= 21.7 °C
Initial temperature of NaOH(aq) – T_2	= 22.1 °C
Highest temperature during experiment	= 28.6 °C
ΔT	=

a) i) In experiment 1, calculate which reactant is in excess. (Show your working clearly.)

ii) In experiment 1, calculate the enthalpy change during the reaction. You may wish to use the data booklet to help you.

b) Calculate ΔT for experiment 2.

c) Outline a third experiment which would have to be carried out in order to confirm Hess's Law.

d) Suggest a precaution which should be taken to minimise heat loss during the experiments.

8 The equation for the formation of benzene from carbon and hydrogen is as follows:

$$6C(s) + 3H_2(g) \rightarrow C_6H_6(l)$$

Use enthalpies of combustion from your data booklet to calculate the enthalpy of this reaction.

9 The equation for the complete hydrogenation of ethyne is shown below:

$$C_2H_2(g) + 2H_2(g) \rightarrow C_2H_6(g)$$

The structure of ethyne is as shown below.

$$H-C\equiv C-H$$

Figure 15.13

Calculate the enthalpy change of this reaction using

a) enthalpies of combustion

b) bond enthalpies.

10 Carbon disulfide, CS_2, is an inflammable liquid producing CO_2 and SO_2 when it burns.

The equation for the formation of carbon disulfide from carbon and sulfur is shown below along with the enthalpy change for the reaction.

$$C(s) + 2S(s) \rightarrow CS_2(l)$$
$$\Delta H = 88 \, kJ \, mol^{-1}$$

Use this information and the enthalpies of combustion of carbon and sulfur to calculate the enthalpy of combustion of carbon disulfide.

11 Use bond enthalpies to calculate the enthalpy change for this reaction:

$$N_2(g) + 3H_2(g) \rightarrow 2NH_3(g)$$

12* Hess's Law can be used to calculate the enthalpy change for the formation of ethanoic acid from its elements.

$$2C(s) + 2H_2(g) + O_2(g) \rightarrow CH_3COOH(l)$$

Calculate the enthalpy change for the above reaction, in $kJ \, mol^{-1}$, using information from the data booklet and the following data:

$$CH_3COOH(l) + 2O_2(g) \rightarrow 2CO_2(g) + 2H_2O(l)$$
$$\Delta H = -876 \, kJ \, mol^{-1}$$

16 Oxidising and reducing agents

One of the attractions of studying chemistry is being able to watch spectacular chemical reactions. For example, if aluminium is added to iron(III) oxide and heated, a vigorous reaction takes place causing molten iron to form.

$$\text{aluminium} + \text{iron(III) oxide} \rightarrow \text{aluminium oxide} + \text{iron}$$

$$Al + Fe_2O_3 \rightarrow Al_2O_3 + Fe$$

This highly exothermic reaction is known as a thermite reaction. So much heat is produced that the iron formed is actually molten. It can be used as a source of molten iron to repair railway tracks, and has also been used by the military as thermite bombs.

Figure 16.1 Thermite reaction

The thermite reaction is an example of a **displacement reaction**. This involves a more reactive metal displacing a less reactive metal from a compound. In this case, aluminium displaces iron from iron oxide. This happens when the metal added has a greater tendency to lose electrons and form ions than the metal being displaced. In other words, the atoms of the metal added (aluminium in this case) lose electrons to the ions of the metal being displaced (Fe^{3+} in this case).

Ion–electron equations are used in chemistry to show the loss and gain of electrons.

$$Al \rightarrow Al^{3+} + 3e^-$$

This equation shows an aluminium atom losing three electrons. This is known as an **oxidation** reaction.

$$Fe^{3+} + 3e^- \rightarrow Fe$$

This equation shows an iron(III) ion gaining three electrons. This is known as a **reduction** reaction.

> Many chemists use the mnemonic OILRIG to help them remember what happens during oxidation and reduction: Oxidation Is Loss, Reduction Is Gain.

As the two reactions happen at the same time, the reaction is known as a **redox reaction**.

The two ion–electron equations can be combined to produce a balanced ionic equation for the overall redox reaction:

$$Al + Fe^{3+} \rightarrow Al^{3+} + Fe$$

In the redox equation, the electrons are not shown since the electrons lost by the aluminium atom are gained by the iron ion.

Oxidising agents and reducing agents

When we examine a redox reaction, we find that one of the reactants is acting as a **reducing agent** and the other reactant is acting as an **oxidising agent**. In the previous example, the aluminium atom is acting as a reducing agent as it is causing the iron(III) ion to gain electrons. The iron(III) ion is an oxidising agent as it is causing the aluminium atom to lose electrons.

> A reducing agent is a substance which donates electrons.

> An oxidising agent is a substance which accepts electrons.

This is illustrated in the two examples below.

1   Zinc displaces copper from a solution containing copper(II) ions.

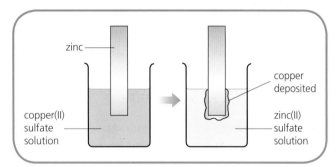

Figure 16.2 Zinc reacting with copper(II) to produce copper metal and zinc ions

$$\text{Oxidation: } Zn(s) \rightarrow Zn^{2+}(aq) + 2e^-$$

$$\text{Reduction: } Cu^{2+}(aq) + 2e^- \rightarrow Cu(s)$$

$$\text{Redox: } Cu^{2+}(aq) + Zn(s) \rightarrow Cu(s) + Zn^{2+}(aq)$$

Cu^{2+} is the oxidising agent. Zn is the reducing agent.

2   Zinc displaces silver from a solution containing silver(I) ions.

In this example the ion–electron equations show that each zinc atom loses two electrons while each silver ion gains only one electron. Therefore, the second ion–electron equation must be doubled to balance the number of electrons lost and gained, so that the redox equation can be obtained in the same way as in the previous example.

Note that the total charge on each side of the redox equation is the same.

$$\text{Oxidation: } Zn(s) \rightarrow Zn^{2+}(aq) + 2e^-$$

$$\text{Reduction: } Ag^+(aq) + e^- \rightarrow Ag(s) \ (\times 2)$$

$$\text{Redox: } 2Ag^+(aq) + Zn(s) \rightarrow 2Ag(s) + Zn^{2+}(aq)$$

Ag^+ is the oxidising agent. Zn is the reducing agent.

In each of the above examples the negative ions present in the solutions have not been included or even referred to since they do not take part in the reaction. It is usual practice to omit such spectator ions from redox equations.

Electronegativity

Electronegativity is a useful guide for predicting whether something will act as an oxidising or reducing agent. For example, fluorine has the highest electronegativity of all the elements with a value of 4.0. This shows that fluorine has a strong attraction for electrons and so will act as a strong oxidising agent. This should make sense when we think about how fluorine reacts; a fluorine atom will gain an electron to form a fluoride ion (F^-).

Most non-metals tend to act as oxidising agents since they accept electrons readily to form negatively-charged ions, such as Cl^-, Br^-, O^{2-}. Overall, the best oxidising agents are the halogens (group VII).

Metals tend to act as reducing agents since they donate electrons readily to form positively-charged ions, such as Na^+, Mg^{2+}, Al^{3+}. Again, electronegativity is a good guide here as metals have low electronegativity values. For example, the alkali metals have the lowest electronegativity values of all the elements. This makes them the best reducing agents.

Questions

1   For each of the displacement reactions described below
   a) write down the relevant ion–electron equations and use them to work out the redox equation (do not include spectator ions)
   b) label the oxidising agent and the reducing agent.
   i) Copper metal reacts with silver(I) nitrate solution to form copper(II) nitrate solution and silver.
   ii) Chromium metal reacts with nickel(II) sulfate solution to form chromium(III) sulfate solution and nickel.

Compounds as oxidising and reducing agents

So far we have dealt with relatively simple ion–electron equations which involve simple ions and atoms or molecules. An examination of the electrochemical series shows that compounds can also act as oxidising and reducing agents. For example, potassium

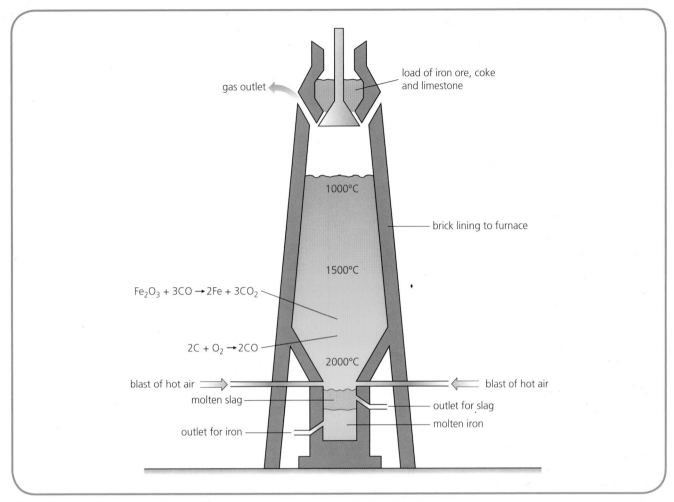

gas outlet

load of iron ore, coke and limestone

1000°C

brick lining to furnace

1500°C

$Fe_2O_3 + 3CO \rightarrow 2Fe + 3CO_2$

$2C + O_2 \rightarrow 2CO$

2000°C

blast of hot air

blast of hot air

molten slag

outlet for slag

outlet for iron

molten iron

Figure 16.3 Carbon monoxide acts as a strong reducing agent in the blast furnace.

permanganate is a strong oxidising agent. This is shown quite spectacularly when potassium permanganate is added to glycerol. The glycerol is oxidised to produce carbon dioxide and water in a very exothermic reaction.

Carbon monoxide is an example of a compound that behaves as a strong reducing agent. In industry, the blast furnace is used to extract iron from iron(III) oxide. This requires iron(III) ions to be reduced to iron. Carbon monoxide is generated in the blast furnace and reduces the iron ions to iron atoms as shown in Figure 16.3.

The electrochemical series

An examination of the electrochemical series also gives us a good indication of the ability of an element or compound to act as an oxidising or reducing agent:

> Elements and compounds at the top right of the electrochemical series are strong reducing agents.

> Elements and compounds at the bottom left of the electrochemical series are strong oxidising agents.

Both dichromate ($Cr_2O_7^{2-}$) and permanganate (MnO_4^-) are found at the bottom of the electrochemical series. These ions are examples of oxyanions. Oxyanions are negative ions which contain oxygen combined with another element. Another example of this type of ion is the sulfite ion, SO_3^{2-}. Equations involving oxyanions are more complex.

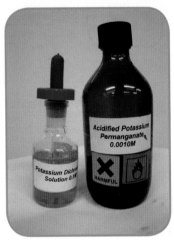

Figure 16.4 Acidified potassium permanganate and acidified potassium dichromate are common oxidising agents.

Writing ion–electron and redox equations

The following three examples of redox reactions are given to emphasise two main points, namely to show how to write:

- ion–electron equations which involve oxyanions

- balanced redox equations for more complex reactions.

State symbols have been omitted so as not to 'overload' the equations with information. The first named is the oxidising agent in each case.

1 Bromine water and sodium sulfite solution

Sodium ions do not appear in any of the following equations as they are spectator ions.

Bromine molecules are reduced to bromide ions.

$$Br_2 + 2e^- \rightarrow 2Br^-$$

brown   colourless

Sulfite ions are oxidised to sulfate ions. Both ions are colourless.

$$SO_3^{2-} \rightarrow SO_4^{2-}$$

The formation of sulfate ions can be shown by testing the solution with barium chloride solution. The white precipitate of barium sulfate formed is insoluble in

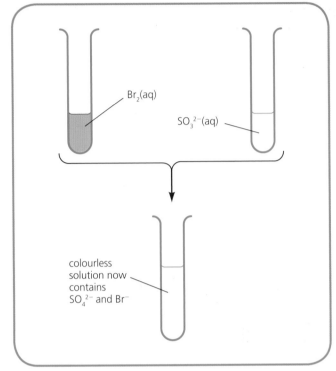

Figure 16.5 Bromine water reacting with sodium sulfite solution

hydrochloric acid. Sulfite ions also form a white precipitate, $BaSO_3$, with barium chloride but it is soluble in $HCl(aq)$.

Instructions for balancing a complex ion–electron equation

1   Check that the main element reacting (not oxygen) is balanced.

2   Add water to balance the oxygen atoms.

3   Add H^+ ions to balance the hydrogen atoms.

4   Add electrons to the same side as the H^+ ions so that both sides of the equation have the same charge.

Now we can apply these rules to our example:

$$SO_3^{2-} \rightarrow SO_4^{2-}$$

1   There is one sulfur atom on each side so there is no need to balance.

2   The oxygen atoms are not balanced. Add one water molecule to the left-hand side:

$$SO_3^{2-} + H_2O \rightarrow SO_4^{2-}$$

3 Add two hydrogen ions to the right-hand side to balance the hydrogens:

$$SO_3^{2-} + H_2O \rightarrow SO_4^{2-} + 2H^+$$

4 Add two electrons to the right-hand side so that both sides of the equation have a 2– charge:

$$SO_3^{2-} + H_2O \rightarrow SO_4^{2-} + 2H^+ + 2e^-$$

This ion–electron equation for the conversion of sulfite into sulfate is now complete. The two ion–electron equations can now be combined to give the balanced redox equation as follows.

$$Br_2 + 2e^- \rightarrow 2Br^-$$

$$SO_3^{2-} + H_2O \rightarrow SO_4^{2-} + 2H^+ + 2e^-$$

$$Br_2 + SO_3^{2-} + H_2O \rightarrow SO_4^{2-} + 2H^+ + 2Br^-$$

2 Acidified potassium permanganate solution reacting with iron(II) sulfate solution

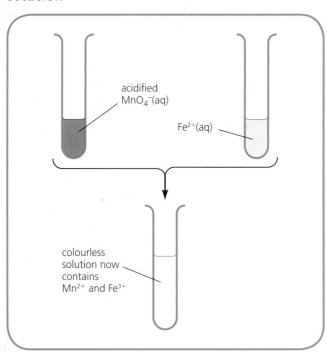

Figure 16.6 Acidified potassium permanganate reacting with iron(II) ions

K^+ and SO_4^{2-} are spectator ions.

Iron(II) ions are oxidised to iron(III) ions:

$$Fe^{2+} \rightarrow Fe^{3+} + e^-$$

The formation of iron(III) ions can be shown by testing the solution with ammonium thiocyanate solution. This gives a dark blood-red solution in the presence of iron(III) ions.

Permanganate ions are reduced to manganese(II) ions:

$$MnO_4^- \rightarrow Mn^{2+}$$

$$\text{purple} \qquad \text{colourless}$$

The ion–electron equation can be completed in a similar way to the previous example by applying our simple rules.

1 Both sides of the equation have one Mn ion.

2 Add $4H_2O$ to the right-hand side to balance the oxygen atoms:

$$MnO_4^- \rightarrow Mn^{2+} + 4H_2O$$

3 Add $8H^+$ to the left-hand side to balance the number of hydrogens:

$$MnO_4^- + 8H^+ \rightarrow Mn^{2+} + 4H_2O$$

4 Add five electrons to the left-hand side so that both sides of the equation have the same charge:

$$MnO_4^- + 8H^+ + 5e^- \rightarrow Mn^{2+} + 4H_2O$$

The final ion–electron equation can be checked against the equation for permanganate in the data booklet. This equation shows that the permanganate ion can only act as an oxidising agent when H^+ ions are present, in other words the permanganate solution must be acidified.

The two ion–electron equations can now be combined to give the balanced redox equation. To balance the number of electrons lost and gained, the equation involving iron ions has to be multiplied by five.

$$5Fe^{2+} \rightarrow 5Fe^{3+} + 5e^-$$

$$MnO_4^- + 8H^+ + 5e^- \rightarrow Mn^{2+} + 4H_2O$$

$$MnO_4^- + 8H^+ + 5Fe^{2+} \rightarrow Mn^{2+} + 5Fe^{3+} + 4H_2O$$

Charges:

1–	8+	10+		2+	15+	0
	17+				17+	

The total charge is the same on each side of the redox equation.

3 Dilute nitric acid reacting with copper

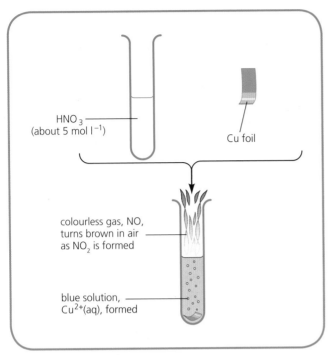

HNO$_3$
(about 5 mol l^{-1})

Cu foil

colourless gas, NO,
turns brown in air
as NO$_2$ is formed

blue solution,
Cu^{2+}(aq), formed

Figure 16.7 Copper reacting with nitric acid

Copper atoms are oxidised to copper(II) ions:

$$Cu \rightarrow Cu^{2+} + 2e^-$$

Nitrate ions are reduced to nitrogen monoxide, NO, a colourless gas which forms brown fumes of nitrogen dioxide in contact with air.

$$NO_3^- \rightarrow NO$$

This equation is balanced by applying the usual steps to give:

$$NO_3^- + 4H^+ + 3e^- \rightarrow NO + 2H_2O$$

In order to write the balanced redox equation it is necessary to multiply the equation involving copper by three and the equation involving nitrate ions by two.

$$3Cu \rightarrow 3Cu^{2+} + 6e^-$$

$$2NO_3^- + 8H^+ + 6e^- \rightarrow 2NO + 4H_2O$$

$$\overline{3Cu + 2NO_3^- + 8H^+ \rightarrow 3Cu^{2+} + 2NO + 4H_2O}$$

Note that the total charge (6+) on each side of the redox equation is again the same.

It would appear that there are no spectator ions in this reaction but a closer look at the redox reaction shows a difference in the number of hydrogen ions and nitrate ions. Nitric acid contains equal numbers of these ions. The six extra nitrate ions not shown in the redox equation are spectator ions.

> ### Questions
>
> 2 In each of the following examples complete the ion–electron equation and indicate whether it represents a reduction or an oxidation.
>
>   a) MnO$_2$(s) changes to permanganate ions, MnO$_4^-$(aq).
>
>   b) FeO$_4^{2-}$(aq) in acidic solution are converted to Fe^{3+}(aq).
>
>   c) V^{3+}(aq) are converted to VO$_3^-$(aq).

Using the electrochemical series to write redox equations

In the electrochemical series, ion–electron equations are listed with electrons on the left-hand side, in other words as reductions. Each equation is, therefore, written in the form:

$$\text{oxidising agent} + \text{electron(s)} \rightarrow \text{reducing agent}$$

When using equations from this series to write a redox equation it will always be necessary to reverse one of the equations as it appears in the table, since an oxidising agent can only react with a reducing agent and vice versa. To help you to decide which equation to reverse, remember that the starting materials (the reactants) must appear on the left-hand side of the redox equation. These points are illustrated by the following examples.

1 Iron(III) chloride solution oxidises potassium iodide solution to form iron(II) ions and iodine. In this reaction Cl$^-$ and K$^+$ are spectator ions. The relevant ion–electron equations obtained from the electrochemical series are shown below:

$$I_2 + 2e^- \rightarrow 2I^-$$

$$Fe^{3+} + e^- \rightarrow Fe^{2+}$$

Since the reaction is between iron(III) and iodide, the first equation must be reversed to show the iodide as a reactant. The second equation is fine as it shows iron(III) as a reactant. The equation for the reduction of iron(III) ions must be doubled to balance the number of electrons transferred.

$$2I^- \rightarrow I_2 + 2e^-$$

$$2Fe^{3+} + 2e^- \rightarrow 2Fe^{2+}$$

$$2Fe^{3+} + 2I^- \rightarrow 2Fe^{2+} + I_2$$

2 Iron(II) sulfate solution reduces acidified potassium dichromate solution to form iron(III) ions and chromium(III) ions. In this reaction SO_4^{2-} and K^+ are spectator ions. The relevant ion–electron equations from the electrochemical series are:

$$Fe^{3+} + e^- \rightarrow Fe^{2+}$$

$$Cr_2O_7^{2-} + 14H^+ + 6e^- \rightarrow 2Cr^{3+} + 7H_2O$$

The first equation must be reversed and also multiplied by six to balance the number of electrons transferred.

$$6Fe^{2+} \rightarrow 6Fe^{3+} + 6e^-$$

$$Cr_2O_7^{2-} + 14H^+ + 6e^- \rightarrow 2Cr^{3+} + 7H_2O$$

$$Cr_2O_7^{2-} + 14H^+ + 6Fe^{2+} \rightarrow 6Fe^{3+} + 2Cr^{3+} + 7H_2O$$

Questions

3 Check the two redox equations above to see whether the total charge on each side of the equations is balanced.

4 In each of the examples given in Table 16.1, use the information to
   i) identify the reducing agent, the oxidising agent and the spectator ions
   ii) write the balanced redox equation for the overall reaction.

Everyday uses for strong oxidising agents

Hydrogen peroxide is probably one of the most common oxidising agents used in everyday life. Like many oxidising agents, it is a highly effective 'bleach' as it is able to break down coloured compounds. Consequently, it is used to bleach wool, cotton and paper. It is also found in many cosmetic products such as hair-lightening products and teeth-whitening products. Hydrogen peroxide is also an effective antiseptic that can kill bacteria and fungi and deactivate viruses.

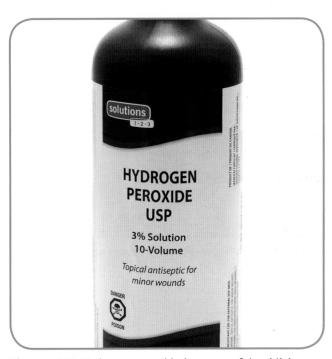

Figure 16.8 Hydrogen peroxide is a powerful oxidising agent.

Reactants	Ion–electron equations
Iodine solution and sodium sulfite solution	$I_2 + 2e^- \rightarrow 2I^-$ $SO_3^{2-} + H_2O \rightarrow SO_4^{2-} + 2H^+ + 2e^-$
Iron(II) sulfate solution and hydrogen peroxide solution	$Fe^{2+} \rightarrow Fe^{3+} + e^-$ $H_2O_2 + 2H^+ + 2e^- \rightarrow 2H_2O$
Tin(II) chloride solution and potassium dichromate solution (acidified)	$Sn^{2+} \rightarrow Sn^{4+} + 2e^-$ $Cr_2O_7^{2-} + 14H^+ + 6e^- \rightarrow 2Cr^{3+} + 7H_2O$

Table 16.1

Potassium permanganate is another strong oxidising agent that has many applications outside the chemistry laboratory. In medicine, it is still used to treat skin infections due to its ability to destroy bacteria and fungi. For example, many people successfully use dilute solutions of potassium permanganate to treat athlete's foot – a fungal infection which tends to affect the skin on the soles of the feet and between the toes. It is also used to maintain the health of fish in fish ponds or tanks as they can be vulnerable to infection. Potassium permanganate is highly effective at destroying the bacteria and fungi that commonly infect fish while also killing the small parasites that inhabit the pond water.

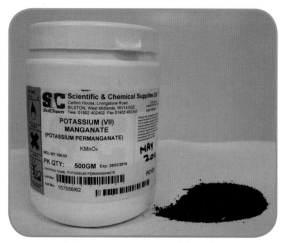

Figure 16.9 Potassium permanganate is used to prevent disease in fish.

Checklist for Revision

- I can identify a substance as acting as an oxidising or reducing agent.

- I can write balanced redox equations.

- I understand the relationship between electronegativity and the ability of a substance to act as an oxidising or reducing agent.

- I can use the electrochemical series to pick out highly effective oxidising agents and reducing agents.

- I can write ion–electron equations for more complex oxidations and reductions involving compounds.

- I know examples of everyday oxidising agents and I know why they are used.

Key Terms

The words and phrases below were introduced in this chapter.

Their definitions are given in the chemical dictionary.

displacement reaction

electrochemical series

oxidation reaction

oxidising agent

redox reaction

reducing agent

reduction reaction

spectator ions

Study Questions

1 Potassium permanganate solution, acidified with dilute sulfuric acid, is decolourised by iron(II) sulfate solution. Refer to the ion–electron equations in the data booklet.

Which ion is the reducing agent in this reaction?

A H^+

B Fe^{2+}

C MnO_4^-

D SO_4^{2-}

2 $$Br_2 + 2I^- \rightarrow I_2 + 2Br^-$$

Which substance involved in this redox reaction has been oxidised?

A Br_2

B I_2

C I^-

D Br^-

3 $$MnO_2 \rightarrow Mn^{2+}$$

Part of an ion–electron equation is shown above. When the equation is complete, the left-hand side will include

A $4H^+ + 2e^-$

B $2H^+ + 4e^-$

C $4H^+ + 4e^-$

D $2H^+ + 2e^-$

4* In which of the following reactions is a positive ion reduced?

A Iodide → iodine

B Nickel(II) → nickel(III)

C Cobalt(III) → cobalt(II)

D Sulfate → sulfite

5* Which of the following is a redox reaction?

A $Mg + 2HCl \rightarrow MgCl_2 + H_2$

B $MgO + 2HCl \rightarrow MgCl_2 + H_2O$

C $MgCO_3 + 2HCl \rightarrow MgCl_2 + H_2O + CO_2$

D $Mg(OH)_2 + 2HCl \rightarrow MgCl_2 + 2H_2O$

6* a) In acid solution, iodate ions, $IO_3^-(aq)$, are readily converted into iodine. Write an ion–electron equation for this half-reaction.

b) Use the equation to explain whether the iodate ion is an oxidising or reducing agent.

7 a) In acid solution, dichromate ions, $Cr_2O_7^{2-}(aq)$, are readily converted into Cr^{3+} ions. Write an ion–electron equation for this half-reaction.

b) Use the equation to explain whether the dichromate ion is an oxidising or reducing agent.

8 Write ion–electron equations for the following changes:

a) $Br_2 \rightarrow BrO_3^-$

b) $V^{2+} \rightarrow VO_3^-$

9 Use the electrochemical series to identify

a) the three best oxidising agents

b) the three best reducing agents.

10* The number of moles of carbon monoxide in a sample of air can be measured as follows.

Step 1 The carbon monoxide reacts with iodine(V) oxide, producing iodine.

$$5CO(g) + I_2O_5(s) \rightarrow I_2(s) + 5CO_2(g)$$

Step 2 The iodine is then dissolved in potassium iodide solution and titrated against sodium thiosulfate solution.

$$I_2(aq) + 2S_2O_3^{2-}(aq) \rightarrow S_4O_6^{2-}(aq) + 2I^-(aq)$$

a) Write the ion–electron equation for the oxidation reaction in Step 2.

b) Name a chemical that can be used to indicate when all of the iodine has been removed in the reaction taking place in Step 2.

11* Uranium ore is converted into uranium(IV) fluoride, UF_4, to produce fuel for nuclear power stations.

In one process, uranium can be extracted from the uranium(IV) fluoride by a redox reaction with magnesium, as follows:

$$2Mg + UF_4 \rightarrow 2MgF_2 + U$$

a) Give another name for this type of redox reaction.

b) Write the ion–electron equation for the reduction reaction that takes place.

c) The reaction with magnesium is carried out at a high temperature. The reaction vessel is filled with argon rather than air. Suggest a reason for using argon rather than air.

12* Some carbon monoxide detectors contain crystals of hydrated palladium(II) chloride. These form palladium in a redox reaction if exposed to carbon monoxide.

$$CO(g) + PdCl_2.2H_2O(s) \rightarrow CO_2(g) + Pd(s)$$
$$+ \ 2HCl(g) + H_2O(l)$$

a) Write the ion–electron equation for the reduction step in this reaction.

b) Another type of detector uses an electrochemical method to detect carbon monoxide.

At the positive electrode

$$CO(g) + H_2O(l) \rightarrow CO_2(g) + 2H^+(aq) + 2e^-$$

At the negative electrode

$$O_2(g) + 4H^+(aq) + 4e^- \rightarrow 2H_2O(l)$$

Combine the two ion–electron equations to give the overall redox equation.

Activities

1 Find out about the use of hydrogen peroxide in everyday products such as teeth whiteners. What concentration is supplied? What safety precautions must be taken? How are the solutions stored? Can you explain the safety precautions/storage conditions using your knowledge of chemistry?

2 Strong oxidising agents are used in medicine to treat skin diseases. Find out about 'Condy's Fluid'. What is it? What is it used to treat? What are the side effects?

3 Find out about the use of potassium permanganate 'ping pong balls' to fight forest fires.

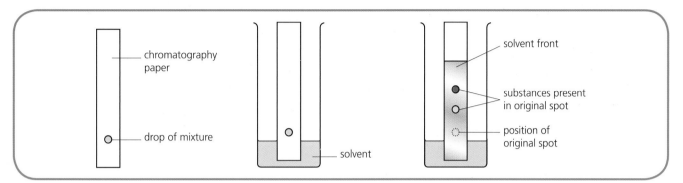

Figure 17.1 Paper chromatography

Chromatography is a powerful technique that allows chemists to separate the components of a mixture. Perhaps the most common example encountered in chemistry kits and school laboratories is paper chromatography used to separate the dyes in ink or coloured compounds in sweets. An illustration of this is shown in Figure 17.1.

Paper chromatography illustrates the basic principles of the separation technique. A small sample of the mixture is placed at the bottom of the paper and the paper is then placed in a solvent. By capillary action, the solvent moves up the paper. Some compounds in the mixture will move rapidly up the paper with the solvent, other compounds will move much more slowly, if at all, and will be found lower down the paper. Thus, the components of the mixture are separated. It is common to measure the distance the sample has moved from its original starting point and compare it with the distance the solvent has moved from the starting point to calculate ratios known as Rf values.

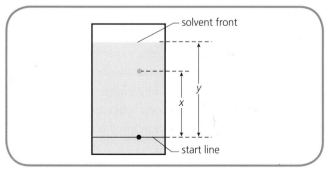

Figure 17.2 Measuring the distance components move in chromatography

Every type of chromatography has a **mobile phase** and a **stationary phase**. In the case of paper chromatography, the wet paper is the stationary phase and the solvent is the mobile phase. The separation occurs because the molecules in the mixture have different polarities and/or size. For example, imagine trying to separate a mixture containing a very polar molecule and a less polar molecule. If a polar solvent is used, such as ethanol, then the polar molecule would rise up the paper much faster than the less polar molecule as the polar molecule is more strongly attracted to the mobile phase. Larger molecules tend to take a longer time to move up the paper compared with smaller molecules.

Chromatography is a good tool for checking the progress of a chemical reaction. For example, Figure 17.3 shows the chromatogram for samples P, Q, R and S from an esterification reaction.

Component P = pure ester

Component Q = the reaction mixture after 10 minutes

Component R = the alcohol used to make the ester

Component S = the carboxylic acid used to make the ester

Spots P, R and S are known as reference samples. By comparing spot Q with the reference samples we can deduce that Q still contains alcohol (R) and carboxylic acid (S) and has yet to form any ester (P). The advantage of this method is that the reaction can continue while the chromatography is being carried out. A result such as the one shown indicates that the

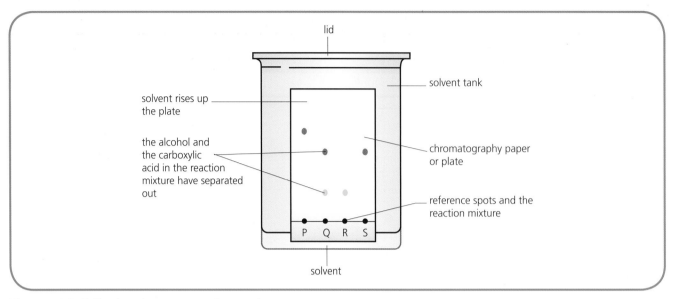

Figure 17.3 Following the progress of a reaction

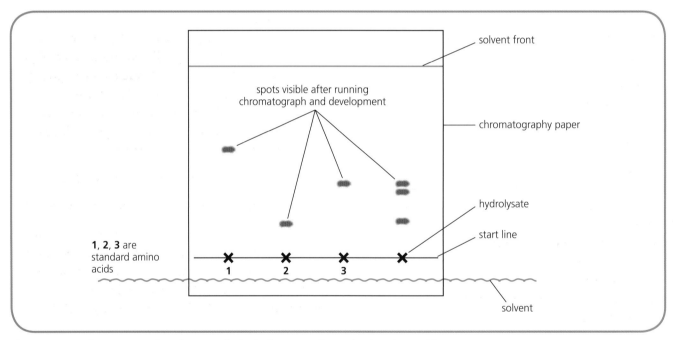

Figure 17.4 Chromatography of a protein hydrolysate and standard amino acids

alcohol and carboxylic acid have still to react to form the ester, or that the quantity of ester produced is so small that it cannot be detected. Thus, the reaction should be left for much longer.

As well as following the course of a reaction, chromatography is also useful for identifying the products of a reaction. Figure 17.4 shows the results of chromatography of a protein hydrolysis experiment.

The hydrolysed protein is spotted onto filter paper, with solutions of known amino acids alongside. The

paper is placed in a tank containing a solvent of propanol and water. When the solvent front has almost reached the top of the paper, the paper is removed and then the colourless amino acids are made visible by spraying with ninhydrin. The paper is then heated after which pink, blue or brown spots appear. Sprays such as ninhydrin are used to help us see the spots on the chromatogram as some spots are not visible to the naked eye. Another method of visualisation involves looking at the chromatogram under UV light since most organic molecules will be visible under UV.

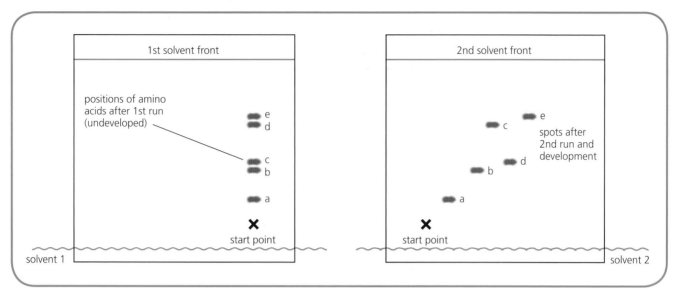

Figure 17.5 Chromatography of a protein hydrolysate by the two-way method

In the example shown in Figure 17.4, the hydrolysed protein appears to contain amino acids '2' and '3' and some other amino acid which is not '1'.

In practice the separation achieved by this method is not good so two-way chromatography is used with two different solvents. Figure 17.5 illustrates the result of such an experiment.

The same hydrolysed protein is used on its own and the paper placed for a fixed time in each solvent in turn. After removal from the second solvent, development with ninhydrin is carried out. To identify the resultant spots, the same process is repeated under identical conditions using each amino acid in turn on separate sheets of paper. Spots are identified by superimposing these separate chromatograms on the original chromatogram.

In modern laboratories, chromatography is usually carried out using much more sophisticated apparatus. Techniques such as GLC (gas liquid chromatography) and HPLC (high performance liquid chromatography) are frequently carried out to help identify the components of a mixture and/or detect impurities. Both of these techniques use the same principles as paper chromatography, in other words

- there is a stationary phase and a mobile phase

- components separate out based on their size/polarity.

In **gas liquid chromatography** the mobile phase is an inert gas, such as nitrogen or helium, and the stationary phase is a high-boiling-point liquid adsorbed onto an inert solid that is placed in a long coiled column. A diagram of a typical GLC is shown in Figure 17.6.

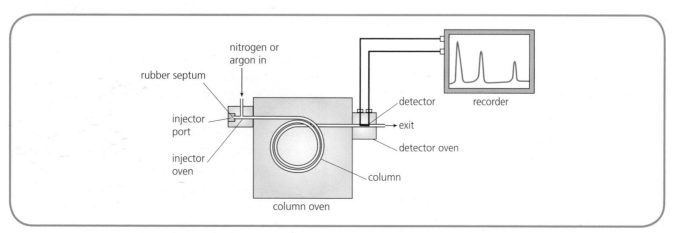

Figure 17.6 Gas liquid chromatography

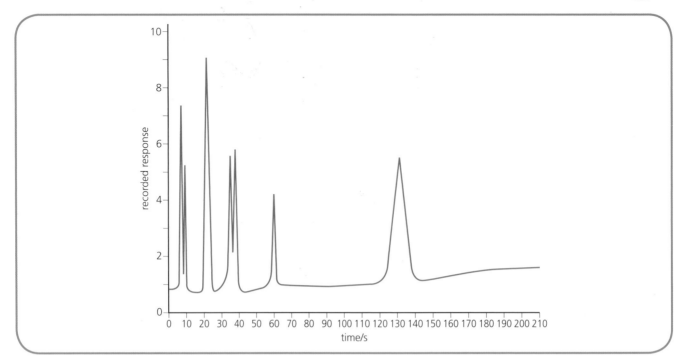

Figure 17.7 A typical result from a GLC

A typical chromatogram obtained from GLC (and HPLC) shows the quantity of component on the y-axis and the **retention time** on the x-axis. The retention time is the time it takes the component to reach the detector. A typical GC chromatogram is shown in Figure 17.7.

The retention times can give us some information about the components if we know the nature of the stationary and mobile phases. For example, if the stationary phase is a polar liquid we would expect polar compounds to have a longer retention time than non-polar compounds since the polar components would be attracted to the stationary phase. Non-polar molecules would not be attracted to the stationary phase. They would be carried very quickly through the column by the carrier gas resulting in a very short retention time.

The chromatogram shows that the components have separated out. On its own, such a graph would be pretty useless. Most chromatography experiments would involve running an experiment where a compound of interest is also passed through the GLC. For example, if forensic scientists were investigating a house fire where it was suspected that petrol was used to start the fire deliberately, several samples would have to be analysed by chromatography. A sample of material from the house could be placed in a sealed bag which would then be heated (for example in an oven) to produce gases from any volatile liquids from the material. A syringe could then be used to remove the gases and inject them into the GLC. Samples of petrol could then be analysed by the same method and the chromatograms obtained could be compared. If some of the peaks match, in other words the retention times are the same, then this would provide some evidence that petrol may have been used.

Figure 17.8 GLC is commonly used to investigate the cause of fires.

Checklist for Revision

- I know the basic principles of chromatography.
- I can interpret a simple chromatogram.
- I can explain the difference in separation of two compounds based on their size or polarity.

Key Terms

The words and phrases below were introduced in this chapter.

Their definitions are given in the chemical dictionary.

chromatography

gas liquid chromatography

mobile phase

retention time

stationary phase

Study Questions

1* When a fire has been started deliberately, gas liquid chromatography (GLC) can be used to identify the tiny amounts of fuel or flammable liquid used to help start the fire.

a) Diesel contains a mixture of non-polar molecules of different sizes.

Below are the chromatograms recorded using a normal sample of diesel and a sample of diesel that has been heated until around 90% of the diesel had evaporated.

Explain how these chromatograms show that large molecules have longer retention times than small molecules in this type of chromatography.

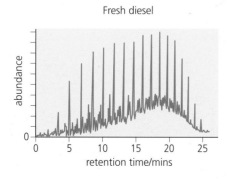

Fresh diesel

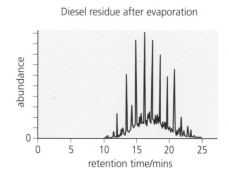

Diesel residue after evaporation

Figure 17.9

b) A suspicious house fire was found to have started in a chair.

An almost empty bottle of paint thinner was found in a suspect's car.

In the house there were two cans of furniture polish which might have been used to clean the chair at some time.

The chromatograms obtained from the remains of the chair, the paint thinner and the furniture polishes are shown in Figure 17.10.

Which of the substances tested were present on the armchair?

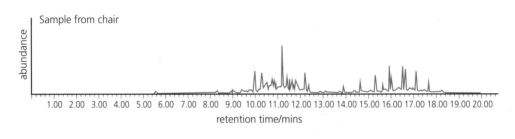

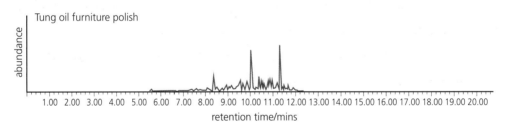

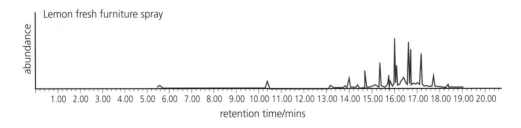

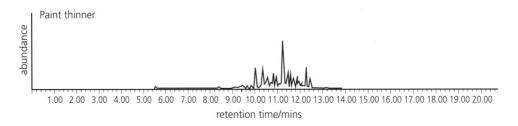

Figure 17.10

2 Column chromatography can be used to separate the components from a reaction. Figure 17.11 shows column chromatography being used to separate two compounds from a mixture. The solvent used was hexane.

Explain which compound, the green or yellow component, is likely to be most polar.

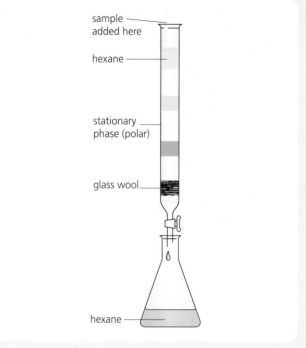

Figure 17.11

1 Find out how chromatography is used to distinguish fake malt whisky from real malt whisky.

2 Research the use of chromatography by forensic scientists investigating illegal drugs.

3 How are sniffer dogs and portable gas chromatography units used to detect explosives?

4 How is chromatography used to detect doping in athletes?

18 Volumetric analysis

Consider the reaction between hydrochloric acid and sodium hydroxide:

$$HCl(aq) + NaOH(aq) \rightarrow NaCl(aq) + H_2O(l)$$

This equation is our starting point for investigating the useful technique of volumetric analysis. This type of analysis allows us to calculate the quantity or concentration of a reacting compound provided we have accurate information about one of the reactants. For example, the concentration of a sodium hydroxide solution can be determined by carrying out a titration with an accurate concentration of hydrochloric acid. The hydrochloric acid would be known as a **standard solution**. A standard solution is a solution of known concentration.

The steps for this are shown in Figures 18.1, 18.2 and 18.3.

The hydrochloric acid is added from the burette until the **indicator** changes colour. The point at which neutralisation occurs is known as the **end point** of the titration. When this point is reached, the volume of acid required is read from the burette. This volume, along with the accurate concentration of acid, can be used to calculate the concentration of sodium hydroxide. Worked Example 1 illustrates how this can be done.

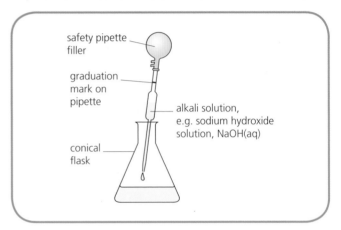

Figure 18.1 Add in a fixed volume of NaOH using a pipette

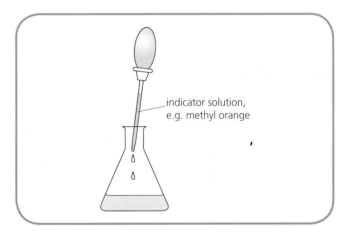

Figure 18.2 Add in a suitable indicator

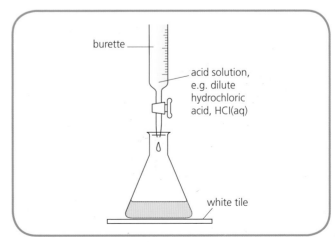

Figure 18.3 Add acid from the burette

Worked Example 1

$25\,cm^3$ of sodium hydroxide solution was added to a flask and titrated with $0.1\,mol\,l^{-1}$ hydrochloric acid. The volume of hydrochloric acid required to neutralise the sodium hydroxide was found to be $10.0\,cm^3$. Use these results to calculate the concentration of the sodium hydroxide solution.

$$HCl(aq) + NaOH(aq) \rightarrow NaCl(aq) + H_2O(l)$$

	HCl(aq)	NaOH(aq)
Mole ratio	1	1
Concentration	$0.1\,mol\,l^{-1}$	?
Volume	$10\,cm^3$	$25\,cm^3$

Table 18.1

From the information given, the number of moles of hydrochloric acid reacting can be calculated using the equation moles = CV, where V is measured in litres.

$$Moles = 0.1 \times 0.01 = 0.001$$

From the mole ratio, 1 mole of HCl reacts with 1 mole of NaOH.

Thus, 0.001 moles of HCl would react with 0.001 moles of NaOH.

$$Concentration\ of\ NaOH = \frac{moles}{volume} = \frac{0.001}{0.025}$$
$$= 0.04\,mol\,l^{-1}$$

Worked Example 2

In a titration, it was found that $10\,cm^3$ of potassium hydroxide was neutralised by $0.05\,mol\,l^{-1}$ sulfuric acid. The volumes of sulfuric acid used in the titration are recorded in Table 18.2.

Titration	Volume of $0.05\,mol\,l^{-1}$ sulfuric acid/cm^3
1	18.0
2	17.4
3	17.3

Table 18.2

Calculate the concentration of the potassium hydroxide given that potassium hydroxide reacts with sulfuric acid according to the equation shown.

$$2KOH(aq) + H_2SO_4(aq) \rightarrow K_2SO_4(aq) + 2H_2O(l)$$

Calculation:

$$Average\ volume\ of\ sulfuric\ acid = \frac{17.3 + 17.4}{2}$$
$= 17.35\,cm^3$ (see Appendix: Researching chemistry for more details on calculating the average and eliminating rogue data)

Number of moles of sulfuric acid reacting
$$= CV = 0.05 \times 0.01735 = 0.00087$$

According to the equation, 1 mole of H_2SO_4 reacts with 2 moles of KOH.

Thus, 0.00087 moles of H_2SO_4 will react with 0.0017 moles of KOH.

$$Concentration\ of\ KOH = \frac{moles}{volume} = \frac{0.0017}{0.01}$$
$$= 0.17\,mol\,l^{-1}$$

Questions

1 $25\,cm^3$ of sodium carbonate solution was neutralised by $17\,cm^3$ of $0.1\,mol\,l^{-1}$ hydrochloric acid. Calculate the concentration of the sodium carbonate solution given the following equation:

$$Na_2CO_3(aq) + 2HCl(aq) \rightarrow 2NaCl(aq) + H_2O(l) + CO_2(g)$$

2 Rhubarb leaves contain the poisonous acid oxalic acid, $(COOH)_2$. A student found it required $12\,cm^3$ of $0.001\,mol\,l^{-1}$ NaOH(aq) to react with $20\,cm^3$ of a solution from rhubarb leaves. Calculate the concentration of oxalic acid in this solution given the following equation:

$$(COOH)_2 + 2NaOH \rightarrow Na_2(COO)_2 + 2H_2O$$

Redox titrations

The previous examples have illustrated the idea of determining the concentration of an unknown solution from an acid–base reaction. Volumetric analysis can also be applied to a redox reaction. For example, the concentration of a solution of a reducing agent can be determined using a solution of a suitable oxidising agent of known concentration provided that:

1   The balanced redox equation is known or can be derived from the relevant ion–electron equations.

2   The volumes of the reactants are accurately measured by pipette and burette.

3   Some method of indicating the end point of the titration is available.

Two examples of redox titrations are given below. A brief outline of the experimental procedure is followed by a specimen calculation. In Worked Example 3 the concentration of a reducing agent, iron(II) sulfate solution, is found by titrating it against an oxidising agent, potassium permanganate solution, of known concentration. In Worked Example 4, a redox titration is used to find the mass of vitamin C in a tablet.

Worked Example 3

To determine the concentration of an iron(II) sulfate solution by titration with a potassium permanganate solution of known concentration

$20\,cm^3$ of iron(II) sulfate solution is transferred by pipette to a conical flask and excess dilute sulfuric acid is added. Potassium permanganate solution $(0.02\,mol\,l^{-1})$ is added from the burette until the contents of the flask just turn from colourless to purple, initial and final burette readings being noted. The titration is repeated to obtain concordant titres.

Since the permanganate solution is so strongly coloured compared with the other solutions, the reaction is self-indicating and the change at the end point from colourless to purple is quite sharp.

Calculate the concentration of an iron(II) sulfate solution given that $20.0\,cm^3$ of it reacted with $24.0\,cm^3$ of $0.02\,mol\,l^{-1}$ potassium permanganate solution. The redox equation for the reaction is

$$MnO_4^- + 8H^+ + 5Fe^{2+} \rightarrow 5Fe^{3+} + Mn^{2+} + 4H_2O$$

According to the equation, 1 mole of MnO_4^- oxidises 5 moles of Fe^{2+}.

Number of moles of MnO_4^- used $= CV = 0.02 \times 0.024$
$$= 4.8 \times 10^{-4}$$

Hence, number of moles of Fe^{2+} present
$$= 5 \times 4.8 \times 10^{-4} = 2.4 \times 10^{-3}$$

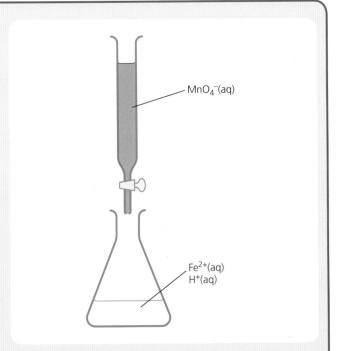

Figure 18.4 The redox titration between permanganate and iron(II) is an example of a self-indicating reaction since the purple colour of permanganate appears once all the iron(II) ions have reacted.

This is contained in $20\,cm^3$, i.e. 0.02 litres.

Hence, concentration of $Fe^{2+}(aq)$, $C = \dfrac{2.4 \times 10^{-3}}{0.02}$
$$= 0.12\,mol\,l^{-1}$$

Since 1 mole $FeSO_4(aq)$ contains 1 mole of $Fe^{2+}(aq)$, the concentration of $FeSO_4(aq) = 0.12\,mol\,l^{-1}$

Worked Example 4

How much vitamin C is present in a vitamin C tablet?

When vitamin C ($C_6H_8O_6$) reacts with iodine, the vitamin C is oxidised and the iodine is reduced:

$$C_6H_8O_6 \rightarrow C_6H_6O_6 + 2e^- + 2H^+$$

$$I_2 + 2e^- \rightarrow 2I^-$$

$$\overline{C_6H_8O_6 + I_2 \rightarrow 2I^- + C_6H_6O_6 + 2H^+}$$

The redox equation shows that 1 mole of iodine reacts with 1 mole of vitamin C. The mass of vitamin C in a tablet can, therefore, be determined by titrating a fixed volume of vitamin C solution with an iodine solution of known concentration. A method for doing this is outlined below.

A vitamin C tablet is dissolved in deionised water (about 50 cm³) in a beaker and transferred with washings to a 250 cm³ standard flask. The flask is made up to the mark, stoppered and inverted several times to ensure thorough mixing.

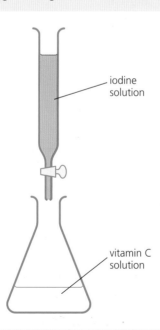

iodine solution

vitamin C solution

Figure 18.5 Titrating a vitamin C solution with iodine solution

A pipette is used to transfer 25 cm³ of this solution to a conical flask and a few drops of starch indicator are added. Iodine solution of known concentration is added from the burette until the first sign of a permanent blue–black colour is seen. The titration is repeated, with dropwise addition of the iodine solution as the end point is approached, to obtain concordant titres.

A solution of vitamin C was prepared as described above and 25 cm³ of this solution was titrated against 0.031 mol l⁻¹ iodine solution using starch indicator. The average titre was 17.6 cm³. Calculate the mass of vitamin C (formula: $C_6H_8O_6$) in the original tablet.

The redox equation is

$$C_6H_8O_6 \quad + \quad I_2 \rightarrow 2I^- + C_6H_6O_6 + 2H^+$$

$$1\,mole \qquad 1\,mole$$

Moles of iodine = CV
$$= 0.031 \times 0.0176$$
$$= 5.456 \times 10^{-4}$$

Hence, number of moles of vitamin C in 25 cm³ (i.e. in the conical flask) = 5.456×10^{-4}

Number of moles of vitamin C in 250 cm³ (i.e. in the standard flask) = 5.456×10^{-3}

This is the number of moles of vitamin C in the original tablet.

Gram formula mass of vitamin C ($C_6H_8O_6$) = 176 g

Mass of vitamin C present in the tablet
$$= 176 \times 5.456 \times 10^{-3}$$
$$= 0.960\,g$$

Questions

3 Calculate the concentrations of the solutions given in italics in the following examples.

a) 12.5 cm³ of an *iodine* solution reacts with 20.0 cm³ of 0.1 mol l⁻¹ sodium sulfite solution.

The redox equation for the reaction is
$$I_2 + SO_3^{2-} + H_2O \rightarrow 2I^- + SO_4^{2-} + 2H^+$$

b) 25.0 cm³ of an *iron(II) sulfate* solution reacts with 20.0 cm³ of 0.5 mol l⁻¹ hydrogen peroxide solution.

The redox equation for the reaction is
$$2Fe^{2+} + H_2O_2 + 2H^+ \rightarrow 2Fe^{3+} + 2H_2O$$

c) 15.0 cm³ of a *tin(II) chloride* solution reacts with 25.0 cm³ of 0.2 mol l⁻¹ potassium dichromate solution which has been acidified with dilute H_2SO_4.

The redox equation for the reaction is
$$3Sn^{2+} + Cr_2O_7^{2-} + 14H^+ \rightarrow 3Sn^{4+} + 2Cr^{3+} + 7H_2O$$

Checklist for Revision

- I can use balanced chemical equations to calculate the quantity of an unknown reactant using information from a titration experiment.
- I can use balanced redox equations to calculate the quantity of an unknown reactant using information from a redox titration experiment.
- I know what is meant by the terms 'indicator', 'end point' and 'standard solution'.
- I know that redox titrations involving potassium permanganate are self-indicating.

Key Terms

The words and phrases below were introduced in this chapter.

Their definitions are given in the chemical dictionary.

end point

indicator

standard solution

Study Questions

1* What volume of sodium hydroxide solution, concentration 0.4 mol l⁻¹, is needed to neutralise 50 cm³ of sulfuric acid, concentration 0.1 mol l⁻¹?

A 25 cm³
B 50 cm³
C 100 cm³
D 200 cm³

2* Sugars, such as glucose, are often used as sweeteners in soft drinks.

The glucose content of a soft drink can be estimated by titration against a standardised solution of Benedict's solution. The copper(II) ions in Benedict's solution react with glucose as shown.

$$C_6H_{12}O_6(aq) + 2Cu^{2+}(aq) \rightarrow Cu_2O(s) + 4H^+(aq) + 2H_2O(l) + C_6H_{12}O_7(aq)$$

a) What change in the ratio of atoms present indicates that the conversion of glucose into the compound with molecular formula $C_6H_{12}O_7$ is an example of oxidation?

b) In one experiment, 25.0 cm³ volumes of a soft drink were titrated with Benedict's solution in which the concentration of copper(II) ions was 0.500 mol l⁻¹. The following results were obtained.

Titration	Volume of Benedict's solution/cm³
1	18.0
2	17.1
3	17.3

Table 18.3

Average volume of Benedict's solution used
= $17.2\,cm^3$

i) Why was the first titration result not used in calculating the average volume of Benedict's solution?

ii) Calculate the concentration of glucose in the soft drink, in $mol\,l^{-1}$.

Show your working clearly.

3 The concentration of an aqueous solution of hydrogen peroxide can be determined in a redox titration with cerium(IV) sulfate solution, $Ce(SO_4)_2(aq)$.

The relevant ion–electron equations are

$$H_2O_2 \rightarrow O_2 + 2H^+ + 2e^-$$

$$Ce^{4+} + e^- \rightarrow Ce^{3+}$$

a) Write the balanced equation for the redox reaction.

b) Name the oxidising agent and the spectator ions present.

c) In an experiment $20.0\,cm^3$ of hydrogen peroxide solution required $15.6\,cm^3$ of $0.092\,mol\,l^{-1}$ cerium(IV) sulfate solution to reach the end point. Calculate the concentration of the solution of hydrogen peroxide.

4* Seaweeds are a rich source of iodine in the form of iodide ions. The mass of iodine in a seaweed can be found using the procedure outlined below.

a) Step 1

The seaweed is dried in an oven and ground into a fine powder. Hydrogen peroxide solution is then added to oxidise the iodide ions to iodine molecules. The ion–electron equation for the reduction reaction is shown.

$$H_2O_2(aq) + 2H^+(aq) + 2e^- \rightarrow 2H_2O(l)$$

Write a balanced redox equation for the reaction of hydrogen peroxide with iodide ions.

b) Step 2

Using starch solution as an indicator, the iodine solution is then titrated with sodium thiosulfate solution to find the mass of iodine in the sample. The balanced equation for the reaction is shown.

$$2Na_2S_2O_3(aq) + I_2(aq) \rightarrow 2NaI(aq) + Na_2S_4O_6(aq)$$

In an analysis of seaweed, $14.9\,cm^3$ of $0.00500\,mol\,l^{-1}$ sodium thiosulfate solution was

required to reach the end point. Calculate the mass of iodine present in the seaweed sample.

5* Chlorine and sodium hydroxide are important industrial chemicals. Both are produced by the electrolysis of sodium chloride solution.

a) Bromine can be obtained by bubbling chlorine gas through a solution of bromide ions.

$$Cl_2(g) + 2Br^-(aq) \rightarrow Br_2(aq) + 2Cl^-(aq)$$

Name this type of reaction.

b) The hypochlorite ion, $ClO^-(aq)$, acts as a bleaching agent in solution.

i) Most household bleaches are made by reacting sodium hydroxide with chlorine. Sodium hypochlorite, sodium chloride and water are formed.

Write a balanced equation for the reaction.

ii) When $ClO^-(aq)$ acts as bleach, it reacts to produce the $Cl^-(aq)$ ion.

$$ClO^-(aq) \rightarrow Cl^-(aq)$$

Complete the above to form the ion–electron equation.

6* For people who suffer from bronchitis, even low concentrations of ozone, O_3, irritate the lining of the throat and can cause headaches.

NO_2 gas from car exhausts reacts with oxygen to form ozone as follows

$$O_2(g) + NO_2(g) \rightleftharpoons NO(g) + O_3(g)$$

Car exhaust fumes also contain volatile organic compounds (VOCs), which can combine with NO gas.

a) Explain how a rise in VOC concentration will change the ozone concentration.

b) In an experiment to measure the ozone concentration of air in a Scottish city, 10^5 litres of air were bubbled through a solution of potassium iodide. Ozone reacts with potassium iodide solution, releasing iodine.

$$2KI(aq) + O_3(g) \rightarrow I_2(aq) + O_2(g) + H_2O(l) \qquad + 2KOH(aq)$$

The iodine formed was titrated with $0.01\,mol\,l^{-1}$ sodium thiosulfate solution, $Na_2S_2O_3(aq)$, using starch indicator.

$$I_2(aq) + 2S_2O_3^{2-} \rightarrow 2I^-(aq) + S_4O_6^{2-}(aq)$$

The results of three titrations are shown in the table.

Experiment	Volume of thiosulfate solution/cm³
1	22.90
2	22.40
3	22.50

Table 18.4

i) What colour change would show that the titration was complete?

ii) Taking the volume of sodium thiosulfate solution to be 22.45 cm³, calculate the volume of ozone in one litre of air.

(Take the molar volume of ozone to be 24 litres mol^{-l}.)

Appendix: Researching chemistry

The scientific discoveries that have taken place over the last 50 years are amazing! Developments in the areas of new medicines, digital technology, alternative energies, explosives and food technology represent a small list of the new developments to which British chemists have contributed. A fundamental part of scientific discovery involves researching what has been done before and researching what other scientists are currently working on. Researching chemistry is a unit of the Higher Chemistry course that will help you to develop lab, research and data-handling skills. This chapter will give a brief overview of the lab- and data-handling skills and should be used alongside other assignments that are at the core of this unit.

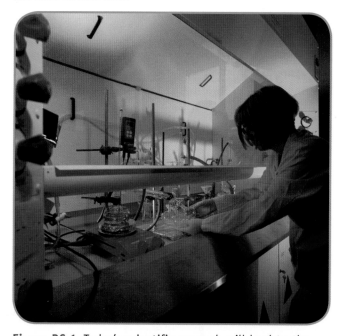

Figure RC.1 Today's scientific research will lead to the development of new products and technologies in the future.

As a developing chemist, you are in the process of refining practical skills that can be applied to make new compounds or analyse existing substances. It is an important part of your training that you can select appropriate apparatus, know how it is used and recognise its limitations. For the Higher course, you should be familiar with, and know how to use, the apparatus listed in Table RC.1.

You should also be familiar with, and know how to carry out, the techniques listed in Table RC.2.

Distillation
Filtration
Methods for collecting a gas: over water or using a gas syringe
Safe heating methods: using a Bunsen, water bath or heating mantle
Titration
Use of a balance

Table RC.2

The limitations of the apparatus should influence your choice of equipment for carrying out a technique. This is discussed in the examples which follow.

Distillation

Distillation is used to separate liquids with different boiling points such as ethanol (bp = 79 °C) and water (bp = 100 °C). The liquid with the lowest boiling point will distil first. Distillation can also be used to recover a solvent from a solution. For example, if a new solid compound has been made and is dissolved

Beaker	Dropper	Pipette filler
Boiling tube	Evaporating basin	Test tubes
Burette	Funnel	Thermometer
Conical flask	Measuring cylinder	Volumetric flask
Delivery tubes	Pipette	

Table RC.1

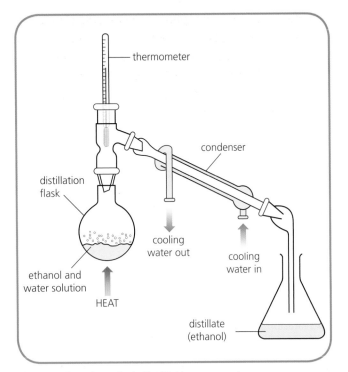

Figure RC.2 A typical distillation apparatus

in an organic solvent, it is common to separate the new compound from the solvent by distillation. This is preferable to evaporation of the solvent as it allows the solvent to be collected so that it can be reused.

An examination of the equipment we use for distillation gives us some insight into the pros and cons of the apparatus we can use for other techniques too.

Choice of thermometer

Thermometers come in a variety of ranges, including $-10-110\,°C$ and $0-200\,°C$. It makes sense to choose a thermometer that covers the range of boiling points of the liquids being separated and is accurate for the temperatures required. For example, if separating liquids with very close boiling points, such as three liquids which boil at $55\,°C$, $65\,°C$ and $80\,°C$, it would not be appropriate to use a thermometer with a large range as the increments on the thermometer would not allow you to distinguish between the liquids. A thermometer with a $0-300\,°C$ range, for example, could have $10\,°C$ as the smallest reading which would make it difficult to control the temperature for distillation involving close-boiling liquids. For the three examples described, it would be better to have a thermometer with a much smaller range, for example $20-100\,°C$, as the increments would be no greater than $1\,°C$.

Choice of heating apparatus

Bunsen burners must be used cautiously if flammable liquids are being distilled. A disadvantage of Bunsen burners is that it can be difficult to control the heating. An advantage is the ability to reach high temperatures. Electric heating mantles allow much greater control of the heating and are safe to use with flammable liquids. Water baths are safe to use, but are very slow to heat, have poor temperature control and cannot heat liquids above the boiling point of water.

Choice of collection flask

It makes sense to choose a flask that can cope with the volume of liquid being distilled! Conical flasks are preferred over beakers as splashes are more contained – they will hit the side of the conical flask. With a beaker, the splashes can often escape through the wide beaker opening.

Evaporation

A solvent can be removed from a solution by leaving it to evaporate in an evaporating basin or heating the solution in an evaporating basin. The disadvantage of this method is that the solvent is 'lost' to the air. Thus, this method would not normally be chosen for harmful or inflammable solvents.

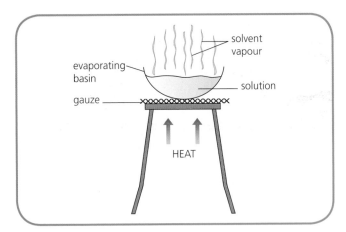

Figure RC.3 Evaporation

Filtration

Filtration is used to collect an insoluble solid from a solid/liquid mixture. Figure RC.4 shows a typical filtration set up.

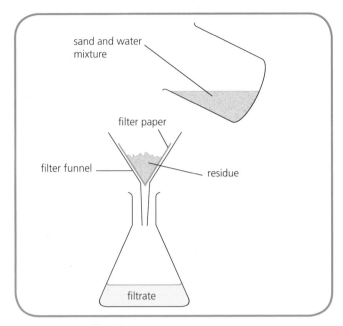

Figure RC.4 Filtration

Methods for collecting a gas

The two main methods for collecting a gas are shown in Figures RC.5 and RC.6.

Collecting a gas over water can be used for gases that are not very soluble in water, for example, any hydrocarbon gas such as methane. If the quantity of gas

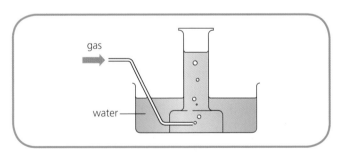

Figure RC.5 Collecting an insoluble gas over water

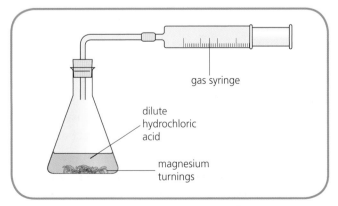

Figure RC.6 Collecting a gas using a gas syringe

is to be determined, an upturned measuring cylinder should be used in place of the gas jar. This method also shows the use of a delivery tube. The apparatus shown in Figure RC.7 could be used to generate a gas which would be connected to the upturned gas jar or gas syringe via a delivery tube.

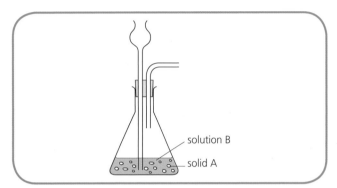

Figure RC.7 Preparing a gas

The gas syringe can be used for both soluble and insoluble gases. It has the advantage that accurate measurements can be determined from reading the scale on the syringe barrel, but there is a limit to the volume of gas that can be collected (usually $100 \, cm^3$).

Safe heating methods

Refer to the earlier section on distillation.

Titration

In the previous chapter, we considered how titrations could be used to determine the quantity or concentration of a reactant. The diagrams in Figure RC.8 illustrate the use of a volumetric flask, pipette, pipette filler, burette and conical flask.

Volumetric flask

This is used to prepare an exact volume of a solution. The solute is dissolved in a beaker of solvent, using a stirring rod to ensure all the solute has dissolved. The solution is transferred to the volumetric flask along with several rinsings from the beaker. The volumetric flask is then made up to the mark. A dropper is usually used to add the final drops of solvent to ensure that the solvent does not go above the line on the flask.

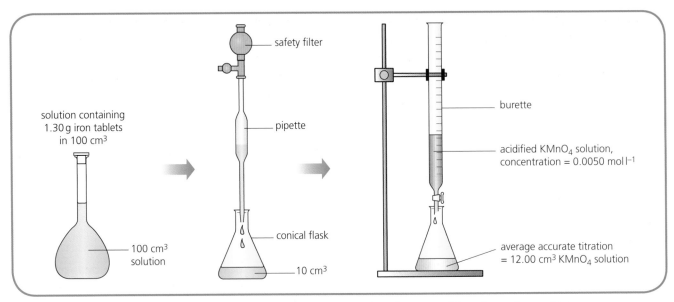

Figure RC.8 Using a standard flask, pipette and burette to determine the mass of iron in an iron tablet.

Pipette

Pipettes are used to transfer exact quantities of liquid. In Figure RC.8, the pipette is being used to transfer 10 cm³ of solution from the standard flask (this is exactly one tenth of the original solution). A pipette filler is used to suck the solution into the pipette.

It is common practice when carrying out a titration to use a pipette to transfer a small volume from the original solution. This allows several samples to be titrated which enables you to assess the **reproducibility** of the technique and helps you to identify **rogue data**. This is discussed later in this chapter.

Burette

Burettes are used to add a liquid during a titration. They are usually filled by adding a funnel to the top of the burette and filling with an appropriate solution from a beaker. A tap is turned to dispense solution from the burette and a measurement is read from the scale on the side of the burette. The funnel should never be left in the burette during a titration and the space below the tap must be full of the solution before any readings are taken.

In the example shown, the end-point of the titration is indicated by the potassium permanganate colour appearing (colourless → purple). This is an example of a self-indicating titration. It will, therefore, not require an indicator.

When using glassware in chemistry, it is vital that the equipment is free from contamination. To prevent dilution of the solutions it is essential to rinse the pipette and burette with the solutions to be used in them before they are filled. For example, if a pipette is being used to transfer 0.1 mol l⁻¹ hydrochloric acid, some of the acid can be used to rinse the pipette.

Use of a balance

There is more than one method for using a balance to measure a mass accurately. A common method is known as weighing by difference. Imagine preparing a sugar solution that must contain an accurate mass of approximately 5.00 g of sugar. Approximately 5 g of the sugar would be transferred to a weighing bottle (off the balance to minimise chemical contamination of the balance), the sugar poured into the vessel where it is to be dissolved and the weighing bottle reweighed. The difference in mass indicates the exact mass transferred.

The accuracy of apparatus

The apparatus chosen for an experiment must be appropriate and take into account the correct degree of accuracy. For example, if you were asked to measure 5.00 g of sugar, you would have to ensure that the balance being used was accurate to two decimal places. Use of a one-decimal-place balance to measure 5.00 g of sugar would be inaccurate, as 5.0 g could represent 5.04 g or 4.95 g whereas 5.00 g could represent 5.004 g or 4.995 g. Clearly, the two-decimal-place balance is much more accurate.

When measuring solutions, you have the choice of using beakers, measuring cylinders and pipettes. The pipette is the most accurate piece of apparatus and would be the sensible choice for measuring volumes where accuracy is important. Burettes can be used to dispense non-standard volumes accurately.

The uncertainty value associated with a piece of apparatus can give some information about the accuracy of the apparatus. For example, a 10 cm³ pipette with an uncertainty of ± 0.08 cm³ is less accurate than a 10 cm³ pipette with an uncertainty of ± 0.02 cm³. The examples used with the balances could be used to show that the two-decimal-place balance has an uncertainty of ± 0.005 g and the one-decimal-place balance has an uncertainty of ± 0.05 g. This comparison makes it obvious that the two-decimal-place balance is more accurate.

Analysis of data

The results from experiments that involve measuring, such as titrations, give us data that we can use in calculations. It is important that the data we use are meaningful and correct. As part of the Researching Chemistry unit, you should be familiar with calculating averages, eliminating rogue data, drawing graphs (scatter and best fit line/curve) and interpreting graphs.

Titration results are commonly encountered in the Higher course, such as those given in Table RC.3.

Titration	Volume of solution/cm³
1	25.5
2	35.5
3	23.8
4	23
5	23.7

Table RC.3

There are two results in this table that could be used to calculate the average titration volume. Results 3 and 5 are within 0.1 cm³ of each other. The average (mean) volume is found by adding these two values and dividing the answer by two:

$$\frac{23.8 + 23.7}{2} = 23.75 \text{ cm}^3$$

Titration 1 represents the rough titration and cannot be used to calculate an average.

Titration 2 looks like a 'rogue' volume and can be discarded. Perhaps the experimenter made a mistake in their calculation or during the experiment.

Titration 4 cannot be used as it has not been quoted to the correct degree of accuracy. We do not know whether 23 represents 23.0, 23.1, 23.2 etc. This result would have to be discarded too.

Reproducibility

An experiment classed as being reproducible is one that provides the same answer, within equipment error, when repeated. For example, the results from an experiment to measure the volume of gas released when magnesium was reacted with hydrochloric acid are shown in Tables RC.4 and RC.5. Both students carried out the experiment three times.

Student A

Experiment	Volume of gas/cm³
1	55
2	54
3	55

Table RC.4

Student B

Experiment	Volume of gas/cm³
1	10
2	18
3	24

Table RC.5

We would say that the results from student A are reproducible. The results from student B are not reproducible. Errors in equipment, for example a leaky gas syringe, could lead to problems with reproducibility or it could be errors in the technique such as gas escaping at the start of the experiment before the student connects the flask to the gas syringe.

Key Terms

The words and phrases below were introduced in this appendix.

Their definitions are given in the chemical dictionary.

distillation

reproducibility

rogue data

Study Questions

1* Which of the procedures would be best for obtaining sodium chloride from a mixture of sodium chloride and silver chloride?

A Add water, filter and collect residue.

B Add water, filter and evaporate filtrate.

C Add hydrochloric acid, filter and collect residue.

D Add sodium hydroxide solution, filter and evaporate residue.

2* Potassium permanganate is a very useful chemical in the laboratory.

a) Solid potassium permanganate can be heated to release oxygen gas. This reaction can be represented by the equation shown below.

$$KMnO_4(s) \rightarrow K_2O(s) + MnO_2(s) + O_2(g)$$

Balance the above equation.

b) An acidified potassium permanganate solution can be used to determine the concentration of a solution of iron(II) sulfate by a titration method.

i) Apart from taking accurate measurements, suggest two points of good practice that a student should follow to ensure that an accurate end-point is achieved in a titration.

ii) In a titration, a student found that an average of $16.7 \, cm^3$ of iron(II) sulfate solution was needed to react completely with $25.0 \, cm^3$ of $0.20 \, mol \, l^{-1}$ potassium permanganate solution.

The equation for the reaction is

$$5Fe^{2+}(aq) + MnO_4^-(aq) \rightarrow 5Fe^{3+}(aq) + Mn^{2+}(aq)$$
$$+ 8H^+(aq) \qquad\qquad + 4H_2O(l)$$

Calculate the concentration of the iron(II) sulfate solution, in $mol \, l^{-1}$.

Show your working clearly.

3* Sulfur dioxide is added to wine as a preservative. A mass of 20 to 40 mg of sulfur dioxide per litre of wine will safeguard the wine without affecting its taste.

The concentration of sulfur dioxide in white wine may be found by titration with a standard solution of iodine.

Describe clearly, with full experimental detail, how $0.05 \, mol \, l^{-1}$ iodine solution would be diluted to give $250 \, cm^3$ of $0.005 \, mol \, l^{-1}$ solution.

4* An experiment was carried out to determine the rate of the reaction between hydrochloric acid and calcium carbonate chips. The rate of this reaction was followed by measuring the volume of gas released over a certain time.

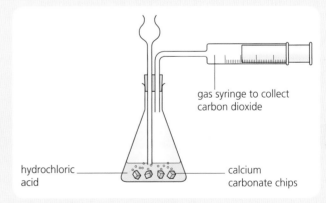

gas syringe to collect carbon dioxide

hydrochloric acid

calcium carbonate chips

Figure RC.9

Describe a different way of measuring volume in order to follow the rate of this reaction.

5* Carbon monoxide is a product of the reaction of carbon dioxide with hot carbon. The carbon dioxide is made by the reaction of dilute hydrochloric acid with solid calcium carbonate.

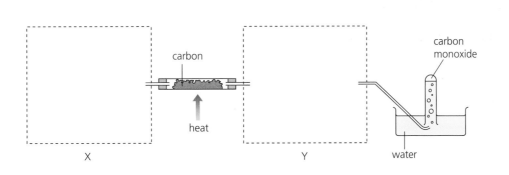

Figure RC.10

Unreacted carbon dioxide is removed before the carbon monoxide is collected by displacement of water.

Copy and complete the diagram to show how the carbon dioxide can be produced at X and how the unreacted carbon dioxide can be removed by bubbling it through a solution at Y.

Normal laboratory apparatus should be used in your answer and the chemicals used at X and Y should be labelled.

6* The picture shows a trainee technician taking a burette reading while carrying out a permanganate titration.

Identify four points of bad practice in his technique.

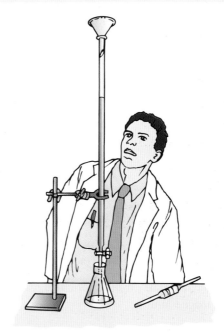

Figure RC.11

End-of-course questions

All of the questions in this section come from past Higher examination papers and are reproduced here with permission from the Scottish Qualifications Authority.

Part 1: Multiple choice questions

1 Which of the following solids has a low melting point and a high electrical conductivity?

A Iodine

B Potassium

C Silicon oxide

D Potassium fluoride

2 Which covalent gas dissolves in water to form an alkali?

A HCl

B CH_4

C SO_2

D NH_3

3 Hydrochloric acid reacts with magnesium according to the following equation:

$$Mg(s) + 2H^+(aq) \rightarrow Mg^{2+}(aq) + H_2(g)$$

What volume of $4\,mol\,l^{-1}$ hydrochloric acid reacts with 0.1 mol of magnesium?

A $25\,cm^3$

B $50\,cm^3$

C $100\,cm^3$

D $200\,cm^3$

4 Two identical samples of zinc were added to an excess of two solutions of sulfuric acid, concentrations $2\,mol\,l^{-1}$ and $1\,mol\,l^{-1}$, respectively.

Which of the following would have been the same for the two samples?

A The total mass lost

B The total time for the reaction

C The initial reaction rate

D The average rate of evolution of gas

5 1mol of hydrogen gas and 1mol of iodine vapour were mixed and allowed to react. After t seconds, 0.8 mol of hydrogen remained.

The number of moles of hydrogen iodide formed at t seconds was

A 0.2

B 0.4

C 0.8

D 1.6

6

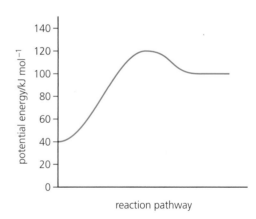

reaction pathway

Which of the following sets of data applies to the reaction represented by the above energy diagram?

	Enthalpy change	Activation energy/$kJ\,mol^{-1}$
A	Exothermic	60
B	Exothermic	80
C	Endothermic	60
D	Endothermic	80

7 A small increase in temperature results in a large increase in rate of reaction. The main reason for this is that

   A more collisions are taking place

   B the enthalpy change is lowered

   C the activation energy is lowered

   D many more particles have energy greater than the activation energy.

8 Which type of bonding can be described as intermolecular?

   A Covalent bonding

   B Hydrogen bonding

   C Ionic bonding

   D Metallic bonding

9 Which statement may be correctly applied to silicon?

   A It consists of discrete molecules.

   B It has a covalent network structure.

   C It has delocalised electrons.

   D It is a covalent molecular solid.

10 The shapes of some common molecules are shown below and each contains at least one polar bond. Which molecule is non-polar?

   A   H — Cl

   B $H\diagdown O\diagup H$

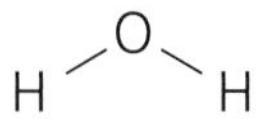

   C   O = C = O

   D $\begin{array}{c} H \\ | \\ C \\ Cl \diagup \ \ \diagdown Cl \\ Cl \end{array}$

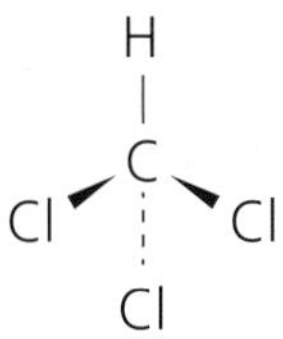

11 $2NO(g) + O_2(g) \rightarrow 2NO_2(g)$

   How many litres of nitrogen dioxide gas could theoretically be obtained in the reaction of 1 litre of nitrogen monoxide gas with 2 litres of oxygen gas? (All volumes are measured under the same conditions of temperature and pressure.)

   A 1

   B 2

   C 3

   D 4

12 Which of the following gases has the same volume as 128.2 g of sulfur dioxide gas? (All volumes are measured under the same conditions of temperature and pressure.)

   A 2.0 g of hydrogen

   B 8.0 g of helium

   C 32.0 g of oxygen

   D 80.8 g of neon

13 Which of the following is the strongest van der Waals' force?

   A Covalent bond

   B Permanent dipole–permanent dipole interactions

   C Hydrogen bond

   D London dispersion forces

14 Which of the following is the strongest oxidising agent?

   A Li

   B MnO_4^-

   C $Cr_2O_7^{2-}$

   D F_2

15 Which of the following compounds does not have isomeric structures?

   A C_2HCl_3

   B $C_2H_4Cl_2$

   C Propene

   D Propan-1-ol

16 Which of the following structural formulae represents a tertiary alcohol?

A

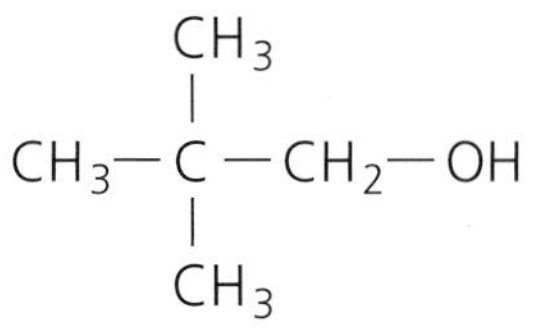

$$CH_3-\underset{\underset{CH_3}{|}}{\overset{\overset{CH_3}{|}}{C}}-CH_2-OH$$

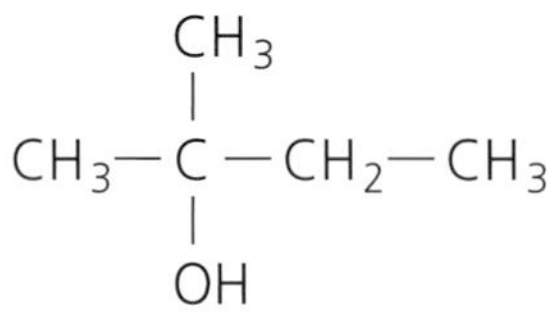

B

$$CH_3-\underset{\underset{OH}{|}}{\overset{\overset{CH_3}{|}}{C}}-CH_2-CH_3$$

C

$$CH_3-CH_2-CH_2-\underset{\underset{OH}{|}}{\overset{\overset{H}{|}}{C}}-CH_3$$

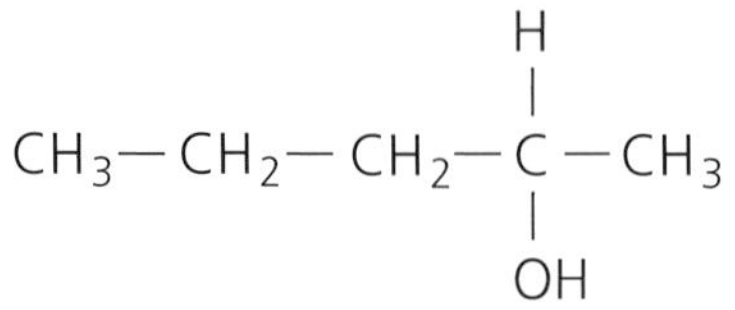

D

$$CH_3-CH_2-\underset{\underset{OH}{|}}{\overset{\overset{H}{|}}{C}}-CH_2-CH_3$$

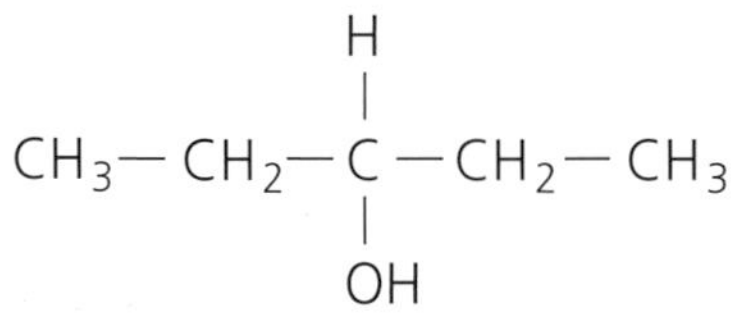

17 An ester has the structural formula:

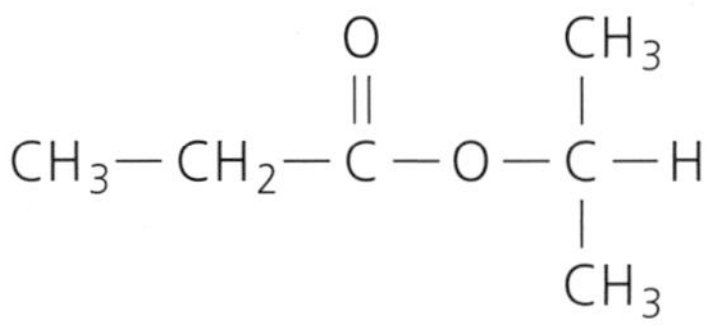

$$CH_3-CH_2-\overset{\overset{O}{||}}{C}-O-\underset{\underset{CH_3}{|}}{\overset{\overset{CH_3}{|}}{C}}-H$$

On hydrolysis, the ester would produce

A ethanoic acid and propan-1-ol

B ethanoic acid and propan-2-ol

C propanoic acid and propan-1-ol

D propanoic acid and propan-2-ol.

18 Which of the following substances acts as a soap?

A Calcium stearate

B Stearic acid

C Potassium stearate

D Ethyl stearate

19 Which reaction can be classified as reduction?

A $CH_3CH_2OH \rightarrow CH_3COOH$

B $CH_3CH(OH)CH_3 \rightarrow CH_3COCH_3$

C $CH_3CH_2COCH_3 \rightarrow CH_3CH_2CH(OH)CH_3$

D $CH_3CH_2CHO \rightarrow CH_3CH_2COOH$

20 Which of the following is an isomer of hexanal?

A 2-methylbutanal

B 3-methylpentan-2-one

C 2,2-dimethylbutan-1-ol

D 3-ethylpentanal

21 Which statement cannot be applied to fats and oils?

A They produce carboxylic acids when hydrolysed.

B They produce glycerol when hydrolysed.

C They are esters.

D They are held together by hydrogen bonds.

22 Which of the following molecules would be found when a protein is completely hydrolysed?

A CH_3-NH_2

B CH_3-COOH

C $CH_3-\overset{\overset{O}{||}}{C}-\underset{\underset{H}{|}}{N}-CH_3$

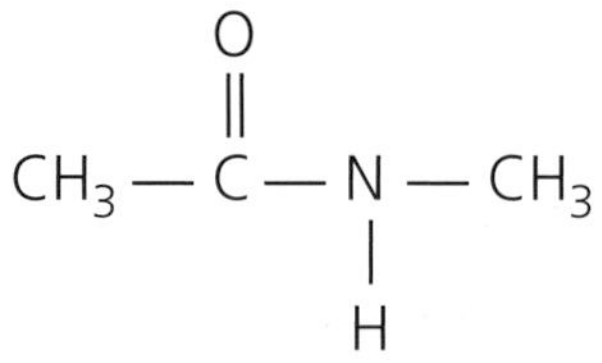

D H_2N-CH_2-COOH

23 Proteins can be denatured under acid conditions. During this denaturing, the protein molecule

   A changes shape

   B is dehydrated

   C is neutralised

   D is polymerised.

24 When 3.6 g of butanal (relative formula mass = 72) was burned, 134 kJ of energy was released.

   From this result, what is the enthalpy of combustion, in kJ mol^{-1}?

   A −6.7

   B +6.7

   C −2680

   D +2680

25 A mixture of sodium chloride and sodium sulfate is known to contain 0.6 mol of chloride ions and 0.2 mol of sulfate ions.

   How many moles of sodium ions are present?

   A 0.4

   B 0.5

   C 0.8

   D 1.0

26 Chemical reactions are in a state of dynamic equilibrium only when

   A the reaction involves zero enthalpy change

   B the concentrations of reactants and products are equal

   C the rate of the forward reaction equals that of the backward reaction

   D the activation energies of the forward and backward reactions are equal.

27 During a redox process in acid solution, iodate ions, $IO_3^-(aq)$, are converted into iodine, $I_2(aq)$.

$$IO_3^-(aq) \rightarrow I_2(aq)$$

   The numbers of $H^+(aq)$ and $H_2O(l)$ required to balance the ion–electron equation for the formation of 1 mol of $I_2(aq)$ are, respectively

   A 3 and 6

   B 6 and 3

   C 6 and 12

   D 12 and 6.

28 In which of the following reactions is hydrogen gas acting as an oxidising agent?

   A $H_2 + C_2H_4 \rightarrow C_2H_6$

   B $H_2 + Cl_2 \rightarrow 2HCl$

   C $H_2 + 2Na \rightarrow 2NaH$

   D $H_2 + CuO \rightarrow H_2O + Cu$

29 The mean bond enthalpy of the N–H bond is equal to one third of the value of ΔH for which of the following changes?

   A $NH_3(g) \rightarrow N(g) + 3H(g)$

   B $2NH_3(g) \rightarrow N_2(g) + 3H_2(g)$

   C $NH_3(g) \rightarrow \frac{1}{2}N_2(g) + 1\frac{1}{2}H_2(g)$

   D $2NH_3(g) + 1\frac{1}{2}O_2(g) \rightarrow N_2(g) + 3H_2O(g)$

30 Given the equations

   $Mg(s) + 2H^+(aq) \rightarrow Mg^{2+}(aq) + H_2(g)\ \Delta H = a\,J\,mol^{-1}$

   $Zn(s) + 2H^+(aq) \rightarrow Zn^{2+}(aq) + H_2(g)\ \Delta H = b\,J\,mol^{-1}$

   $Mg(s) + Zn^{2+}(aq) \rightarrow Mg^{2+}(aq) + Zn(s)\ \Delta H = c\,J\,mol^{-1}$

   then, according to Hess's Law

   A c = a – b

   B c = a + b

   C c = b – a

   D c = – b – a.

Part 2: Extended answer questions

1 The melting and boiling points and electrical conductivities of four substances are given in the table.

Substance	Melting point/ °C	Boiling point/ °C	Solid conducts electricity?	Melt conducts electricity?
A	92	190	no	no
B	1050	2500	yes	yes
C	773	1407	no	yes
D	1883	2503	no	no

Copy and complete the table below by adding the appropriate letter for each type of bonding and structure.

Substance	Bonding and structure at room temperature
	covalent molecular
	covalent network
	ionic
	metallic

(2)

2 The elements in the second row of the Periodic Table are shown below.

Li	Be	B	C	N	O	F	Ne

a) Why does the atomic size decrease crossing the period from lithium to neon? (1)

b) Use the electronegativity values to explain why nitrogen chloride contains pure covalent bonds. (1)

c) The hydrides of carbon, CH_4, and fluorine, HF, have very different boiling points. Explain why HF has a much higher boiling point than CH_4. (3)

d) The Periodic Table groups together elements with similar properties. In most Periodic Tables hydrogen is placed at the top of group I, but in some it is placed at the top of group VII.

Using your knowledge of chemistry, comment on why hydrogen can be placed in both group I and group VII. (3)

3 Alkanes and alkenes can react with bromine. Alkanes react via a free radical mechanism to produce a substitution product. Alkenes react to form an addition product.

a) Draw the product formed when ethene reacts with 1 mole of Br_2. (1)

b) Ethane reacts with bromine to produce bromoethane and hydrogen bromide:

$$C_2H_6 + Br_2 \rightarrow C_2H_5Br + HBr$$

i) Using bond enthalpy values, calculate the enthalpy change, in $kJ\,mol^{-1}$, for this reaction. Assume that this is a gas phase reaction. (2)

ii) Calculate the atom economy for the production of bromoethane. (1)

c) The initiation step for the reaction of bromine with ethane is:

$$Br–Br \rightarrow Br^{\cdot} + Br^{\cdot}$$

Write chemical equations for the two propagation steps. (2)

d) Explain why the reaction of bromine with ethane occurs in daylight but does not occur in darkness. (1)

4 Hydrogen sulfide, H_2S, is the unpleasant gas produced when eggs rot.

a) **i)** The gas can be prepared by the reaction of iron(II) sulfide with dilute hydrochloric acid. Iron(II) chloride is the other product of the reaction.

Write a balanced chemical equation for this reaction. (1)

ii) Iron metal is often present as an impurity in iron(II) sulfide.

Name the other product which would be formed in the reaction with dilute hydrochloric acid if iron metal is present as an impurity. (1)

b) The enthalpy of combustion of hydrogen sulfide is $-563\,kJ\,mol^{-1}$.

Use this value and the enthalpy of combustion values in the data booklet to calculate the enthalpy change for the reaction

$$H_2(g) + S(s) \rightarrow H_2S(g)$$
$$(rhombic)$$

Show your working clearly. (2)

5 An ester can be prepared by the following sequence of reactions.

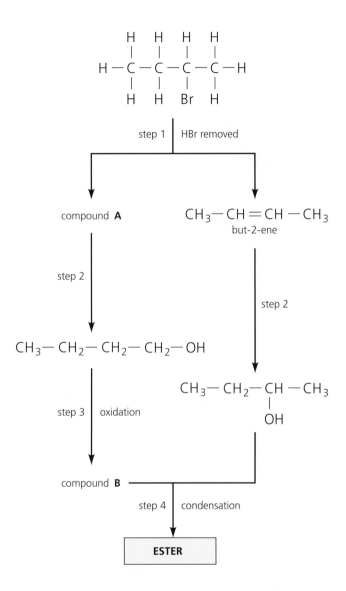

a) i) Draw a structural formula for compound A. (1)

ii) But-2-ene and compound A undergo the same type of reaction in Step 2.

Name this type of reaction. (1)

iii) Acidified potassium dichromate solution can be used to carry out Step 3.

Suggest an alternative to acidified potassium dichromate which could be used to carry out Step 3. (1)

iv) Name compound B. (1)

b) i) What evidence would show that an ester had been formed in Step 4? (1)

ii) Give one use for esters. (1)

6 A student added 0.20 g of silver nitrate, $AgNO_3$, to 25 cm³ of water. This solution was then added to 20 cm³ of 0.0010 mol l⁻¹ hydrochloric acid as shown in the diagram.

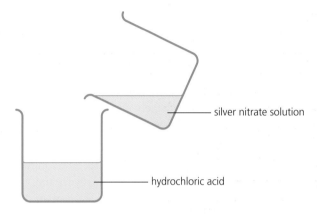

The equation for the reaction which occurs is

$$AgNO_3(aq) + HCl(aq) \rightarrow AgCl(s) + HNO_3(aq)$$

a) Name the type of reaction which takes place. (1)

b) Show by calculation which reactant is in excess. Show your working clearly. (2)

7 When sodium hydrogencarbonate is heated to 112 °C it decomposes and the gas carbon dioxide is given off:

$$2NaHCO_3(s) \rightarrow Na_2CO_3(s) + CO_2(g) + H_2O(g)$$

The following apparatus can be used to measure the volume of carbon dioxide produced by the reaction.

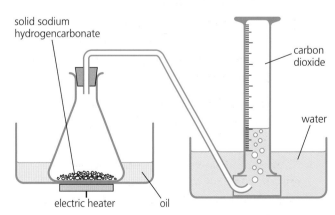

a) Why is an oil bath used and not a water bath? (1)

b) i) Calculate the theoretical volume of carbon dioxide produced by the complete decomposition of 1.68 g of sodium hydrogencarbonate. (Take the molar volume of carbon dioxide to be 23 litres mol^{-1}.) Show your working clearly. (2)

ii) Assuming that all of the sodium hydrogencarbonate is decomposed, suggest why the volume of carbon dioxide collected in the measuring cylinder would be less than the theoretical value. (1)

c) Sodium hydrogencarbonate costs £5.84 for 1 kg, 95% of which is sodium hydrogencarbonate.

Calculate the cost of 1.68 g of pure sodium hydrogencarbonate. (2)

8 Many of the flavour and aroma molecules found in foods are aldehydes and ketones. Although aldehydes and ketones have different structures, they both contain the carbonyl functional group.

a) In what way is the structure of an aldehyde different from that of a ketone? (1)

b) i) As a result of the difference in structure, aldehydes react with Tollens' reagent but ketones do not.

In the reaction of propanal with Tollens' reagent, silver ions are reduced to form silver metal.

Copy and complete the following ion–electron equation for the oxidation. (1)

$$C_3H_6O \rightarrow C_2H_5COOH$$

ii) Name the compound with formula C_2H_5COOH. (1)

iii) Name the type of compounds added to foods to prevent oxidation. (1)

c) As a result of both containing the carbonyl group, aldehydes and ketones react in a similar way with hydrogen cyanide.

The equation for the reaction of propanal and hydrogen cyanide is shown.

i) Suggest a name for this type of reaction. (1)

ii) Draw a structure for the product of the reaction between propanone and hydrogen cyanide. (1)

9 Vitamin C is required by our bodies for producing the protein, collagen. The structure of collagen is formed from the protein bonding to form sheets that support skin and internal organs.

a) i) Name the type of bonding which occurs between protein molecules. (1)

ii) Part of the structure of collagen is shown.

Draw a structural formula for an amino acid that could be obtained by hydrolysing this part of the collagen. (1)

b) A standard solution of iodine can be used to determine the mass of vitamin C in orange juice.

Iodine reacts with vitamin C as shown by the following equation.

$$C_6H_8O_6(aq) + I_2(aq) \rightarrow C_6H_6O_6(aq) + 2H^+(aq) + 2I^-(aq)$$
vitamin C

In an investigation using a carton containing 500 cm^3 of orange juice, separate 50.0 cm^3 samples were measured out. Each sample was then titrated with a 0.0050 mol l^{-1} solution of iodine.

The results from the titration are shown in the table.

Experiment	Volume of iodine/cm³
1	23.0
2	21.5
3	21.3

i) Titrating the whole carton of orange juice would require large volumes of iodine solution. Apart from this disadvantage give another reason for titrating several smaller samples of orange juice. (1)

ii) Calculate the number of moles of iodine reacting with the vitamin C in 50.0 cm³ of orange juice. (1)

iii) Use the result from part ii) to calculate the mass of vitamin C, in grams, in the 500 cm³ carton of orange juice. Show your working clearly. (2)

10 An industrial method for the production of ethanol is outlined in the flow diagram.

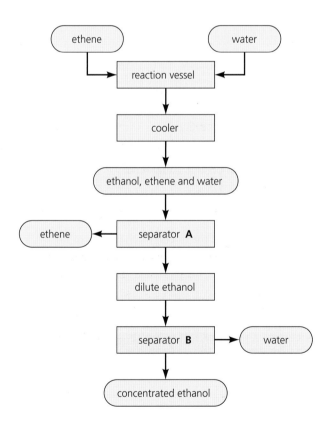

a) i) Unreacted ethene is removed in separator A. Suggest how the separated ethene could be used to increase the efficiency of the overall process. (1)

ii) Name the process that takes place in separator B. (1)

b) In the reaction vessel, ethanol is produced in an exothermic reaction.

$$C_2H_4(g) + H_2O(g) \rightleftharpoons C_2H_5OH(g)$$

i) Name the type of chemical reaction that takes place in the reaction vessel. (1)

ii) What evidence is there that the reaction of ethene with water is exothermic? (1)

iii) What would happen to the equilibrium position if the temperature inside the reaction vessel was increased? (1)

iv) If 1.64 kg of ethanol (relative formula mass = 46) is produced from 10.0 kg of ethene (relative formula mass = 28), calculate the percentage yield of ethanol. (2)

c) State the name of the method used to produce ethanol from fruit sugars. (1)

11 Fats and oils can be reacted with sodium hydroxide to produce soaps.

a) Explain why fats have a higher melting point than oils.

In your answer, refer to the structure of fats and oils and the intermolecular bonds. (3)

b) By referring to the structure of soap, explain how soap can help oil and water to mix. (3)

12 A student used the simple laboratory apparatus shown to determine the enthalpy of combustion of methanol, CH_3OH.

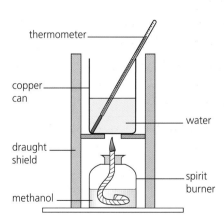

The student measured the change in mass of the methanol so that the mass of methanol burned could be calculated. She also measured the volume of water, the starting temperature of the water and the highest temperature of the water.

a) Describe how the student should use the thermometer to accurately record the highest temperature of the water. (1)

b) In an experiment, the following results were obtained.

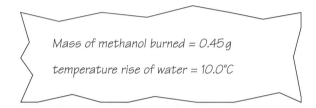

Mass of methanol burned = 0.45 g

temperature rise of water = 10.0°C

Given that the volume of water heated was 100 cm^3, calculate the enthalpy of combustion, in kJ mol^{-1}, for methanol. (3)

c) A more accurate value for the enthalpy of combustion can be obtained using a bomb calorimeter.

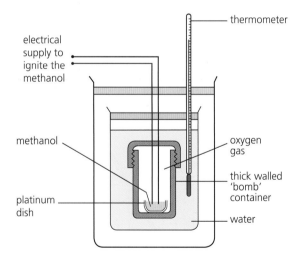

Give two reasons why the value obtained for the enthalpy of combustion of methanol is more accurate using this method than the student's first method. (2)

13 Gas chromatography can be used to identify chemicals. Two chromatograms from samples of petrol are shown below.

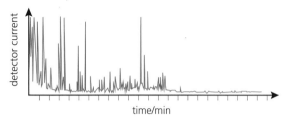

Petrol sample taken after 10 minutes

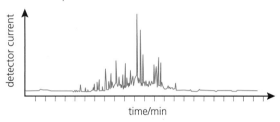

Petrol sample taken after 200 minutes

a) The carrier gas used for the chromatography was nitrogen. Suggest why this gas is used. (1)

b) Suggest why the samples have different chromatograms. (1)

14 A proton NMR spectrum can be used to help identify the structure of an organic compound.

The three key principles used in identifying a group containing hydrogen atoms in a molecule are as follows:

1. The position of the line(s) on the x-axis of the spectrum is a measure of the 'chemical shift' of the hydrogen atoms in the particular group.

Some common 'chemical shift' values are given in the table below.

Group containing hydrogen atoms	Chemical shift
$-CH_3$	1.0
$-C{\equiv}CH$	2.7
$-CH_2Cl$	3.7
$-CHO$	9.0

2. The number of lines for the hydrogen atoms in the group is n + 1 where n is the number of hydrogen atoms on the carbon atom next to the group.

3. The maximum height of the line(s) for the hydrogen atoms in the group is relative to the number of hydrogen atoms in the group.

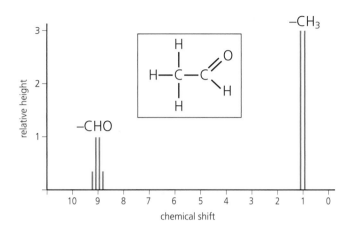

The spectrum for ethanal is shown above.

a) The chemical shift values shown in the table are based on the range of values shown in the data booklet for proton NMR spectra.

Use the data booklet to find the range in the chemical shift values for hydrogen atoms in the following environment: (1)

b) A carbon compound has the following spectrum.

Draw a structural formula for this compound. (1)

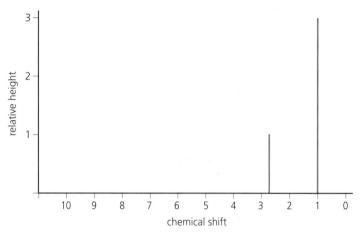

c) Draw the spectrum that would be obtained for chloroethane. (1)

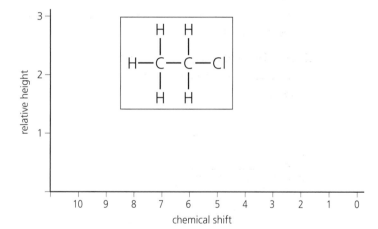

Chemical dictionary

A

Activated complex: An unstable arrangement of atoms formed at the maximum of the potential energy barrier during a reaction.

Activation energy: The energy required by colliding molecules to form an activated complex.

Addition: A reaction in which two or more molecules combine to produce a larger molecule and nothing else.

Alcohols: Carbon compounds which contain the hydroxyl functional group, –OH.

Aldehydes: Carbon compounds which contain the –CHO functional group. They are formed by oxidation of primary alcohols and they oxidise to produce carboxylic acids.

Alkanals: A homologous series of aldehydes, general formula $C_nH_{2n}O$. The first member is methanal, HCHO.

Alkanes: A homologous series of saturated hydrocarbons, general formula C_nH_{2n+2}. The first member is methane, CH_4.

Alkanoic acids: A homologous series of carboxylic acids, general formula $C_nH_{2n}O_2$. The first member is methanoic acid, HCOOH.

Alkanols: A homologous series of alcohols, general formula $C_nH_{2n+1}OH$. The first member is methanol, CH_3OH.

Alkanones: A homologous series of ketones, general formula $C_nH_{2n}O$. The first member is propanone, CH_3COCH_3.

Alkenes: A homologous series of unsaturated hydrocarbons, general formula C_nH_{2n}. Each member contains a carbon–carbon double bond. The first member is ethene, $CH_2=CH_2$.

Alkyl group: A group of carbon and hydrogen atoms forming a branch in a carbon compound, for example methyl group, CH_3-; ethyl group, C_2H_5-.

Amide link: Group of atoms formed by condensation polymerisation of amino acids in the formation of protein chains. The amide link is –CO–NH– and occurs between each pair of amino acid residues in the chain. Also called a **peptide link**.

Amino acids: Compounds of general formula, $H_2NCHRCOOH$ – where R is, for example, H, CH_3, $C_6H_5CH_2$ – which link by condensation reaction to form proteins. Essential amino acids cannot be synthesised by an animal and must be present in its diet.

Antioxidant: Compounds that slow oxidation reactions. They are commonly added to food to prevent edible oils becoming rancid. Examples include vitamins E and C.

Atom economy: A measure of the proportion of reactants that have been converted into products. It is calculated by using the formula,

$$\text{atom economy} = \frac{\text{mass of desired product}}{\text{total mass of reactants}} \times 100$$

Reactions with a high atom economy are desirable.

Atomic number: The number of protons in the nucleus of an atom.

Average rate: The change in mass or concentration of a reactant or product divided by the time interval during which the change occurs.

B

Bonding continuum: A concept applied to bonding. Ionic and covalent bonding lie at opposite ends of the bonding continuum with polar covalent bonding in between.

C

Carbonyl group: The functional group present in ketones, C=O (also present in aldehydes as part of their functional group, –CHO, and in carboxylic acids as part of their functional group, –COOH).

Carboxyl group: The functional group present in carboxylic acids, –COOH. The name derives from the fact that the carboxyl group contains a **carb**onyl and hyd**roxyl** group.

Carboxylic acids: Carbon compounds which contain the carboxyl functional group. Ethanoic acid is an example of a carboxylic acid.

Catalyst: A substance which speeds up a reaction without itself being used up. It lowers the activation energy of the reaction.

Catalyst poisoning: This occurs when a substance forms strong bonds with the surface of a catalyst thus reducing its efficiency.

Chromatography: A technique for separating substances. Molecules of different size or polarity can be separated by this technique which uses a mobile phase of gas or liquid passing over a stationary phase of a solid or a liquid-impregnated solid.

Closed system: Reversible reactions will only reach a state of dynamic equilibrium when the reaction takes place in a reaction vessel that prevents reactants and products escaping.

Collision geometry: A term used to describe the way reactants collide with each other.

Collision theory: A theory used to explain the factors which lead to a successful reaction. It explains how altering variables, such as temperature, can affect the speed of the reaction. The theory requires reactants to i) collide, ii) have the correct collision geometry and iii) have a minimum energy (the activation energy) before a reaction occurs.

Concentration: The amount of solute dissolved in a given volume of solution. The usual units are moles per litre ($mol\,l^{-1}$).

Condensation polymerisation: A process whereby many small molecules (monomers) join to form a large molecule (a polymer), with water or other small molecules formed at the same time. Forming a protein from amino acids is an example of condensation polymerisation.

Condensation reaction: A reaction where molecules join together by the elimination of a small molecule, such as water.

Covalent atomic radius: A useful measure of atomic size, being half the distance between the nuclei of two covalently-bonded atoms of an element. Covalent bond lengths between any two atoms can be obtained by adding the appropriate covalent atomic radii.

Covalent bonding: Bond formed between two atoms by the sharing of a pair of electrons. This usually occurs between non-metal atoms.

Covalent network: A very strong and stable structure formed by certain elements (such as B, C diamond and Si) and certain compounds (for example SiC and SiO_2). All the atoms are held together by strong covalent bonds. Consequently, covalent network compounds are all solids at room temperature and have very high melting points.

Cracking: The breaking up of larger hydrocarbon molecules (usually alkanes) to produce a mixture of smaller molecules (usually alkanes and alkenes). Heat alone is used in thermal cracking. The use of a catalyst (in catalytic cracking) allows the process to be carried out at a lower temperature.

Cycloalkanes: A homologous series of saturated ring molecules with general formula C_nH_{2n}. The simplest is cyclopropane, C_3H_6.

D

Dehydration: The removal of water from a single compound, for example dehydration of ethanol, C_2H_5OH, produces ethene, C_2H_4.

Dehydrogenation: The removal of hydrogen from a single compound, for example dehydrogenation of propane, C_3H_8, produces propene, C_3H_6.

Delocalised electrons: Electrons which are not confined to a single orbital between a pair of atoms, for example in metallic bonding. Delocalised electrons are free to move away from the atom they came from.

Denaturing of proteins: Altering the shape of a protein by an increase in temperature or a reduction in pH. Loss of enzyme activity is one important consequence.

Displacement: A redox reaction where a metal high in the electrochemical series reacts with a compound of a metal lower in the electrochemical series.

Distillation: A process used for separating liquid mixtures. A liquid is boiled and its vapour then condensed to collect pure samples of the liquid. It is used to increase the percentage of ethanol after fermentation.

E

Electrochemical series: A list of chemicals arranged in order of their increasing ability to gain electrons, in other words in order of increasing oxidising power.

Electrolysis: The process that occurs when a current of electricity is passed through a molten electrolyte (resulting in decomposition) or an electrolyte solution (which results in decomposition of the solute and/or the water).

Electron: A particle that moves around the nucleus of an atom. It has a single negative charge but its mass is negligible compared with that of a proton or neutron.

Electronegativity: The strength of the attraction by an atom of an element for its bonding electrons. If the electronegativities of two atoms sharing electrons are similar, the bond will be almost purely covalent. The greater the difference in electronegativities, the more likely the bond is to be polar covalent, or even ionic.

Empirical formula: Shows the simplest ratio of atoms in a compound, for example CH_3 is the empirical formula for ethane (molecular formula C_2H_6).

Emulsion: A mixture of liquids where small droplets of one liquid are dispersed in another liquid. Emulsions of oil and water are commonly found in food.

Endothermic reaction: A reaction in which heat energy is absorbed from the surroundings. It has a positive enthalpy change (ΔH).

End point: The point in a titration where the indicator changes colour to indicate that the reaction is complete.

Enthalpy change: The difference in heat energy between reactants and products in a reaction.

Enthalpy of combustion: The enthalpy change when one mole of a substance is completely burned in oxygen.

Enthalpy of neutralisation of an acid: The enthalpy change when the acid is neutralised to form one mole of water. The enthalpy of neutralisation of a base can be similarly defined.

Enthalpy of solution: The enthalpy change when one mole of a substance is dissolved in sufficient water to form a dilute solution.

Enzyme: A globular protein which is able to catalyse a specific reaction.

Equilibrium: State attained in a reversible reaction when forward and reverse reactions are taking place at the same rate.

Essential amino acids: Amino acids that cannot be made by the body. They must be obtained from the diet.

Essential oils: Oils extracted from plants. They usually have distinctive smells, are non-polar, volatile and often contain compounds known as terpenes.

Esters: Carbon compounds formed when alcohols react with carboxylic acids by condensation.

Exothermic reaction: A reaction in which heat energy is released to the surroundings. It has a negative enthalpy change (ΔH).

F

Fats: Esters formed from one molecule of glycerol and three molecules of (usually saturated) long-chain carboxylic acids. The compounds have melting points high enough to be solid at room temperature. See also **oils**.

Fatty acids: Carboxylic acids formed from the hydrolysis of fats and oils.

Feedstock: A substance derived from a raw material which is used to manufacture another substance.

Fermentation: The process, catalysed by enzymes in yeast, which converts sugars into ethanol and carbon dioxide. This is known as alcoholic fermentation.

Free radical: Highly reactive atoms or molecules with unpaired electrons.

Free radical scavenger: A compound added to plastics, cosmetics and foods to prevent free radical reactions. They react with free radicals to produce stable molecules. This terminates the reaction.

Functional group: A group of atoms or type of carbon–carbon bond which provides a series of carbon compounds with its characteristic chemical properties, for example –CHO, –C=C–.

G

Gas liquid chromatography (GLC): A technique used to separate mixtures in the gas phase.

Glycerol: Propane-1,2,3-triol. Formed from the hydrolysis of fats and oils.

Group: A column of elements in the Periodic Table. The values of a selected physical property show a distinct trend of increase or decrease down the column. The chemical properties of the elements in the group are similar.

H

Haber Process: The industrial production of ammonia from nitrogen and hydrogen using high pressure and temperature, with iron as a catalyst.

Hardening: The process of hydrogenating an oil to produce a more solid compound.

Hess's Law: The enthalpy change of a chemical reaction depends only on the chemical nature and physical state of the reactants and products and is independent of any intermediate steps.

Homologous series: A group of chemically similar compounds which can be represented by a general formula. Physical properties change progressively through the series, for example the alkanes, general formula C_nH_{2n+2}, show a steady increase in boiling point.

Hormones: Chemicals, often complex proteins, which regulate metabolic processes in the body. An example is insulin which regulates sugar metabolism.

Hydration: The addition of water to an unsaturated compound, for example the hydration of ethene, C_2H_4, produces ethanol, C_2H_5OH.

Hydrocarbon: A compound containing the elements carbon and hydrogen only.

Hydrogenation: The addition of hydrogen to an unsaturated compound, for example hydrogenation converts alkenes to alkanes and oils into fats.

Hydrogen bonds: Intermolecular forces of attraction. The molecules must contain highly polar bonds in which hydrogen atoms are linked to very electronegative nitrogen, oxygen or fluorine atoms. The hydrogen atoms are then left with a positive charge and are attracted to the electronegative atoms of other molecules. They are a specific, stronger type of permanent dipole–permanent dipole interaction.

Hydrolysis: The breaking down of larger molecules into smaller molecules by reaction with water.

Hydrophilic: A term used to describe molecules, or parts of a molecule, which are attracted to water. For example, the –OH group in alcohols is hydrophilic.

Hydrophobic: A term used to describe molecules, or parts of a molecule, which repel water and will not bond to water. For example, the long hydrocarbon chains in fats and oils are hydrophobic.

Hydroxyl group: The –OH group. It is found in alcohols.

I

Indicator: A chemical dye added to a titration to detect the end point.

Intermolecular bonds: Bonds between molecules, such as London dispersion forces, permanent dipole–permanent dipole interactions and hydrogen bonds. They are much weaker than intramolecular bonds.

Intramolecular bonds: Bonds within molecules, such as covalent and polar covalent bonds.

Ion–electron equation: An equation that shows either the loss of electrons (oxidation) or the gain of electrons (reduction).

Ionic bond: Bond formed as a result of attraction between positive and negative ions.

Ionisation: The loss or gain of electrons by neutral atoms to form ions, for example

$$Na(g) \rightarrow Na^+(g) + e^-$$

$$Cl(g) + e^- \rightarrow Cl^-(g)$$

'Ionisation enthalpy' is usually reserved for enthalpy changes referring to the formation of positive ions.

Ions: Atoms or groups of atoms that possess a positive

or negative charge due to loss or gain of electrons, for example Na^+ and CO_3^{2-}.

Isomers: Compounds which have the same molecular formula but different structural formulae.

Isotopes: Atoms of the same element which have different numbers of neutrons. They have the same atomic number but different mass numbers.

K

Ketones: Carbon compounds that contain the carbonyl group (C=O). They are formed from the oxidation of secondary alcohols. Unlike aldehydes, ketones cannot be oxidised using mild oxidising agents.

L

Lattice: The three-dimensional arrangement of positive and negative ions in the solid, crystalline state of ionic compounds.

Le Chatelier's Principle: If any change of physical or chemical conditions is imposed on any chemical equilibrium then the equilibrium alters in the direction which tends to counteract the change of conditions.

London dispersion forces: The weak forces of attraction between all atoms and molecules, caused by temporary dipoles.

M

Mass number: The total number of protons and neutrons in the nucleus of an atom.

Metallic bonding: The bonding responsible for typical metallic properties such as malleability, ductility and electrical conductivity in metals and alloys. Each atom loses its outer electrons to form positive ions. These ions pack together in a regular crystalline arrangement with the electrons delocalised through the structure, binding the ions together.

Miscibility: The ability of liquids to mix perfectly together. In contrast, immiscible liquids form clearly defined layers with the denser liquid forming the lower layer.

Mobile phase: In chromatography, the moving part of the process, for example the inert gas in GLC which carries the mixture of compounds through the column, or the solvent in paper chromatography which carries the mixture of compounds up the paper.

Molar bond enthalpy: The energy required to break one mole of covalent bonds. Values are listed in the data booklet.

Molar volume: The volume of one mole of a gas at a specified temperature and pressure.

Mole: The gram formula mass of a substance. It contains 6.02×10^{23} formula units of the substance.

Molecular formula: A formula which shows the number of atoms of the different elements that are present in one molecule of a substance.

Molecule: A group of atoms held together by covalent bonds.

Monatomic: A term used to describe the noble gases since they are composed of individual atoms which do not bond to each other. They are held together by London dispersion forces in the liquid and solid state.

N

Neutron: A particle found in the nucleus of an atom. It has the same mass as a proton but no charge.

Non-polar covalent bond: A covalent bond where both atoms share the electrons equally. This occurs between all elements that exist as molecules, such as Cl_2 and S_8, since the atoms joining are identical. It also occurs in compounds where the bonding atoms have a small difference in electronegativity, such as hydrocarbons.

Nucleus: The extremely small centre of an atom where the neutrons and protons are found.

O

Oils: Esters formed from one molecule of glycerol and three molecules of (usually unsaturated) carboxylic acids. Oils have melting points low enough to be liquid at normal room temperature. See fats.

Oxidation: A process in which electrons are lost.

Oxidising agent: A substance that gains electrons, in other words is an electron acceptor.

P

Peptide link: See amide link.

Percentage yield: This is the actual yield of substance obtained divided by the theoretical yield calculated from the balanced equation then multiplied by 100.

Period: A horizontal row in the Periodic Table.

Periodic Table: An arrangement of the elements in order of increasing atomic number, with chemically similar elements occurring in the same main vertical columns (groups).

Permanent dipole–permanent dipole interactions: The attraction between molecules which possess a permanent dipole because of the presence of polar bonds.

pH: A measure of the acidity of a solution.

Pickling: A method used to preserve foods by storing them in vinegar.

Polar covalent bonds: Bonds formed between non-metallic atoms by sharing a pair of electrons. If the atoms have considerably different electronegativities, the electrons are not shared equally, the more electronegative atom becoming slightly negative in comparison with the other atom. As a result the bond is 'polar', for example $H^{\delta+} - Cl^{\delta-}$.

Polymer: A very large molecule that is formed by the joining together of many smaller molecules (monomers).

Polymerisation: The process whereby a polymer is formed.

Proton: A particle found in the nucleus of an atom. It has a single positive charge and the same mass as a neutron.

R

Rate of reaction: A measure of the speed of a chemical reaction.

Raw material: A useful substance for the chemical industry which is found naturally, for example crude oil, water, air, metallic ores, coal, etc. Feedstocks are obtained from raw materials.

Redox reaction: A reaction in which reduction and oxidation take place. Electrons are lost by one substance and gained by another.

Redox titration: An experiment in which the volumes of aqueous solutions of a reducing agent and an oxidising agent, which react together completely, are measured accurately. The concentration of one of the reactants can then be determined provided the concentration of the other reactant is known.

Reducing agent: A substance that loses electrons, in other words is an electron donor.

Reduction: A process in which electrons are gained.

Relative atomic mass: The average mass of one atom of an element on a scale where one atom of $^{12}_{6}C$ has a mass of 12 units exactly.

Renewable energy source: One which will not run out in the foreseeable future, such as solar, wind and tidal power or fuel obtained from crops.

Reproducibility: Results obtained from an experiment are said to be reproducible if the same data can be obtained when the experiment is repeated. An experiment with good reproducibility will produce the same results when carried out again and again.

Retention time: The length of time it takes a substance to reach the detector, in a chromatography experiment, after being injected into the chromatography column.

Reversible reaction: One which proceeds in both directions, for example:

$$N_2 + 3H_2 \rightleftharpoons 2NH_3$$

Rogue data: Results obtained from an experiment that are unusual/do not fit the pattern of expected results. Usually caused by experimental error.

S

Saturated hydrocarbon: A hydrocarbon in which all carbon–carbon covalent bonds are single bonds.

Screening: The ability of electrons in the inner energy levels of an atom to reduce the attraction of the nuclear charge for the electrons of the outermost levels.

Soaps: Salts of fatty acids, e.g. sodium stearate. Soaps have an ionic head that is water soluble and a covalent tail that is soluble in oil.

Spectator ion: An ion which is present in a reaction mixture but takes no part in the reaction.

Standard solution: A solution of known concentration.

State symbols: Symbols used to indicate the state of atoms, ions or molecules: (s) = solid; (l) = liquid; (g) = gas; (aq) = aqueous (dissolved in water).

Stationary phase: In chromatography, the phase other than the mobile phase. For example, the liquid in GLC.

Strong acids and alkalis: Acids and alkalis that are fully dissociated into ions in solution. Strong acids include hydrochloric, nitric and sulfuric acids. Strong alkalis include sodium and potassium hydroxides.

Structural formula: A formula that shows the arrangement of atoms in a molecule or ion. A full structural formula shows all of the bonds, for example, propane:

$$
\begin{array}{ccccccc}
 & H & & H & & H & \\
 & | & & | & & | & \\
H- & C & - & C & - & C & -H \\
 & | & & | & & | & \\
 & H & & H & & H & \\
\end{array}
$$

A shortened structural formula shows the sequence of groups of atoms, for example, propane: $CH_3CH_2CH_3$.

T

Temporary dipole: Formed in all atoms where an excess of electrons is formed at one part of the atom. Temporary dipoles are the basis for London dispersion forces.

Terpene: Unsaturated compounds found in many plant oils. They are formed from the joining together of isoprene units.

Transition metals: The elements which form a 'bridge' in the Periodic Table between groups II and III, for example, iron and copper.

Triglyceride: The molecules found in fats and oils. They are formed from one glycerol molecule joining to three fatty acid molecules.

U

Unsaturated compounds: Compounds in which there are carbon–carbon double or triple bonds, such as alkenes, alkynes and vegetable oils.

V

Van der Waals' forces: The forces of attraction that occur between all atoms and molecules. They are known as intermolecular forces and include hydrogen bonding, permanent dipole–permanent dipole interactions and London dispersion forces. Van der Waals' forces are much weaker than covalent bonds.

Variable: Something that can be changed in a chemical reaction such as temperature, particle size, concentration, etc.

Viscosity: A description of how 'thick' a liquid is, for example, engine oil is 'thicker' (more viscous) than petrol.

W

Weak acids and alkalis: Acids and alkalis that do not dissociate fully into ions in solution. Weak acids include most carboxylic acids, carbonic acid and sulfurous acid. Weak alkalis include ammonia.

Periodic Table of the Elements

Group I Group II

Group III Group IV Group V Group VI Group VII Group 0

1.0		
H		
hydrogen		
1		

Key

1.0	relative atomic mass
H	symbol
hydrogen	name
1	atomic number

Transition elements

4.0
He
helium
2

6.9	9.0
Li	**Be**
lithium	beryllium
3	4

10.8	12.0	14.0	16.0	19.0	20.2
B	**C**	**N**	**O**	**F**	**Ne**
boron	carbon	nitrogen	oxygen	fluorine	neon
5	6	7	8	9	10

23.0	24.3
Na	**Mg**
sodium	magnesium
11	12

27.0	28.1	31.0	32.1	35.5	40.0
Al	**Si**	**P**	**S**	**Cl**	**Ar**
aluminium	silicon	phosphorus	sulfur	chlorine	argon
13	14	15	16	17	18

39.1	40.0	45.0	47.9	51.0	52.0	54.9	55.8	58.9	58.7	63.5	65.4	69.7	72.6	74.9	79.0	79.9	83.8
K	**Ca**	**Sc**	**Ti**	**V**	**Cr**	**Mn**	**Fe**	**Co**	**Ni**	**Cu**	**Zn**	**Ga**	**Ge**	**As**	**Se**	**Br**	**Kr**
potassium	calcium	scandium	titanium	vanadium	chromium	manganese	iron	cobalt	nickel	copper	zinc	gallium	germanium	arsenic	selenium	bromine	krypton
19	20	21	22	23	24	25	26	27	28	29	30	31	32	33	34	35	36

85.5	87.6	88.9	91.2	92.9	95.9		101.1	102.9	106.4	107.9	112.4	114.8	118.7	121.8	127.6	126.9	131.3
Rb	**Sr**	**Y**	**Zr**	**Nb**	**Mo**	**Tc**	**Ru**	**Rh**	**Pd**	**Ag**	**Cd**	**In**	**Sn**	**Sb**	**Te**	**I**	**Xe**
rubidium	strontium	yttrium	zirconium	niobium	molybdenum	technetium	ruthenium	rhodium	palladium	silver	cadmium	indium	tin	antimony	tellurium	iodine	xenon
37	38	39	40	41	42	43	44	45	46	47	48	49	50	51	52	53	54

132.9	137.3		178.5	181.0	183.9	186.2	190.2	192.2	195.1	197.0	200.6	204.4	207.2	209.0			
Cs	**Ba**		**Hf**	**Ta**	**W**	**Re**	**Os**	**Ir**	**Pt**	**Au**	**Hg**	**Tl**	**Pb**	**Bi**	**Po**	**At**	**Rn**
caesium	barium		hafnium	tantalum	tungsten	rhenium	osmium	iridium	platinum	gold	mercury	thallium	lead	bismuth	polonium	astatine	radon
55	56		72	73	74	75	76	77	78	79	80	81	82	83	84	85	86

	226.0										
Fr	**Ra**		**Rf**	**Db**	**Sg**	**Bh**	**Hs**	**Mt**	**Uun**	**Uuu**	**Uub**
francium	radium		rutherfordium	dubnium	seaborgium	bohrium	hassium	meitnerium	unununilium	unununium	ununbium
87	88		104	105	106	107	108	109	110	111	112

Lanthanides

138.9	140.1	140.9	144.2		150.4	152.0	157.3	158.9	162.5	164.9	167.3	168.9	173.0	175.0
La	**Ce**	**Pr**	**Nd**	**Pm**	**Sm**	**Eu**	**Gd**	**Tb**	**Dy**	**Ho**	**Er**	**Tm**	**Yb**	**Lu**
lanthanum	cerium	praseodymium	neodymium	promethium	samarium	europium	gadolinium	terbium	dysprosium	holmium	erbium	thulium	ytterbium	lutetium
57	58	59	60	61	62	63	64	65	66	67	68	69	70	71

Actinides

227.0	232.0	231.0	238.0	237.0										
Ac	**Th**	**Pa**	**U**	**Np**	**Pu**	**Am**	**Cm**	**Bk**	**Cf**	**Es**	**Fm**	**Md**	**No**	**Lr**
actinium	thorium	protactinium	uranium	neptunium	plutonium	americium	curium	berkelium	californium	einsteinium	fermium	mendelevium	nobelium	lawrencium
89	90	91	92	93	94	95	96	97	98	99	100	101	102	103

Relative atomic masses are shown only for elements which have stable isotopes or isotopes with very long half-life.

Index

Answers to In-Text Questions

Chapter 1: Controlling the rate of reation

1 a) $1.5 \times 10^{-3}\,\text{mol}\,l^{-1}\,s^{-1}$

b) $1.0 \times 10^{-3}\,\text{mol}\,l^{-1}\,s^{-1}$

2

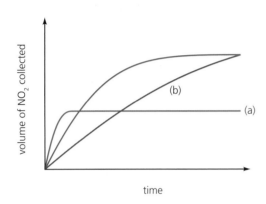

3 a) Decreasing concentration of acid/H^+ ions as the reaction proceeds.

b)

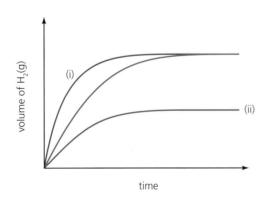

4 Burning phosphorus: low activation energy; burning magnesium: high activation energy

5 a) Reaction C

b) (i) E_A: Reaction A: 50 kJ; B: 30 kJ; C: 40 kJ

(ii) ΔH: Reaction A: -10 kJ; B: -40 kJ; C: 20 kJ

c) (i) Reaction A **(ii)** Reaction B

Chapter 2: The Periodic Table: bonding and structure

1 Aluminium has three outer electrons compared with sodium's one outer electron. These electrons delocalise leading to greater conductivity for aluminium.

2 Diamond has a network covalent structure. Sulfur has S_8 covalently bonded molecules that are held together by London dispersion forces. It takes much more energy to break the covalent bonds in diamond than to break the London dispersion forces in sulfur, to separate the molecules.

Chapter 3: Trends in the Periodic Table

1 a) K has one more energy level than Na (giving more screening between the nucleus and the outermost electron).

b) Both sodium and chlorine have the same number of electron shells. However, the chlorine atom has a higher nuclear charge. This attracts the outer electrons more strongly causing a decrease in atomic size.

2 a) $596 + 1160 = 1756\,\text{kJ mol}^{-1}$

b) $584 + 1830 + 2760 = 5174\,\text{kJ mol}^{-1}$

3 Xe has the largest noble gas atoms, which means that the electron to be removed to create Xe^+ will be furthest from the nucleus. Hence, the first ionisation enthalpy of Xe is the lowest of any of the noble gases.

Chapter 4: Bonding in compounds

1 a) 2.0 **b)** 1.7 **c)** 2.2; CsCl is most ionic and NaI is least

2 Electronegativity difference is 1.4. In fact, it is ionic. You should recognise that it will be, at least, strongly polar.

3 KBr and MgO are most likely to have an NaCl lattice structure as the ion ratio is $1:1$.

4

5 $H^{\delta+}-Cl^{\delta-}$ deflected

O=O not deflected

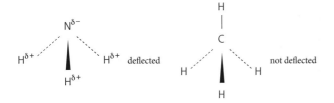

Chapter 5: Alcohols, carboxylic acids and esters

1

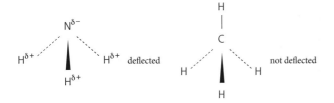

methanol

HO — C — C — H

ethanoic acid

methyl ethanoate (ester produced)

2 $CH_3CH_2CH_2COOH$

butanoic acid

$HOCH_2CH_2CH_3$

propan-1-ol

$CH_3CH_2CH_2COOCH_2CH_2CH_3$

propyl butanoate (ester produced)

3 a) Propyl methanoate, on hydrolysis, produces:

and

b) Methyl benzoate, on hydrolysis produces:

and

4 a) $CH_3CH_2CH_2COOCH_2CH_3 + KOH \rightarrow$
ethyl butanoate
$CH_3CH_2CH_2COO^-K^+ + HOCH_2CH_3$
potassium butanoate   ethanol

b) $CH_3CH_2CH_2CH_2CH_2OOCCH_3 + H_2O \rightarrow$
pentyl ethanoate
$CH_3CH_2CH_2CH_2CH_2OH + HOOCCH_3$
pentan-1-ol   ethanoic acid

Chapter 6: Fats, oils and soaps

1

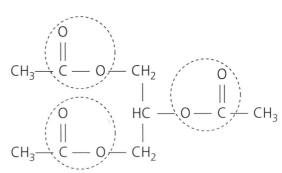

Chapter 8: The chemistry of cooking, and oxidation of food

1 a) 2-methylbutan-2-ol (tertiary)

b) 2,2-dimethylbutan-1-ol (primary)

c) 4-methylpentan-2-ol (secondary)

2 a) i)

$$CH_3CHCH_2CH_2C\diagdown\substack{O\\H}$$ with CH_3 branch

ii) made by oxidising 4-methylpentan-1-ol

b) i)

$$CH_3CHCCH_3$$ with CH_3 branch and $=O$

ii) made by oxidising 3-methylbutan-2-ol

3 a) 4-ethylhexan-3-one

b) 3,3-dimethylbutanal

4 a) $CH_3OH \rightarrow HCHO \rightarrow HCOOH$

O:H ratio: $1:4 = 0.25:1$ $1:2 = 0.5:1$ $2:2 = 1:1$

In each step the O:H ratio is increasing, i.e. oxidation is taking place.

b) (i) $C_4H_9OH \rightarrow C_3H_7CHO \rightarrow C_3H_7COOH$

      butan-1-ol   butanal   butanoic acid

O:H ratio: $1:10 = 0.1:1$ $1:8 = 0.13:1$ $2:8 = 0.25:1$

(ii) $C_3H_7CH(OH)CH_3 \rightarrow C_3H_7COCH_3$

      pentan-2-ol   pentan-2-one

O:H ratio: $1:12 = 0.08:1$ $1:10 = 0.1:1$

Chapter 10: Skin care

1 Initiation

$Cl-Cl \rightarrow Cl^\bullet + Cl^\bullet$

Propagation

$Cl^\bullet + C_2H_6 \rightarrow {}^\bullet C_2H_5 + HCl$

${}^\bullet C_2H_5 + Cl_2 \rightarrow C_2H_5Cl + {}^\bullet Cl$

Termination

$Cl^\bullet + Cl^\bullet \rightarrow Cl_2$

${}^\bullet C_2H_5 + Cl^\bullet \rightarrow C_2H_5Cl$

${}^\bullet C_2H_5 + {}^\bullet C_2H_5 \rightarrow C_4H_{10}$

Chapter 12: Calculations from equations

1 176 g

2 176 g

3 56.1 g

4 159 g

5 0.1 mol l^{-1}

6 2 mol l^{-1}

7 100 cm^3

8 22.5 cm^3

9 329 cm^3

10 a) Moles of Mg $= \dfrac{0.6}{24.3} = 0.025$; moles of HCl $= 2 \times 0.04 = 0.08$

1 mole of Mg reacts with 2 moles of HCl

0.025 moles of Mg requires 0.05 moles of HCl

Therefore, HCl is in excess.

b) Moles of excess acid $= 0.08 - 0.05 = 0.03$ moles

c) A titration with alkali could be carried out.

11 a) Moles of Zn $= \dfrac{2.6}{65.4} = 0.04$; moles of copper(II) sulfate $= 0.03$

Therefore, the zinc is in excess since 1 mole of zinc reacts with 1 mole of $CuSO_4$.

b) Mass of Cu $= 0.03 \times 63.5 = 1.91$ g

c) Add excess acid to react with the remaining zinc (the copper will not react with dilute acid) and then filter to remove the remaining copper.

12 25 000 cm^3

13 a) (i) 0.96 litres **(ii)** 120 litres

b) (i) 3 moles **(ii)** 0.015 moles

14 a) 4.81 litres

b) 2.4 litres

15 600 litres

16 30 cm^3 O_2; 60 cm^3 NO_2

17 100 cm^3 O_2; 60 cm^3 CO_2; 80 cm^3 H_2O

18 a) (i) 400 cm^3 O_2 **(ii)** 200 cm^3 CO_2

b) (i) 32.5 litres O_2 **(ii)** 20 litres CO_2

19 a) Moles Al $= \frac{2.7}{27} = 0.1$ moles; moles HCl $= 0.2$ moles

1 mole of Al reacts with 3 moles of HCl therefore 0.1 moles requires 0.3 moles. The aluminium is in excess in this reaction.

b) $0.1 \times 24 = 2.4$ litres

20 a) (i) $CH_4(g) + 2O_2(g) \rightarrow CO_2(g) + 2H_2O(l)$

10 cm³ methane requires 20 cm³ of oxygen. Oxygen is, therefore, in excess.

(ii) 5 cm³ oxygen; 10 cm³ carbon dioxide

b) (i) $C_3H_8(g) + 5O_2(g) \rightarrow 3CO_2(g) + 4H_2O(l)$

10 cm³ propane requires 50 cm³ of oxygen. Propane is, therefore, in excess.

(ii) 5 cm³ propane; 15 cm³ carbon dioxide

Chapter 13: Percentage yield and atom economy

1 82.8%

2 4.33 g

3 45.9%

4 100%

Chapter 14: Equilibria

1 Bleaching action

a) decreases   **b)** decreases   **c)** increases

2 a) Rate increases   **b)** Yield decreases

3 a) Reaction 2   **b)** Reaction 1

4 a) Equilibrium reached faster.

b) Yield increases.

5 H_2SO_4 dissolves, effectively absorbing H_2O, equilibrium goes to the right, yield of ester increases. As H_2SO_4 dissolves, H^+ is formed, this acts as a catalyst, equilibrium reached faster.

Chapter 15: Chemical energy

1 $-877.8\,kJ\,mol^{-1}$

2 a) $-1254\,kJ\,mol^{-1}$

b) This is much less than the data booklet value. The main sources of error are likely to be incomplete combustion of propanol and heat losses to the surroundings.

3 $34.8\,kJ\,mol^{-1}$

4 $-40.1\,kJ\,mol^{-1}$

5 $-54.3\,kJ\,mol^{-1}$

6 $-56.85\,kJ\,mol^{-1}$

7 $226\,kJ\,mol^{-1}$

8 $-202\,kJ\,mol^{-1}$

9 a) $-140\,kJ\,mol^{-1}$

b) $-778\,kJ\,mol^{-1}$

Chapter 16: Oxidising and reducing agents

1 (i) a) $Cu \rightarrow Cu^{2+} + 2e^-$

$Ag^+ + e^- \rightarrow Ag$

Redox equation: $Cu + 2Ag^+ \rightarrow Cu^{2+} + 2Ag$

b) Oxidising agent $= Ag^+$; Reducing agent $= Cu$

(ii) a) $Cr \rightarrow Cr^{3+} + 3e^-$

$Ni^{2+} + 2e^- \rightarrow Ni$

Redox equation: $2Cr + 3Ni^{2+} \rightarrow 3Ni + 2Cr^{3+}$

b) Oxidising agent $= Ni^{2+}$; Reducing agent $= Cr$

2 a) $MnO_2 + 2H_2O \rightarrow MnO_4^- + 4H^+ + 3e^-$ Oxidation

b) $FeO_4^{2-} + 8H^+ + 3e^- \rightarrow Fe^{3+} + 4H_2O$ Reduction

c) $V^{3+} + 3H_2O \rightarrow VO_3^- + 6H^+ + 2e^-$ Oxidation

3 1) $2Fe^{3+}$ + $2I^-$ $\rightarrow$ $2Fe^{2+}$ + I_2

Charge: $6+$ $2-$ $4+$ 0

Charge on LHS $= 4+$; Charge on RHS $= 4+$. In other words, the total charge on each side is the same.

2) $Cr_2O_7^{2-}$ + $14H^+$ + $6Fe^{2+}$ $\rightarrow$ $6Fe^{3+} + 2Cr^{3+} + 7H_2O$

Charge:

$2-$ $14+$ $12+$ $18+$ $6+$ 0

Charge on LHS $= 24+$; Charge on RHS $= 24+$. In other words, the total charge on each side is the same.

4 (i)

	Reducing agent	Oxidising agent	Spectator ion(s)
a)	SO_3^{2-}	I_2	Na^+
b)	Fe^{2+}	H_2O_2	SO_4^{2-}
c)	Sn^{2+}	$Cr_2O_7^{2-}$	K^+ and Cl^-

(ii) a) $I_2 + SO_3^{2-} + H_2O \rightarrow 2I^- + SO_4^{2-} + 2H^+$

b) $2Fe^{2+} + H_2O_2 + 2H^+ \rightarrow 2Fe^{3+} + 2H_2O$

c) $3Sn^{2+} + Cr_2O_7^{2-} + 14H^+ \rightarrow 3Sn^{4+} + 2Cr^{3+} + 7H_2O$

Chapter 18: Volumetric analysis

1 $0.034\,mol\,l^{-1}$

2 $0.0003\,mol\,l^{-1}$

3 a) $0.16\,mol\,l^{-1}$

b) $0.8\,mol\,l^{-1}$

c) $1.0\,mol\,l^{-1}$

Answers to Study Questions

Chapter 1: Controlling the rate of reaction

1 D

2 a) **(i)** $1\,cm^3\,s^{-1}$

    (ii) $0.167\,cm^3\,s^{-1}$

b)

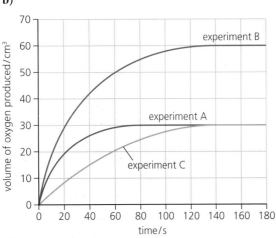

3 B

4 a) $190\,kJ$ **b)** $-20\,kJ$; exothermic

c)

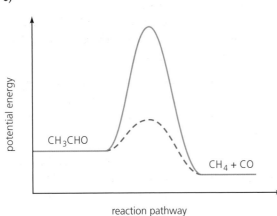

5 a) $H^+(aq)$ are not used up.

b)

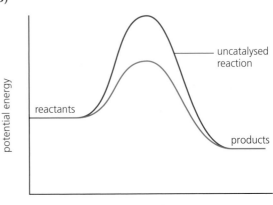

Chapter 2: The Periodic Table: bonding and structure

1 molecular

2 London dispersion forces

3 network

4 A

5 C

6 B

7 C

8 a) Fullerene consists of discrete molecules; diamond is a covalent network.

  b) Helium is an unreactive gas. If air is present, the graphite will burn.

  c) If it decolourises bromine water, it is unsaturated. If not, it is saturated.

9 In descending order: e, b, d, c, a

Chapter 3: Trends in the Periodic Table

1 D

2 B

3 B

4 a) Electronegativity

b) It decreases

5 a) The ionic radius for element 13 is less than that of Mg^{2+} but more than that of B^{3+}. The ionic radius for element 15 is greater than that of N^{3-}.

b) (i) H^+ has no electrons.

(ii) Li^+ has more protons than H^- and therefore greater nuclear attraction for the same number of electrons.

c) N^{3-} has one more electron energy level.

6 a) Chlorine has a greater nuclear charge.

b) Si^{4+} has two layers of electrons; P^{3-} has three layers of electrons.

Chapter 4: Bonding in compounds

1 polar

2 large

3 hydrogen bonding

4 A

5 A

6 C

7 C

8 D

9 A

10 a) (i) It decreases due to increasing nuclear charge.

(ii) It increases due to more energy levels.

b) Caesium and fluorine

11 a) No, as ions are not free to move.

b) Yes, as outer electrons are delocalised.

c) No, as it is covalent.

12 a) Methanol and hydrazine

b) Hydrogen bonds are stronger than London dispersion forces so molecules are more strongly attracted to each other.

c) Heavier molecules have more electrons and therefore have stronger London dispersion forces between molecules.

13 a) Group 0 or noble gases

b) C and S have the same electronegativity.

c) Going down the group, atoms have more energy levels. The inner levels have a screening effect so the ability to attract bonding electrons decreases despite the greater nuclear charge.

14 a) More electrons are present so the London dispersion forces increase in strength. It therefore takes more energy to separate the molecules so boiling points are higher.

b) Unlike the other hydrides, H_2O has much stronger hydrogen bonding between molecules. It takes more energy to break the strong hydrogen bonds, hence the higher boiling point.

15 a) Permanent dipole−permanent dipole interactions are an example of an intermolecular attraction (or force) between molecules.

b) In HCN, the biggest difference in electronegativity is between C and N. As N has a higher electronegativity, it carries a small negative charge and the C carries a small positive charge. The charges on HCN molecules allow them to form pdp−pdp attractions to other HCN molecules.

16 Hydrogen is a gas as the forces between hydrogen molecules are the weak London dispersion forces, which are easily overcome at room temperature.

The London dispersion forces are caused by the movement of electrons. This gives rise to an instantaneous dipole which induces a dipole in a neighbouring hydrogen molecule. This allows the molecules to attract each other. The attraction is known as the London dispersion force.

17 Ammonia has a relatively high boiling point as hydrogen bonding can occur between ammonia molecules; hydrogen bonding is a strong intermolecular force of attraction.

Hydrogen bonding arises as there is a big difference in electronegativity between N and H atoms. The N and H bond is therefore very polar.

Chapter 5: Alcohols, carboxylic acids and esters

1 A

2 D

3 A

4 a) (i) Methyl ethanoate

(ii) Condensation

(iii)

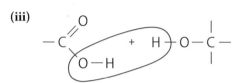

b) (i) An oily layer forms and there is a distinctive smell.

(ii) It removes water from the reaction thus preventing hydrolysis of the ester. It acts as a catalyst for the reaction.

5

$$H-\overset{\overset{O}{\|}}{C}-O-\overset{\overset{CH_3}{|}}{\underset{|}{C}}-\overset{\overset{H}{|}}{\underset{H}{C}}-\overset{\overset{H}{|}}{\underset{H}{C}}-\overset{\overset{H}{|}}{\underset{H}{C}}-H$$

or

$$CH_3$$
$$HCOOCHCH_2CH_2CH_3$$

6 2-methylpropan-1-ol and butanoic acid

7 a) Ethanoic acid

b) The alcohol and ester are flammable.

8 a) Ethyl butanoate

b) An oily layer would form.

Chapter 6: Fats, oils and soaps

1 D

2 C

3 D

4 a) Each glycerol molecule has three −OH groups which condense with three acid molecules to form a triglyceride molecule.

b) They become saturated **or** hydrogen adds across the carbon−carbon double bonds.

c) Carbon−carbon double bonds

5 a) Two

b) $C_{18}H_{36}O_2$

c) Glycerol **or** propane-1,2,3-triol

$$CH_2OH$$
$$|$$
$$CHOH$$
$$|$$
$$CH_2OH$$

6 a) Glycerol **or** propane-1,2,3-triol

b) Carbon−carbon double bond

c) Hydrogenation **or** addition (of hydrogen) **or** hardening

7 a) The molecule contains −OH groups which are water soluble and hydrocarbon chains which are insoluble in water/soluble in non-polar solvents.

b) 2.5 cm³

8 Fat molecules are mainly saturated; oil molecules are unsaturated. This allows fat molecules to pack closer together. This efficient packing allows more intermolecular bonding to take place. Thus, more energy must be supplied to separate fat molecules.

Chapter 7: Proteins

1 B

2 C

3 a)

b)

c) It may become hydrolysed when heated in water.

4 a)

Any

$$\underset{\underset{}{|}}{\overset{\overset{O}{\|}}{-C}} \underset{\underset{}{|}}{\overset{\overset{H}{|}}{-N}} -$$

b)

$$\underset{\underset{H}{|}}{\overset{\overset{H}{|}}{H-N}} \underset{\underset{CH_3}{|}}{\overset{\overset{}{|}}{-C}} \overset{\overset{O}{\|}}{-C} -OH$$

or

$$\underset{\underset{}{|}}{\overset{\overset{H}{|}}{H-N}} \underset{\underset{CH_2}{|}}{\overset{\overset{H}{|}}{-C}} \overset{\overset{O}{\|}}{-C} -OH$$
$$\underset{\underset{CH_3}{|}}{\overset{}{H-C-CH_3}}$$

or

$$\underset{\underset{CH_2}{|}}{\overset{\overset{H\ H}{|\ |}}{H-N-C}} \overset{\overset{O}{\|}}{-C} -OH$$

with benzene ring and OH

5 a) Amino acids

b) The breaking down of larger molecules into smaller molecules using water.

c) Ester

Chapter 8: The chemistry of cooking and oxidation of food

1 secondary

2 increased

3 carbonyl

4 blue-green

5 C

6 D

7 B

8 D

9 a)

$$-C-C-C-C-OH$$

or

$$HO-C-C-C-C-$$

b)

$$-C-C-C-C-$$ with OH on third carbon

c)

$$-C-C-C-C-$$ with OH on second carbon

10 a) Butan-2-ol

b)

$$CH_3 \underset{\underset{CH_3}{|}}{\overset{\overset{OH}{|}}{-C}} -CH_3$$

11 a) I is butan-1-ol, II is butan-2-ol, III is 2-methylpropan-2-ol, IV is 2-methylpropan-1-ol.

b) I and IV are primary, II is secondary, III is tertiary.

c) (i) D is the tertiary alcohol, i.e. D is III.

(ii) A & B are primary; C is secondary, i.e. C is II.

(iii) D, when dehydrated, gives a branched alkene. I cannot do so but IV will, so B is I and A is IV.

12 a) (i) Both compounds are esters.

(ii) React both compounds with bromine water. Only geranyl acetate will decolourise bromine water.

b) Dotted line from one O to the H of the other molecule's OH or a dotted line from one H of the OH to the O of the other molecule's OH.

c)

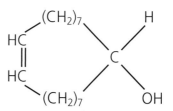

13 a) In an aldehyde, the carbonyl group is at the end of the carbon chain/the carbonyl group has one hydrogen attached.

In a ketone, the carbonyl group is not at the end of

the carbon chain/the carbonyl group does not have any hydrogen atoms attached.

b) **(i)** Blue → red

  (ii) $C_3H_6O + H_2O → C_2H_5COOH + 2H^+ + 2e^-$

Chapter 9: Fragrances

1 a)

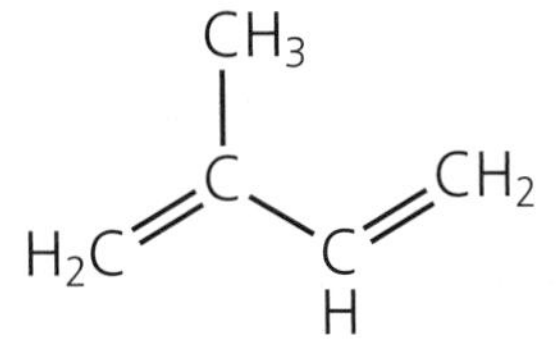

$$\begin{array}{c}
CH_3 \\
| \\
C \\
\end{array}$$
H_2C \quad CH_2

(structure with CH_3, H_2C, C, CH_2, C, H)

b) Number of moles of bromine required = CV
   = $1.2 \times 0.0475 = 0.057$

1 mole of Br_2 will react with 1 mole of double bonds.

$0.057 \div 0.019 = 3$, i.e. 3 moles of Br_2 are required for 1 mole of terpene. Therefore the terpene is A.

c)

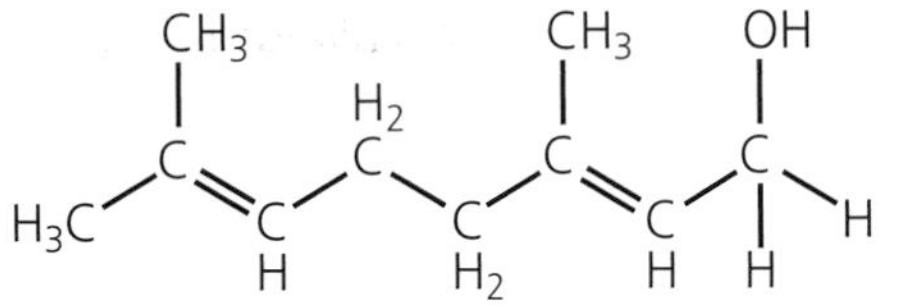

(structure with CH_3, H_2, CH_3, OH, H_3C, H, H_2, H, H)

2 a)

(structure with $(CH_2)_7$, H, HC, C, HC, $(CH_2)_7$, OH, OH)

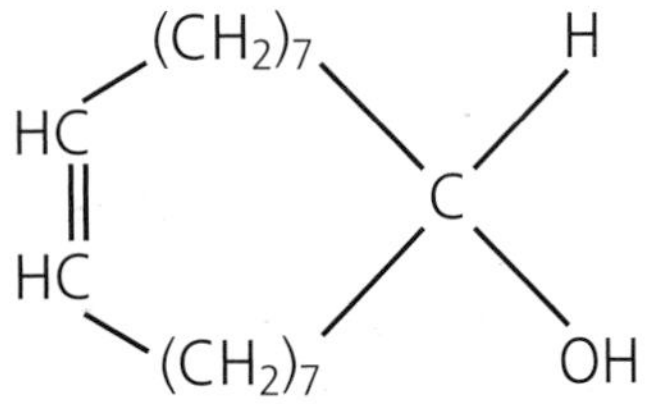

b) Any set of five carbon atoms, four connected in a line with one branching from carbon 2 of this chain.

Chapter 10: Skin care

1 A

2 a) Light

 b) Propagation and termination

 c) b = Br$^•$ + Br$^•$, c = Br$^•$, d = $^•CH_3$, e = $^•CH_3$, f = Br$^•$

3 a) Initiation

   $F−F → F^• + F^•$

   Propagation

   $F^• + C_3H_8 → {}^•C_3H_7 + HF$

${}^•C_3H_7 + F_2 → C_3H_7F + F^•$

Termination

$F^• + F^• → F_2$

${}^•C_3H_7 + F^• → C_3H_7F$

${}^•C_3H_7 + {}^•C_3H_7 → C_6H_{14}$

b) Initiation

   $Br−Br → Br^• + Br^•$

   Propagation

   $Br^• + H_2 → {}^•H + HBr$

   ${}^•H + Br_2 → HBr + {}^•Br$

   Termination

   $Br^• + Br^• → Br_2$

   ${}^•H + Br^• → HBr$

   ${}^•H + {}^•H → H_2$

4 The energy required to break the halogen bonds is less than the energy required to break the C−H (or H−H) bond. (The bond enthalpies for the halogen bonds are much lower than the bond enthalpies for H−H or C−H bonds.)

Chapter 11: Getting the most from reactants: designing an industrial process

1 B

2 a)

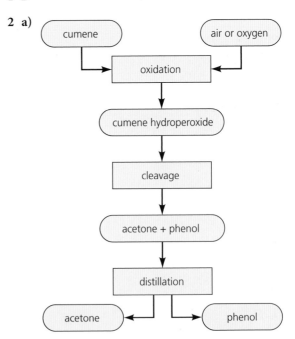

b) Any two of: energy costs, availability of feedstocks, number of stages involved, market for by-product(s), waste disposal or emissions to the air

3 a) (i) $CH_4(g) + H_2O(g) \rightleftharpoons CO(g) + 3H_2(g)$

730 °C, 30 atmospheres pressure, nickel oxide catalyst

(ii) $CO(g) + H_2O(g) \rightleftharpoons CO_2(g) + H_2(g)$

330 °C, iron oxide catalyst

b) It reacts with some hydrogen to produce more steam.

c) This is to avoid poisoning of the catalysts used in the subsequent stages.

d) $K_2CO_3 + H_2O + CO_2 \rightarrow 2KHCO_3$

4 a) HCl, C_2H_4, CH_2ClCH_2Cl

b) $CH_2ClCH_2Cl \rightarrow CH_2{=}CHCl + HCl$

c) Distillation

d) Neutralisation

5 a) Ammonia, carbon dioxide and sea water

b) $Ca(OH)_2 + 2NH_4Cl \rightarrow CaCl_2 + 2NH_3 + 2H_2O$

c) It forms insoluble magnesium carbonate (which can be removed by filtration).

d) Any two from: recycling of NH_3 and/or CO_2, energy saving by burning coke in **A**, sea water is a raw material **or** is cheap, continuous process, $CaCl_2$ by-product.

Chapter 12: Calculations from equations

1 720 g

2 a) $C + 2Cl_2 \rightarrow CCl_4$

b) 7.1 g

3 a) $S + O_2 \rightarrow SO_2$

b) 25.6 g

4 a) $C + \frac{1}{2}O_2 \rightarrow CO$

b) 1.4 g

5 9.95 g

6 180 g

7 6.62 g

8 798 tonnes

9 0.15 mol l^{-1}

10 3 mol l^{-1}

11 40.8 g

12 a) Moles of lead nitrate = 0.004; moles of KI = 0.006

0.004 moles of lead nitrate requires 0.008 moles of KI, so lead nitrate is in excess.

b) 1.383 g

13 D

14 a) (i) Moles of lead(II) carbonate = 0.011; moles of nitric acid = 0.02

0.011 moles of lead(II) carbonate require 0.022 moles of nitric acid for complete reaction, so the lead carbonate is in excess.

(ii) 0.02 moles nitric acid → 0.01 moles of lead(II) nitrate = 3.312 g

b) (i) Moles of Al = 0.3; moles of HCl = 1

0.3 moles of Al require 0.9 moles of HCl, so HCl is in excess.

(ii) Moles of aluminium chloride formed = 0.3 moles = 40.05 g

15 B

16 B

17 D

18 2.32 g

19 a) Moles of iron sulfide = 0.34; moles of HCl = 0.5

0.34 moles of FeS require 0.68 moles of HCl to react, therefore FeS is in excess.

b) 6 litres

20 a) 45.9

b) These liquids would not turn into a gas using this apparatus as the highest temperature they can be heated to is 100 °C (the boiling point of water).

21 a) $CO + \frac{1}{2}O_2 \rightarrow CO_2$

b) CO_2

c) 80 cm^3 (of CO_2 would be removed)

d) 110 cm^3 of oxygen

22 a) $C_2H_2 + 2\frac{1}{2}O_2 \rightarrow 2CO_2 + H_2O$

b) 95 cm^3 O_2 (excess); 100 cm^3 CO_2

Chapter 13: Percentage yield and atom economy

1 a) 88.89%   **b)** 100%

2 a)

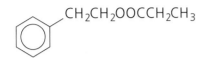

$CH_2CH_2OOCCH_2CH_3$

b) 90.8%

c) 1.48 tonnes of propanoic acid requires 2.44 tonnes of phenylethanol for complete reaction.

d) 2.49 tonnes

3 a) 50%

b) 4.27 g

c) 35%

4 a) 100%

b) 56%

5 0.73 kg

6 a) 51%

b) 100%

7 100%

Chapter 14: Equilibria

1 constant

2 left

3 decreases

4 endothermic

5 B

6 B

7 D

8 A

9 a) It would increase as a temperature fall favours the exothermic reaction.

b) A stronger industrial plant would be needed, costing more to build and maintain.

10 a) The enthalpy change is positive **or** the reaction is endothermic.

b) The position of equilibrium moves to counteract the applied change. An increase in pressure pushes the equilibrium in the direction of fewer moles of gas, i.e. towards reactant side, therefore less product.

c) It increases.

d) It is unchanged.

11 a) **(i)** It moves to the right.

(ii) It moves to the left.

(iii) No effect

b) Nitric acid

12 a) This occurs when the rate of the forward reaction equals the rate of the reverse reaction.

b) Increasing the temperature lowers the yield of ammonia, i.e. it favours the reverse reaction. Therefore, this is endothermic and the forward reaction is exothermic.

c) **(i)** 40%

(ii) Unreacted gases are recycled.

Chapter 15: Chemical energy

1 B

2 B

3 A

4 $-50.2 \, kJ \, mol^{-1}$

5 17.8 °C

6 a) 0.218   **b)** 15.8 g

7 a) **(i)** Acid is in excess, 0.05 mol of HCl to 0.04 mol NaOH and mole ratio in the equation is 1:1.

(ii) $-42.8 \, kJ$

b) 6.7 °C

c) Determine the enthalpy of solution of NaOH(s) in water **or** measure temperature change when 1 g of NaOH(s) is added to 50 cm³ of water.

d) Carry out the reactions in a polystyrene cup.

8 $46 \, kJ \, mol^{-1}$

9 a) $-312 \, kJ \, mol^{-1}$

b) $-303 \, kJ \, mol^{-1}$

10 $-1076 \, kJ \, mol^{-1}$

11 $-85 \, kJ$

12 $-484 \, kJ \, mol^{-1}$

Chapter 16: Oxidising and reducing agents

1 B

2 C

3 A

4 C

5 A

6 a) $2IO_3^- + 12H^+ + 10e^- \rightarrow I_2 + 6H_2O$

b) The iodate ion is being reduced so it is acting as an oxidising agent. (The reaction shown only works if iodate can react with ten electrons. Another substance must lose these electrons (oxidation) to allow iodate to react. We can say that iodate has caused another substance to be oxidised.)

7 a) $Cr_2O_7^{2-} + 14H^+ + 6e^- \rightarrow 2Cr^{3+} + 7H_2O$

b) The dichromate ion is an oxidising agent (as per Q6b).

8 a) $Br_2 + 6H_2O \rightarrow 2BrO_3^- + 12H^+ + 10e^-$

b) $V^{2+} + 3H_2O \rightarrow VO_3^- + 6H^+ + 3e^-$

9 a) The three best oxidising agents: $Cl_2(g)$, $MnO_4^-(aq)$ and $F_2(g)$

b) The three best reducing agents: Li, Cs and Rb

10 a) $2S_2O_3^{2-} \rightarrow S_4O_6^{2-} + 2e^-$

b) Starch

11 a) Displacement

b) $U^{4+} + 4e^- \rightarrow U$

c) Argon is unreactive (air contains oxygen which would react with the Mg).

12 a) $Pd^{2+} + 2e^- \rightarrow Pd$

b) $2CO(g) + O_2(g) \rightarrow 2CO_2(g)$

Chapter 17: Chromatography

1 a) During evaporation, smaller molecules lost; evaporated sample has peaks with shorter RT missing

b) Paint thinner and lemon fresh furniture spray

2 The yellow component is likely to be most polar as it is sticking to the stationary phase. (The green component is moving further down the column with the mobile phase (hexane) which suggests that the green component is more strongly attracted to the hexane. In other words, the green component is more likely to be non-polar.)

Chapter 18: Volumetric analysis

1 A

2 a) Increase in the O:H ratio (or decrease in the H:O ratio)

b) **(i)** This was a rough titration − it is not concordant with the other two results.

(ii) $0.172 \, mol \, l^{-1}$

3 a) $2Ce^{4+} + H_2O_2 \rightarrow 2Ce^{3+} + O_2 + 2H^+$

b) Cerium(IV) ions; sulfate ions

c) $0.036 \, mol \, l^{-1}$

4 a) $H_2O_2 + 2H^+ + 2I^- \rightarrow I_2 + 2H_2O$

b) $0.00945 \, g$

5 a) Redox reaction or displacement

b) **(i)** $2NaOH + Cl_2 \rightarrow NaClO + NaCl + H_2O$

(ii) $ClO^- + 2H^+ + 2e^- \rightarrow Cl^- + H_2O$

6 a) VOCs remove NO; this shifts the equilibrium to the right which results in the ozone concentration increasing.

b) **(i)** Blue/black → colourless

(ii) $2.695 \times 10^{-8} \, litres$

Appendix: Researching chemistry

1 B

2 a) $2KMnO_4 \rightarrow K_2O + 2MnO_2 + \frac{1}{2}O_2$

b) **(i)** Any two from: flask should be swirled; read at eye level; white tile under flask/beaker; paper on burette for easier reading; titrate slowly; add solution dropwise (at end); take funnel out; keep washing flask down

(ii) $1.5 \, mol \, l^{-1}$

3 Use a pipette to add $25 \, cm^3$ of the $0.05 \, mol \, l^{-1}$ iodine solution to a $250 \, cm^3$ standard flask, with rinsings. Make up to the mark with water.

4 Collect the gas in an upturned measuring cylinder filled with water.

5 A suitable diagram showing any workable method of producing CO_2 with calcium carbonate and dilute hydrochloric acid labelled and removing CO_2 with chemical labelled, such as sodium hydroxide solution, lime water, alkali.

6 Any four from: no eye protection; burette reading is not at eye level; open lab coat; filter funnel is still in the burette; the pipette is not securely held on the bench.

Answers to End-of-Course Questions

Part 1: Multiple choice questions

1 B

2 D

3 B

4 A

5 B

6 D

7 D

8 B

9 B

10 C

11 A

12 B

13 C

14 D

15 A

16 B

17 D

18 C

19 C

20 B

21 D

22 D

23 A

24 C

25 D

26 C

27 D

28 C

29 A

30 A

Part 2: Extended answer questions

1

A	covalent molecular
D	covalent network
C	ionic
B	metallic

2 a) As you go across the period, the nuclear charge increases. This pulls the electrons closer to the nucleus resulting in a decrease in atomic size.

b) N and Cl have an equal pull on electrons as they have identical electronegativity values (3.0). The electrons are, therefore, shared equally.

c) The bonding between HF molecules is mainly hydrogen bonding. The bonding between CH_4 molecules is London dispersion forces. It takes more energy to break the hydrogen bonds between HF than it does to break the London dispersion forces between methane as hydrogen bonds are much stronger.

d) Due to the nature of the open-ended question, there are several possible answers, as shown below.

Arguments for group VII: Hydrogen is like a halogen because

♦ it is diatomic

♦ hydrogen atoms require a single electron to achieve a full stable shell

♦ it is very reactive

♦ hydrogen atoms form one bond

♦ hydrogen can form H^- ions.

Arguments for group I: Hydrogen is like a group I element because

♦ it has one outer electron

♦ it is highly reactive

♦ it forms a single bond, etc.

♦ it can form H^+ ions, etc.

3 a)

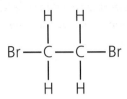

b) **(i)** $-39\,\text{kJ}\,\text{mol}^{-1}$

(ii) 57%

c) $Br^{\bullet} + C_2H_6 \rightarrow {}^{\bullet}C_2H_5 + HBr$

$^{\bullet}C_2H_5 + Br_2 \rightarrow C_2H_5Br + {}^{\bullet}Br$

d) Light is required to start the reaction as the light supplies the energy to break the Br—Br bond.

4 a) **(i)** $FeS + 2HCl \rightarrow FeCl_2 + H_2S$

(ii) Hydrogen

b) $-20\,\text{kJ}\,\text{mol}^{-1}$

5 a) **(i)**

$CH_3CH_2CH = CH_2$ or

[structural formula: H—C—C—C=C with H substituents]

(ii) Hydration **or** addition (of water)

(iii) Hot copper oxide or acidified potassium permanganate.

(iv) Butanoic acid

b) **(i)** Fruit smell **or** oily layer on water

(ii) Flavourings **or** perfumes **or** solvents

6 a) Precipitation

b) $AgNO_3$ is in excess, $1.18 \times 10^{-3}\,\text{mol}$ compared with only $2 \times 10^{-5}\,\text{mol}$ of HCl.

7 a) A water bath can only heat to 100 °C.

b) **(i)** 0.23 litres

(ii) Some of the CO_2 will dissolve in the water./ There could be leaks in the system./The theoretical volume is only obtained under standard conditions of temperature and pressure — as this experiment proceeds, both temperature and pressure will change. This will affect the final volume produced.

c) 10.33p (to obtain 1.68 g pure requires 1.768 g of $NaHCO_3$ of 95% purity)

8 a) The carbonyl group is at the end of the chain in an aldehyde (it is not at the end of the chain in a ketone).

b) **(i)** $C_3H_6O + H_2O \rightarrow C_2H_5COOH + 2H^+ + 2e^-$

(ii) Propanoic acid

(iii) Antioxidants

c) **(i)** Addition or reduction

(ii)

[structural formula] or [structural formula]

9 a) **(i)** Hydrogen bonding

(ii)

[structural formula]

or [structural formula]

or [structural formula]

b) **(i)** It gives you several attempts at the titration so that you can obtain reproducible results.

(ii) 0.000107 moles

(iii) 0.188 g

10 a) **(i)** It can be recycled back into the reaction vessel.

(ii) Distillation

b) **(i)** Hydration or addition of water

(ii) A cooler is required.

(iii) It would shift to the left.

(iv) 10%

c) Fermentation

11 a) As fats are mainly saturated they have a regular 'tuning fork' structure that allows close packing of fat molecules. This close packing allows efficient intermolecular bonding to take place (mainly London dispersion forces). As oil molecules have more double bonds, their molecules have a more irregular structure. Consequently, they cannot pack as closely together which means that the intermolecular bonding is less efficient (weaker). As a result, it takes more energy to separate fat molecules than it does to separate oil molecules.

b) Soaps have a long covalent tail and an ionic head. The covalent tail is non-polar so it is soluble in oil but insoluble in water. The ionic head is soluble in water. This allows the soap molecules to dissolve in both oil and water.

12 a) The student should stir the water with the thermometer, ensuring that the bulb of the thermometer does not touch the walls of the copper can.

b) $-297\,kJ\,mol^{-1}$

c) Complete combustion can take place, the methanol cannot evaporate, and heat lost to the surroundings is minimised.

13 a) Nitrogen is an unreactive gas.

b) The partially-evaporated sample has lower retention times as these are like compounds that have evaporated (they more volatile compounds).

14 a) 5.5−4.5

b)

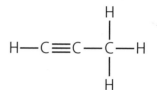

c)

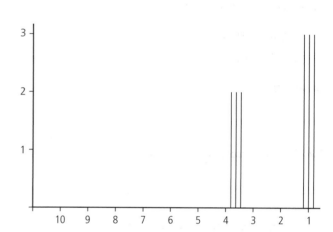